AMERICA'S MOST CHARMING TOWNS & VILLAGES

YOUR PASSPORT TO GREAT TRAVEL!

ADVANCE PRAISE FOR LARRY BROWN'S
AMERICA'S MOST CHARMING TOWNS & VILLAGES

"Chances are, when you drive to Disney World or Yosemite, you'll unwittingly pass by some of the most inviting small towns in America. This book encourages you to stop off at a few of them with profiles of 200 picturesque places travel agents don't know much about ..."
– US News and World Report's **1994 Great Vacation Drives**

Discover the charm and allure of America's most enchanting small towns and villages. Let Larry Brown take you along the open road in search of 200 terrific destinations, with a wide variety of activities, recreation, hikes, strolls, shopping, and much more! From Vermont's classic fall foliage to California's unbeatable wine country, from Southern riverport towns to Midwest farm villages, this captivating travel guide brings you everything you need to have the trip of a lifetime! Every state is represented, every town thoroughly explored.

If you're planning a trip, or just want to learn more about a unique part of American life, you'll want to own **America's Most Charming Towns & Villages**.

ABOUT THE AUTHOR

A native of the Midwest, Larry Brown was educated at the University of Kentucky, University of Edinburgh in Scotland, and Princeton University. He was a member of the psychology faculty at Oklahoma State University from 1961 to 1990. While in Oklahoma, he authored and co-authored numerous research publications, several teaching manuals, and a psychology textbook.

After taking early retirement, Brown turned his attention to three areas of special love: travel, conservation, and American cultural history. He now lives with his wife, Ausma, and their three dogs in Albuquerque, New Mexico.

ACKNOWLEDGMENTS

I am so very grateful to the representatives of hundreds of chambers of commerce, regional and state tourism offices, historical societies, magazines, newspapers, state parks, museums, inns and restaurants. Not only did these folks willingly provide the information and advice I sought, they did so with a friendliness that frequently transformed toil into real enjoyment.

I am also grateful to my publishers, Jonathan Stein and Avery Cardoza, for their help and examples of tireless commitment to travel writing.

Special thanks, above all, to my wife Ausma, for her patience and encouragement.

HIT THE OPEN ROAD WITH OPEN ROAD PUBLISHING!

Open Road Publishing, your passport to great travel, now has guide books to exciting, fun destinations on four continents. It was started by old college pals and veteran travelers who joined forces to bring you the best travel guides available anywhere!

No small task, but here's what we offer:

• All Open Road publications are written by authors, authors with a distinct, opinionated point of view – not some sterile committee or team of writers. Our authors are experts in the areas covered and are polished writers.

• Our guides are geared to people who want great vacations, great value, and great tips for both mainstream tourist sites *and* fun alternatives.

• We're strong on the basics, and we also provide terrific choices for those looking to get off the beaten path and *experience* the country or city – not just *see* it or pass through it.

• Our guides assume nothing. We tell you everything you need to know to have the trip of a lifetime – presented in a fun, literate, no-nonsense style.

• And, above all, we welcome your input, ideas, suggestions to help us put out the best travel guides possible.

AMERICA'S MOST CHARMING TOWNS & VILLAGES

YOUR PASSPORT TO GREAT TRAVEL!

LARRY BROWN

OPEN ROAD PUBLISHING

*Dedicated to all who believe that our small-town
American heritage must be preserved.*

First Edition

Library of Congress Catalog Card No. 94-66037
ISBN 1-883323-09-6

Front Cover photo courtesy of Vermont Department of Travel and Tourism.

Back Cover photos courtesy of Taos County Chamber of Commerce (Taos – Ray Lutz, photographer); New Jersey Division of Travel and Tourism (Cape May) ; and South Dakota Tourism (Deadwood). Inside photos following page 192, in order they appear, are courtesy of: Virginia Division of Tourism; Carson Valley (NV) Chamber of Commerce and Visitors Authority; Michigan Travel Bureau (James Kransburger, photographer); Ferndale (CA) Chamber of Commerce (Bob von Normann, photographer); Missouri Division of Tourism; New York State Department of Economic Development; Leavenworth (WA) Chamber of Commerce; Ohio Division of Travel and Tourism (Gene Allebach, photographer); South Dakota Tourism; New Jersey Division of Travel and Tourism (Jean McDougall, photographer); West Virginia Department of Tourism and Parks (David Fattaleh, photographer); Maryland Office of Tourism Development; Pendleton (SC) District Historical and Recreational Commission; Bucks County (PA) Tourist Commission; Vermont Department of Travel and Tourism.

Maps by Betty Borden.

TABLE OF CONTENTS

Maps are located on the first page of each chapter. They are not drawn to scale, but rather are intended to give you a feel for the general location of each town and village.

INTRODUCTION

AMERICA'S MOST CHARMING TOWNS & VILLAGES is a unique and fascinating travel guide, a book that shows you how to get off the beaten path and enjoy small town America's most enchanting, historical, and fun destinations. If you enjoy historic inns and B&Bs, arts and crafts festivals and shows, antiquing, hiking, cross-country skiing, or just strolling down a quaint Main Street in a new place, then you'll want to own this book.

Each community is described so that its general character and principal points of interest can be noted in a quick scan. Lodging and restaurant suggestions are restricted to B&Bs, historic inns and hotels, and locally-owned eating establishments.

People who enjoy good architecture, history, art, handmade crafts, and natural forms of beauty don't seem to need shopping malls and theme parks for their travel excitement. Walking tours, hiking, fishing, canoeing, sampling local food, relaxing with a book on the veranda, and making new friends at the breakfast table or around the evening fire know what I'm referring to. It's the joy that comes from finding new friends on the open road. And it's the great fun involved in exploring special places – places with character and a sense of place – that seem to live on from a bygone era, hidden over a hill or tucked away in the next valley.

This book will show you where to find beautiful covered bridges and great places to fish. I'll take you to incredible places where waves crash against vintage historic lighthouses. I'll lead you to my favorite white-pillared antebellum Southern homes and through old riverboat port-towns. We'll visit unspoiled steamboat stops along the mighty Mississippi, and travel to villages where you can pick apples and peaches, watch for bald eagles, or linger awhile beside old flower gardens.

I'll show you wonderful wine-tasting villages in California's unbeatable Sonoma Valley. I'll guide you to classic New England commons and show you where to experience picture-perfect fall foliage. And I'll take you to places where spreading vistas are an everyday affair, and where friendly folks can't wait to help you learn more about their hometown.

In the pages that follow you'll also find great places to stay and eat, a wide range of fun sports and recreation activities for individuals and families alike, and perfect escapes for those looking for some solitude and quiet relaxation.

Whether you're planning a trip to one or more of these charming towns or villages, or just want to learn more about some of our historic communities, **AMERICA'S MOST CHARMING TOWNS & VILLAGES** is your indispensable companion. Read on, and have the trip of a lifetime!

PREFACE

There was a time when our country had towns and countryside. Towns were separated by fields and farms and woods. There was little confusion between what was a town and what was countryside. When one began, the other ended.

True, strip development wasn't unknown, especially around our largest cities; but it wasn't the rule for our towns and smaller cities. As late even as the 1950s I remember traveling down a country road one minute and, the next, entering a shaded residential area of Ft. Wayne, Indiana (pop. 134,000 in 1950).

But the map of our country has changed rapidly. Many of our cities and towns and villages now melt into one another or are linked by chains of convenience stores, junkyards, mobile homes, metal prefabs, and strip malls. A few gaps may remain in some of the chains, and by shielding one eye and focusing the other on the gap, it may still be possible to see a bit of the countryside, to imagine what it was like to travel that road 30 or 50 years ago.

The situation is little better within our towns. It can take a good quarter of an hour, or more, to pass through sprawls like Hot Springs, Arkansas, Sierra Vista, Arizona, or Auburn, California, with populations of 30,000 or less. Strip malls and shopping centers, many of them half vacant, sprawl endlessly. In front of and between them lie vast acres of largely unoccupied asphalt. There are empty lots, and there are fast-food restaurants, gas stations, and used-car lots that don't need more than half the land they occupy. Vacant, wasted, or under-utilized land lies everywhere.

And yet on the periphery of the towns new strip malls and shopping centers play leapfrog as businesses compete to see which can get farthest from the town's center. Farms and forests are gutted and villages consumed by the swelling construction. The surrounding countryside is defiled while the town's interior converts to a wasteland. Is there any Western people who appear to have more contempt for their towns and villages than we Americans?

There are still some lovely towns and villages out there, of course, and with a little time and effort — and maybe luck — the traveler can discover them. The bothersome question, though, is whether our grandchildren will want to discover them. There is little satisfaction in discovering something when it is buried in a sea of mobile homes and metal prefabs and other "development."

Defenders of urban sprawl like to throw us the euphemism "progress." What such people badly need is a visit to a community where modern shopping centers, gas stations and other commercial structures have been designed and located so as to *contribute* to the town's charm. Green Valley, Arizona, provides an excellent example of a late 20th century town that is both "progressive" and charming.

Very fortunately, unplanned development is finding a counterforce: love of our country and respect for outr past, combined with an increasing sophistication (and nostalgia) concerning matters of history, architecture, regional diversity — and preservation. Several states have instituted programs to restore and otherwise enhance the beauty of designated "Main Streets." Victorian houses everywhere are undergoing restoration and reappearing as bed and breakfasts. Buildings with even the remotest claim to historic interest bear plaques announcing their membership in one or another registry of historic places.

Interest in preserving human-made beauty is one of the few defenses we have against the continuing transformation of America into one never-ending urban wasteland. (Concern with protecting our natural environment may be the only other.) Anything we can do to promote concern with recapturing the beauty of what remains of another era can only contribute to that defense.

This book was undertaken as one means of promoting preservation: the more we Americans know about our most charming towns and villages, the more we will be inclined to invest our tourist, and even retirement, dollars in those communities. And the greater the investment, the greater the chances for helping these communities survive and encouraging preservation projects elsewhere.

My wife and I have found that there are few experiences more rewarding than discovering a charming town or village. We park our car and, with a couple of hours to spare and a self-guiding tour map in hand, we explore. Some of our fondest memories are of little walking tours of places like Holly Springs, Mississippi and Lindsborg, Kansas.

I hope that the pages that follow will make it just a little easier for others to experience the pleasure that can come from encountering a little bit of the world that belonged to those who came before us. This pleasure can be right up there with the joy that comes from hiking the same woods where our ancestors journeyed, enjoying the food and drink of a two-centuries-old inn, or re-discovering that part of our past that is still alive and well in America's thriving towns and villages.

Larry Brown
May, 1994

PRICE CODES

Brief listings of bed and breakfasts, inns and restaurants accompany the descriptions of many of the towns and villages. Each listing is followed by a price code.

Unless otherwise noted, the coded prices for lodgings refer to rates for a double room (double occupancy):

$ most rooms $40 or less
$$ most rooms in $41 to $70 range
$$$ most rooms $71 or more

The code for the restaurants designates the prices of evening meals, excluding alcoholic beverages, tips or taxes. Prices are per person:

$ most meals $12 or less
$$ most meals in $12 to $25 range
$$$ most meals $26 or more

NOTES FOR THE READER

This guide is intended only as an introduction to a town or village's general character and principal points of interest. More detailed information, including admission fees and schedules and calendars of special events, is available from Chambers of Commerce, visitors bureaus, and (oftentimes) innkeepers. I have noted throughout the book the notation "CoC," which is shorthand for Chamber of Commerce.

The majority of the listed communities publish brochures for self-guided tours. This is sometimes noted, but not always.

Almost all national parks, national monuments, state parks, state historic sites, major museums and large churches are open year-fround. Many other sites and attractions, however, restrict visiting hours or close altogether during the winter months. *Always* inquire in advance when planning a visit after Labor Day and before Memorial Day.

Virtually every community (with some exceptions) sponsors some kind of Christmas celebration. The theme is inevitably "Victorian."

SELECTION OF TOWNS AND VILLAGES

The selection of charming towns and villages was governed by at least three sets of nominations for each state. To obtain the necessary number of nominations it was necessary to gather information from five different sources:

First, nominations were sought from state tourism offices. Each state's tourism department was sent a letter requesting a list of "between one and eight towns/villages" that the office considered to be the most charming. No attempt was made to define "charming" other than to note that the term is subjective and related in meaning to "attractive," "delightful," "captivating" and "alluring."

The criteria for nomination were given as (a) a population no larger than 15,000; (b) historical preservation/restoration (listed as optional); (c) community concern with preservation (also listed as optional); and (d) location within or close to a scenic and/or rural setting. It was stressed that a nominated community did not need to be well-known.

Nominations were received from 50 states. Although several state offices simply forwarded a list of towns (which is all that in fact was requested), many justified their listings with brochures, maps, descriptive material, information on history, and other supporting evidence. The large amounts of time and effort put into the nominations were unexpected – but certainly appreciated!

Nominations made by the editorial offices of regional interest magazines provided a second source of information. A request for nominations was sent to at least one magazine in each state. Each magazine was asked to nominate towns with populations no greater than 15,000 that "are photographed and/or written about most frequently for your publication." The term "charming" appeared in the request but no effort at definition was attempted.

Nominations were received from 33 regional interest magazines. The magazines were:

Aloha
Arizona Highways
Atchinson Magazine
Back Home in Kentucky
Berkshire Magazine
Blue Ridge Country
Colorado Outdoors
Connecticut Magazine
Country Living Magazine (Ohio)
Delaware Today
Florida Living
Georgia Journal
The Iowan Magazine
Kentucky Living
Louisiana Life Magazine
Minnesota Explorer
Mississippi Magazine

Montana Magazine
New Alaskan
New Mexico Magazine
North Carolina Mountains
Oregon Coast Magazine
Outdoor Indiana
Peninsula (California)
Pennsylvania Magazine
The Sandpaper (New Jersey)
South Dakota Magazine
Texas People & Places
Tourist Magazine–A Guide to Middle Tennessee
Vermont Magazine
Virginia Magazine
Wonderful West Virginia Magazine
Yankee Magazine (New Hampshire)

A third kind of information, usually sought when either the first or second category was unavailable for a state, was provided by state historical societies. The letter used for requesting the information was essentially the same as that used for the state tourism offices. Because the term charming often connotes more than simply "historical," nominations by state tourism departments and regional interest magazines were sought before those from historical societies. Nominations from historical societies were obtained for 19 states.

Town and village descriptions appearing in various kinds of travel guides provided the fourth category of information. The travel guide information was often supplemented by recommendations from people familiar with the states. This information, used in selecting towns and villages in seven states, was usually compiled when both magazine and historical society nominations were unavailable. However, the category was used as a fourth category for two states, California and Maine, whose large numbers of charming communities made the use of an additional category especially desirable.

The fifth source of information consisted of listings in national bed-and-breakfast directories. These listings were used to form a list of nominees for each of the 50 states.

The bed and breakfast establishment has become almost an integral part of the charming town. Bed and breakfasts are often structures of some historical interest, and it has been my experience that the people who frequent them are the kind of people who enjoy charming towns. However, the correlation between charm and number of bed and breakfasts in a community is probably less than perfect — many charming villages, especially those outside New England, have no bed-and-breakfasts, or any kind of accommodation for that matter. The bed-and-breakfast nominations were therefore given a secondary, albeit still important role (see below).

The bed-and-breakfast nomination process was straightforward enough: all towns in a given state were ordered in terms of their number of bed and breakfasts and the top eight, which often included ties, were selected for nomination. All towns tying for eighth place were listed, which means that the number of nominations for some states exceeded eight.

In summary then, at least three sets of nominations were obtained for each state. At least two were obtained from the state tourism office, a regional interest magazine, the state historical society and/or listings in national travel guides. A final one was based on bed-and-breakfast listings.

The procedure used in selecting each state's most charming towns and villages consisted of three steps:

First of all, all sets of nominations except those based on the bed-and-breakfast listings were compared for common citations. Any town or village appearing in two or more sets of nominations was automatically selected.

If the number of communities selected in the first step failed to fill the state's allotment, towns that appeared in the bed-and-breakfast nominations and one other set of nominations were selected. If the towns selected by both this and the first step exceeded the state's allotted number, those selected by the present step that had the largest numbers of bed and breakfasts were retained. Towns that were dropped, i.e., those with the fewest bed and breakfasts, were then listed in the appendix as "Also Recommended."

A third step in the selection procedure became necessary when the first two steps failed to meet a state's allotment. In this step, all as-yet-unselected nominees, other than the bed-and-breakfast, were ranked according to their numbers of bed and breakfasts. The state's quota was then filled by selecting the highest ranked towns. When there were ties in the rankings, the selection procedure became more subjective. The final decision was then made on the basis of information from travel guides, personal visits and/or recommendations by people familiar with the communities. When such information was insufficient to allow for a fair selection, the remaining communities were ranked according to their populations (1990 census) and those with the smallest populations selected. This procedure was followed both in completing the state's allotment and in selecting three or four communities for the "Also Recommended" designation.

The selection procedure involved no competition between communities in different states; all competition between states ended with the allotment procedure. It must be remembered, therefore, that the communities listed in this directory are charming only in relation to other communities in the same state.

METHODOLOGY

Allotment of Towns/Villages to States

The procedure used in assigning the 200 towns to the states was a compromise between allotting each state an equal number of towns and allotting towns solely on the basis of population. Departing just a little from the compromise used by the U.S. Constitution in assigning the states representation in Congress, each state was automatically allotted one representative. Assignment of the remaining 150 towns was based on population.

Assigning the towns by population followed several steps:

First, the 1950 U.S. census was used in determining the states' populations. Use of the 1990 census would have penalized several Eastern and Midwestern states, states with an abundance of charming communities, whose share of the population has declined during the last several decades. At the same time, use of a much earlier census, say that of 1900, would have penalized the Western states. The 1950 census was selected as a compromise.

Second, an adjustment was made to prevent states with large urban populations from receiving inflated numbers of towns. This was accomplished by subtracting from each state's population the populations (1950 census) of all cities with 100,000 or more people. This adjustment resulted in a population estimate more closely approximating the actual 1950 rural or semi-rural population.

Third, each state's adjusted population was divided by the total of all adjusted populations (111,328,000) to yield that state's percent share of communities. The product of this value and 200, rounded off to the nearest whole number, yielded the state's number of allotted towns and villages.

Finally, applying a kind of Robin Hood factor, two allotted communities were "stolen" from Pennsylvania (which had received the largest number) and one from each of the next eight of the "wealthiest" states, and the ten stolen slots were assigned to several "deserving states." A deserving state was one that was judged to contain a relatively large number of charming towns and villages for its population.

Determination of "deserving" was admittedly subjective, but the fact of the matter is that, for reasons of history and/or geography, many of our country's most charming towns and villages are located in states with small populations. The best example is Vermont, a state with a tiny population but a superabundance of charm. Two extra communities were assigned to Vermont, and one each to California (whose wealth, natural beauty, and cultural diversity have netted a disproportioinately large number of charming towns), Colorado (which with the removal of Denver had a tiny 1950 population), Delaware, Hawaii, Maine, Montana, New Hampshire and New Mexico.

When two communities selected for a state happened to be neighbors, the communities were paired and counted as one. Such pairing made it possible to assign some states one or two communities more than would otherwise have been allowed.

ALABAMA

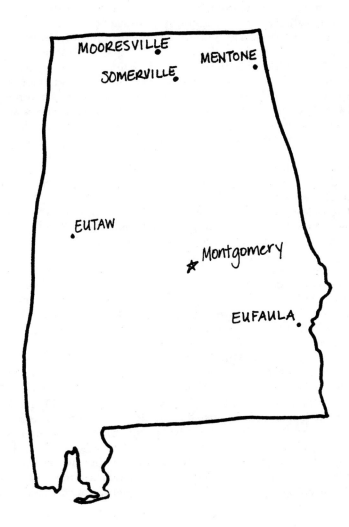

EUFAULA, ALABAMA

Population: 13,220

With antebellum houses, azaleas, dogwoods and a history of wealth centering on cotton, **Eufaula** (you FALL uh) is unmistakably the Deep South. Located on the **Chattahoochee River**, the town was once an ideal riverboat port for planters from across a broad swath of Alabama, Georgia and Florida. And as was so often true in the South during the 1840s and 1850s, the planters and merchants converted their wealth into magnificent homes, churches and other buildings.

Spared by the Yankees (the Confederacy had surrendered by the time Union troops reached the town), many of the antebellum structures still stand. In the post-war years many other beautiful structures went up, and these too have been preserved. The result is that Eufaula, with over 700 historic buildings, boasts Alabama's finest 19th-century small-town commercial district as well as its grandest collection of domestic Italianate architecture. Many of the historic houses are in the Seth Lore-Irwinton Historic District and many of the historic commercial buildings are on Broad Street.

The oldest commercial structure in town — and also the oldest frame structure — is **The Tavern**, originally an 1830s inn, later a Confederate hospital and now a studio and private residence listed on the National Register of Historic Places.

The best-known home is the **Shorter Mansion** (open to the public). Built in 1884 and enlarged and rebuilt in 1906, it is one of Alabama's finest Neoclassical mansions. **Fendall Hall** (1860) is one of the town's finest Italianate mansions. The structure is topped by a square cupola so characteristic of the Italianate style. Waterford chandeliers, hand-stenciled walls and murals grace the interior (shown by appointment).

The **Holleman-Foy Home** (1907) and its columned rotunda entrance provide a magnificent example of turn-of-the-century Neoclassical Eclectic architecture. The house has been in the same family since 1909. Other important Eufaula houses include the Greek Revival **Hart-Milton House** (1843) and **Kendall Manor**, a stately Italianate mansion (listed below as a bed and breakfast).

Brochures for walking and driving tours of the many homes in the historic district are available at the tourism council. Most of the homes are private, but during Eufaula's Pilgrimage in April many of the owners open the doors and allow visitors to explore the rooms and family heirlooms within. The pilgrimage also features open-air art exhibits, tea gardens, concerts and a major antique show.

SPECIAL FEATURES

• Bordered by 640 miles of shoreline, **Lake Eufaula** is sometimes called the *Big Bass Capital of the World.* The 25-year-old reservoir is surrounded by many weedy sloughs and stump rows and is dotted with 48 fish attractors. Two full-service marinas and many public-use areas serve fishermen as well as other water sportsmen.

Sheppard Cottage, the oldest residence in Euraula (1837), can be visited simply by entering the Eufaula/Barbour County Tourism Council. The twice-weekly local newspaper carries the phrase, "Symbol of the Old South, Cradle of the New."

WHERE TO STAY

Kendall Manor B&B, 534 W. Broad St., (205) 687-8847. Ca. 1859 Italianate home with columned veranda and distinctive cupola, 16-ft ceilings, full breakfasts. $$$

St. Mary's B&B, 206 Rivers Ave., (205) 687-7195. Ca. 1850 Italianate home with pumpkin pine floors and oriental rugs, private baths, bicycles. $$

WHERE TO EAT

Dogwood Inn Restaurant, 214 N. Eufaula Ave., (205) 687-5629. In ca. 1905 home, prime rib, specialty desserts, Friday seafood buffet. $ to $$

Lakeview Restaurant, US 82 & Riverside Dr., (205) 687-2021. Overlooking Lake Eufaula, catfish steaks, Southern dishes. $ to $$

Old Mexico, 114 N. Eufaula Ave., (205) 687-7770. Authentic Mexican cuisine served in historic Bluff City Inn. $ to $$

FURTHER INFORMATION

Eufaula/Barbour County Tourism Council, P. O. Box 1055, Eufaula, AL 36072 (800) 524-7529.

DIRECTIONS

From Montgomery, US 82 southeast through Union Springs to Eufaula.

EUTAW, ALABAMA

Population: 2281

Eutaw is the seat of Greene County, a county known for its meandering rivers and white-pillared plantation houses. Located on the black, fertile soil of west Alabama, Greene County was (and to some extent still is) cotton country. Both the county and Eutaw fully participated in the romantic "Golden Era" of the plantation south, the period between 1840 and 1860.

In large part because of the defense provided by the rivers surrounding the town, Union troops showed little interest in harming Eutaw, and much of the old town therefore survives. In the center of town is a charming public square, and on the square sits a lovely little Greek Revival **courthouse** (1839/68). Rural, and distant from anything that isn't, the place smacks of another era. The town even boasts a country store with a high ceiling that still delivers groceries and cuts off pieces of cheese from a large round (called "hoop" cheese).

A few of Eutaw's buildings are open to the public, others are not. In cases of doubt, simply ask — you'll find that Eutaw is an especially friendly town.

The meticulously restored **Kirkwood Mansion** (1860) is one of the most impressive of Eutaw's more than 40 antebellum structures. The four-story mansion is lined on two sides with massive columns, and has iron balconies and four tall chimneys. Also striking are the **Captain Edwin Reese House** (1858), with four two-story fluted Ionic columns, and the Greek Revival **Coleman-Banks House** (ca. 1847). On the grounds of the latter are the original smokehouse and kitchen/wash-house.

One of the most interesting of the non-residential structures is the 1851 Greek Revival **First Presbyterian Church**. The church's slave gallery is still in place, as are the original whale-oil pulpit lamps.

SPECIAL FEATURES

• Ionic-columned **Thornhill** (1833) and what is possibly Alabama's most beautiful mansion, **Rosemount** (1832-39), are located in the tiny community of Forkland, 13 miles south of Eutaw on US 43.

> *Eutaw only came into being because, in 1838, Greene County needed a new government seat.*
> *As with many Southern counties, the timber industry is today more important to Greene County than cotton.*

WHERE TO STAY

A Humble Bed & Breakfast, 401 Main St., (205) 372-9297. Stately 1840 home, elegantly appointed rooms with period antiques, on National Register. $$

Kirkwood B&B, 111 Kirkwood Dr., (205) 372-9009. Carrara marble mantels, Waterford crystal chandeliers, wooded gardens. $$$

WHERE TO EAT

Cotton Patch, P. O. Box 270, (205) 372-4235. Old-fashioned fried chicken the specialty. $ to $$

FURTHER INFORMATION

Green County Historical Society, 310 Main St., Eutaw, AL 35462 (205) 372-2871.

DIRECTIONS

From Birmingham, I 20 southwest to exit 40, AL 14 south to Eutaw.

MENTONE, ALABAMA

Population: 474

Wilderness, rippling streams, and spectacular mountain views may not be among the images conjured up by the mention of Alabama, yet these are the very kinds of things that describe the mountain-top village of **Mentone** in lovely northeastern Alabama. They are also the kinds of things that make Mentone so many places in one: In the warmer months, an artist colony, a golf resort, a dude ranch, a nature lover's paradise; in the winter, the nation's southernmost ski resort. During all times of the year, shops along the town square and elsewhere offer a variety of unique mountain arts and crafts. A good example are *Gourdies* — dolls made from gourds.

The cooler temperatures and clear mountain air attracted visitors here throughout the 19th century, but it wasn't until the construction of the **Mentone Springs Hotel** in the 1880s that the village began to enjoy widespread popularity as a vacation retreat. The hotel was an active resort from the late 19th century to the early 1930s. Today, no longer a hotel, the building stands as a reminder of another era.

St. Joseph's-on-the-Mountain Episcopal Church began as a log cabin in 1870 and with the help of donated furnishings and decorations ended up a lovely church. The stained-glass windows, more than a century old, were hand-painted and fired in France.

SPECIAL FEATURES

• One of the best ways to take in the area's scenery is to drive south seven miles to **DeSoto State Park**. The top sites are **Little River Canyon**, one of the deepest gorges east of the Mississippi River, and the majestic 110-ft **DeSoto Falls**.

Mentone averages about 10 degrees F. cooler than the surrounding valley.

WHERE TO STAY

Blossom Hill B&B (and Herb Farm), Rt. 1 (Box 177C), (205) 634-4673. Borders Little River Canyon, gardens, air conditioning. $$

Madaperca, H. C. 68 (Box 20), (205) 634-4792. "A riverside retreat" atop Lookout Mountain, private baths, today's conveniences. $$

Mentone Inn B&B, P. O. Box 284, (205) 634-4836. Historic mountain retreat, natural wood beauty, private baths, country breakfasts. $$

Shady Grove Dude Ranch, (205) 634-4344. One hundred miles of wilderness trails for part-time cowboys and nature enthusiasts. $

WHERE TO EAT

Cragsmere Manna Restaurant and Gardens, DeSoto Parkway, (205) 634-4677. Fine dining in one of oldest houses on mountain. $ to $$

Log Cabin Deli, Rt. 1 (Box 300), (205) 634-4560. Building originally an Indian fur-trading post. $

Ye Olde Heritage House Restaurant, 1 Hotel Square, (205) 634-4040.   In historic Mentone Springs Hotel, atop mountain. $

FURTHER INFORMATION

DeKalb County Tourist Association, P. O. Box 1165, Fort Payne, AL 35967 (205) 845-3957.

DIRECTIONS

From Chattanooga, I 59 south to exit 231, south on AL 117 to Mentone.

MOORESVILLE, ALABAMA

Population: About 60

Mooresville was incorporated in 1818, making it the oldest incorporated community in Alabama. Both Andrew Johnson and James A. Garfield spent time here years before their presidential days. Small then and small now, the village doesn't go much farther than three or four blocks in any direction. Almost all of its buildings are on the National Register, and all but one or two are lived or worked in. Though out of the past, picturesque little Mooresville is a living village.

Bypassed by the interstate, the village is kind of tucked away, unknown even to people in nearby towns. On most maps of the state it looks as though the village has disappeared into some kind of urban sprawl connecting **Decatur** and **Huntsville**. In actual fact, the community is surrounded by cotton fields. Large towns are not far away, and many of the townspeople commute to them, but Mooresville still retains its rural charm — and setting. It is peaceful here.

Spanning as they do more than 150 years, Mooresville's buildings vary in style, size and construction. Some are brick, some are white or pastel frame. All are shaded by beautiful old oaks, magnolias and other trees. The town's most famous building is probably the **Mooresville Post Office,** which has been in continuous use since 1844. The wooden cubby holes receiving mail today are the same that received mail in Civil War times.

Two churches are of special historic interest. One, the circa 1820 restored red brick **community church,** still has one of the original chandeliers and the slave balcony (though boarded up after the Civil War). The pulpit of the second, the 1854 white-frame **Church of Christ,** was where Garfield, then a teacher, read from the Bible.

Among the other buildings of special note is the old stagecoach stop/tavern, currently undergoing restoration, and two houses dating from around 1825 that owe their survival to Union generals who ordered that they not be vandalized.

SPECIAL FEATURES

• The **Old State Bank** in neighboring Decatur is the oldest bank in the state (1833). Recently restored, the bank was one of only four buildings in Decatur still standing at the end of the Civil War. Decatur is also home to two well-preserved Victorian residential areas.

• Mooresville borders the **Wheeler National Wildlife Refuge**, the largest wildlife refuge in Alabama. The refuge includes a wildlife interpretive center and an observation platform from which migratory waterfowl may be viewed.

> *Only ancient cedars lining the front walk remain of the Female Institute (1830). The institute, which had 55 "lady pupils," was destroyed by Union soldiers.*

WHERE TO STAY

Dancy-Polk House, 901 Railroad St. (in Decatur), (205) 353-3579. Restored 1829 Palladian home on National Register, Union headquarters during Civil War, antiques. $$

WHERE TO EAT

Ol' Heidelberg, 6125 University Dr. (in Huntsville), (205) 922-0556. German and American dishes, locally popular. $ to $$.

Simp McGee, 725 Bank St. (in Decatur), (205) 353-6284. Cajun cooking, seafood, steaks, red beans and smoked sausage, gumbo, etouffees. $ to $$.

FURTHER INFORMATION

Alabama Mountain Lakes Association, P. O. Box 1075, Mooresville, AL 35649 (800) 648-5381.

DIRECTIONS

From Huntsville, I 565 west to Mooresville exit (just east of I 65).

SOMERVILLE, ALABAMA

Population: 208

Known as *Morgan County's Grand old Gal*, **Somerville** is one of those rare little towns where the flavor of the Old South — the real Old South — still lingers. Of course, some of the new has invaded the town. The **Town Hall** is new, for example, and there are telephones (at least in some of the buildings) and electricity. But as an old-fashioned stroll around the square should make clear, very little has happened here since the 19th century.

Settled around 1818, Somerville was a 19th-century cotton town. It served as the county seat until 1891, when despite an uproar and even threats of violence, county government was moved to Decatur. Then total quiet took over. In recent years the town has become a home for people working in Decatur and Huntsville, and this, combined with the beginnings of tourism, has stirred up some activity – but not much.

Somerville's most imposing building, and one straight out of the Old South, is the partially renovated **Old Morgan County Courthouse** (1837). The two-story Federal-syle brick structure, listed on the National Register, is Alabama's oldest courthouse. The bell in the belfry is still rung to welcome in each new year. (An appointment is advised for visitors wishing to tour the interior — check at the Town Hall.)

Sprinkled about town are a number of old homes, all private residences. Architecturally the most interesting is the **Rice House** (circa 1835), a Federal-style Tidewater-type cottage. On the National Register, the one-and-a-half-story house has original woodwork and mantels. The house is unique in that the brick was laid in Flemish bond around the entire building rather than just in front.

Other interesting houses include the restored **Gilchrist-Williams House** (probably mid-19th-century), the late 19th-century **Lyle House** and the antebellum **Mikell House**, with original Federal woodwork. The 1880 **Binford-Peck House** was home to the town's telephone switchboard during the 1930s. A visit to the lovely old **Somerville Cemetery** can provide an excellent lesson in history.

SPECIAL FEATURES
• **Huntsville** is home to the **US Space and Rocket Center** (hands-on exhibits, Spacedome Theater, bus tours of NASA's Marshall Space Flight Center). Among the city's many other attractions is the **Twickenham Historic District**, containing one of Alabama's largest and finest collections of antebellum homes.

WHERE TO STAY AND WHERE TO EAT
See previous selection, "Mooresville, Alabama."

> *To avoid what could have been an unpleasant confrontation over moving the county seat (in 1891), people from Decatur quietly removed the county records from Somerville by night.*

FURTHER INFORMATION
Town Hall, Somerville, AL 35670, (205) 778-8282

DIRECTIONS
From Birmingham, I 65 north to exit 328, Al 36 east to AL 67, AL 67 north to Somerville.

Note: I wish to thank historian David W. Whitehorn, author of *Historic Somerville*, for providing some of the information for this selection. A copy of *Historic Somerville* may be obtained by writing the Somerville Public Library, P. O. Box 178, Somerville, AL 35670.

ALASKA

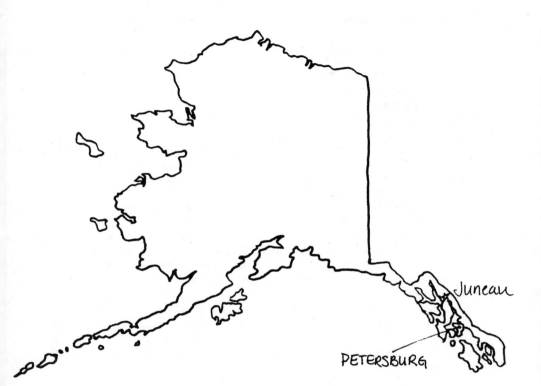

Juneau

PETERSBURG

PETERSBURG, ALASKA

Population: 3,207

From the docks of **Petersburg's** harbor you can see snow-capped mountains, their upper reaches partly obscured by clouds, their lower reaches dark with forests. They rise steeply from the fjords. This is southeast Alaska's **Inside Passage**, not Norway, but it could be either.

Petersburg, or *Little Norway*, was settled by Norwegians (1897), and the heritage is still very important. The town sponsors an annual **Little Norway Festival** (see below), rosemaling decorates old Scandinavian-style frame buildings, and fishing and logging continue to dominate daily lives, just as in the Old Country (although tourism is making an entry).

One of the most picturesque of the older buildings is the the **Sons of Norway Hall** (1912), a National Historic Site, constructed on pilings over a slough. Next to the hall is the *Valhalla*, a Viking ship built in 1976 to participate in the US Bicentennial Parade of Ships in New York Harbor.

The **Clausen Memorial Museum** has a number of unusual attractions. Among them is the giant lens from the Cape Decision Lighthouse, a 126.5-pound King Salmon, and "Fisk" (Norwegian for "fish"), a lovely fountain sculpture.

Although small, Petersburg is a major fishing port — 10th in the country — and visitors enjoy exploring the docks of the three colorful harbors. The most popular catches are salmon (summer), halibut and herring (spring), crab (winter), and shrimp (all year).

Petersburg offers a variety of boat charters and rentals for fishing, sightseeing, whale watching and wildlife observing. Air charters are also available for sightseeing. This is the **Alaska Panhandle**, Alaska's *banana belt*, and so the weather is much milder and far more supportive of outdoor activities than in more northerly parts of the state.

SPECIAL FEATURES

• People in Norwegian, Viking, and Valkyrie costumes dance, feast, compete and have a good time at the **Little Norway Festival**, held on the weekend closest to May 17 (Norwegian Independence Day). This is the time to sample from an authentic Smorgasbord.

• Several Petersburg companies offer boat tours of beautiful **LeConte Glacier**, the world's southernmost active tidal glacier. The glacier can also be toured by air.

> *Alaskan King Crabs can have a "wingspan" of up to eight feet.*
> *One of the best places to see bears is from the Fredrick Point Boardwalk, a nearby scenic hiking trail.*

WHERE TO STAY

Jewels by the Sea B&B, P. O. Box 1662, (907) 772-3620. Beachfront home, gallery, full breakfasts. $$ to $$$

Scandia House, P. O. Box 689, (800) 722-5006. Old World hotel, central location, complimentary breakfasts. $$ to $$$

Water's Edge B&B, P. O. Box 1201, (907) 772-3736. Beachfront, private baths, kitchenette, courtesy transportation. $$ to $$$

Sing Lee B&B, P. O. Box 1625, (907) 772-4700. On Historic Sing Lee Alley, full breakfasts, evening snacks. $$ to $$$

WHERE TO EAT

Beachcomber Inn, P. O. Box 570, (907) 772-3888. Waterfront dining, local seafood and steaks, dock facility, courtesy van. $$

FURTHER INFORMATION

Petersburg Chamber of Commerce, P. O. Box 649, Petersburg, AK 99833 (907) 772-3646.

DIRECTIONS

Petersburg is on an island, so you'll have to make arrangements to get here by boat or plane. **Alaska Airlines** offers jet service to Petersburg from Seattle and Anchorage, and **Wings of Alaska** offers scheduled service between Petersburg and other Alaskan cities. A spectacularly beautiful trip to Petersburg aboard a large ship (and ferry) is available through **Alaska Marine Highway**, Bellingham, Washington.

ARIZONA

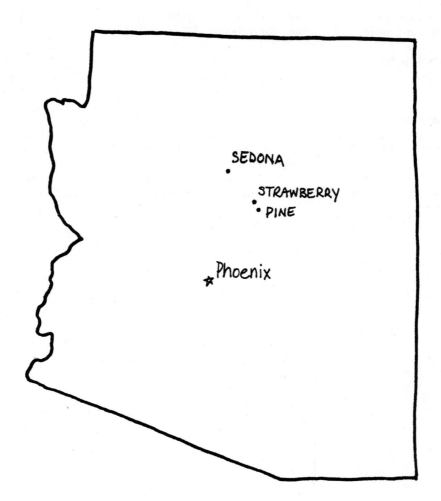

PINE/STRAWBERRY, ARIZONA

Population: 3,905

You'll find little mention of **Pine** (elev. 5,500 ft.) or its sister community **Strawberry** (elev. 6,000 ft.) in most travel guides. In fact, there are people born and raised in Arizona who have never even heard of them. But those who have visited the Pine/Strawberry area rank it very high on their list of favorite places.

Nestled in **Pine Creek Valley**, Pine and Strawberry enjoy an especially peaceful and beautiful setting. Mormon pioneers settled Pine in 1879; many of their descendants still live here. Strawberry, just three miles up the road and settled about the same time, was named after the wild strawberries growing in the area. Although updated to serve a variety of 20th-century purposes, many of the original rock and log cabins remain in the area.

The **Pine and Strawberry Museum**, located in the **Old Mormon Church** in Pine, is a nice place to begin your visit. On display are artifacts from local archaeological digs, memorabilia from early pioneer days and old photographs.

The old **Strawberry schoolhouse** is Arizona's oldest standing schoolhouse. Constructed in 1885, the inside walls were decorated with wainscoting and wallpaper — elegant for a frontier schoolhouse. The interior has been restored and the building is now a state historical site

The mountains, forests, lakes and streams are custom-ordered for fishing, camping, hiking and backbacking. There are also scenic drives for the less energetic. The CoC has maps and information on trails.

SPECIAL FEATURES

• **Tonto Natural Bridge**, three miles south of pine, has become one of Arizona's most popular state parks. The bridge is thought to be the largest natural travertine bridge in the world, with a span that is 183 feet high. Also in the park is an historic lodge (1927), on the National Register, that is filled with antiques and heirlooms of the family that discovered and settled the surrounding little valley.

> *The first European to see Tonto Natural Bridge was Dave Gowan, a Scottish prospector who in 1877 stumbled across the bridge while being chased by Apaches.*
>
> *Pine and Strawberry are nestled in the largest stand of ponderosa pine in the world.*

WHERE TO STAY

Strawberry Lodge, P. O. Box 331, (602) 476-3333. Mountain lodge, fireplaces, balconies, rustic bar. $$

WHERE TO EAT

Strawberry Lodge (see above). Variety of steaks, prime rib (the Saturday special), homemade pies. $ to $$.

FURTHER INFORMATION

Pine/Strawberry Chamber of Commerce, P. O. Box 196, Pine, AZ 85544 (602) 476-3547.

DIRECTIONS

From Flagstaff, I-17 south to Camp Verde exit, AZ 260 east to AZ 87/260, AZ 87/260 south to Pine and Strawberry.

SEDONA, ARIZONA

Population: 7720

It's hard to imagine that any town lying at the mouth of **Oak Creek Canyon** in central Arizona could avoid a listing in this book. The towering red rocks, fiery in the sun, dramatic in any season, make the area one of the most photographed in the country. Arizonans claim that "God created the Grand Canyon but He lives in Sedona." But even without the surroundings, **Sedona** has much to offer the visitor: first-class art galleries, boutiques, upscale restaurants, luxury resorts.

Sedona boasts over 40 galleries exhibiting creations by some of the most talented artists and craftspeople in the country. The Mexican-style **Tlaquepaque shopping village** is especially recommended for lovers of charm. Even people who hate to shop will enjoy a stroll through the village's quaint courtyards.

Dramatic country like this is hardly of recent discovery: Native American settlers were attracted to the area hundreds of years ago. The remains of prehistoric cultures — cliff dwellings, villages, petroglyphs and pictographs — abound in the Sedona region.

The touring options form an appetizing menu: in addition to the usual driving, walking and hiking tours, there are airplane, helicopter, even hot-air balloon tours for seeing the scenery. The back country, and the ancient Indian ruins in particular, can be explored by guided jeep or horseback tours. Jeeps can also be rented for self-guided touring.

SPECIAL FEATURES

• Some of the most photographed scenery in the world can be seen at **Red Rock Crossing**, a few miles west of town.

• A few miles southwest of town is **Red Rock State Park**, an environmental park where hikers, bikers, and others can experience first-hand the contrast between the coolness of tree-lined **Oak Creek** and the barrenness of the red cliffs and spires.

• To the north, **Oak Creek Canyon**, a gorge with streams and waterfalls between sheer rock walls, provides one of the most scenic drives in the country.

• A natural water slide at **Slide Rock State Park** tempts everyone, adult as well as kid, to jump in and go with the current. There are also natural swimming pools and opportunites for trout fishing.

With over three million visitors in 1992, Sedona rivals the Grand Canyon in popularity.

A veritable back lot for Hollywood, many celebrities have worked and/or lived in Sedona. Among them: John Wayne, Elvis Presley, Lucille Ball, Orson Welles, Walt Disney.

WHERE TO STAY

Bed & Breakfast at Saddle Rock Ranch, P.O. Box 10095, (602) 282-7640. Three-acre historic country estate, rock fireplaces, private baths, incredible views. $$$

Briar Patch Inn, HC 30 Box 1002, (602) 282-2342. Cottages on bank of creek in Oak Creek Canyon, Arizona Indian and Mexican decor, fireplaces, library, full breakfasts. $$$

Canyon Villa B&B Inn, 125 Canyon Circle Dr., (800) 453-1166. Elegantly decorated rooms, stained-glass windows, red rock views, gourmet breakfasts, heated pool. $$$

Casa Sedona B&B Inn, 55 Hozoni Dr., (800) 525-3756. Individually appointed guest rooms, red rock setting, fireplaces, library, Southwestern breakfasts. $$$

Lantern Light Inn, 3085 W. US 89A, (602) 282-3419. Country French antique decor, private entries, private baths, tree-lined grounds, full breakfasts. $$$

WHERE TO EAT

L'Auberge de Sedona, P. O. Box B, (800) 272-6777. Gourmet French cuisine in a Country French inn. $$$

Enchantment's Yavapai Room, 525 Boynton Canyon Rd., (800) 826-4180. Sonoran Free Range Chicken Breast, Enchantment Beef Wellington. $$$

The Heartline Cafe, 1610 W. Highway 89A, (602) 282-0785. Inventive menu of European/Mediterranean/Asian ancestry. $$

The Hideaway, P.O. Box 1757, (602) 282-4204. Italy on the banks of Oak Creek. $

Pietro's Classic Italian Restaurant & Cafe, 2445 W. Highway 89A, (602) 282-2525. Name says it all, wide range of choices. $$

FURTHER INFORMATION

Sedona-Oak Creek Canyon Chamber of Commerce, P. O. Box 478, Sedona, AZ 86336 (602) 282-7722.

DIRECTIONS

From Flagstaff, US Alt. 89 south to Sedona.

ARKANSAS

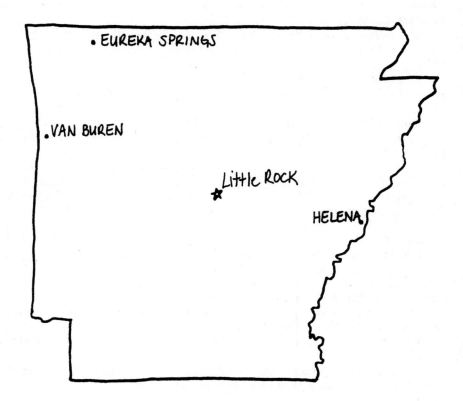

• EUREKA SPRINGS

• VAN BUREN

Little ROCK
☆

HELENA

EUREKA SPRINGS, ARKANSAS

Population: 1900

Eureka Springs is a beautifully unique blend of the Victorian and the Ozarks. The colorful array of Victorian buildings earned the entire downtown shopping district and residential area a listing on the National Register of Historic Places. But there are also narrow, winding mountain streets and lovely limestone walls built from native stone. Streets are sometimes hundreds of feet higher, or lower, than adjacent streets. And when streets cross, they never do so at right angles. You're in the **Ozarks**.

Belief in the healing powers of its spring waters was Eureka Springs's fore-bear. The town grew as thousands of health seekers journeyed, first by stagecoach and later by train, to the bathhouses of the growing resort. Today the town's native limestone buildings, "gingerbread" houses, shaded trails, springs and gaze-bos preserve the Victorian atmosphere.

Eureka Springs is to be explored by some combination of trolley and foot, probably in that order. There are no fewer than six trolley routes, each desig-nated by a color displayed on a sign in the front window, and they serve most of the town's places of lodging. Information on the trolley routes and a copy of the *Scenic Walking Tours* booklet can be obtained at the CoC.

Two Victorian homes are open to the public: the **Queen Anne Mansion** (1891), with exceptional interior oak and cherry woodwork, and lovely **Rosalie** (1880s), with period furnishings and accessories.

Just west of town (on US 62W) are two especially inspiring attractions, the exquisitely beautiful **Thorncrown Chapel**, an architectural masterpiece, and the **Eureka Springs Botanical Gardens**. The gardens span 33 acres of informal grounds and display a variety of hardwood trees and native plants.

SPECIAL FEATURES

· The **Eureka Springs and North Arkansas Railway** offers a 4-mile excursion (departing hourly) through the Ozarks. A more leisurely tour of the mountains is available by cruise boat on scenic **Beaver Lake**.

> *Eureka Springs is home to the regionally famous Great Passion Play, a spectacular outdoor drama depicting the life, death and resurrection of Christ. Known as an artists' colony as early as the 1930s and 1940s, Eureka Springs is now one of the most respected fine arts centers of the mid-South.*

WHERE TO STAY

5 Ojo Inn, 5 Ojo St., (501) 253-6734. 1992 restoration award, fireplaces, private baths, Jacuzzis, gourmet breakfasts. $$$

Crescent Hotel, 75 Prospect St., 1-800-342-9766. Historic "Queen of the Ozarks," National Landmark, spacious Victorian guest rooms, restaurant, carriage rides. $$ to $$$

Dairy Hollow House, 515 Spring St., (501) 253-7444. Regional antiques, quilts, fresh flowers, murder mystery weekends, one of region's finest. $$$

Heartstone Inn B&B/Cottages, 35 Kingshighway, (501) 253-8916. Circa 1882 home, antiques, private baths, TV, tree-shaded decks, gourmet breakfasts, regional and national citations. $$ to $$$

Palace Hotel & Bath House, 135 Springs St., (501) 253-7474. Restored Victorian hotel in historic district, bathhouse. $$$

WHERE TO EAT

Dairy Hollow House, 515 Spring St., 1-800-562-8650. Apple-glazed Cornish Game Hen, Smoked Trout Mousse with Watercress, one of best in Ozarks, by reservation only. $$ to $$$

DeVito's Restaurant, 5 Center St., 253-6807. Authentic Italian cuisine, trout, seafood. $$

Eurekan Dining Car, 299 N. Main/Ark. 23N, (501) 253-9623. Service aboard railroad dining car. $$

Spring Street House Restaurant, 124 Spring St., (501) 253-8558. Regional and continental cuisine in Victorian setting. $ to $$

Victorian Sampler Restaurant, 33 Prospect, (501) 253-8374. Home-cooked meals, daily specials. $$

FURTHER INFORMATION

Eureka Springs Chamber of Commerce, Box 551, Eureka Springs, AR 72632 (501) 253-8737.

DIRECTIONS

From Springfield (Missouri), US 65 south to US 62, west to Eureka Springs.

HELENA, ARKANSAS

Population: 7,491

Situated on a rise overlooking the Mississippi, **Helena** was described by Mark Twain as occupying "one of the prettiest situations on the river." Although much of Arkansas belongs geographically and culturally to the mid-South, Helena is definitely part of the Deep South. The second oldest city in Arkansas (founded in 1820), its history is that of steamboats, cotton and the Mississippi Delta. Helena was the home of seven Confederate generals; it is now home to a major blues festival.

The **Cherry Street Historic District** is a well-preserved business district of the late 19th and early 20th centuries. The district's appearance and ambience are those of a traditional river town. A top site is the new **Delta Cultural Center**, an important regional museum (costing $8.5 million) that chronicles the history of the Delta and its people. The center is housed in the 1903 **Helena Train Depot**.

Helena has a handsome collection of antebellum, Victorian and Edwardian homes. Many are listed on the National Register of Historic Places. (Some offer tours by appointment — check with the CoC). Three important antebellum homes are **Estevan Hall**, a magnificent home preserved by the descendants of the original owners; the 1860 red brick **Moore-Hornor Home**, with 18-ft. ceilings and parlor doors that still bear shell marks from the Battle of Helena (see below); and the spacious 1858 Greek Revival **Tappan-Pillow Mansion**, with the original two-room brick kitchen out back.

Among the most elegant of the postbellum houses are the Italianate **Hornor-Gladin House** (1880), with original fireplaces and mantels, and the grand Georgian-Revival **West-Webb House** (1900), with parquet floors and quarter-sawn oak woodwork.

High on Crowley's Ridge, the **Confederate Cemetery** offers a panoramic view of the Mississippi River. Another view of the water may be enjoyed from the boardwalk of **Riverfront Park**.

The restored **Old Almer Store**, constructed in 1872 of cypress, was once a market for dairy products and, later, a neighborhood grocery. Entered on the National Register, the store now serves as an area-wide arts and crafts cooperative.

SPECIAL FEATURES

• Both the **St. Francis National Forest** and the **White River National Widlife Refuge** offer superb opportunities for fishing and wildlife observation.

> *The Battle of Helena was fought in 1863 as a Confederate attempt to relieve pressure on Vicksburg downriver. The Confederate troops suffered heavy casualties.*
>
> *The riverboats Delta Queen and Mississippi Queen often put into Helena so that their passengers may tour Cherry Street.*
>
> *The bridge at Helena is the only Mississippi River bridge between West Memphis (to the north) and Lake Village (to the south).*

WHERE TO STAY

Edwardian Inn, 317 Biscoe St., (501) 338-9155. Restored turn-of-century mansion, original fireplace mantels, private baths, TV and phones, one of the South's finest. $$

WHERE TO EAT

Bell's, 115 Cherry St., (501) 338-6655. Prime rib, seafood, steaks. $ to $$

Casqui Restaurant, 101 Missouri St., (501) 338-3565. Home-cooked foods served buffet style. $

FURTHER INFORMATION

Phillips County Chamber of Commerce, 111 Hickory Hill Dr., Helena, AR 72342, (501) 338-8327

DIRECTIONS

From Little Rock, I 40 east to exit 216 (Brinkley), US 49 southeast to Helena.

VAN BUREN, ARKANSAS

Population: 14,979

Largely bypassed by much larger Fort Smith, across the Arkansas River, **Van Buren** retains much of the quaint ole' river town atmosphere. Narrow **Main Street**, which looks pretty much like it did 100 years ago, has appeared in several films and in the TV mini-series *The Blue and The Gray*. The street has seen everything from wagon trains to Union and Confederate troops to stagecoaches headed west. And wagons hauling freight to and from the many steamboats on the Arkansas. More than 70 buildings in the Main Street area are on the National Register of Historic Places.

Crawford County Courthouse, built in 1841 and rebuilt in 1877, is the oldest active county courthouse west of the Mississippi. The Seth Thomas clock in the tower has been tolling the hour for nearly 120 years.

The elegant 1890s **King Opera House** is currently undergoing restoration; Jenny Lind and William Jennings Bryant appeared here.

Van Buren's shops, known and respected throughout western Arkansas and eastern Oklahoma, display dolls, stained glass, jewelry, cutlery, quilts, pottery and other items handmade by local artists. The emphasis is on the handcrafted and the Victorian. The fine arts are also represented.

SPECIAL FEATURES

• On Saturdays from April through November, the **Scenic Ozark Railway** offers three-hour excursions to the mountain village of **Winslow**. Passengers relax in early 1900s cars with restored inlaid mahogany interiors as they travel over trestles and through a tunnel built in 1882. The train embarks from the **Old Frisco Depot**, now restored and housing a railroad museum as well as the CoC.

• The towering bluffs along the Arkansas River can be seen from the decks of the 138-passenger *Frontier Belle*. The main deck is enclosed.

• Across the river, the **Fort Smith National Historic Site, Belle Grove Historic District** and the **Old Fort Museum** are especially worth a visit.

> *Fort Smith was established in 1817 to help keep peace among the region's Indians.*
>
> *On the back of the river wall in the Mike Meyer Riverfront Park is a mural history of Van Buren painted by Van Buren High School art students.*

WHERE TO STAY

O'Malley's, 600 Main St., (501) 474-4693. In restored beer depot, antiques, full breakfasts, dinner theater also on premises. $$

Old Van Buren Inn, 633 Main St., (501) 474-4202. Second floor of High Victorian bank building, said to be haunted. $$$

WHERE TO EAT

Cottage Cafe, 810 Main St., (501) 474-9895. "Country-style" menu, breakfasts/lunches, very popular with locals. $

O'Malley's (see above). Varied menu. dinner theater. $ to $$.

FURTHER INFORMATION

The Van Buren Chamber of Commerce, P. O. Box 652, Van Buren, AR 72956, (800) 332-5889.

DIRECTIONS

From Little Rock, I 40 west to exit 5 (Van Buren/Fort Smith exit).

CALIFORNIA

FERNDALE

FORT BRAGG
MENDOCINO   NEVADA CITY
GUALALA
HEALDSBURG
Sacramento
SONOMA

HALF MOON BAY

SOLVANG

AVALON

AVALON, CALIFORNIA

Population: 2918

There are few communities in Southern California that can equal **Avalon's** quaintness. There are *none* that can equal the beauty of its setting — the blue harbor, coastal hillsides, beaches, crystal-clear water and clear skies (except when the wind's blowing from Los Angeles). Situated on lovely **Santa Catalina Island** off the California coast, Avalon has been a popular pleasure resort since the 1890s.

Avalon is small, no more than about one square mile in area, and so its winding streets can be explored by foot. Foot is the best way to absord the late 19th-century charm of this village, but there are others: tram tours, bus tours, golf carts. Overlooking a gorgeous harbor, and ocean beyond, the village could be on the French or Italian Riviera.

The 1929 art deco **Casino Building**, situated on one side of the harbor, is one of Avalon's top sites. The building includes the **Avalon Theatre** and **Casino Ballroom**. The Avalon Theatre, known for its excellent acoustics and murals by John Gabriel Beckman, has a full-scale pipe organ whose largest pipe measures 16 feet and shortest a mere 1/4 inch. The circular Casino Ballroom, the largest of its type in the world, was a symbol of the Big Band Era of the '30s, '40s, and '50s (daily walking tours available).

Avalon's underwater scenery is spectacular; the octopus, barracuda, spiny lobsters, kelp forests, even wrecks make snorkeling and scuba diving very popular. There are glass-bottom boat tours, night as well as day, for underwater sight-seers who wish to remain dry.

SPECIAL FEATURES

• The **Seal Rocks** down the coast can be visited by tour boat (migratory sea lions rather than seals sun on the rocks).

> *Santa Catalina was once used as a base by Yankee, Russian and other sailors and hunters in the sea-otter trade.*
> *About 86% of the island is owned by the Santa Catalina Island Conservancy, a nonprofit group whose mission is to restore and preserve the land in a natural state.*
> *Avalon is known for its fresh seafood, especially the swordfish.*

WHERE TO STAY

Catalina Island Seacrest Inn, 201 Clarissa, (310) 510-0196. Country decor, close to beach, lace and wicker sun room, TV. $$$

Garden House Inn, 125 Clarissa Avenue, (310) 510-0356. 1927 house, steps from beach, ocean view terraces, antiques, wine/appetizers. $$$

Gull House, Box 1381, (310) 510-2547. Spacious suites and rooms, fireplaces, TV, patio with pool, spa. $$$

Inn on Mt. Ada, 398 Wrigley Rd., (310) 510-2030. 1921 Georgian Colonial-style mansion overlooking bay, on National Register, private baths, golf cart, all meals included. $$$

The Old Turner Inn, 232 Catalina Ave., (310) 510-2236. Quiet setting in heart of Avalon, antiques, handmade linens, private baths, fireplaces, evening wine/appetizers $$$

WHERE TO EAT

Armstrong's Fish Maraket & Seafood Restaurant, 306 Crescent Ave., (310) 510-0113. Fresh seafood dining on Avalon Bay, mesquite charbroiled fish. $$

Blue Parrot Restaurant, 205 Crescent Ave., (310) 510-2465. Cool tropical atmosphere, view of Avalon Bay. $

Channel House Restaurant, 205 Crescent, (310) 510-1617. European flair, tableside Caesar salad & flambe desserts. $$

Luau Larry's, 509 Crescent Ave., (310) 510-1919. Oceanfront, spirits,oysters, entertainment. $

Ristorante Villa Portofino, 111 Crescent Ave., (310) 510-0508. Northern Italian cuisine, oceanfront site, seafoods, pastas, reservations advised. $$

FURTHER INFORMATION

Catalina Island Chamber of Commerce & Visitor's Bureau, P. O. Box 217, Avalon, CA 90704, (310) 510-1520.

DIRECTIONS

Boats depart for Catalina Island from Long Beach, San Pedro, San Diego, Oceanside and Newport Beach. Year-round helicopter service is available from most of the same ports. Check with the CoC for scheduling.

FERNDALE, CALIFORNIA

Population: 1,331

The "**Victorian Village of Ferndale**" is tucked between the Eel River and northern California's *Lost Coast*. Although geographically one of California's most western towns, Ferndale is architecturally one of the state's most eastern. **Main Street** (on the National Register) as well as the side streets are bordered by carefully restored, brightly painted Victorian buildings. Even the Victorian public restrooms are beautifully painted. The nicely kept gardens add to the color, and the palm trees, camellias and other lush plants impart a unique, almost enchanting beauty that sets the town apart from most other Victorian communities.

Situated in a rich dairying region, Ferndale became the agricultural center of northern California during the final decades of the 19th century. The area's wealth helped build ornate Victorian homes, nicknamed *Butterfat Palaces*. The town changed very little after the late 1800s. In the 1960s, the picturesque buildings were discovered by artists and craftspeople and Ferndale's revitalization was underway. Today the thriving Main Street is lined with specialty shops, an old-fashioned mercantile, antique stores, and at least seven studios/galleries.

The principal architecture of the historic homes is Gothic Revival and Stick, although Queen Anne and other Victorian styles are never far away. Some of the commercial structues are late Victorian, some early Modernistic (1920-1936). Much of the picturesque town can be taken in on a 2-hr. walking tour, especially with the assistance of the CoC's visitors' guide. An excellent stop on the tour, if not in fact its starting point, is the **Ferndale Museum**. Among the museum's displays are Victorian room settings, a working seismograph (earthquakes are not unknown here) and early agricultural equipment.

The **Ferndale Reportory Theatre** stages comedies, mysteries, the classics and, most popular of all, musicals. The performances, acclaimed and offered year-round, have played no small part in putting Ferndale back on the map.

SPECIAL FEATURES

• Ferndale consistently ranks in the top 20 of Audubon bird counts, with 355 varieties of birds spotted in the area. Good locations for bird watching, and nature watching in general, are the **Eel River State Wildlife Area**, the **Humboldt Bay National Wildlife Refuge** and Ferndale's own **Russ Park**, a 105-acre wilderness preserve.

• One of the best ways to see the the giant redwoods is to take a trip along the **Avenue of the Giants**, a winding stretch of old US 101 southeast of Ferndale.

> *California's Lost Coast is accessible only by foot (or maybe helicopter). Expect to spend several days on the trek.*

WHERE TO STAY

Gingerbread Mansion Inn, 400 Berding St., (707) 786-4000. Restored 1899 home, one of best in California, four parlors, private baths, English garden, full breakfasts, afternoon tea and cake, bicycles. $$$

Shaw House Inn B&B, P.O. Box 1125, (707) 786-9958. 1854 Gothic Revival home, cozy fireplaces, private balconies, fresh flowers, sumptuous breakfasts, afternoon teas. $$ to $$$

WHERE TO EAT

Bibo and Bear, 460 Main St., (707) 786-9484. Fresh local seafood, Raspberry Chicken, Kiwi Amaretto Shrimp. $ to $$

Diane's, 553 Main St., (707) 786-4950. Special place for lunch, everything freshly made from local produce. $

Victorian Inn, 400 Ocean Ave., (800) 576-5949. No menu — entrees changed daily. $$

FURTHER INFORMATION

Ferndale Chamber of Commerce, P. O. Box 325, Ferndale, CA 95536, (707) 786-4477.

DIRECTIONS

From San Francisco, US 101 north to Fernbridge/Ferndale exit (south of Eureka), west to Ferndale.

FORT BRAGG, CALIFORNIA
Population: 6,078

Fort Bragg is a lumber town, and it has been for most of its history. But Fort Bragg is really several towns, and therein lies its charm.

There is first of all Fort Bragg the American home town. The facades of early 1900s buildings along **Main Street** are painted in Victorian four-color schemes and decorated with canvas awnings. Bungalows of the Craftsman and other traditional California styles bring down-home warmth to the adjacent neighborhoods.

Then there is Fort Bragg the coastal resort, with inns, fine restaurants and other amenities for visitors wishing to enjoy the rugged Pacific scenery. Magnificent headlands, coves, natural arches, redwood forests, beaches and tidepools are just minutes away, even by foot.

Fort Bragg is also a fishing village. Down in **Noyo Harbor** is a commercial fishing fleet along with everything needed to service it. There are also facilities for recreational craft. Seafood restaurants, fishing charters and boat excursions cater to the tourist, and add to the color.

An art center is beginning to look as though it may be Fort Bragg's newest identity. Several good galleries have grown up, including the **Northcoast Artist's Cooperative.** The **Fort Bragg Center for the Arts** sponsors exhibitions of photographs, weavings, collage art, sculpture and other media.

Fort Bragg's logging history is recalled in two museums. The **Guest House Museum**, a handsome three-story 1892 home, displays photos and other artifacts of the lumber industry. The **Fort Bragg Depot**, a new marketplace museum, houses historic trains and logging artifacts under the same roof with little shops, a food court and art gallery.

SPECIAL FEATURES
• The famous California Western Railroad *Skunk* trains run 40 miles from Fort Bragg to the inland town of **Willits**. Once a logging railroad, the *Skunk* line delivers mail and groceries to remote areas. The line's half-day and full-day roundtrips through the redwoods have become one of Fort Bragg's top attractions. Sometimes the "trains" operate as motorcars on rails, at other times passenger cars are pulled by diesel or historic steam locomotives.

• **MacKerricher State Park** north of town has miles of beautiful beaches.

> *Visitors to Glass Beach, once the town dump, can find interesting, often attractive ocean-cleansed glass and pottery shards.*
>
> *The 1906 Earthquake devastated Fort Bragg as well as San Francisco. However, San Francisco's demand for lumber to rebuild brought prosperity to Fort Bragg.*

WHERE TO STAY
Avalon House B&B, 561 Stewart St., (707) 964-5555. Restored turn-of-century Craftsman-style home, antiques, private baths, extra-thick towels. $$$

Glass Beach B&B Inn, 726 N. Main St., (707) 964-6774. Fireplaces, private baths, hot tub, full country breakfasts. $$ to $$$

The **Grey Whale Inn,** 615 N. Main St., (800) 382-7244. Views of ocean or town, private baths, individually decorated rooms. $$$

Harbor Lite Lodge, 120 N. Harbor Dr., (707) 964-0221. Overlooking picturesque Noyo Harbor, private balconies, TV and telephones, landscaped grounds. $$ to $$$

Noyo River Lodge, 500 Casa del Noyo, (800) 628-1126. 1868 lumber baron's home perched on bluff, large deck, private baths, antiques and comforters, suites. $$$

WHERE TO EAT

Coast Hotel Cafe, 101 N. Franklin, (707) 964-6446. In restored historic Coast Hotel, King Salmon steamed with lemon dill beurre blanc, Breast of Chicken en Papilotte. $ to $$

North Coast Brewing Co., 444 N. Main St., (707) 964-2739. "Great Dinners - Serious Brew - Seafood Headquarters." $ to $$

The Restaurant, 418 N. Main St., (707) 964-9800. 1895 hospital (but doesn't look like one), original oils by Olaf Palm. $$ to $$$

The Wharf Restaurant, Noyo Harbor, (707) 964-4283. Overlooking river and ocean, fresh seafood, steaks. $ to $$

FURTHER INFORMATION

Fort Bragg-Mendocino Coast Chamber of Commerce, P. O. Box 1141, Fort Bragg, CA 95437, (707) 961-6300.

DIRECTIONS

From San Francisco, US 101 north to CA 20 (at Willits), CA 20 west to Fort Bragg.

GUALALA, CALIFORNIA

Population: About 1,200

Very few towns can compete with **Gualala** (pronounced "guah LAH lah") as a place of retreat. The little town hugs the Pacific Ocean along CA 1, a road far from the interstates and other crowded tourist ducts. The important part, though, is what lies between CA 1 and the Pacific: bold headlands, sweeping redwood forests, spectacular offshore rock formations. It is here that the hiker can face the wind on a lonely blufftop trail, or climb down to watch the waves break on a lonely beach, or explore an isolated cove.

Coastal scenery like this inspires. Place it not far from several heavily populated areas (to the south) and people who can afford it are going to move here. And that's exactly what's happening. Upscale developments are appearing in the hills about Gualala, and upscale shops are appearing in Gualala. Because the cultural climate is ideal for people with creative talents and a special love of nature, there are now probably more art galleries in Gualala than groceries.

The **Gualala Arts Center** provides a major source of nourishment for the town's artistic efforts. The center sponsors concerts, theater productions, and classes and maintains two galleries with changing exhibits.

River fishing and ocean rock fishing are popular pastimes here. Rock picking and free diving for abalone are becoming popular. The **Gualala River** is excellent for swimming and canoeing. Bicyclists as well as hikers will find trails offering breathtaking views of the ocean.

SPECIAL FEATURES

• The **Point Arena Lighthouse** north of town is the second tallest lighthouse on the West Coast. The lighthouse was built in 1908 to replace an earlier one destroyed by the San Francisco Earthquake. Maintained by a non-profit organization, the lighthouse and small adjacent museum are open to the public.

> *Jack London used to stay at the Gualala Hotel when he came here to fish. Naturally air-conditioned, Gualala's temperature rarely rises above 80° F.*

WHERE TO STAY

Gualala Hotel, CA 1, (707) 884-3441. Restored historic hotel, game room, library, wine shop, dining room. $$

Whale Watch Inn By the Sea, CA 1, (800) 942-5342. Contemporary inn with five buildings, beach access by private stairway, spectacular views, down comforters, full breakfasts. $$$

The Old Milano Hotel, CA 1, (707) 884-3256. B&B inn with ocean views, National Historic Monument, dining room. $$$

WHERE TO EAT

The Old Milano Restaurant, (see above). International entrees, fresh local produce prepared with Continental flair, reservations. $$ to $$$

St. Orre's Restaurant, CA 1, (707) 884-3335. In onion-domed building on landscaped grounds, California and Continental cuisines. $$$

FURTHER INFORMATION

Mendocino Coast Chamber of Commerce, P. O. Box 1141, Fort Bragg, CA 95437, (707) 961-6300.

DIRECTIONS

From San Francisco, CA 1 north (along Pacific) to Gualala.

HALF MOON BAY, CALIFORNIA

Population: 8,886

Boasting miles of beautiful beaches and rugged bluffs, and separated from San Francisco by a half hour's drive and from the Silicon Valley by a coastal mountain range, it's only to be expected that **Half Moon Bay** should be a popular

Bay Area retreat. The town is also the floriculture center of the **San Mateo Coast**; fields of flowers can be seen from the road, and fresh cut flowers are a given in area homes, inns and restaurants.

San Mateo County's first settlement (once known as Spanishtown), many of the homes and commercial structures in Half Moon Bay's historic district date to the 19th century. Restored storefronts provide an interesting backdrop for art and craft galleries, restaurants and quaint gift shops. Group walking tours may be arranged through the CoC.

The **James Johnston House**, outside of town, is a saltbox structure (ca. 1855) whose design was probably copied from the builder's Ohio home. Now on the National Register, plans call for the house and grounds to open after restoration is completed.

Located just north of town, **Pillar Point Harbor** is a bustling haven for pleasure craft and a commercial fishing fleet. The colorful harbor offers full marina services.

Widely known for its natural coastal beauty and abundant flora and fauna, Half Moon Bay provides a rich menu of recreational and sightseeing options. To list a few: whale-watching tours (January–April), air-taxi rides, horseback riding along the cliffs, salmon and rock fishing (charters available), sailing, beachcombing. Cyclists will fine a 12-mile coastal bicycle trail and golfers a course that overlooks the Pacific. Half Moon Bay also has an interesting variety of night clubs.

SPECIAL FEATURES

• A nature lover's paradise, the Half Moon Bay area offers the visitor a choice among a variety of field trips. Some suggestions:

For birdwatching — **Pescadero Marsh National Preserve**

For hiking/biking among giant trees and wildflowers — **Purissima Creek Redwoods**

For touring elephant-seal breeding grounds (December–March) —**Año Nuevo State Reserve** (reservations necessary)

For tide pooling — **Fitzgerald Marine Reserve**

• Visitors may pick their own berries, pumpkins, and kiwi at farms along the coastline.

WHERE TO STAY

Mill Rose Inn, 615 Mill St., (800) 900-7673. English country inn, European antiques, hand-painted fireplace tiles, private baths, TV/video players/phones, afternoon wine and cheese. $$$

Old Thyme Inn, 779 Main St., (415) 726-1616. 1899 Queen Anne home, English herb garden, antiques, private baths, sherry and candies. $$$

The Pillar Point Inn, P. O. Box 388 (El Granada), (415) 728-7377. Harborside inn, fireplaces, European-style feather beds, private baths, TV, phones, afternoon tea/beverages. $$$

San Benito House, 356 Main St., (415) 726-3425. Decorative pieces from Europe, contemporary paintings, English-style garden, sauna, glass-walled deck, restaurant. $$ to $$$

The Zaballa House B&B Inn, 324 Main St., (415) 726-9123. Circa 1859 home, antiques, oil paintings, old grandfather clocks, private baths, full breakfasts, beverages. $$ to $$$

WHERE TO EAT

Moss Beach Distillery, Beach Way & Ocean Blvd. (Moss Beach), (415) 728-5595. Spectacular views, ghosts, murder mystery dinners, champagne brunches. $$

San Benito House, (see above). "Salmon with a red pepper, toasted almond, and green olive butter served with a corn pancake." $ to $$

The Shore Bird, P. O. Box 40 (El Granada), (415) 728-5541. "Cape Cod on the California Coast," seafood. $$

FURTHER INFORMATION

Half Moon Bay Coastside Chamber of Commerce, 520 Kelly Ave., Half Moon Bay, CA 94019, (415) 726-8380

DIRECTIONS

From San Francisco, CA 1 south to Half Moon Bay.

HEALDSBURG, CALIFORNIA

Population: 9,469

Healdsburg is a model American town set in California wine country. The life and geography of the town center on a square, called **Healdsburg Plaza**, that dates back to the 1850s. The **bandstand** is the site of summer concerts; everything from Dixieland and Cajun to opera is performed for an audience seated, and sometimes picnicking, on the lawn. Every May, just before the **Healdsburg Country Fair**, about everyone in town marches around the square in an FFA/4H parade.

Spreading out from the square is a delightful town, with beautifully restored houses that span a good stretch of American history. The best way to see Healdsburg is to park (there are no parking meters) and, of course, stroll about the square. Here there are craft shops, art galleries and more good bakeries than is probably healthy for a town this size. Just off the plaza are antique shops and collectives representing over 100 dealers.

Reminding the visitor that this is after all wine country, several wineries have tasting rooms on the square. The tasting rooms are especially warm and natural places, with wood panelling and friendly greeters. Visitors receive a serving of one ounce or less of each wine they select. There's no need to swallow the wine: Little buckets take care of drivers and others who'd rather settle just for the taste. And all of this is for free — tasting rooms in Sonoma County do not charge.

SPECIAL FEATURE

• More than 50 **wineries** surround Healdsburg, making a trip into the countryside part of the itinerary. There are also farms, many open to the public, that grow asparagus, nectarines, popcorn, raspberries, kiwi fruit, winter squash and dozens of other fruits and vegetables. Most of the farms participate in Healdsburg's farmers' market, held at least one day each week from May through December. Farm directories and maps can be obtained at CoCs across Sonoma County.

> *Many Italian prospectors and miners settled around Healdsburg after the Gold Rush because the country reminded them of Northern Italy.*
> *Healdsburg is the only town in Sonoma County that always has fireworks on the 4th of July.*

WHERE TO STAY

The George Alexander House, 423 Matheson St., (707) 433-1358. Charming 1905 Victorian with quatrefoil windows, private baths, fireplaces, Oriental rugs, full breakfasts. $$ to $$$

Camelia Inn-Bed & Breakfast, 211 North St., (707) 433-8182. 1869 Italianate townhome, twin marble parlor fireplaces, antiques, villa-style swimming pool, full breakfasts. $$ to $$$

Grape Leaf Inn, 539 Johnson St., (707) 433-8140. Restored 1900 Queen Anne home, private baths, full breakfasts, afternoon wines and cheeses. $$ to $$$

Healdsburg Inn on the Plaza, 110 Matheson St., (707) 433-6991. Downtown Victorian inn, private baths, clawfoot tubs and fluffy towels, full breakfasts on roof garden/solarium. $$ to $$$.

Madrona Manor, 1001 Westside Rd., (800) 258-4003. Full-service inn in a mansion, 18 fireplaces, eight secluded acres, swimming pool, restaurant. $$$

WHERE TO EAT

Bistro Ralph, 109 Plaza St., (707) 433-1380. Simple food prepared by chef trained in France, seafood specialties. $$ to $$$

Jacob Horner's, 106 Matheson St., (707) 433-3939. Blueberry Pork Tenderloin, Mahi Mahi with Pineapple and Tomatillo $$ to $$$

Madrona Manor, (see above). Ca. 1881 Victorian mansion serving modified Classical French, prix fixe menu. $$$

Matuszek's, 345 Healdsburg Ave., (707) 433-3427. Czech and California-style cuisines done up in picture-book beauty and flavor. $$

Tre Scalini, 241 Healdsburg Ave., (707) 433-1772. The calamata olive and roasted red pepper oil baguette is a favorite baked good. $$ to $$$

FURTHER INFORMATION

Healdsburg Area Chamber of Commerce, 217 Healdsburg Ave., Healdsburg, CA 95448, (800) 648-9922.

DIRECTIONS

From San Francisco, US 101 north to Healdsburg.

MENDOCINO, CALIFORNIA

Population: 1008

When leaving CA 1 to enter **Mendocino**, take the northern approach (Lansing Street). Before you will appear a charming New England-like village looking down upon the blue Pacific. It's a beautiful sight.

Many of the loggers and mill workers attracted to Mendocino by the redwoods came from New England, hence the Cape Cod or Down East ambience of the village they built. After the mill operations ceased in the 1930s, the town went into a sort of hibernation and remained there until artists and others rediscovered its charm. Today there is a commitment by the people to preserve that charm; there's even an historical review board whose function it is to preserve Mendocino's traditional appearance.

Main Street is a wonderful juxtaposition of shops and businesses on one side and headlands (called palisades in southern California) and ocean on the other. On the street is the **Mendocino Presbyterian Church** (1868), the oldest Presbyterian church in continous operation in the state. The historic **Ford House** (1854), also on the street, is now a museum and visitor center for **Mendocino Headlands State Park** (see below).

The 1861 **Kelley House**, built of rough-sawn redwood boards, was erected by an early Mendocino entrepreneur. The house, gardens and spring-fed duck pond are now a museum.

Along Main and the several inland streets are some first-class art galleries and an unusually broad variety of unique shops. The **Mendocino Art Center** is the arts headquarters, with galleries, an art shop, library, gardens, classes and a theater.

SPECIAL FEATURES

• Mendocino is surrounded by **Mendocino Headlands State Park** Get a map of the park at Ford House and take in the sights, sounds and smell of the ocean from a walk on the headlands. Guided tours are sometimes available.

• Aquatic opportunities include deep-sea fishing, whale watching (winter months), snorkeling, and canoeing on Big River.

> *Scenes for the "Maine" village of Cabot Cove in the TV series "Murder, She Wrote" were in fact filmed in Mendocino.*
> *Mendocino's first known settler was the sole survivor of an 1850 shipwreck.*

WHERE TO STAY

Blair House Inn, Ford and Little Lake Sts., (707) 937-1800. Jessica Fletcher's house in TV series "Murder, She Wrote." $$$

The Headlands Inn, Howard and Albion Sts., (707) 937-4431. Restored 1868 building, fireplaces, private baths, "creative" full breakfasts. $$$

Joshua Grindle Inn, P. O. Box 647, (707) 937-4143. 1879 New England farmhouse on two landscaped acres, ocean views, fireplaces, antiques, private baths, full breakfasts. $$$

Mendocino Hotel and Garden Suites, 45080 Main St., (800) 548-0513. Established 1878, antiques, comforters, telephones, beautifully appointed dining rooms and lounges, gardens. $$$

The Whitegate Inn, 499 Howard St., (800) 531-7282. Victorian home, antiques, ocean views, fireplaces, private baths, gourmet breakfasts. $$$

WHERE TO EAT

Cafe Beaujolais, 961 Ukiah St., (707) 937-5614. Bread baked daily in wood-fired oven, regionally acclaimed. $$

Chocolate Moosse, 10390 Kasten st., (707) 937-4323. Seafood, pasta, delicious desserts, expresso. $ to $$

MacCallum House Restaurant, 45020 Albion St., (707) 937-5763. 111-year-old Victorian mansion, American Mediterraneau dining. $$

Mendocino Hotel, (see above), (707) 937-0511. Victorian dining room, Continental cuisine. $$$

955 Ukiah St. Restaurant, 955 Ukiah St., (707) 937-1955. "Casual elegance," California-French cuisine. $$

FURTHER INFORMATION

The Mendocino Coast Chamber of Commerce, P. O. Box 1141, Fort Bragg, CA 95437, (707) 961-6300.

DIRECTIONS

From San Francisco, CA 1 north to Mendocino.

NEVADA CITY, CALIFORNIA

Population: 2855

Colorfully painted buildings, balconies, winding streets and natural-gas lights. Place all of this in the pine forests of the Sierra foothills and the result is a very pretty town with a truly distinctive charm.

Nevada City began in 1849 with a store selling miners' supplies. One year later the town had a government, post office, and population of some 10,000! Since that year the population has swung up and down, mostly down. Today, what began as a Gold Rush mining town is a kind of living museum with a reputation that attracts artists, musicians, writers — and visitors. Strict building codes and underground wiring throughout help preserve that reputation.

Nevada City's downtown, full of interesting shops, is listed on the National Register of Historic Places. Of special interest is the **National Hotel** (1854-57), California's oldest continuously-operating hotel (see listing below). Herbert Hoover, Lola Montez, Jane Wyman, Martha Raye and Tim Conway are among the many notables who have entered its doors. The square grand piano in the lobby once journeyed around Cape Horn, and the ornate back bar was originally the dining room buffet in the Spreckels mansion in San Francisco. Horse-drawn carriage tours can be taken from the hotel.

The Victorian bell tower and gingerbread trim of **Firehouse No. 1** were added after the building's constructioin in 1861. Its contemporary,**Firehouse No. 2** (1861), continues in use. The **Nevada Theatre** (1865) is the state's oldest building constructed as a theater. Musicians, actors, and others still perform here.

The many restored homes, some of them historic, merit a drive or walk through the neighborhoods surrounding the downtown. Evening strolls along the gas-lighted streets downtown are popular here — people describing the setting usually use the word "romantic."

SPECIAL FEATURE

• **Grass Valley**, similar to Nevada City in charm and history, is just two miles away in the next valley.

> *In the general election of 1856 only Sacramento and San Francisco cast more ballots than Nevada City.*
> *During the 1960s and '70s hippies and back-to-the-landers began opening shops and other small businesses in the decaying downtown. Such efforts contributed much toward putting the town back on the map.*

WHERE TO STAY

Deer Creek Inn, 116 Nevada St., (800) 655-0363. 1870s Queen Anne home, picturesque creekside setting, gardens, private baths, "hearty" breakfasts. $$$

Downey House Bed & Breakfast Inn, 517 W. Broad St., (800) 258-2815. 1869 Eastland home, fragrant gardents, veranda, sweeping views of town, private baths, buffet breakfasts. $$$

Grandmere's Bed & Breakfast Inn, 449 Broad St., (916) 265-4660. Three-story 1856 Colonial Revival home on National Register, lawns and gardens, private baths, full breakfasts. $$$

National Hotel, 211 Broad St., (916) 265-4551. Oldest continuously operating hotel west of Rockies (1854-1857), a Who's Who of famous guests, Victorian dining room, saloon, pool. $$ to $$$

Red Castle Inn, 109 Prospect St., (916) 265-5135. 1857 Gothic Revival landmark, terraced gardens, verandas, private baths, Indian pudding or Miner's biscuits sometimes on breakfast menu. $$$

WHERE TO EAT

Country Rose, 300 Commercial St., (916) 265-6248. Country French. $$

Creekside Cafe, 101 Broad Street, (916) 265-3445. Lunch or dinner inside or out on deck, bar. $$

Friar Tuck's Restaurant & Wine Bar, 111 N. Pine St., (916) 265-9093. Dinner house, fondue, steaks, fish, bar, entertainment. $$

Posh Nosh, 318 Broad St., (916) 265-6064. Deli menu at lunch, California cuisine at dinner. $$

Selaya's, 320 Broad St., (916) 265-5697. International, dinner only. $$

FURTHER INFORMATION

Nevada City Chamber of Commerce, 132 Main St., Nevada City, CA 95959, (916) 265-2692.

DIRECTIONS
From Sacramento, I 80 north to Auburn, CA 49 north to Nevada City.

SOLVANG, CALIFORNIA
Population: 4,741

Separated from the Pacific by a coastal mountain range to the south, but open to climate-moderating ocean breezes from the west, lovely **Santa Ynez Valley** is sunny, temperate, and smog-free. The gently rolling valley is home to vineyards, horse ranches, apple orchards and, as unlikely as it may seem, the *Danish Captial of America*, **Solvang**.

Solvang (*sunny field* in Danish) was founded in 1911 by Danes from the Midwest seeking to establish a West Coast Danish colony and folk school. Over the years the town began to look more and more Danish as the townspeople, perhaps encouraged by visits from Danish royalty, turned increasingly to Danish-style architecture. Today the buildings sport exteriors of timber-framed white stucco, sloping green copper or wood shingle roofs, and lots of gables and dormers and towers. Up on top are hand-carved storks, down below are cobblestone sidewalks, outdoor cafes and shops with leaded-glass windows. There are four windmills; one still turns. Visiting Danes say that the town looks more like Denmark than Denmark.

Specific Danish sites include the **Little Mermaid**, a half-scale copy of the original in Copenhagen harbor, and the **Bethania Lutheran Church**, a typical rural Danish church with hand-carved pulpit and a scale model of a Danish sailing ship hanging from the ceiling. The half-timbered **Elverhoy Museum**, once a residence, presents the story of Solvang with old photographs, crafts, period rooms, and other exhibits. The **Hans Christian Andersen Museum** honors the life and work of the father and master of the modern fairy tale.

Solvang's most historic site is entirely non-Danish. The adobe **Mission Santa Ines**, established in 1804 as the 19th of the 21 missions built in California by Spanish Franciscan priests, has been beautifully restored (visitors welcome). The chapel, in continuous use since 1817, is decorated with murals by Indian artists as well as by masterpieces of Moorish art and sculpture. The **Mission Museum** displays a number of treasures, among them 16th-century church vestments. On the grounds are the cemetery and semi-formal gardens. Plans exist for restoring the mission village and quadrangle.

Solvang boasts no fewer than 350 shops! Danish offerings include pastries (of course), music boxes, porcelain figurines, knitted sweaters, folk art, handmade lace and Danish costumes. The shops are also noted for their selections of paintings and antiques.

Tours of Solvang may be taken on the *Honen*, a replica of a turn-of-the-century Copenhagen streetcar pulled by a pair of Belgian draft horses. Carriage tours are also offered. Gliders and bicycles provide two of the best ways to tour the valley; the air currents are ideal for the former, and the many delightful country roads are designed for the latter.

Critically acclaimed musicals, dramas, and comedies are staged in Solvang's outdoor **Festival Theater** from summer through early fall by the **Pacific Conservatory of the Performing Arts Theaterfest** And four spectacular area golf courses offer a variety of golfing challenges.

SPECIAL FEATURES

• Over 20 **Santa Barbara County wineries** are open to visitors, most without appointment. Many provide picnic tables. A wine touring map may be picked up at the vistiors center.

• **Lake Cachuma**, 15 minutes southeast, is home to a host of wildlife, including 275 species of birds. Eagle boat cruises (in winter) and boat rentals are available.

• The Pacific Ocean may be enjoyed at **Gaviota State Park** and **Refugio** and **El Capitan** state beaches.

> *All classic grape varieties can be grown in Santa Barbara County because of the many micro-climates.*

WHERE TO STAY

The Inn at Petersen Village, 1576 Mission Dr. (800) 321-8985. Replica of Danish village, garden, private baths, TV, "European buffet" breakfasts, dining room, wine hour with grand piano music. $$$

Los Olivios Grand Hotel, P.O. Box 526 (Los Olivios), (800) 446-2455. Exquisite little hotel, antiques, fireplaces, TV, pool, superb dining room, bicycles. $$$

Storybook Inn B&B, 409 First St., (805) 688-1703. Fireplaces, European beds, private baths, full gourmet breakfasts, wine/hors d'oeuvres hour, nightly homemade desserts. $$$

WHERE TO EAT

Ballard Store, 2449 Baseline Ave. (Ballard), (805) 688-5319. Continental menu, rack of lamb, fresh fish, bouillabaisse, abalone, all local wines. $$

Danish Inn Restaurant, 1547 Mission Dr., (805) 688-4813. Danish Smorgasbord, Danish specialties, steak, prime rib, fresh fish. $$

Scott's California Cafe and Wine Bar, 435 First St., (805) 686-8666. Gourmet American menu, regionally famous salads, daily fish and pasta specials.

FURTHER INFORMATION

Solvang Convention & Visitors Bureau, P.O. Box 70, Solvang, CA 93464, (800) 468-6765.

DIRECTIONS

From Los Angeles, US 101 west to Buellton, CA 246 east to Solvang.

SONOMA, CALIFORNIA

Population: 8,121

Old adobe buildings look on as children on the plaza play or point at ducks in the pond. Fountains splash as people enjoy their lunches or simply relax under the trees. This could so easily be Old Mexico. Only, of course, it's not. But it does have a Mexican ancestry.

Mission San Francisco Solano de Sonoma was founded in 1823, when California was still a province of Mexico. The mission was the last and most northerly of California's 21 Franciscan missions. A few years after the mission was built, Mexican General Mariano Vallejo, headquartered here, laid out the enormous 8-acre **Sonoma Plaza** (1834). The plaza was to become the center of Sonoma.

Still the center of Sonoma, the plaza today is bordered by old adobe buildings, lovely historic hotels (see listing below), art galleries and a host of inviting specialty shops. The best known of the buildings erected during Mexican times is the adobe **San Francisco Solano Mission church**, built by General Vallejo in 1840 to replace an earlier structure. The attached padres' quarters date to about 1825 and are Sonoma's oldest structure. The 1836 **Sonoma Barracks** and 1850s **Toscano Hotel** (originally a general store and library) join the mission church in making up the **Sonoma State Historic Park**.

Among the historic houses on or near the plaza are the 1840s **Salvador Vallejo Home**, the 1836 adobe "Casa Grande" and the 1847 **Nash-Patton Adobe**. A house of special interest away from the plaza is **Lachryma Montis**, the two-story Gothic Revival house built in 1851 by the now-American General Vallejo as his permanent home. The house, designated a state historical monument, was prefabricated and shipped around the Horn. Check with the Sonoma Valley Visitors Bureau on the plaza for touring information on these and many other historic buildings.

Sonoma's association with wine is nearly as old as the town itself. Cuttings of the Mission grape, used to make wines for the Mass, were brought to Sonoma as early as 1825 by Franciscan missionaries. The real birth of the wine industry, however, dates to 1857 when a Hungarian nobleman introduced cuttings of old-world varietals to the area and established **Buena Vista Winery**. Lining the beautiful Tuscany-like **Sonoma Valley** are now 36 or so wineries and some 6,000 acres of vineyards. Most of the tasting rooms along the 17-mile-long valley are open year round, and tastings are free in about 99% of them.

SPECIAL FEATURES

• Jack London built his hillside ranch, which he called his Beauty Ranch, near Glen Ellen north of Sonoma. What is now **Jack London State Historic Park** comprises about 800 acres of trees and spectacular scenery. On the grounds are the **House of Happy Walls** built in 1919 by London's widow, Charmian, and the remaining walls of **Wolf House**, a stone mansion that mysterously burned a few days before the Londons were due to move in. London memorabilia are on display in The House of Happy Walls.

• The **Sonoma Valley** is made-to-order for picnics. Pick up some local cheese, French bread and other items from the specialty food shops around the plaza and journey out to the vineyards to purchase a bottle of wine. Many of the wineries have set aside picturesque areas for picnics.

> *Sonoma Valley wines are by custom served only in distinctive blue-stemmed wine glasses.*

WHERE TO STAY

El Dorado Hotel, 405 First St. W., (707) 996-3030. French windows and terraces, bed linens of goose down, heated pool. $$$

Sonoma Mission Inn & Spa, P. O. Box 1447, (707) 938-9000. Lovely historic Spanish-mission-style hotel, extensive grounds. $$$

Swiss Hotel, 18 W. Spain St., (707) 938-2884. 1830s home converted to hotel in late 1800s, 1934 bar, signed celebrity photos. $$$

Thistle Dew Inn, 171 W. Spain St., (800) 382-7895. Antique arts and crafts furniture, gourmet breakfasts, bicycles $$$

Trojan Horse B&B, 19455 Sonoma Hwy., (800) 899-1925. Turn-of-century estate with antiques, gardens, outdoor Jacuzzi, bicycles. $$$

WHERE TO EAT

Della Santina's, 101 E. Napa St., (707) 935-0576. Trattoria, rosticceria, pasticceria. $ to $$

Eastside Oyster Bar & Grill, 133 E. Napa St., (707) 939-1266. Fresh seafood and Sonoma County products, garden patio. $ to $$

Cafe at the Feed Store, 529 First St. Wl, (707) 938-2122. In 1921 Feed Store Building, delightful cafe and bakery, garden patio. $

Murphy's Irish Pub, 464 First St. E., (707) 935-0660. Pub food, pasties, Irish stouts and international ales. $

Ristorante Piatti, in El Dorado Hotel (see above). Regional Italian cuisine, specialties from wood-burning oven and rotisserie. $ to $$

FURTHER INFORMATION

Sonoma Valley Visitors Bureau, 453 First Street East, Sonoma, CA 95476, (707) 996-1090.

DIRECTIONS

From San Francisco, US 101 north to CA 37, CA 37 northeast to CA 121, CA 121 north to CA 12, CA 12 north to Sonoma.

COLORADO

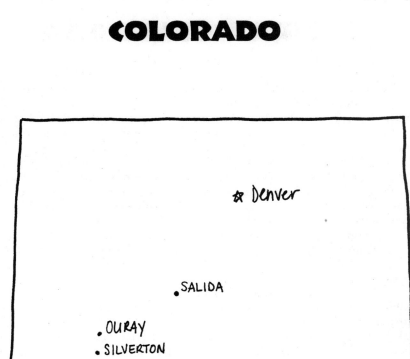

OURAY, COLORADO

Population: 644

Travelers sometimes allot a couple of hours to **Ouray** before speeding on to their next destination. They often come back, but this time for a week, or more. True, Ouray is a quaint old Victorian mining town with no traffic lights, malls, freeways or fast-food restaurants. But Ouray is more than that, as visitors soon discover. Ouray is also a popular spa, and it is also the *Jeep Capital of the World*.

All of Ouray is a National Historic District. The buildings, most of them restored, go back to the last two decades of the 19th century and the first decade of the 20th. Although quiet and charming today, Ouray was once wild and wide open: not a few of the structures that now house respectable bed & breakfasts, restaurants and residences were once saloons, brothels and cribs.

The **Ouray County Museum** is the best place to start a tour of the town. The museum, once a miners' hospital (1887), contains 27 room-sized exhibits of everything from a cellblock out of the old **Ouray Jail** to a child's bedroom to an outstanding mineral collection.

Sweet, hot mineral water (105 degrees) flowing from **Box Canyon** heats buildings, fills hotel hot tubs and vaporcaves, and pours into the **Ouray Hot Springs Pool**. The latter is divided into several sections of differing temperatures. The hottest is a soaking section, the coolest a diving and lap lane section. The complex, which also includes a fitness center and park, is very popular in the winter, especially after a day of crosscountry skiing or ice climbing.

Ouray's **Chipeta Opry Show**, one of the finest of its kind anywhere, features country music, western music, '50s music, gospel, an Elvis tribute and a patriotic revue.

SPECIAL FEATURE

• The surrounding country, some of the most beautiful in the world, is laced with old mule trails, stage coach trails and mining roads that have found new life as 4-wheel-drive roads. Along these roads are old mines and boarding houses, ghost towns, alpine flowers, waterfalls and other treasures. The best way to do these roads is by guided tour, at least on the first time out. Once you think you'd be comfortable driving along the top of a 3,000-foot canyon, go for a rental.

> *Scenes from "True Grit" and "How the West Was Won" were filmed in the Ouray area.*

WHERE TO STAY

The Damn Yankee B&B, 100 6th Ave., (800) 845-7512. Distinctive custom-built B&B inn, gourmet breakfasts. $$ to $$$

Historic Western Hotel Bed l& Breakfast, 210 7th Ave., (303) 325-4645. Restored hotel built in 1891 as a "miner's palace," "hearty" breakfasts. $$

Main Street B&B's, 322 Main St., (303) 325-4871. Charming turn-of-the-century houses with decks, private baths, TV, some kitchen suites. $$ to $$$

The Manor B&B, 317 2nd St., (303) 325-4574. Restored 1890 Georgian Victorian hybrid on National Register, private baths, hot tub, afternoon refreshments. $$ to $$$

St. Elmo Hotel, 426 Main St., (303) 325-4951. Established 1898, antiques, stained glass, polished wood and brass trim, private baths. $$ to $$$

WHERE TO EAT

Bon Ton Restaurant, (See St. Elmo Hotel). Italian cuisine, fresh seafood, award-winning wine list. $ to $$

Coachlight, 118 W. 7th Ave., (303) 325-4361. Charming Victorian setting (1888), once a brothel, a favorite Ouray dinner house. $ to $$

Outlaw Restaurant & Mountain Cookout, 610 Main, (303) 325-4366/4458. Popular steak house, Western flair, home of Outlaw Mountain Cookout. $ to $$

The Pinon Restaurant and Tavern, 737 Main St., (303) 325-4334/7303. Classic international recipes with home-style flair, tavern deck with mountain views, reservations recommended. $ to $$

Pricco's, 736 Main St., (303) 325-4040. Steaks, seafood, pasta, patio dining in historic building, summer only. $ to $$

FURTHER INFORMATION

Ouray Chamber Resort Association, P. O. Box 145, Ouray, CO 81427, (800) 228-1876.

DIRECTIONS

From Denver, I 70 west to exit 37 (before Grand Junction), CO 141 south to US 50, US 50 south to US 550 (at Montrose), US 550 south to Ouray.

SALIDA, COLORADO

Population: 4,737

Salida (pronounced "sa LYE da") is easy to picture — simply conjure up an image of what a Colorado town ought to look like: tree-shaded streets (including a turn-of-the-century main street) nestled in a valley surrounded by snow-capped mountains, crystal-clear streams and lakes, wildflower-covered slopes, and bright yellow aspens against Colorado blue skies. It is with good reason that Salida has been nicknamed the *Heart of the Rockies.*

Established in 1880, Salida has an agricultural, mining and railroad history. The historic district, made up of late 19th- and early 20th-century homes and business structures, is one of the largest in Colorado listed on the National Register of Historic Places.

One of the most active of the historic sites is the **Salida Hot Springs Pool and Mixed Baths,** the largest indoor hot springs pool in Colorado. As popular today as 50 years ago, the odorless mineral waters are used for everything from swimming and water games to arthritis classes. There are three pools in addition to private hot baths.

Sometimes called the *Banana Belt* because of its surprisingly mild climate, Salida is a year-round sportsman's paradise. Kayak racing, hiking, backpacking, golfing, horseback riding and four-wheeling are all popular. The **Monarch Ski Area** is just minutes away. For mountain bikers there are leisurely rides, rides in the mid-ability range, and rides like the Monarch Crest Trail, considered one of the best in the world.

The **Arkansas River**, which flows through Salida, offers guided family float trips, high-adventure white-water trips, and everything in between, including fishing excursions. Trips vary from quarter-day to several-day and offer splendid opportunities to view wildlife and majestic scenery. Large brown, rainbow, cutthroat, and brook trout are plentiful in the Arkansas and in countless streams, lakes, and beaver ponds.

SPECIAL FEATURES

• The high country and several ghost towns can be visited by half-day to all-day car tours. A four-wheel drive isn't necessary. Check with the CoC for routings.

• **Buena Vista**, another 19th-century Colorado town with a quaint downtown area, is 25 miles north of Salida.

> *One of the most beautiful of the town's seasonal attractions occurs each year right after Thanksgiving when some 22,000 colored lights are strung in the shape of an enormous Christmas tree on the side of Tenderfoot Hill.*
>
> *The Salida area is sometimes called the "14ers Region" because of the number of peaks over 14,000 feet in the Sawatch Range to the west.*
>
> *Over 40 percent of the trout used to stock Colorado's waters come from nearby Mt. Shavano Fish Hatchery.*

WHERE TO STAY

Castillo de Caballeros, P. O. Box 89, (719) 539-2002. High on Pinon Hill, hot tub on deck, piano, bottomless pot of coffee, overnight stabling. $ to $$

The Century House B&B, 401 E. 1st St., (719) 539-7064. 103-year-old French Victorian home, antiques, close to downtown. $ to $$

The Gazebo Country Inn B&B, 507 E. Third St., (719) 539-7806. 1901 home with white picket fence, porch swing, full breakfasts. $$

The Poor Farm Country Inn, 8495 County Rd. 160, (719) 539-3818. Renovated 1892 brick poor farm, 100-year-old library lounge, wine. $$

Plum Tree Inn, 247 E. Sackett St., (719) 539-7812. 1890s inn, large gathering room, hot tub room, bunks available, downtown location. $

WHERE TO EAT: A SAMPLE

First Street Cafe, 137 E. First St., (719) 539-4759. Local favorite, Mexican platters, vegetarian dishes, daily specials. $

Mama D's Sandwich Joint, 140 F St., (719) 539-2228. Chicago-style sandwich joint, popular lunch spot, framed caricatures on wall. $

Mt. Shavano Inn, 1220 E. US 50, (719) 539-4561. Extensive steak and seafood menus. $ to $$

FURTHER INFORMATION

Heart of the Rockies, 406 W. Rainbow Boulevard, Salida, CO 81201, (719) 539-2068.

DIRECTIONS

From Denver, I 25 south to exit 102 (Pueblo), US 50 west to Salida.

SILVERTON, COLORADO

Population: 716

Nestled in a narrow valley in the county with the highest mean elevation of any county in the United States, **Silverton's** "low" altitude is a mere 9,318 feet. At this altitude you may need a blanket on a summer evening, but on a sunny day in winter you can sport in the snow with a t-shirt instead of a jacket or sweater. The surrounding countryside is 100% scenery — there's not so much as one acre of agriculture in the entire county.

Victorian Silverton, now a National Historic Landmark, is one of the best-preserved but least-discovered of Colorado's romantic old mining camps. Having never experienced a major fire (unlike most mining towns) Silverton retains most of its original homes and commercial buildings. The **museum** next to the county courthouse provides a good short introduction to the town and ideal starting point for a walking tour. The **San Juan County Courthouse** (1907), still in use, is one of the most beautiful in Colorado. Another impressive public building, the native stone **Town Hall** (1909), has been faithfully restored to its original self.

"Notorious" **Blair Street** once housed 40 saloons and brothels, integral parts of every proper mining and railroad town. The street has provided settings for several Western movies.

The **Old Hundred Gold Mine Tour** proves that there are experiences that can be both educational and exciting. The one-hour tour, set up by local miners, consists of a narrow-gauge train ride into an authentic gold mine deep in a mountain. An experienced miner serves as the guide.

There are several options for the evening. Enjoying the saloons, a time-honored recreation in any mining town, is one. Another is attending a production of *A Theatre Group* in the **Miners' Union Theatre**. The company stages the plays of George Bernard Shaw in the summer **Shaw Festival**; a variety of plays are staged the rest of the year.

SPECIAL FEATURE

• One of the best ways to enjoy the area's spectacular scenery is to board a coal-fired, steam-operated train of the **Durango & Silverton Narrow Gauge Railroad Company** for a trip to Durango. The train, serving Silverton since 1882, offers breathtaking views. During some months it is possible to take a railroad-operated bus to Durango and return to Silverton by train the same day.

> *Some of the nation's best 4-wheel-drive roads are in the Silverton area. Check with the CoC for a detailed Jeep map and for information on Jeep rentals and tours.*
>
> *Some of the clearest and cleanest air in the U.S. is just south of Silverton on top of Molas Pass.*

WHERE TO STAY

Christopher House B& B, P. O. Box 241, (303) 387-5857. 1894 home, house of mayor during town's boom days, antiques, fresh wildflowers, full breakfasts. $$

The Grand Imperial Hotel, 1219 Greene St., (303) 387-5527. 1882 hotel, mountain views, private baths, two magnificent back bars, dining room. $$ to $$$

Wingate House B&B, 1045 Snowden St., (303) 387-5520. 1886 home, art, down pillows & comforters, spectacular views from porch. $$

WHERE TO EAT

Bent Elbow Restaurant & Bar, P. O. Box 371, (303) 387-5775. Steaks, Rocky Mountain trout, Mexican dishes. $

Gold King Dining and Hub Saloon, (see Grand Imperial Hotel). Traditional American fare in grand Victorian surroundings. $$

FURTHER INFORMATION

Silverton Colorado Chamber of Commerce, P. O. Box 565, Silverton, CO 81433, (303) 387-5654.

DIRECTIONS

From Denver, I 70 west to exit 37 (before Grand Junction), CO 141 south to US 50, US 50 south to US 550 (at Montrose), US 550 south to Silverton.

CONNECTICUT

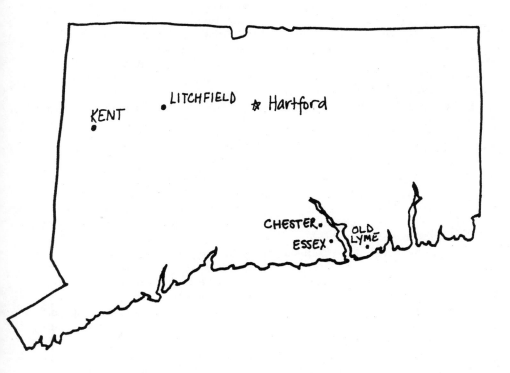

KENT

LITCHFIELD

☆ Hartford

CHESTER

ESSEX

OLD LYME

ESSEX/CHESTER, CONNECTICUT

Population: 2,500/1,563

The pretty villages of **Essex** and **Chester** are the kinds of places you go when you wish to experience that New England of Christmas cards, picture calendars and romantic old movies. Here you can start the day by jogging or biking along a wooded country road past little clusters of white clapboard houses. You can then spend part of the day sightseeing along the beautiful **Connecticut River** and the rest browsing in galleries, boutiques, and sophisticated shops. In the evening you can relax by the fire in a gorgeous old inn after seeing a good play and dining in a world-class restaurant. It doesn't come much better.

The **Connecticut River Museum** in Essex offers a thoroughly enjoyable introduction to the region. Housed in an 1878 dockhouse, the museum's permanent and seasonal exhibits recall the long and colorful history of the Connecticut River and its beautiful valley.

Quaint shops in both villages offer a wide selection of fine and decorative artwork. **The Artisans**, a craft gallery cooperative in Chester, displays paintings, furniture, pottery, clothing and other works of its members. For arts and crafts from another time, there's the colonial **Pratt House** (1732/1734) in Essex, where you'll find Connecticut redware and American furnishings of the 17th, 18th, and 19th centuries among the collections.

The natural beauty of the **Connecticut River Valley** combines with the picturesque beauty of villages like Essex and Chester to make this region an especially attractive one. There are several good ways to take in the beauty. The **Valley Railroad Company** in Essex offers excursions in vintage 1920s' steam trains along the Connecticut River to Chester and back; there's also the option of getting off at **Deep River** for a riverboat cruise. Two-hour cruises on a 70-foot schooner are also available (some summers) out of Essex.

Chester Airport offers 25-minute scenic flights over the lower Connecticut River Valley. For more traditional (and shorter and cheaper) sightseeing, there's the trip across the river on the **Chester-Hadlyme Ferry**, one of the oldest continuously operating ferries in the nation.

The theater has long been important in Connecticut, and Essex and Chester maintain the tradition. Among the best-known productions are those of the **Ivoryton Playhouse** near Essex (summer repertory), the **National Theatre of the Deaf** in Chester (performances in sign language and spoken words), and the **Goodspeed-at-Chester/Norma Terris Theatre** (new musicals-in-progress).

> *Although there is still some commerce and light industry in the region, Essex has evolved into a definitely upscale residential community.*

WHERE TO STAY

Riverwind Inn B&B, 209 Main St. (Deep River), (203) 526-2014. Romantic restored 1830 home, informal country atmosphere, private baths, full breakfasts. $$$

The Inn at Chester, 318 W. Main St., (203) 526-9541. 1776 inn in country setting, lovely gardens, private baths, health club. $$$

The Copper Beech Inn, 46 Main St. (Ivoryton), (203) 767-0330. Elegant Victorian home and gardens, private baths, famed restaurant. $$$

Griswold Inn, 36 Main St. (Essex), (203) 767-1776. Lovely country hotel, handsome barroom, historic collection of marine art, private baths, charming dining rooms. $$$

The Ivoryton Inn, 115 Main St. (Ivoryton), (203) 767-0422. 18th-century inn, individually decorated rooms, restaurant. $$ to $$$

WHERE TO EAT

The Copper Beech Inn, (see above). Fine French country cuisine. $$ to $$$

Fiddlers Seafood Restaurant, 4 Water St. (Chester), (203) 526-3210. "Fresh and innovative seafood at its best," Lobster au Peche, Oysters Imperial. $$

Fine Bouche, Main St. (Centerbrook), (203) 767-1277. Classical French, grilled salmon, sauteed trout. $$

Griswold Inn, (see above). Classic American dishes and traditional New England fare, famous meat pies, own sausages. $$

Restaurant du Village, 59 Main St. (Chester), (203) 526-5301. Award-winning, regional French cuisine. $$$

FURTHER INFORMATION

Connecticut Valley Tourism Commission, 393 Main St., Middletown, CT 06457, (203) 347-6924.

DIRECTIONS

From New Haven, I 95 east to exit 69, CT 9 north to Essex.

KENT, CONNECTICUT

Population: 2,900

The three parallel lines on the map signify that **Kent** is nestled in some special countryside. One of the lines is scenic U.S. 7 winding its way through the **Litchfield Hills.** A second is the **Housatonic River,** flowing alongside the highway. The third, a little to the west, is the **Appalachian Trail,** synonymous with breathtaking scenery. In addition to its lovely countryside, Kent has many beautiful mementos of some three centuries of history. The village also offers some fabulous shopping.

The sites of Kent are neatly ordered along the three parallel lines. Approaching from the south, the visitor first passes **Bull's Bridge,** already in place at the time of the Revolution, and one of the only two covered bridges in Connnecticut open to automobiles. The bridge and the falls beneath it are very frequently viewed through camera lenses.

Kent Center, a little more up the highway, is the place for antiques, fine arts and both traditional and contemporary American arts and crafts, including hand-carved signs and some of the finest and most unusual clothing around.

Two miles north of Kent Center is the **Sloane-Stanley Museum**. The museum features works of art by noted author and artist, Eric Sloane. There is also a re-creation of Sloane's studio, an extensive collection of Early American woodworking tools and implements, and the remains of the **Kent Iron Furnace**, in operation from 1826 to 1892.

Yet a little farther north is the **Flanders Historic District**, a cluster of houses that were once part of the center of Kent. Especially noteworthy here is the**Seven Hearths**, the 1754 home of the great portrait painter, George Lawrence Nelson. The home, now a museum, displays an impressive collection of Nelson's artwork and lithographs.

SPECIAL FEATURES

 • **Kent Falls State Park**, north on US 7, is known for its 200-foot cascade, the largest in the state.

> *With its iron ore and many smelting furnaces, this part of Connecticut was able to supply the Continental Armies in the War for Independence with hundreds of cannon.*

WHERE TO STAY

Chaucer House, 88 N. Main St., (203) 927-4858. Colonial home, large lawns and maple trees, convenient location, "English hospitality," "bountiful" breakfasts. $$$

Constitution Oak Farm, Beardsley Rd., (203) 354-6495. 1830s home on 200-acre farm, near Lake Waramaug, period furnishings. $$$

The Country Goose B&B, 211 Kent Cornwall Rd., (203) 927-4746. 18th century colonial house, antiques, guest library, garden flowers, home baking. $$$

Fife 'n Drum, US 7, (203) 927-3509. Elegant guest rooms, private baths, TV, award-winning restaurant. $$$

Mavis' B&B, 230 Kent Cornwall Rd., (203) 927-4334. 1860 Greek Revival home, cozy den, private baths, also cottage apartment. $$$

WHERE TO EAT

Bulls Bridge Inn, 333 Kent Rd., (203) 927-1617. American menu, steaks, chicken, fresh grilled seafood. $$

The Cornucopia Restaurant, 24 S. Main St., (203) 927-3136. Contemporary American cuisine created from Asian and European influences. $$

Villager Restaurant, Main St., (203) 927-3945. Home-style cooking in cozy and friendly atmosphere. $

FURTHER INFORMATION

The Litchfield Hills Travel Council, P. O. Box 1776, Marble Dale, CN 06777, (203) 868-2214.

DIRECTIONS

From New York City, I 684 north to I 84, east to exit 7, north on US 7 to Kent.

LITCHFIELD, CONNECTICUT

Population: 1378

Litchfield is one of the finest examples of mid and late 18th century architecture in the U.S. It is also one of the most beautiful colonial villages in New England. The village has been compared with Williamsburg, Virginia; the difference is that Williamsburg is a reconstruction and Litchfield is the real thing.

The **Litchfield Green** was laid out in the 1770s and hasn't changed much since. On the Green are exactly what ought to be there: quaint shops, restaurants, art galleries and, of course, a **Congregational Church** (1829) that is one of the most photographed in New England.

Grand maple-lined streets, gracious old homes and gentrification carry the colonial spell beyond the **Green.** Along CT 63 north and south of the Green lie a living museum of gorgeous Georgian buildings. To name just three: the house once owned by **Benjamin Tallmadge** (ca 1760), an aide to George Washington; **Sheldon's Tavern** (1760), where George Washington really did sleep; and the birth site of **Harriett Beecher Stowe** (1775), author of *Uncle Tom's Cabin.*

Also on CT 63 (South) is the **Tapping Reeve House and Law School**, the country's first law school (1774). Graduates included Vice Presidents Aaron Burr and John C. Calhoun, three Supreme Court justices, and well over a hundred cabinet members, governors and members of Congress. The house, with finely furnished period rooms, and school are open to the public.

The **Litchfield Historical Society Museum** has seven galleries featuring an especially fine selection of early Americana. The museum also traces the history of Litchfield from Indian country to the village as it is today.

> *Litchfield's beautiful homes and tree-lined streets belie its early history as a manufacturing center.*
>
> *Just west of town is Connecticut's largest natural lake, Bantam Lake. Bordering the lake is White Memorial Foundation, a 4,000-acre nature sanctuary.*
>
> *White Flower Farm, with 5 acres of display gardens, is nationally known for its English tuberous begonias.*

WHERE TO STAY

The Litchfield Inn, Rte. 202, (203) 567-4503. Country inn, roaring fireplaces, private baths, TV and phones, restaurant, hor d'oeuvres. $$$

Toll Gate Hill Inn & Restaurant, Rte. 202 and Tollgate Rd., (203) 567-4545. 1745 restored tavern in National Register, private baths, TV and phones, restaurant, outdoor decks. $$$

WHERE TO EAT

Toll Gate Hill Inn & Restaurant, (see above). Early American setting with contemporary American menu, award-winning restaurant. $$ to $$$

The Village Restaurant, 25 West St., On the Green, (203) 567-8307. Sauteed salmon, Maryland crab cakes, home-made desserts. $$

West Street Grill, West St., On the Green, (203) 567-3885. "New lighter approach" with "old-fashioned flavors," reputedly one of best in Connecticut. $$ to $$$

FURTHER INFORMATION
Litchfield Hills Travel Council, P. O. Box 1776, Marble Dale, CT 06777, (203) 868-2214.

DIRECTIONS
From Hartford, US 202 east to Litchfield.

OLD LYME, CONNECTICUT

Population: village less than 1,000

It sometimes happens that the best of an era becomes concentrated in one small spot on the map. When that happens, the beauty of the spot can become almost overwhelming. A common human reaction seems to be to grab a brush or a camera, as though caging the beauty were the only way to control it. And so it's been with **Old Lyme**.

Through the 18th century and well into the 19th, some of the most fortunate beneficiaries of the region's maritime commerce, including sea captains, built grand homes along **Lyme Street**. A few of the earliest houses were pre-Georgian; later ones displayed Georgian, Greek Revival, Italianate, and various mixtures of styles. The houses were, and are, separated by stone walls and vast, beautifully groomed grounds. Those on one side of the street back onto the **Lieutenant River**, and so views of water and salt marshes enter the scene.

It was only a matter of time before the landscape would begin attracting serious artists. And so it did, in 1899; from that year until 1937 Old Lyme was home to one of the country's first art colonies, and the center of American Impressionism. At the heart of the activity was Florence Griswold, daughter of a sea captain and heiress to one of Lyme Street's lovely mansions. Griswold didn't have the money to maintain the home, and so turned to innkeeping. The house-turned-inn became home to the art colony, and Florence Griswold became the colony's friend and advocate.

Sitting proudly on five landscaped acres, the 1817 Georgian mansion is now the **Florence Griswold Museum**. Painted on the doors and wooden dining-room panels of the house are various works of "Miss Florence's" boarders. Each has its story. The museum also presents four exhibitions each year of works from the Barbizon and American Impressionist schools of painting. A museum of history as well as art, the house features several period room settings.

Art is also exhibited at other addresses on Lyme Street. Housed in a Federal-style home (1817, on National Register), the **Lyme Academy of Fine Arts** exhibits paintings, sculptures and other works by students, faculty and others. The gallery of the **Lyme Art Association** offers year-round shows of works by association members.

Even with its art aside, beautiful Old Lyme is worth some serious exploring. A National Historic District, the village is a living museum of gracious old mansions. It is also a center for fine antiques.

SPECIAL FEATURE

• Down the coast in the southeastern corner of the state is another quintessential New England seaside village, **Stonington Borough.** The borough is home to the last commercial fishing fleet in Connecticut. Of special note here are the **Old Lighthouse Museum** and the many fine examples of 18th- and 19th-century architecture. The main street is flanked by boutiques, antique shops and several fine restaurants.

> *Sound View Beach is a public beach with parking and other facilities. Local residents tend to avoid the place during the warmer months.*

WHERE TO STAY

Bee & Thistle Inn, 100 Lyme St., (203) 434-1667. Restored 1756 home with riverside setting, lovely carved staircase, sunlit porches. $$$
Old Lyme Inn, 85 Lyme St., (203) 434-2600. Restored 1850s mansion, Empire and Victorian furnishings, private baths. $$$

WHERE TO EAT

Bee & Thistle Inn, (see above). Highly rated, American cuisine, romantic setting with fireplaces. $$ to $$$
Old Lyme Inn, (see above). Highly rated, innovative menu, white table cloths with a single rose, royal blue chairs and rug. $$$

FURTHER INFORMATION

Southeastern Connecticut Tourism District, P. O. Box 89, New London, CT 06320, (800) 863-6569; **Florence Griswold Museum,** 96 Lyme St., Old Lyme, CT 06371, (203) 434-5542.

DIRECTIONS

From New Haven, I 95 east to exit 70, CT 156 south to Old Lyme.

DELAWARE

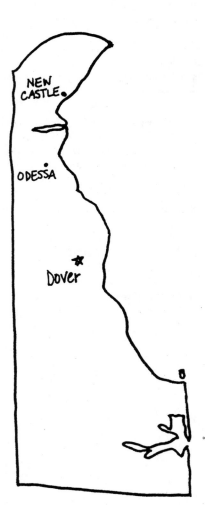

NEW CASTLE, DELAWARE

Population: 4,837

Located on the Delaware River just south of Wilmington, **New Castle** is one of our country's finest but least known colonial treasures. In the historic part of town there are not only buildings but whole streets, some even cobbled, that look very much like they did 200 years ago. Although a town today, New Castle was once a prosperous colonial city. Which is what makes New Castle's historic district so very precious — it isn't a reconstructed village, it's a preserved 18th-century American city!

When an 18th-century American city enters the 21st century largely intact, something in history took a wrong turn. And so it did. During the 1600s New Castle shifted back and forth between Swedish, Dutch and English control. In the 1700s the town became the capital of the colony and, later, state of Delaware. It also became the largest city in Delaware, and one known for its wealth and refinement.

Following the Revolution, the town prospered as a transportation and trade center; then, it happened: around 1840, long-distance rail lines were laid through Wilmington, not New Castle. The town/city remained virtually forgotten until rediscovery in the early 1920s.

New Castle's *Heritage Trail* comprises 26 historic sites, some of them entire streets or rows of houses. The buildings, usually brick, were built throughout the 18th and into the early 19th centuries. They show several architectural styles, including Dutch, Georgian, and Federal (Adam). Most of the houses are private residences.

The **Court House** was the colonial capitol between 1732 (date of construction) and 1777, when Dover became Delaware's capital. Standing on the edge of the **Green** (1655), the building is now a Delaware State Museum Site. The prisoners' dock, witness stand and judge's bench can be seen in the restored courtroom. Group tours may be arranged.

Immanuel Episcopal Church (1703; tower, 1822), was the first parish of the Church of England in Delaware. The church was rebuilt, using the original walls, after a fire in 1980. Signers of the Declaration of Independence, governors and other historic figures are buried in the cemetery. Another important church, the **New Castle Presbyterian Church** (1707), was restored to its original appearance after World War II.

There are three house museums, all with period furnishings. The first, the **Dutch House** (1700), is a rare and relatively undisturbed example of a house common in colonial times. Standing in contrast, the elegant **Amstel House** (1738) was the home of Governor Van Dyke. George Washington attended a wedding here in 1784. The third house is the Federal-style **George Read II House** (1801); with its 22 rooms and 14,000 square feet, it was once the largest house in the state. The formal garden, installed in 1847, is the oldest surviving garden in Delaware.

SPECIAL FEATURES

• Many historic homes and gardens are open to the public on *A Day in Old New Castle*, held the third Saturday in May.

• Several lovely, historic mansions and gardens in or near Wilmington, several miles to the north, are open to the public. One of the most celebrated is **Winterthur**, where American decorative arts from 1640 to 1860 are displayed in two buildings on a nearly 1,000-acre estate. In one, a gallery, is an introductory exhibition; in the second, the mansion of Henry Francis du Pont, are 175 period room settings (guided tours). **Rockwood** (1851), another 19th-century estate, provides a superb example of Rural Gothic architecture and Gardenesque landscape design.

> *The interior and basement of the hexagonal Old Library Museum (1892) are illuminated in part by skylights and light-sinks.*

WHERE TO STAY

The David Finney Inn, 216 Delaware St., (800) 334-6640. Historic inn with origins in 1600s, antique pieces, private baths. $$ to $$$

Jefferson House B&B, 5 The Strand, (302) 323-0999. 1790s river-front hotel/ residence, antique furnishings, Jacuzzi, private baths, private entrances, efficiencies. $$ to $$$

Terry House B&B, 130 Delaware St., (302) 322-2505. Circa 1860 brick town house, spacious rooms, TV, private baths, porches. $$ to $$$

William Penn Guest House, 206 Delaware St., (302) 328-7736. Restored 1682 home, reputed lodging place of William Penn, antiques. $$

WHERE TO EAT

The David Finney Inn, (see above). Fine meals served in antique-furnished dining room or on courtyard overlooking gardens. $$

Newcastle Inn Restaurant, Cobblestone Market St., (302) 328-1798. Dishes ranging from traditional colonial fare to authentic French entrees. $$

FURTHER INFORMATION

New Castle Visitors Bureau, P. O. Box 465, New Castle, DE 19720, (800) 758-1550; and **George Read II House**, 42 The Strand, New Castle, DE 19720, (302) 322-8411.

DIRECTIONS

From Wilmington, DE 9 south to New Castle.

ODESSA, DELAWARE

Population: About 300

Rural **Odessa**, known until 1855 as **Cantwell's Bridge**, prospered during the 18th and 19th centuries from grain shipping and, later, the peach trade. The sources of prosperity didn't last, however, and the town's growth came to an end. Many handsome buildings from the 18th and 19th centuries survived, in large part because Odessa's commercial life had always proceeded in cooperation rather than competition with existing buildings. Today the buildings, some exquisitely restored, line the tree-shaded brick sidewalks of an especially delightful little chunk of another era.

Four of the town's most historic buildings are grouped as the **Historic Houses of Odessa**, owned and operated by the Winterthur Museum and Gardens. The buildings are open to the public. Group tours are available by reservation (groups may enjoy boxed lunches — see below — or a formal coffee/tea).

The first of the Historic Houses of Odessa, the **Corbit-Sharp House** (1771/1774), is the finest example of mid-Georgian architecture in the state. Landscaped with sweeping lawns and formal gardens, the house is beautifully furnished in the style of the late 18th century.

The stately **Wilson-Warner House** (1769) typifies a simpler form of Georgian architecture commonly found in Delaware. Itemized lists of the house's contents from 1829 have aided the Winterthur Museum in selecting and arranging the furnishings. In the rear of the house are beehive ovens and a muskrat-skinning shack.

One of Delaware's oldest houses, the early 18th-century **Collins-Sharp House**, was formed by joining two small houses. The log-and-frame house serves as a center for the museum's hands-on educational programs for children.

The Federal-style "brick hotel" (1822), originally a hotel and later a residence, is now a gallery housing the country's largest collection of Belter furniture. (Belter was a mid 19th-century manufacturer known for his technologically innovative, highly carved creations. The furniture's style is described as "Rococo Revival," but most people today would describe it simply as Victorian — and elegantly uncomfortable.)

There are several lovely private homes in Odessa whose doors open as part of the annual "Christmas in Odessa," first weekend in December. One of them, the circa 1780 **January House**, commands a spectacular view of the **Appoquinimink Creek** and surrounding marshland. Another, the **Charles T. Polk House** (1852), is a grand mansion exemplifying the late Federal style.

SPECIAL FEATURES

• **DE 9**, which passes just to the east of town, is listed by the state as a scenic drive.

• To the southeast of Odessa on DE 9 is the 15,122-acre **Bombay Hook National Wildlife Refuge**, a haven for waterfowl. Within the refuge are auto tour routes, walking paths, and observation trails and towers. The **Allee House**, a circa 1753 brick plantation house, is also part of the refuge (open to the public).

In 1855 the town optimistically renamed itself Odessa after the great Russian grain-shipping port.

WHERE TO STAY

Cantwell House B&B, P. O. Box 2, (302) 378-4179. Ca. 1840 house with Colonial antiques, private baths. $$ to $$$

WHERE TO EAT

Historic Houses of Odessa will reserve box lunches for groups of 15 or more. The lunches (which include beverages, linens and flatware) may be set up in any of several lovely locations. Menu options range from a fresh deli tray to a croissant box lunch to a lunch consisting of an entree with full accompaniments, including freshly baked pies and cakes.

FURTHER INFORMATION

Historic Houses of Odessa, P. O. Box 507, Odessa, DE 19730, (302) 378-4069.

DIRECTIONS

From Wilmington, US 13 south to Odessa.

FLORIDA

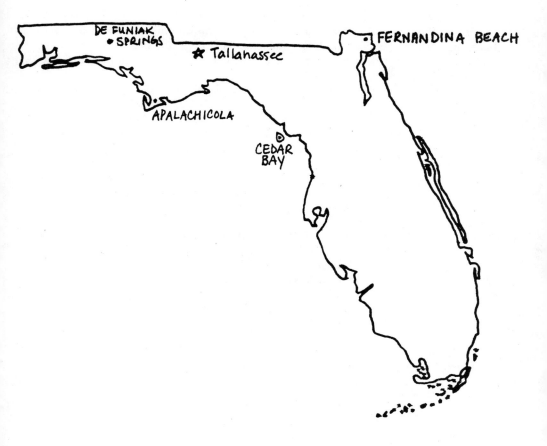

APALACHICOLA, FLORIDA

Population: 2,602

If the United States were to be divided according to its various brands of charm, the **Florida Panhandle** would receive a separate listing. For it is here that the South begins to take on a hint of the tropics, and the mix can be lovely, even haunting. A very good example is **Apalachicola**, where antebellum homes and other buildings out of history share a water-surrounded town with fishing and shrimping vessels from the Gulf of Mexico.

Located at the mouth of the **Apalachicola River**, the port was one of the busiest on the Gulf in the 19th century. Before the Civil War steamboats carried cotton, timber and other products up and down the river between here and Georgia and elsewhere. In more recent times the economy has shifted to seafood; the surrounding waters now produce most of Florida's oysters and a major part of the shellfish.

Nestled as it is on Florida's *Forgotten Coast*, Apalachicola is a quiet town with one traffic light and no shopping mall within 50 miles. The historic district and fishing and shrimping boats have been joined by art galleries, an old-fashioned soda fountain and families busy restoring the old houses. There are also two small but interesting museums: the **John Gorrie State Museum** and the **museum of the St. Vincent National Wildlife Refuge**. The former features a replica of the world's first ice machine, invented by Gorrie. The latter, with exhibits and information on coastal wildlife, is located in town because the refuge itself occupies a barrier island accessible only by private boat.

Apalachicola is obviously the place for those who love oysters, shrimp, scallops, crayfish and/or fresh fish. The seafood industry is honored the first Saturday in November with the celebration of the **Florida Seafood Festival**. Among the festival's highlights are demonstrations of boat building and netmaking, an oyster-shucking contest, the blessing of the fleet, and arts and crafts exhibits.

SPECIAL FEATURES

• **St. George Island State Park**, located 10 miles east and south of Apalachicola and reached by toll bridge, is considered one of Florida's most beautiful state parks. The island park has nine miles of undeveloped beaches and dunes. Along the island's beaches, salt marshes and forests of slash pines and live oaks dwell osprey, raccoons, ghost crabs, diamondback terrapin and many species of shorebirds.

> *If you're thinking about building condominiums here, beware. Land for development is scarce and the ecological health of the Apalachicola River and surrounding waters is taken very seriously.*
>
> *Private boaters headed for the St. Vincent National Wildlife Refuge should be prepared for the mosquitoes and other discomforts of this coastal wilderness.*

WHERE TO STAY

The Gibson Inn, Apalachicola, (904) 653-2191. Restored 1907 hotel, private baths, television, restaurant and bar. $$

The Witherspoon Inn, 94 5th St., (904) 653-2215. Restored ca. 1871 boarding house, period furniture, private baths, spacious porch beneath ancient oak. $$ to $$$

WHERE TO EAT

Apalachicola Seafood Grill & Steakhouse, 100 Market St., (904) 653-9510. Renovated to the original downtown cafe, freshest seafood, world-famous "Death by Chocolate!" $ to $$

The Gibson Inn, (see above). Grouper Papilliote, Oysters Remick, Shrimp-Scallop-Crab Dijon. $$

The Riverfront Restaurant, 123 Water St., (904) 653-8139. Fresh local seafood, oyster bar, panoramic view of river. $ to $$

FURTHER INFORMATION

Apalachicola Bay Chamber of Commerce, 57 Market Street, Apalachicola, FL 32320, (904) 653-9419.

DIRECTIONS

From Tallahassee, US 319/98 south to Apalachicola.

CEDAR KEY, FLORIDA

Population: 668

Three miles out in the **Gulf of Mexico** there is a little island community with just one main street, one grocery store and no stoplights. The houses of tabby and wood, with gables and porches, are home to families who have lived here for generations and who continue to maintain the island's traditions and memories. **Cedar Key's** atmosphere is something that has become very, very rare — something called Old Florida.

The island's 200-year history is highlighted in both the **Cedar Key State Museum** and the **Cedar Key Historical Society Museum.** Inquire at the CoC for information on a walking tour of the historic district. But take your time — hurrying doesn't agree with Cedar Key's culture, nor climate.

Very appropriately, this part of Florida's coast is called the *Nature Coast.* Cedar Key and the other tiny keys around it are a naturalist's paradise, with hundreds of species of birds and animals. Strolling along the shorelines and marshes is a favorite way to pass the time. Ospreys build their nests, Great Blue Herons and egrets wade the waters, pelicans dive and fish, dolphins play.

Cedar Key is understandably popular with seafood lovers. This is the place to sample, or gorge on if you like, smoked mullet, grouper, clams, shrimp, stone crab claws, blue crabs, soft shell crabs, oysters — all fresh from the Gulf.

SPECIAL FEATURE

• A pastime designed for lovers of charm is renting a johnboat and exploring the many uninhabited keys in the surrounding waters. In addition to the abundant wildlife, there's an 1850s lighthouse and artifacts, exposed by the shifting sands, from ancient Indian communities.

> *Naturalist John Muir walked 1000 miles in 1867 to reach his destination here. He wrote, "Today I reached the sea and many gems of tiny islets called keys."*
>
> *There are probably more artists and writers per capita on Cedar Key than in any other Florida town.*

WHERE TO STAY

Cedar Key B&B, P. O. Box 700, (904) 543-9000. Restored 1880 home, canopied by old live oaks, rocking chairs on verandas, private baths, tea/baked goods. $$

Island Hotel, P. O. Box 460, (904) 543-5111. 1859 inn on National Register, long balcony with rockers, private baths, some feather beds, full breakfasts, seafood restaurant. $$$

WHERE TO EAT

The Captain's Table, west end of pier, (904) 543-5441. Lunch and dinner upstairs over the water, seafood and steaks. $

The Heron, P. O. Box 358, (904) 543-5666. Gourmet seafood restaurant in restored Victorian setting. $ to $$

The Island Hotel (see above). Distinctively Cedar Key menu, soft shell and stone crabs, homemade poppy-seed bread. $ to $$

The Island Room at Cedar Cove, P. O. Box 716, (904) 543-6520. Elegant dining at water's edge, seafood and steaks, variety of pasta presentations. $

The Seabreeze on the Dock, P. O. Box 520, (904) 543-5738. Dining over the water, seafood, steaks handcut by chef. $

FURTHER INFORMATION

Cedar Key Area Chamber of Commerce, P. O. Box 610, Cedar Key, FL 32625, (904) 543-5600.

DIRECTIONS

From Tallahassee, US 19 east to Fl 24 (Otter Creek), west to Cedar Key.

DEFUNIAK SPRINGS, FLORIDA

Population: 5,120

One natural and one human event combined to produce what may be the most unique 1-mile hike in the country. The natural event was the formation of a spring-fed lake, 60 feet deep and about one mile in circumference, almost perfectly round. It was inevitable that such a beautiful little lake would make **DeFuniak** (pronounced "dee FEW nee ack") **Springs** a rather special kind of town.

The human event was the establishment of the winter capital of **Chautauqua** on the shores of the lake. Chautauqua was an institution formed in upstate New York in the latter part of the 19th century to provide summer cultural, educational and religious programs (see Chautauqua, New York). From 1885 until the early 1920s the institution migrated to DeFuniak Springs for a winter session. Some of the people who migrated with it built handsome houses around the lake and, in some cases, became permanent residents.

The path about the lake therefore offers vistas of crystal-clear water on one side and a series of grand late 19th- and early 20th-century homes on the other. The CoC distributes a map and description of the buildings for a self-guided tour. Motorists may take the tour by following **Circle Drive.**

The most prominent of the buildings is the **Chautauqua Auditorium** (1885, expanded in 1909), which once housed an auditorium with 4,000 inclined seats, as well as halls and classrooms. The building was reduced in size and altered in appearance by a 1975 hurricane.

One of the smallest buildings on the lake is the **Walton-DeFuniak Library,** which claims to be the "oldest structure in Florida built as a library and still serving that purpose." Inside is a substantial collection of swords and other weaponry.

Houses make up the majority of the buildings and illustrate a wide array of turn-of-the-century architectural styles. One of the most noteworthy is **Dream Cottage** (ca. 1888), a Gothic Stick chalet-style house built by Wallace Bruce, American ambassador to Scotland. Four bells hanging from the gable produce a range of tones when stirred by the wind.

Two other especially impressive houses are **Magnolia House** (1887), which boasts 50 windows and 12 magnolia trees, and the **Elliot Home** (1907), decorated with massive Doric columns, five soaring chimneys and an octagonal tent-roofed tower. The latter house was used to entertain celebrities during the Chautauqua sessions.

SPECIAL FEATURES
• An annual modern-day **Chautauqua Festival** is held around the lake in April.
• The beaches of the **Gulf of Mexico** are only a half hour's drive to the south.

On the lake is a circa 1840 magnolia tree with a spreading crown of 72 feet and a trunk with a circumference of 12 1/2 feet.

WHERE TO STAY
Live Oaks B&B, 405 Live Oak Ave., (904) 892-0849. Ca. 1887 home within walking distance of lake. $$

Sunbright Manor B&B, 606 Live Oak Ave., (904) 892-0656. Ca.1886 Queen Anne home on National Register, once home of Florida governor, full Florida breakfasts served on original Jewel Tea china. $$ to $$$

WHERE TO EAT
Busy Bee Cafe, 2 N. 7th St., (904) 892-6700. A re-creation of original turn-of-the-century DeFuniak eatery, lunches. $

Edie's, 301 N. 9th St., (904) 892-4847. Unusual daily luncheon specials. $

Mia's Cafe & Gourmet Market, 24 Baldwin Ave., (904) 892-6427. Soups, salads, daily luncheon entree specials. $

FURTHER INFORMATION
Walton County Chamber of Commerce, P. O. Box 29, DeFuniak Springs, FL 32433, (904) 892-3191.

DIRECTIONS
From Tallahassee, I 10 west to exit 14 (DeFuniak Springs exit).

FERNANDINA BEACH, FLORIDA
Population: 8,765

American Victoriana and an ocean beach make an unlikely couple, albeit an engaging one. When the setting is palmetto Florida, the coupling is even more unlikely and engaging. Add to the scene draping Spanish moss and the scent of magnolias and you'll understand the lure of the old seaport of **Fernandina Beach** on **Amelia Island**.

There was a time back in the 19th century when it looked as though Fernandina Beach might become a major resort center. But then, in the parting years of the century, tycoon Henry M. Flagler's East Coast Railroad bypassed the village on its way south. The railroad — and more reliably warm winter temperatures — carried tourists farther south. Today Fernandina Beach, more Southern than Floridian, boasts some 450 structures built before 1927, and more than 50 blocks of the downtown area form an historic district listed on the National Register.

The **Palace Saloon** is Florida's oldest tavern (1878). The 40-foot handcarved mahogany bar, the stuff of which great saloons are made, provides just one of several reasons why the visitor might want to step inside. General Ulysses S. Grant once stayed at the **Florida House Inn**, another gem in the historic district, now authentically restored and still very much in business (see listing below).

Centre Street, the hub of the district, has been returned to a turn-of-the-century shopping district with gas lanterns and cobblestone walks. A number of homes in the district are separately listed on the National Register; several are bed and breakfast inns (see below).

SPECIAL FEATURES
• Construction on the brick fort in nearby **Ft. Clinch State Park** began in 1847, and continued during the Union occupation in the latter part of the Civil War, but was never completed because of obsolescence. The soldiers' barracks, prison, guardhouse, and a wooden drawbridge are among the structures that can be visited. State park reenactors portray Union troops performing daily duties such as cooking and repairing rifles. Candlelight tours are conducted on some weekends. The park's unspoiled beaches afford a view of a Florida that has largely disappeared.

•**Amelia Island** has 13 miles of dunes and white sand beaches. Beachside horseback riding and fresh and saltwater fishing are among the many activities that this beautiful island offers.

> *Amelia Island is sometimes called the "Isle of Eight Flags," because it is the only land in the United States that has been under eight flags.*
>
> *Fernandina Beach, which boasts a modern shrimp industry, is home to the world's larger producer of handmade shrimp nets.*

WHERE TO STAY

Bailey House, P. O. Box 805, (904) 261-5390. 1895 Queen Anne, on National Register, antiques, private baths, bicycles, beach towels. $$ to $$$

Florida House Inn, 22 S. 3rd St., (800) 258-3301. Oldest continuously operated hotel in Florida, wonderful old dining room. $$ to $$$.

Posada San Carlos, 212 Estrada St., (904) 277-2274. Once a sea pilot's home, overlooking entrance to harbor. $$$

WHERE TO EAT

Beech Street Grill, 801 Beech St., (904) 277-3662. Continental and nouvelle cuisine, solid wine list, one of best in state. $$

Brett's Waterway Cafe, Fernandina Beach Marina, (904) 261-2660. Great views of Intracoastal Waterway, fresh catch of the day. $$

Florida House Inn, (see above). Oldest dining room in state, Southern delicacies served boarding-house style. $

FURTHER INFORMATION

Amelia Island Chamber of Commerce, P. O. Box 472, Fernandina Beach, FL 32034, (800) 226-3542.

DIRECTIONS

From Jacksonville, I 95 north to exit 129, FL A1A east to Amelia Island.

GEORGIA

DAHLONEGA, GEORGIA

Population: 3,086

Dahlonega is probably the only town in the country where you can pan for gold in the morning, shop for Appalachian crafts in the afternoon, dine on fried chicken served country-style in the evening, and canoe the next morning on a mountain stream. Nestled in the foothills of the beautiful **Blue Ridge Mountains**, picturesque Dahlonega obviously has a story to tell.

Twenty years before gold was discovered in California, the Cherokee Nation in northern Georgia saw the first major gold rush in the United States. The smell of gold attracted thousands to the area in 1828, and prospectors continued coming for the next 20 years. Dahlonega (accent on second syllable) did well: over $6 in gold was coined by the U.S. Branch Mint in Dahlonega between 1838 and 1861.

Gold is still very much a part of the Dahlonega scene. The **Gold Museum,** once the **Lumpkin County Courthouse** (1836), is the oldest public building in north Georgia. (It is also one of the state's most visited historic sites.) Here are displayed gold coins minted at Dahlonega as well as locally discovered gold nuggets, one over 5 ounces.

Consolidated Mines, the largest gold mining operation east of the Mississippi (closed in the 1930s), offers tours which include a trip down a 250-foot hole (called the *Glory Hole*). Here and at several other places in the area visitors preferring the do-it-yourself (and keep-what-you-find) route are welcome to pan for gold. Check with the CoC for sites and information. Prospecting equipment is available in shops in town and at the panning sites. Trying to "find color" is Dahlonega's most popular visitor pastime.

Around the square and on the surrounding streets are dozens of charming 19th-century houses and other buildings listed on the National Register of Historic Places. Local crafts and gold jewelry are among the items of special regional interest offered in Dahlonega's many colorful shops. See the welcome center for walking and auto tours.

SPECIAL FEATURES
• What with 47% of Lumpkin County in national forest, and the **Appalachian Trail** and the **Desoto Falls Scenic Area** just a few miles away, hiking, camping, fishing and canoeing opportunities abound.

> *The Smith House (1884) is a 70-year-old restaurant, an old-fashioned mountain inn (see listings below), and beloved town landmark.*
>
> *A prospecting party from nearby Auraria founded the first settlement at the present site of Denver, Colorado and named it after their hometown (Aurora is now a major Denver suburb).*

WHERE TO STAY
Mountain Top Lodge, P. O. Box 150, (800) 526-9754. Secluded mountain location, antique-filled rooms, private baths, outdoor spa with view. $$ to $$$

Royal Guard Inn B&B, 203 S. Park St., (706) 864-1713. Close to square, private baths, full breakfasts, wine & cheese. $$

The Smith House, 202 S. Chestatee St., (800) 852-9577. Renovated inn, wide verandas, on vein of Dahlonega gold. $ to $$

Worley Homestead Inn, 410 W. Main St., (706) 864-7002. Historic home (ca. 1845/1872), antiques, "gourmet" breakfasts, horseback riding. $$

WHERE TO EAT

The Smith House (see above). Fried chicken, sweet baked ham, beef stew, dumplings, angel biscuits, fried okra, candied yams, family-style service. $

Wagon Wheel Restaurant, US 19 North, (706) 864-6677. Country cooking, all-you-can-eat catfish, cafeteria or menu. $

FURTHER INFORMATION

Dahlonega-Lumpkin County Chamber of Commerce, 101 South Park St., Dahlonega, GA 30533, (706) 864-3711.

DIRECTIONS

From Atlanta, US 19 to north to Dahlonega.

HELEN, GEORGIA

Population: 300

The **"Alpine Village of Helen"** is a picture-book Bavarian village nestled among the mountains, forests, lakes and waterfalls of northeast Georgia. Viewed from afar, the village is a cluster of old-world towers, rust-colored roofs and gabled Bavarian facades.

Closer up, the place becomes a colorful mosaic of cobblestone alleys, balconies, outdoor cafes and cascading flower baskets. Some of the townspeople dress in Bavarian attire.

Helen's story has a much larger Cinderella component than do the stories of most towns. It seems that in the late 1960s several local businessmen decided that bleak little Helen could stand some improvement. The men turned to John Kollock, a local artist, and within a week were presented with a set of watercolor sketches of an Alpine Helen. Liking what they saw, a decision was made to proceed.

The transformation quickly became a community affair. Business people renovated their shops, the city put up quaint street lights and planters, and the townsfolk planted trees and flowers. New businesses put up new buildings. Power lines went underground. The work is still in progress.

More than 200 specialty and import shops now line Helen's streets and alleys. There is also a delightful collection of pubs and lodgings. The restaurant menus are about as loyal to their German and Austrian counterparts as menus on this side of the Atlantic are likely to get. For those not wishing to tour the town on foot, there are horse-drawn buggies and a village trolley.

Because the **Chattahoochee River** runs right through town, Helen is able to provide a morning of shopping to one part of the family while offering tubing, canoeing or trout fishing to another. Golfing is also an option. Hiking, backpacking and horseback riding are just a few of the other activities pursued in the area. The **Appalachian Trail** passes north of town.

SPECIAL FEATURES

• **Unicoi State Park**, just north of Helen, provides a scenic setting for canoeing and fishing. The park also has public beaches and a dining room.

• Beginning just outside of town, the **Richard B. Russell Scenic Highway** (GA 348) winds through a particularly beautiful section of Georgia's **Blue Ridge Mountains**.

> *Helen's 6-to-8-week Oktoberfest attracts as many as 150,000 visitors.*
> *Artist Kollock's Alpine images were inspired by a stay in Bavaria with the army.*

WHERE TO STAY

Dutch Cottage B&B, P. O. Box 757, (706) 878-3135. "A Dutch setting with Southern hospitality," shuttle service to town, buffet breakfasts. $$

Nacoochee Valley Guest House, P. O. Box 249 (Sautee), (706) 878-3830. Turn-of-century home overlooking Nacoochee Valley, spacious rooms, gourmet dining room. $$ to $$$

The Stovall House Country Inn & Restaurant, GA 255 N (Box 1476) (Sautee), (706) 878-3355. Restored circa 1837 home on National Register, private baths, family antiques. $$$

WHERE TO EAT

Alt Heidelberg, White Horse Sq., (706) 878-2986. Sauerbraten, Wiener Kalbs Schnitzel, Baurenwurst, Chicken a la Mozart, Georgia Mountain Trout. $ to $$

Hofbrauhaus Inn, 1 Main St., (706) 878-2248. Extensive Bavarian/French/Italian/seafood menu, three dining rooms. $ to $$

Nacoochee Valley Guest House, (see above). Shrimp Scampi, Beef Wellington, Chicken Picatta, napoleons & tarts, reservations a must. $ to $$

The Stovall House Country Inn & Restaurant, (see above). Stuffed Chicken the house specialty, Fresh Mountain Trout, pastas, phyllo, daily specials. $ to $$

FURTHER INFORMATION

Alpine Helen/White County Convention & Visitors Bureau, P. O. Box 730, Helen, GA 30545, (706) 878-2181.

DIRECTIONS

From Atlanta, I 85 northeast to exit 45, I 985 north to Gainesville, US 129 north to GA 75, GA 75 north to Helen.

MADISON, GEORGIA

Population: 3483

Gone With the Wind was a work of fiction, but a Grand Old South did in fact exist in Georgia, at least for a fortunate few. General Sherman's march to the sea was not a work of fiction, but a few scenes from Georgia's Old South did survive the devastation. **Madison** was one of them. The town's National Historic District is an image from another era; parts of it are virtually the same today as they were on the eve of the Civil War. Maybe they're even prettier.

The town lay smack in the middle of Sherman's path, and yet survived. It seems that as the Yankees advanced, a delegation of men led by Senator Joshua Hill pleaded with the general to spare the town. Sherman obliged — although the railroad station and some surrounding plantations were kindled — and the town was subsequently known as "the town Sherman refused to burn."

The CoC, housed in the 1887 city hall and fire station, provides a brochure and tape for a walking tour of the historic district. Among the over 100 structures on the tour are three whose doors are regularly open to the public: the Greek Revival **Heritage Hall** (ca 1825), currently the home of the **Morgan County Historical Society**; the **Madison-Morgan Cultural Center**, a restored 1895 Romanesque Revival school building housing a museum, original classroom and antique auditorium; and the **African-American Museum**, housed in a recently restored home and displaying paintings and other works of art and memorabilia that honor the area's Black heritage.

Many of the houses are shown during tours in May and December. Private tours of some may also be arranged during other months. Whether their doors are open or not, the unusually well restored and maintained homes in the historic district merit a walk- or drive-by.

Three antebellum churches also merit a visit: the **Advent Episcopal Church** (ca. 1842) with its wrought-iron chandeliers and slave gallery, now used for the organ and choir; the **Madison Baptist Church** (1858), built by bricks handmade by slaves on a local plantation; and the "Old English"-style **Presbyterian Church** (1842), whose silver communion service, still in use, was stolen during the Civil War and later returned by Federal orders. The churches are usually open daily.

Madison's preserved downtown is the kind designed to delight antique hunters, casual shoppers and just plain lovers of charm. There are brick sidewalks, two old-fashioned soda fountains, and interesting shops. One of the largest antique shops is located in an 1890s hotel building.

Madison was once described as the "wealthiest and most aristocratic town" on the stagecoach route between Charleston and New Orleans.

With 19,000 acres, Lake Oconee, east of town, is the largest power-company lake in Georgia.

WHERE TO STAY

Note: All four of the B&Bs listed below are in the historic district.

Boat House Victorian B&B, 383 Porter St., (706) 342-3061. Restored early Victorian home, antiques, private baths, full breakfasts. $$$

The Brady Inn, 250 N. Second St., (706) 342-4400. Victorian cottage, period antiques, private baths, full breakfasts, dinners available. $$$
Burnett Place, 317 Old Post Rd., (706) 342-4034. Restored 1830 Federal-style home, period furnishings, private baths, full breakfasts. $$$
Turn of the Century Victorian B&B, 450 Pine St., (706) 342-1890. 1890s home, antiques, full breakfasts, reservations required. $$$

WHERE TO EAT
Ye Olde Colonial Restaurant, 108 E. Washington St., (706) 342-2211. Southern cooking served cafeteria-style in old bank building. $

FURTHER INFORMATION
Madison-Morgan County Chamber of Commerce, P. O. Box 826, Madison, GA 30650, (706) 342-4454.

DIRECTIONS
From Atlanta, I 20 east to exit 51, north on US 129.

ST. MARYS, GEORGIA
Population: 8,187

With lovely antebellum buildings, gentle breezes off the sea, and wide avenues shaded by ancient live oaks, **St. Marys** is a town of many memories and moods. As the gateway to **Cumberland Island National Seashore** (see below) and neighbor to a naval base, St. Marys has a present and future as well as a past; but it is quiet here, and very beautiful.

Turbulent is perhaps the best term to describe St. Marys's past. Settled in 1787, the town has known smuggling, a slave trade, the scourge of yellow fever, periods of economic depression, and ravaging by the British in the War of 1812 and the Yankees in the Civil War. But there have also been times of peace and — thanks to shipping, timber, shrimping and, more recently, a paper mill and submarine base — periods of prosperity.

A 20-block area in the older section of town has been placed on the National Register of Historic Places. The streets in this district are the same as on the original 1788 town map and bear the names of the town's founders.

Orange Hall, St. Marys's venerable landmark, is a circa 1830 Greek Revival Mansion built by the town's first Presbyterian minister. The house is listed on the National Register and now serves as a welcome center for the tourism council (open daily).

Among the historic district's antebellum buildings are several churches with interesting credentials. **The First Presbyterian Church** (1808) is the oldest Presbyterian church in continuous use in Georgia. **St. Marys Methodist Church** (1858), organized in 1799, is the Mother Church of Methodism in Florida (which begins just across the St. Marys River). And the **Old Catholic Church** is housed in the oldest masonry bank building still standing in Georgia (1837).

The "**Toonerville Trolley**" is probably the district's most unique possession. A passenger rail car on the **St. Marys Railroad** from 1928 until 1938, the trolley was made famous in the nationally syndicated comic strip *Wash Tubbs and Easy* in 1935. It is still operated on special occasions.

Soldiers of every American war, yellow fever victimns, Acadians and others are buried in **Oak Grove Cemetery**. The oldest marked gravesites are dated 1801.

Surrounded by water, St. Marys is an ideal spot for photographers, hikers, bikers, birders, fishermen and boaters. A good place to see the flora and fauna is on a nature trail at **Crooked River State Park**. Visitors are welcome on the greens of nearby **Osprey Cove Golf Course**.

SPECIAL FEATURES

• Boats depart daily from St. Marys for **Cumberland Island National Seashore**, located on the southernmost of Georgia's sea islands. Here there are 16 miles of undisturbed white-sand beach bordered by sand dunes that rise as high as 40 feet. Herds of horses graze openly on the island, and loggerhead turtles come ashore to lay their eggs. No vehicles are available, so walking and swimming (no lifeguards) are the only ways of moving about.

• On some Sundays the boat to Cumberland Island puts in at **Plum Orchard Dock**. Plum Orchard is a magnficent thirty-room mansion constructed by Lucy Carnegie for her son and his wife in 1898. The building is currently undergoing restoration.

> *The Washington Pump, still around, was the only source of fresh water during the tidal wave of 1880.*
> *Many sites in the historic district are marked in Braille for sight-impaired visitors.*

WHERE TO STAY

Goodbread House B&B, 209 Osborne St., (912) 882-7490. Carefully restored ca. 1870 home, each room with own fireplace and bath, complimentary wine and cheese. $$

Riverview Hotel, 105 Osborne St., (912) 882-3242. 1916 hotel on banks of river, veranda with rocking chairs, private baths. $ to $$

The Historic Spencer House Inn, 101 E. Bryant St., (912) 882-1872. Renovated 1872 hotel, original mouldings and wide-planked floors, three verandas. $$ to $$$

WHERE TO EAT

Seagle's Restaurant, in Riverview Hotel (see above). Fresh seafood, steaks, picnic lunches with basket and checkered tablecloth. $

FURTHER INFORMATION

St. Marys Tourism Council, P. O. Box 1291, St. Marys, GA 31558, (912) 882-6200.

DIRECTIONS

From Jacksonville (FL), I 95 north to exit 2, GA 40 east to St. Marys.

ST. SIMONS ISLAND, GEORGIA

Population: 12,026

One of Georgia's *Golden Isles*, **St. Simons Island** is a place of palmettos, azaleas and lush green lawns set against sunny blue skies and ocean waters. It's a place steeped in time, with historic buildings — both actual and remembered — and old oaks draped with Spanish moss. To the scene, the late 20th century has added golf courses, gardens and resorts with swimming pools and chaise longues. The climate is delightfully moderate.

Once inhabited by Guale Indians and, for a spell, Spanish missionaries, St. Simons Island was settled in 1736 by James Edward Oglethorpe. Oglethorpe and his followers built **Fort Frederica** to protect against and help contain the Spanish to the south. Later, grand plantations grew up as European markets paid high prices for long-staple sea-island cotton. The plantations were destroyed in the Civil War, but several of their sites (and names) survive.

Fort Frederica (1736) is now a national monument. Only the tabby powder magazine remains intact, but the foundations of many of the other buildings have been excavated, researched and identified. Costumed interpreters assist visitors and demonstrate the everyday activities of the fort's early inhabitants.

St. Simon Lighthouse (1872) is one of the oldest lighthouses in continuous use in the United States. The charming lighthouse keeper's cottage (1872) now houses the **Museum of Coastal History,** operated by the Coastal Georgia Historical Society. Included in the museum's exhibits are an old photograph collection and plantation memorabilia.

Another 19th-century structure, **Christ Church** (1886), is distinguished by its trussed Gothic roof and lovely stained-glass windows. Part of the credence table and an inset in the altar are from the altar of the original church (1820), destroyed in the Civil War.

St. Simons is home to colonies of artists and writers. As might be expected, there are several art and antique galleries. The merchandise in the town's many unique specialty shops varies from middle range to the strictly discriminating.

The *Island Players* perform professional dramatic and musical productions in the **Old Casino Building.** Most of the island's entertainment is quite understandably out-of-doors: pier fishing, off-shore fishing, crabbing, sailing, golfing and tennis. There are several miles of beaches, with full beach facilities, and many miles of bike paths. Sailboats and equipment for other water sports can be rented.

SPECIAL FEATURES

• Among the many points of interest in the historic city of **Brunswick,** on the mainland, are the **Old Town Historic District** (turn-of-the-century homes), the 900-year-old **Lovers' Oak,** shrimp docks and the magnificently situated **Overlook Park.**

• Georgia's other Golden Isles, all close by, are **Jekyll Island, Sea Island,** and **Little St. Simons Island.** The latter is accessible only by boat.

John and Charles Wesley, Anglican missionaries, were part of Oglethorpe's group of settlers. John Wesley later founded the Methodist Church, in England. Methodists regard St. Simons as the place where the Wesleys "sowed the seeds of Methodism."

The English actress Fanny Kemble spent time on St. Simons Island in 1838-1839. In her Journal of a Residence on a Georgia Plantation she expressed horror over slavery. Later published, the journal inflamed anti-slavery sentiment in the North and in England and is believed to have contributed to England's decision to refrain from aiding the Confederacy.

WHERE TO STAY

Note: Several bed and breakfasts may be found in Brunswick; lodging on St. Simons Island is largely confined to hotels, motels, and resorts.

WHERE TO EAT

Blanche's Courtyard, 440 Kings Way, (912) 638-3030. Unique Bayou-Victorian atmosphere, seafood and steaks, broiling the house specialty. $ to $$

Chelsea, 1226 Ocean Blvd., (912) 638-2047. American regional cuisine, fresh seafood, prime New York sirloin, pastas, popular. $ to $$

Frederica House, 3611 Frederica Rd., (912) 638-6789. Steaks, grilled fish, shellfish, Lime Pie, Georgia Pecan Pie, a local favorite. $$

Mullet Bay, 512 Ocean Blvd., (912) 638-0703. Fresh fish, seafood platters, "land platters," pasta. $ to $$

Poor Stephen's, 1617 Frederica Rd., (912) 638-7316. Scallops, crab cakes, baby back ribs, spaghetti, popular hangout. $ to $$

FURTHER INFORMATION

St. Simons Island Chamber of Commerce and Visitors Center, 530-B Beachview Dr., St. Simons Island, GA 31522, (912) 638-9014.

DIRECTIONS

From Jacksonville (FL), I 95 north to exit 6, US 17 east to St. Simons Island causeway.

HAWAII

HALEIWA

Honolulu

HANA

HALEIWA (OAHU), HAWAII

Population: 2,442

Haleiwa's brand of charm is one of the most delightfully unusual in the country. The old wooden buildings along the main road, or **Kam** (short for **Kamehameha**) **Highway**, look very much like those you might find in an old Western town. Yet many of the shops sell clothing and supplies for distinctly non-Old-West surfers, snorkelers and other ocean sports fans. In the restaurants, surf enthusiasts mingle with art enthusiasts attracted by Haleiwa's first-rate galleries. Down the road lies a picturesque little harbor offering charters for deep-sea fishing. And then come miles of coastline boasting some of the most beautiful beaches in the world!

Oahu's **North Shore**, on which Haleiwa rests, is the world's surfing capital. Most of the year the waters are quiet, ideal for all kinds of water activities. But from November through January the waters become very active (and dangerous) — and a paradise for professional surfers. As an example, the average height of the winter waves at **Sunset Beach** is 15 feet. Monster waves measuring 35 and 40 feet are not unknown. Surfers from around the world come to meet the challenge, and surfing spectators follow for the excitement and beauty.

Haleiwa (pronounced "hah lay EE vah") is of course also active during the winter months, in concert with the swells and those who ride and watch them. But during the rest of the year the town, like the water, is quiet. This is a part of Oahu that is still largely rural. The area is in fact called "the country." There are still pineapple fields here, and even a surviving sugar mill. Proud of its plantation/rural heritage, Haleiwa actively strives to preserve it. The facades of historic wood buildings are protected, and the historic appearance of Kamehameha Highway is maintained by imposing strict design codes on new construction. The result is a lovely little rural town on Hawaii's most urbanized island.

SPECIAL FEATURES

• Down the coast just a few miles is one of Hawaii's most beautiful and historic properties, 1,800-acre **Waimea Falls Park**. The park is home to native birds and animals and to thousands of tropical plants displayed in more than 30 gardens. The lush, exotic grounds and the 45-foot waterfall may be toured by foot and/or by open-air tram. Among the park's many attractions are cliff divers, demonstrations of traditional Hawaiian games and performances by a resident hula troupe.

• A garden featuring a variety of pineapple plants is open to the public at the **Dole Plantation** near **Wahiawa**.

> *Parks and Recreation personnel at the Surf Center at Haleiwa Alii Beach Park offer information on North Shore beaches, free use of ocean-sport gear and free surfing and windsurfing lessons.*

WHERE TO STAY

For information on bed and breakfast accommodations in Hawaii, contact:

Bed & Breakfast Honolulu, 3242 Kaohinani Dr., Honolulu, HI 96817, (808) 595-7533, (800) 288-4666 from U.S. Mainland, Fax (808) 595-2030.

WHERE TO EAT

Kua Aina, Kam Hwy. Tiny and popular, known for "world-famous" hamburgers.

Jameson's by the Sea, Kam Hwy., (808) 637-4336. Relaxed sunset dining, views of Queen Liliuokalani's fishpond. $$ to $$$

Proud Peacock Restaurant, Waimea Falls Park, (808) 638-8531. Casual dining, gorgeous views, reservations recommended. $ to $$

Rosie's Cantina, Haleiwa Shopping Plaza, (808) 637-3538. "The friendliest place in Haleiwa," Mexican dinners. $

Steamer's Bar and Restaurant, Haleiwa Shopping Plaza, (808) 637-5071. Gourmet menu, outdoors dining, one of best on North Shore. $$$

FURTHER INFORMATION

North Shore News, P. O. Box 1117, Haleiwa, Oahu, HI 96712, (808) 637-3138.

DIRECTIONS

From Honolulu, I H1 west to HI 99, HI 99 north to HI 83, HI 83 north to Haleiwa.

HANA (MAUI), HAWAII

Population: about 1,200

Once a bustling sugar town, historic **Hana** is today a country-quiet village famed for its untouched natural beauty and relaxed lifestyle. Far from the intense development elsewhere on Maui, this is a peaceful tropical paradise, the enchanting Hawaii of picture postcard and movie. This is the Hawaii where swimmers may choose between a tropical pool or one of several ocean beaches — a black one, a red one and a silver one.

Consistent with its gorgeous setting, Hana has little commercial development. And what little there is can be interesting. For example, the bank has a sign announcing that the doors are open from 3:00 to 4:30 p.m. daily, except on Fridays, when closing time is extended to 6:00. And **Hasegawa's General Store**, in business since 1910, stocks horseshoe nails, barbed wire, and bolo knives side by side with potato chips and pickled turnips.

One of the most interesting of Hana's historic structures is the **Wananalua Church** (ca. 1840), built of lava rock. The area is rich with archeological remnants from the early Hawaiian culture; most are unmarked, however, so inquire locally for information.

Driving to Hana is itself an eye-dazzling adventure. The narrow coastal road (HI 360) twists along cliffs, over streams and waterfalls and through lush tropical foliage. People who have counted them report that the road has over 600 curves and 55 or so one-lane bridges. Allow about 3 hours each way.

Most visitors to Hana stay in towns like **Wailea** and **Kapalua** and take tour vans or rental cars out to Hana and back the same day. The area may also be reached by two commuter airlines, **Island Air** and **Air Molokai.**

SPECIAL FEATURES

• Eleven miles down the coast from Hana is **Ohe'o Gulch,** renowned for its series of lovely stream-carved pools and tropical rain forest setting. Trails lead to several waterfalls. The gulch is a section of **Haleakala National Park.**

• Cabins and camping are available at nearby **Waianapanapa State Park.** The park features a cave and scenic hiking trails along the shore.

> *One of the most popular tourist items in Hana is a t-shirt proclaiming that its wearer has "Survived the Road to Hana."*

WHERE TO EAT

Main Dining Room, Hotel Hana Maui, P. O. Box 9, (808) 248-8211. Outdoor dining on bluff overlooking ocean, tropical gardens. $$$

FURTHER INFORMATION

Maui Visitors Bureau, 250 Alamaha St., Ste. N-16, Kahului, HI 96732, (808) 871-8691.

DIRECTIONS

From Kahului, HI 360 east to Hana.

Note: I wish to thank Carl Lindquist, long-time Hana resident and author of *On the Hana Coast,* for his contributions to this piece. *On the Hana Coast* may be obtained by writing P. O. Box 507, Hana, Hawaii 96713.

IDAHO

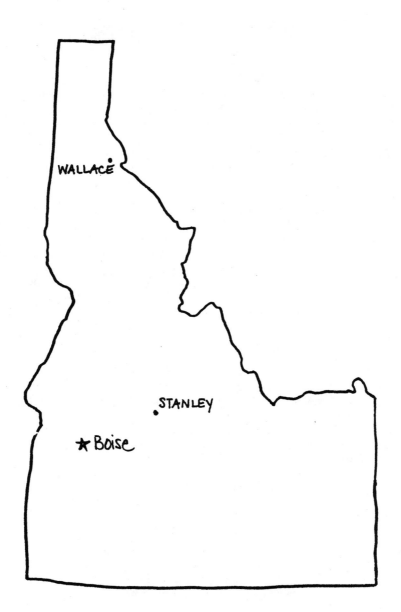

STANLEY, IDAHO

Population: 71

Only 71 souls and sundry aspens, pines and firs live along **Stanley's** few streets. The streets are gravel, even the main street, and there are no sidewalks. Many of the homes are old cabins. Yet the town, elevation 6,260 feet, is surrounded by some of the most glorious scenery on the continent.

Situated on the Salmon River in the northern part of the spectacular **Sawtooth National Recreation Area,** Stanley is nestled among pristine mountain ranges, 300 glacial lakes and dense forests. Three **National Forest Scenic Byways** — the **Sawtooth,** the **Ponderosa Pine** and the **Salmon River** — converge on the town. Stanley was obviously designed for the nature lover, the outdoor sportsperson, the photographer and the artist.

The **Stanley Museum** displays artifacts and photographs from the early days of the Sawtooth Valley and the Stanley Basin. The **Custer Museum,** 30 minutes north of town, features a ghost town and mining-history museum. Interesting old tombstones can be found in **Boot Hill Cemetery,** near the museum.

Virtually every land sport — and many of the water ones, too — known to the Western world can be pursued in these parts. Outfitters and guides abound. For snowmobilers there is the groomed *Highway to Heaven* trail from Boise or Lowman to Stanley. For hut skiiers there are stationary circular tents with bunks, cooking equipment, and wood stoves. For wilderness floaters there is the **Middle Fork** of the beautiful Salmon River (three- to six-day trips by raft, oar boat, and paddle boat can be arranged in Stanley).

And for people in a hurry there are scenic air tours.

SPECIAL FEATURE

• The **Sawtooth National Recreation** area is an eye-dazzling wilderness tamed only by the occasional guest ranch, resort and horse trail. This is the kind of country that deserves to be seen from the back of a horse, and outfitters and guides are available to help you do just that.

> *Stanley really consists of two towns, incorporated upper Stanley and unincorporated lower Stanley. The two are about two miles apart and have different histories.*

WHERE TO STAY

Idaho Rocky Mountain Ranch, HC 64 (Box 9934), (208) 774-3544. One of Idaho's oldest and finest guest ranches. $$$

Redfish Lake Lodge, P. O. Box 9, (208) 774-3536. Marina with boat rentals, horseback riding, lakeside dining. $$ to $$$

Sawtooth Hotel, P. O. Box 52, (208) 774-9947. Early 20th-century hotel, quilts, "world-famous" sourdough pancakes, fishing guides. $ to $$

WHERE TO EAT

Idaho Rocky Mountain Ranch, (see above). Historic lodge dining room, guitar serenades, spectacular views, reservations. $ to $$

Stanley Kasino Club, Downtown Stanley, (208) 774-3516. Nightly pasta specials, "Idaho's finest beef and poultry." $ to $$

FURTHER INFORMATION
Stanley-Sawtooth Chamber of Commerce, P. O. Box 8, Stanley, ID 83278, (208) 774-3411.

DIRECTIONS
From Boise, ID 21 east and north to Stanley.

WALLACE, IDAHO
Population: 1010

The buildings of the late 19th century Western mining towns were put up quickly, crudely and cheaply. A goodly number of them served as saloons and/or cheap hotels and/or brothels. Yet today many of the descendants of these mining camps are among the West's most charming places. And so it is with **Wallace,** now listed on the National Historic Register and featuring turn-of-the-century buildings, unique shops, art galleries, museums, even a melodrama.

Wallace's history is nicely wrapped up in its nickname, *The Silver Mining Capital of the World.* At the turn of the century Wallace was the center of action in the **Silver Valley,** a scenic valley that happens to be one of the richest mining districts on the planet. As might be expected, most of Wallace's top attractions relate in one way or another to silver.

The displays and exhibits of the **Wallace District Mining Museum** portray without glamour life as it was in the old mines and mining camps. A 20-minute video show discusses the history and technology of mining. Included in the exhibits are old photographs, a collection of paintings by James R. Buckham (born and raised in Wallace), and the world's largest silver dollar, weighing in at 150 pounds.

The bricks used to build the **Northern Pacific Depot,** now a railroad museum, served as ballast in sailing ships coming over from China. The restored building houses photographs and artifacts from the mining district's early days. The escorted tour of the **Sierra Silver Mine** proceeds through an underground tunnel that stretches for five blocks. Along the way is a 149-ft shaft now filled with water. A guide explains and demonstrates mining procedures, equipment and safety precautions. A trolley carries visitors to and from the mine's entrance.

Some of Wallace's attractions are seasonal, but many are not. Skiers and other off-season visitors will discover that Wallace's charm can be enjoyed year-round.

SPECIAL FEATURE
• The Wallace CoC distributes instructions for a scenic and historical loop that includes a "living ghost town," gold rush camps, ancient towering cedars, and the spot where Wyatt Earp owned and operated a saloon.

> *Wallace was established in 1884 by prospector William R. Wallace, cousin to novelist, general, and statesman Lew Wallace.*
>
> *Idahoans are proud to boast that the Silver Valley is the only place in the world that has produced a <u>billion</u> ounces of silver in less than a century.*

WHERE TO STAY

Jameson B&B, 304 6th St., (208) 556-1554. In restored turn-of-the-century hotel, period furnishings and decor. $$

WHERE TO EAT

Jameson Restaurant & Saloon (see above). Restored 1900 dining room, saloon with mirrored back bar. $$

FURTHER INFORMATION

Wallace Chamber of Commerce, P. O. Box 1167, Wallace, ID 83873, (208) 753-7151.

DIRECTIONS

From Spokane (Washington), I 90 east to exit 57 (Wallace exit).

ILLINOIS

GALENA

GENEVA

NAUVOO

CARTHAGE

★ Springfield

ELSAH

MAEYSTOWN

GOLCONDA

CARTHAGE, ILLINOIS

Population: 2,657

Settled in 1833, **Carthage** is a pretty little Midwestern town with an old courthouse on a square, a bustling downtown around the square, and tree-lined streets with homes representing over a century of architectural styles. The courthouse and 19th-century commercial buildings about the square have been designated an historic district. There are no discount stores or malls on Carthage's outskirts, so the downtown looks very much like the downtown of a traditional county seat.

The **Hancock County Court House** (1908), an unusually beautiful, all-stone structure, is a favorite subject of photographers, sketchers and painters. Inside is a large genealogical card index and collection of local artifacts.

Carthage is home to an interesting history and natural history museum, the **Alice Kibbe Museum**. The museum features collections of Native American, Mormon, Civil War, and late 19th century artifacts.

The two-story limestone **Old Carthage Jail** is the site of the mob murder of Mormon prophet Joseph Smith and his brother Hyrum in 1844. Now a museum and visitor center, the jail has become a kind of Mormon shrine; thousands of people of the Mormon Church visit the site every year (although non-Mormons are by all means welcome).

SPECIAL FEATURES

• Several charming old two-story farmhouses can be spotted in the countryside around Carthage. Many of the old farmhouses here and elsewhere in the Midwest have weathered away or been destroyed, but fortunately, some farm families have invested considerable time and money to preserve these "gems of the prairie."

> *You'll see fields of corn and soybeans around Carthage, but very few farm animals — farmers say they can no longer afford the feed and other supplies needed to keep livestock.*
>
> *The Great River Road along the Mississippi can be joined just a few miles west of town.*

WHERE TO STAY

The Wright Farmhouse, P. O. Box 110, (217) 357-2421. Restored 19th-century home on a working Illinois farm. $

WHERE TO EAT

Plum Tree Supper Club & Lounge, 69 S. Adams St., (217) 357-3518. Chicken, steaks, seafood, ribs, Mexican dishes, specials. $ to $$.

FURTHER INFORMATION

Carthage Chamber of Commerce, P. O. Box 247, Carthage, IL 62321, (217) 357-3024.

DIRECTIONS
From Peoria, US 24 southwest to US 136, US 136 west to Carthage.

ELSAH, ILLINOIS

Population: 851

Once a steamboat stop on the Mississippi, unspoiled little **Elsah** is the kind of village where you go to pick apples and peaches, watch for bald eagles or linger beside old flower gardens. It's the kind of place where the local restaurant packs picnic lunches for passing bicycles. It's an enchanting spot.

The first village in the country to be listed in its entirety on the National Register of Historic Places, Elsah seems to be charmingly stuck in the last century. Indeed, most of the old and (thanks to stringent codes) new buildings are of an architecture belonging to the 1850-1900 period.

Guarded by bluffs, Elsah offers splendid views of the **Mississippi River Valley**. The riverside beauty can be enjoyed by renting a bike and cycling along the water on the newly paved **Vadalabene Bike Trail**. Horseback and boat rides are also popular. The **Great River Road** (IL 100) from Elsah to Alton offers sweeping views of the river on one side and beautiful limestone cliffs on the other.

SPECIAL FEATURES
• The lovely campus of nearby **Principia College** is worth a special visit. The college was recently placed on the National Register of Historic Places.

• **Pere Marquette Park**, about five miles west of Elsah, is the largest state park in Illinois. The park overlooks the **Illinois River** and boasts an especially beautiful stone lodge (1930s).

• Elsah's charm spills over onto **Grafton**, about 4 miles upriver, and **Alton**, about 10 miles downriver. Both of these towns are noted for their old homes and fabulous antiquing.

> *Part of Elsah, now rebuilt, was damaged by the Great Flood of 1993. Missouri can be easily reached by the ferry from Grafton to Calhoun Point.*

WHERE TO STAY
The Corner Nest B&B, P. O. Box 220, (618) 374-1892. 1883 home with spacious screened-in porch overlooking river, antiques. $$

Green Tree Inn & Mercantile, 15 Mill St., (618) 374-2821. 1850s-style country inn, private baths, gourmet breakfasts. $$ to $$$

The Homeridge B&B, 1470 N. State St. (Jerseyville, IL), (618) 498-3442. Beautiful Italianate home on 18 acres, heated pool, private baths. $$

Maple Leaf Cottage Inn, P. O. Box 156, (618) 374-1684. "Inn-chanting" cottages with antiques, English Herb Garden, private baths. $$$

WHERE TO EAT

Elsah Landing Bakery & Tearoom, 20 LaSalle St., (618) 374-1607. Homemade pastries, own cookbooks, English teas by reservation. $

Elsah Landing Restaurant, 18 LaSalle St., (618) 374-1607. Four homemade soups daily, eight homemade breads, incredible desserts. $

FURTHER INFORMATION

Greater Alton/Twin Rivers Convention & Visitors Bureau 200 Piasa, Alton, IL 62002, (800) 258-6645.

DIRECTIONS

From St. Louis (MO), US 67 north (across Mississippi River) to IL 100, IL 100 north to Elsah.

GALENA, ILLINOIS

Population: 3,647

Surrounded by some of the most beautiful rolling countryside in Ilinois, **Galena** is a little town of historic mansions, handsome brick commercial buildings and churches with hand-carved altars and pulpits. The lure of this delightful place can be underscored by noting that Chicago CEOs have chosen to retire here and that several members of the renowned Chicago Symphony have selected this as their second home.

With economic roots in lead mining, smelting and riverboating, Galena was once the largest Mississippi River port between St. Louis and St. Paul. But the railroad was to replace the riverboat, and this and other developments eventually plunged the town into a depression that lasted from the 1890s until the 1960s. The many grand old buildings were neither modernized nor torn down simply because on one had enough to money to do so. Artists from Chicago began restoring the town in the 1960s and, joined by other groups, changed Galena from a sleepy, decaying river town to one of the most charming and sophisticated spots in Illinois, the Midwest, and the United States.

Galena and **Jo Daviess County** claim more than 50 antique shops (making this a principal Midwestern antiquing center), 60 bed and breakfasts, 20 galleries, 50 private studios, and countless specialty shops. Ranking as one of the most popular destinations in the Midwest, visitors may find accommodations scarce. Reservations are advised — only November and March can be relied on as truly "dead" months.

85% of Galena is listed on the National Register. Architectural styles include Federal, Italianate, Greek Revival, Queen Anne, Romanesque Revival and Galena Vernacular. There are more historic sites here than in many large cities. A good starting point for a tour of the town is the **Galena/Jo Daviess County History Museum**. Housed in an 1858 Italianate mansion, the museum features paintings, toys and dolls, household items, clothing and a Civil War exhibit that includes Thomas Nast's original painting, "Peace in Union."

One of Galena's most famous sites is the **Ulysses S. Grant Home State Historic Site**, the 1860 Italianate home that was presented to Grant in 1865 on his return from the Civil War. The restored home contains original furnishings and personal items of the Grant family.

The Old Market House State Historic Site is an 1845/1846 Greek Revival building that once served as the center of Galena's community life. Among its many functions today are a center for historical and architectural exhibits, an open-air farmer's market during the summer and fall, and a hospitality center during the Christmas season.

Among the historic homes open to the public are the **Dowling House** (1826) and the **Belvedere Mansion and Gardens** (1857). The native limestone Dowling House, Galena's oldest house, contains primitive period furniture and a large collection of Galena pottery. The 22-room Italianate Belvedere Mansion has Victorian furnishings, items from Liberace's estate and the famous green drapes from Tara in *Gone With the Wind*.

Also of interest are the limestone **Galena Post Office** (1857/1859), the second oldest continuously-operating post office in the United States; the Greek Revival **Galena Public Library** (1906), which has a reading room with a mosaic fireplace in the style of Frank Lloyd Wright; and the **Old General Store Museum**, a replica of a 19th-century store complete with pot-belly stove and back-room bar. The **Vinegar Hill Historic Lead Mine and Museum** offers a guided tour of an 1822 underground lead mine.

Recreational opportunites abound in the Galena area. A casino cruise ship plies the nearby **Mississippi River**. Mississippi riverboats also offer sightseeing excursions, including two-day round-trip cruises. Houseboats can also be rented.

Summer sports include hiking, horseback riding and some of the best golfing in the country. With winter come skating, sledding, tobogganing, snow-shoeing and some of the best downhill skiing in the Midwest. Sleighrides are popular. Cultural offerings range from chamber music to bluegrass, from dinner theater to performances by a professional theatrical troupe.

SPECIAL FEATURES

•Check with the Visitor Information Center for help on planning a scenic drive. **Jo Daviess County** is full of winding country roads.

> *Ulysses S. and Julia Dent Grant considered Galena their hometown even though Grant actually lived in the town for no more than a total of about two years.*

WHERE TO STAY

Aldrich Guest House, 900 Third St., (815) 777-3323. 1845 Greek Revival home, antique decor, grand piano, screened porch, library, full breakfasts. $$ to $$$

DeZoya House B&B, 1203 Third St., (815) 777-1203. 1830 limestone Federal house on two acres, antiques and art from Federal period, private baths, full breakfasts. $$$

Hellman Guest House, 318 Hill St., (815) 777-3638. 1895 Queen Anne home overlooking downtown and countryside, private baths, stained glass, antique decor. $$$

The Park Avenue Guest House, 208 Park Ave., (800) 359-0743. 1897 Queen Anne home, screened wrap-around porch, gazebo, private baths, gardens. $$ to $$$

The Steamboat House, 605 Prospect St., (815) 777-3128. 1855 Gothic Revival house, ornate antique decor, parlor fireplaces, private baths, large whirlpool. $$$

WHERE TO EAT

The DeSoto House Hotel, 230 S. Main St., (815) 777-0090. Restored 1855 hotel on National Register, Leadminers Stew, stuffed pork chops, hand-cut Midwestern steaks. $ to $$

Eldorado Grill, 219 N. Main St., (815) 777-1224. Southwestern decor and cuisine, naturally-raised meats and produce, vegetarian dishes. $ to $$

Fried Green Tomato Co., 1301 N. Irish Hollow Rd., (815) 777-3938. In complex of historic brick buildings, country Italian cuisine, by-the-ounce steaks, seafood, reservations suggested. $ to $$

Kingston Inn Restaurant, 300 N. Main St., (815) 777-0451. Continental cuisine and regional American dishes, fresh ocean fish, award-winning wine cellar, singing servers. $ to $$

Lost Art Cafe, 317 S. Main St., (815) 777-2820. Cappuccino, latte, scones, biscotti, cheesecake, veggie sandwiches. $

FURTHER INFORMATION

Galena/Jo Daviess County Convention & Visitors Bureau, 101 Bouthillier St., Galena, IL 61036, (800) 747-9377.

DIRECTIONS

From Chicago, I 90 (Northwest Tollway) to I 39 (Rockford), I 39 (about four miles) to US 20, US 20 west to Galena.

GENEVA, ILLINOIS

Population: 12,617

Flowing just beyond the reach of Chicago's western suburbs is the beautiful Fox River. Each of the towns along the river has a waterside park, and the parks' bike trails have been connected to offer bicyclists, roller bladers, hikers and joggers 25 miles of uninterrupted scenery.

Geneva is one of the prettiest and most historic of the towns along the river. The town's considerable charm is in part due to the convergence of its historic beauty, its 150-year-old reputation as a shopping center and its lovely and unique location. Founded in the 1830s, Geneva has two historic districts and more than 200 homes, churches and other buildings on the National Register of Historic Places. Most of the homes and churches were built in the middle of the 19th century, with the decades of the 1840s, 1850s, and 1860s predominating.

Encouraged by Geneva's beautiful setting — and the tastes of area residents — it was inevitable that during the decades of the 20th century the shops and the historic homes would begin to find each other. And so they did. Geneva boasts over 100 antique shops, galleries, specialty shops, restaurants and cafes, many nestled within the walls of beautiful old homes. The union of upscale shopping with the town's architectural treasures and romantic riverside setting has earned Geneva a respected reputation in Chicagoland, and beyond.

The interior of the **Kane County Courthouse** is laced with wrought-iron balconies from the first to the fourth floors and displays eight large murals by Edward Holslag. The murals provide a good view of the surrounding countryside as it appeared in 1910.

Among the local memorabilia showcased by the **Geneva Historical Society Museum**, in **Wheeler Park**, are furniture made by area cabinetmakers from local walnut and period costumes and hats from the shops of town merchants.

Bikes and roller blades can be rented riverside. The **Fox River bike trails** extend from Aurora to Elgin and beyond, and connect with a vast network of bike paths on Chicago's western outskirts.

SPECIAL FEATURE
• Geneva's lovely **Island Park** is ideal for picnicking.

WHERE TO STAY
The Herrington, 15 S. River Ln., (708) 208-7433. Riverfront inn with Northern European and Scandinavian ambience, fireplaces, whirlpools, riverside gazebo, fitness room, dining room. $$$

Oscar Swan Country Inn, 1800 W. State St., (708) 232-0173. 1902 estate surrounded by seven acres, antiques, pre-arranged meals. $$$

WHERE TO EAT
302 West, 302 W. State St., (708) 232-9302. "Bold new American cuisine in an atmosphere of casual elegance." $$ to $$$

The Little Traveler, 404 S. Third St., (708) 232-6060. Since 1922, thirty-room mansion serving luncheon and snacks all day in Atrium Cafe, luncheon by reservation in Antique Courts. $

Mill Race Inn, 4 E. State St., (708) 232-2030. Country inn serving good food on river's edge for 60 years. $ to $$

Ristorante Chianti, 207 S. Third St., (708) 232-0212. Award-winning Italian cuisine served in casual setting. $ to $$

Riverwalk, 35 N. River Ln., (708) 232-1330. Good food served with dramatic view over Fox River Dam. $ to $$

FURTHER INFORMATION
Geneva Chamber of Commerce, P. O. Box 481, Geneva, IL 60134, (708) 232-6060.

DIRECTIONS
From Chicago, IL 38 west (approx. 20 miles).

GOLCONDA, ILLINOIS

Population: 823

The tiny, sleepy Ohio river town of **Golconda** is the kind of place where a showboat would put in, a Huck Finn would go fishing, and an Aunt Polly would don a bonnet before heading to the store to fetch some thread or a pound of sugar. The big old houses and the turn-of-the-century architecture puts one in mind of a time when steamboat trade could bring prosperity to little river communities. And the rolling hills of the vast **Shawnee National Forest** remind of still isolated country.

Golconda is the place to go to relax, to experience the Ohio the way another generation might (in theory) have experienced it. There are a couple of antique and craft shops on **Main Street** to browse in, and what with the entire town on the National Register, there are lots of old buildings to explore. The town even has one of the finest restaurants in southern Illinois (see below).

Docking facilities and boat rentals are available at the one major new structure in town, the multi-million dollar **Golconda Marina**. Along with great boating and water-skiing, the river also offers terrific fishing.

Golconda is an ideal home base from which to explore the river and the national forest. Spectacular views of the river are available from several points. Two of the best are the **Ohio River Recreation Area** just east of town and the visitors center of the **Smithland Locks and Dam** 15 miles south. The **Shawnee National Forest** is dotted with interesting state parks; two are listed below.

SPECIAL FEATURES

• **Dixon Springs State Park** west of town is noted for its rugged crags, ancient trees, mineral springs and large swimming pool.

• **Cave-In-Rock State Park**, upriver from Golconda, features a large cave in a bluff overlooking the **Ohio River**. The cave was once a roost for robbers preying on pioneers heading west on the river. It also once served as a tavern and as a shelter for travelers.

WHERE TO STAY

The Mansion of Golconda, Box 339, (618) 683-4400. Renovated 1894 home on National Register, richly appointed accommodations, private baths, full breakfasts. $$$

WHERE TO EAT

The Mansion of Golconda (see above). Beautifully decorated dining r o o m s with menu ranging from deep-fried chicken and fiddlers (local delicacy) to "French-inspired and sauced entrees." $ to $$

FURTHER INFORMATION

Southern Illinois Tourism Council, P. O. Box 40, Whittington, IL 62897 (800) 342-3100.

DIRECTIONS

From Paducah (KY), I 24 north (across Ohio River) to exit 16, IL 146 east to Golconda.

MAEYSTOWN, ILLINOIS

Population: 135

Cluster an old stone church, a little stone bridge, an inn, several stores, a few houses, and a handful of outbuildings on the rolling Illinois countryside, and you have the quaint little German village of **Maeystown**. The land was never graded to form level lots; instead, the buildings were set into the hillside. This means that to go upstairs you have the choice between climbing stairs or going outside and climbing a little hill to a door on the next floor. The effect is an integration of building and landscape; the overall result is a village straight out of a storybook.

The entire village of Maeystown, founded in 1852, is listed on the National Register. The village is so tiny that residents report two populations, the one given above and a larger one that includes the dogs and cats (and there are a lot of these around). Some of the more signficant of the buildings include the original **stone church** (1865-67); **the home** (1860-65) **of the town's founder, Jacob Maeys**; and **Zeitinger's Mill** (1859), now the home of the preservation society. The picturesque old one-lane **stone bridge** (1881) is still in use.

Rent a bicycle and tour the village, or let a horse-drawn carriage do it for you. Everyone greets everyone else on the village's half dozen streets, and conversation comes easy. A very pleasant morning or afternoon can be spent by getting to know those lingering in the restaurant, inn, or old-fashioned general store.

SPECIAL FEATURE

• The original powder magazine and reconstructed north wall and guardhouse may be explored at **Fort de Chartres State Historic Site**, several miles south of town on the Mississippi. The original fort (1753) had 3-foot-thick stone walls and was built by the French to protect settlers in Prairie du Rocher.

> *Services at the original stone church were sometimes held in German until 1943.*
>
> *Many of the original barns, smokehouses, summer kitchens, sheds and outhouses are still standing behind the village's homes.*

WHERE TO STAY

Corner George Inn, Main and Mill Sts., (618) 458-6660. Restored 1884 hotel, now country inn B&B, breakfast in the ballroom. $$ to $$$

WHERE TO EAT

Hoefft's Village Inn, Main and Mill Sts., (618) 458-6425. Country cooking, daily specials, homemade pies. $

FURTHER INFORMATION
The Innkeepers, Corner George Inn, Maeystown, IL 62256, (618) 458-6660.

DIRECTIONS
From St. Louis, I 255 (across Mississippi River) to exit 6, IL 3 south to Waterloo, Maeystown Rd. southwest to Maeystown.

NAUVOO, ILLINOIS

Population: 1108

Located on a bluff overlooking the Mississippi, **Nauvoo** (pronounced "NAH voo") is the idyllic early 19th century American town. Lovely shade trees and green parkland blend with stately old brick buildings so beautifully and naturally that cars and RVs look out of place. The atmosphere is small-town and peaceful. There is no commercialization, and in fact you're not likely to come across the town except by a lucky stumble. That is, unless you happen to know something about Mormon history.

Fleeing persecution elsewhere, the Mormons settled in Nauvoo in 1839. There, granted autonomy by the Illinois legislature, they prospered. During the 1840s, Nauvoo, which means *a beautiful place* in Hebrew, became the largest town in Illinois and the 10th largest in the country. Troubles continued to plague the church, however, and following the murder of Mormon leader Joseph Smith, the Mormons left Illinois. Nauvoo was abandoned. In subsequent years, French, German and Swiss settlers came to the area. Wine- and cheese-making came with them.

The best way to explore Nauvoo is by driving tour aided by a map and cassette obtained from the **Nauvoo CoC Uptown Tourist Center** (downtown). The two best-known sites, or clusters of sites, help define the historic district, once inhabited by Mormons. Both are taken from the pages of Mormon history:

On the south side of the historic district is the **Joseph Smith Historic Center** which comprises the log **Homestead** (1803), **Mansion House** (1842), and **Red Brick Store** (1842), all family properties of Joseph Smith. The Red Brick Store displays merchandise typical of the early 1840s. Near the store is the Smith family cemetery, burial place of Joseph Smith and his wife and brother, Emma and Hyrum.

The **LDS Visitors Center**, on the north side of the district, maintains the **Monument to Women Gardens.** The center provides a good introduction to the district and offers guided tours of its many beautifully restored homes and shops.

SPECIAL FEATURE
• Daily demonstrations of Nauvoo's old crafts are provided all over town, and because they are indoors, in all seasons. Woodworking, blacksmith, and cooper demonstrations are just a few that can be seen. All are performed by skilled

artesans — the sheer intelligence and inventiveness of the craftsmanship are guaranteed to amaze.

> *What with the bald eagles wintering in the area, the sleigh bells and the traditional holiday decorations, many find December the best season to visit Nauvoo.*
>
> *Held on July 30-31 and August 3-7, the outdoor musical "City of Joseph" employs song, dance, costumes, fireworks and a computerized sound and lighting system to tell the story of Nauvoo.*

WHERE TO STAY

The Ancient Pines, 2015 Parley St., (217) 453-2767. 140-year-old pines, stained-glass windows, hand-carved woodwork, full breakfasts with homemade bread. $

Mississippi Memories B&B, P. O. Box 291, (217) 453-2771. On banks of Mississippi, wooded setting, large decks, flannel sheets, seasonal fruit and flowers, full breakfasts. $$

Parley Lane B&B, P. O. Box 220, (217) 453-2277. Restored 1830 farmhouse, 80 acres of woodlands, fine antiques, bicycles, pet accommodations. $

WHERE TO EAT

Hotel Nauvoo, IL 96, (217) 453-2211. Country-style buffet in restored home. $ to $$

FURTHER INFORMATION

Nauvoo Tourism, P. O. Box 41, Nauvoo, IL 62354, (217) 453-6648.

DIRECTIONS

From Peoria, US 24 southwest to US 136, US 136 west to IL 96, IL 96 north (along Mississippi River) to Nauvoo.

INDIANA

Indianapolis
✫

METAMORA
•

NASHVILLE
•

MADISON
•

FRENCH LICK
•

CORYDON
•

• NEW HARMONY

CORYDON, INDIANA

Population: 2,661

Here and there among the hills and forests of southern Indiana are little towns that look much as they did 50 years ago, or more. Too small to grow into sprawls, but too big to disappear, such towns somehow hang on, often with the help of tourist dollars attracted by a bit of Hoosier nostalgia. **Corydon** is a wonderful example of such a little town, and it has a lot of genuine Hoosier nostalgia to work with.

Corydon's downtown has an ambience that beautifully complements the Hoosier heritage. Many of the businesses proudly display — and restore and preserve — ornamental iron storefronts from the 1890s. Included among the businesses are specialty shops, antique and art malls, restaurants and a soda fountain. Corydon is especially known for its sculptured art glass objects.

On the square is the charming little **State Capitol Building**, Indiana's first state capitol (1816-1825). The 40-foot-square building, today a state historic site, is made of rough blue limestone and has first-floor walls that are 2 1/2 feet thick.

Not far away is the 1817 Federal-style brick **Governor Hendricks's Headquarters**. This two-story building, open to the public, was the home and headquarters of William Hendricks while he was governor of Indiana (1822-1825). Also near the square is a one-story brick building (1817) that was rented to the state for offices, making it the first state office building (now a private residence).

Two other beautiful old buildings that are open to the public are the **Posey House**, a large brick house built in 1817 (operated as a museum by the D.A.R.), and the **Kintner House**, a delightful B&B inn (see below). Other historic buildings include the restored two-story log **Branham Tavern** (1800), the 1807 log **Westfall House**, and the Federal-style office of the weekly newspaper, the *Corydon Democrat*, originally built as a residence and drug store (1842).

SPECIAL FEATURES

• Scheduled **trains** operate 16-mile excursions on an 1883 scenic railroad. The excursions last about 1 1/2 hours.

• In the rolling countryside not far from Corydon are some of the country's most beautiful caves. The best known, all open to the public, are **Wyandotte Cave, Little Wyandotte Cave, Marengo Cave**, and **Squire Boone Caverns**. Many farmers have wild caves that they allow visitors to explore.

> *The Battle of Corydon Memorial Park south of town was the site of one of the few Civil War battles fought on Northern soil.*

WHERE TO STAY

Kintner House Inn B&B, Capitol & Chestnut sts., (812) 738-2020. Restored 1873 hotel featured on Christmas cards, on National Register, private baths, antiques, inviting large porch. $ to $$$

WHERE TO EAT

Magdalena's Restaurant, on the square, (812) 738-8075. Steak, chicken, seafood, pasta, homemade soups/salads/sandwiches/muffins. $

Overlook Restaurant, P. O. Box 67 (Leavenworth), (812) 739-4264. Spectacular view of Ohio River, fried chicken, country ham, famous coconut cream pie. **$**

FURTHER INFORMATION
Harrison County Chamber of Commerce, 310 N. Elm St., Corydon, IN 47112, (812) 738-2137.

DIRECTIONS
From Louisville (KY), I-64 west to exit 105, IN-135 south to Corydon.

FRENCH LICK, INDIANA
Population: 2,087

Nestled among the scenic knobs of southern Indiana, **French Lick** is, was, and has always been one of the Midwest's great resorts. Belief in the medicinal and generally beneficial effects of the area's mineral waters turned French Lick and the neighboring village of **West Baden Springs** into a fashionable spa as early as the middle of the 19th century. The wealthy and the not-so-wealthy came here to take the waters, promenade and enjoy the restaurants and casinos. Some of the wealthy even came in their own railroad cars. An opera house was built. As the resort seasoned, major-league baseball teams came here to train. The grandest of the spa's hotels, the 6-story **West Baden Springs Hotel,** was built in 1902.

French Lick's popularity continued until the years of the Depression. Thereafter the resort had its ups and downs, but never died. In 1991 the West Baden Springs Hotel, by now renamed the **French Lick Springs Resort** and listed as a National Historic Landmark, underwent extensive restoration. The result is a hotel whose reputation as the largest, most complete all-season resort in the Midwest continues unchallenged. The hotel features an Olympic-sized outdoor pool, a glass-domed indoor pool, two 18-hole golf courses, 18 tennis courts, 30 miles of trails for horseback riding and a health and fitness spa. French Lick and West Baden Springs continue doing what they've been doing so well for over 150 years.

French Lick and West Baden Springs can fill out a pleasant day even for those not staying at the resort. **Main Street** and a couple of adjacent streets in French Lick have an interesting assortment of gift and antique shops as well as the quaint appearance that people expect of southern Indiana. A couple of very pleasant hours can also be spent strolling the beautiful lobby, veranda and vast landscaped grounds of the hotel. On the grounds is the renowned **Pluto Spring**.

Adjacent to the resort is the **Indiana Railway Museum.** Here a 1 3/4-hr. trip can be taken through 20 miles of the **Hoosier National Forest** on the **French Lick, West Baden, and Southern Railroad** Along the way is the 2,200-ft. **Burton Tunnel,** one of the longest railway tunnels in the state. The museum also displays several vintage locomotives and a number of old railroad cars.

The water from one of the artesian mineral springs, the Pluto Spring, was once bottled and widely distributed as "Pluto Water."

WHERE TO STAY

French Lick Springs Resort, French Lick, (800) 457-4042. Historic resort hotel, golf, tennis, swimming pools, stables, health spa, bicycles, restaurants, European and Modified American plans. $$$.

WHERE TO EAT

The **French Lick Springs Resort** features a variety of restaurants, menus and price ranges. Among the more casual, moderately-priced are **LeBistro** and **Pluto's Pavillion**; at the more expensive, gourmet end are the **Hoosier Dining Room** (traditional ballroom) and **Chez James.**

FURTHER INFORMATION

French Lick–West Baden Chamber of Commerce, P. O. Box 347, French Lick, IN 47432, (812) 936-2405.

DIRECTIONS

From Louisville (KY), US 150 northwest to Prospect, IN 56 south to French Lick.

MADISON, INDIANA

Population: 12,006

Every visitor to **Madison** should reserve time for a stroll on the beautiful brick walk along the riverfront. On one side is the **Ohio River**, with the hazy hills of Kentucky beyond, and on the other are the wooded heights and limestone cliffs of Indiana overlooking and sheltering the finest concentration of early 19th century architecture in the Midwest.

Madison's entire downtown, 133 blocks worth, is listed on the National Register of Historic Places. Most of the buildings on **Main Street** — one of the finest in the country — were in place at the time of the Civil War, yet the street is as alive as any main street ever was. Interwoven with the usual businesses, here and on adjacent streets, are some unusually fine antique, craft and specialty shops. The charm of the district reaches a peak at N. Broadway and Main, where a Victorian fountain, called the **Broadway Fountain**, commands a little square. The fountain, originally cast in iron and recast in bronze in 1976, was presented in 1876 to the Philadelphia Centennial Exposition by France.

One of Madison's best-known citizens was financier James Lanier, who loaned financially troubled Indiana money during the Civil War so that the state could equip Union troops. Lanier built a Greek Revival mansion (1844) that has become Madison's most popular attraction. Now the **J. F. D. Lanier State Historic**

Site, the splendid home has period furnishings and a south portico with a commanding view of the **Ohio River** that, by itself, would justify a trip to Madison.

The Greek Revival **Shrewsbury House** (1849) is another lovely Madison landmark. Especially noteworthy inside are the plasterwork and three-story freestanding spiral staircase. The house and its period furnishings are open to public view.

The **Jeremiah Sullivan House** (1818), an outstanding example of Federal architecture, was probably Madison's first mansion (open). Also in the Federal style, the **Masonic Schofield House** (ca. 1816) is believed to be the first two-story brick house/tavern in Madison (open).

The contents, including medical instruments, of **Dr. William D. Hutchings's Office** (1848) are exactly the same as they were at the time of Dr. Hutchings's death in 1903 (open).

SPECIAL FEATURES

• A **riverboat excursion** provides an opportunity to see Madison the way it's been seen by generations of passing steamboats. The autumn foliage can be breathtaking from the water.

• **Hanover College**, founded in 1827, is seven miles west of town. The campus consists of thirty Georgian-style buildings located on a hilltop overlooking the **Ohio River Valley**.

• **IN 56E** offers a picturesque tour of the countryside along the Ohio.

> *The Fair Play Fire Company is Indiana's oldest existing volunteer fire department (1841).*
>
> *Settlers often put into Madison for provisions on their way to their new homes in the Northwest Territory, now the eastern part of the Midwest.*

WHERE TO STAY

Broadway House B&B, 502 Broadway, (800) 767-2207. One of Madison's largest homes, fireplaces, private baths, gourmet breakfasts, view of Broadway Fountain. $$$

Cliff House B&B, 122 Fairmount Dr., (812) 265-5272. 1885 Victorian mansion high above historic district, antiques. $$$

The Elderberry Inn B&B, 411 W. First St., (812) 265-6856. Mid-1890s home next to Lanier Mansion, unique blend of antique and contemporary furnishings, full-course breakfasts. $$$

Main Street B&B, 739 W. Main St., (800) 362-6246. Restored 1840s Greek Revival home in historic district, private baths. $$$

Schussler House B&B, Jefferson St., (800) 392-1931. Restored ca. 1849 Federal/Classic Revival home, antiques, private baths, full breakfasts. $$$

WHERE TO EAT

Bonnie's Landing Riverfront Cafe, Vaughn Dr., (800) 998-2090. Floating site also serves as boat dock, seafood. $

Scotella Restaurant & Winery, Aulenbach Ave., (812) 265-3825. Italian cuisine, Seafood Neptune, Filet Mignon Bologna Style, wines produced on premises. $$

FURTHER INFORMATION

Madison Area Visitors Center, 301 E. Main St., Madison, IN 47250, (812) 265-2956.

DIRECTIONS

From Louisville (Kentucky), I 65 north to exit 33, IN 256 east to Madison.

METAMORA, INDIANA

Population: about 200

Tiny **Metamora's** (first) golden days came in the 1840s and 1850s when the village prospered as a port on the 76-mile-long **Whitewater Canal** (1845). Floods, mismanagement, the coming of the railroad and other factors ganged up on the canal, and the old waterway fell into disrepair. And so it remained until the 1940s, when the Indiana Department of Natural Resoures acquired 14 miles of it and began restoration. Included in the restoration was a covered aqueduct, built in 1843, that carried the canal 16 feet over **Duck Creek.**

Today, the restored canal, aqueduct and working grist mill make up the **Whitewater Canal State Historic Site.** A horse-drawn canal boat, the *Ben Franklin III*, takes on passengers and travels through the aqueduct, the only operational covered-bridge aqueduct in the United States (hourly departures).

With well over 100 shops, the village has become so popular that it now counts Nashville, Indiana (see below) as its main rival. Many of the shops are housed in quaint 19th-century houses and other buildings. The goods and wares include dolls, oak and cherry furniture, paintings, oak baskets, candles, homemade horseradish, wooden folk art, Amish cheese, wood signs, nutcrackers, quilts, tinware and ceramics. Shoppers come from as far away as Cincinnati, Indianapolis, Dayton, and Louisville.

SPECIAL FEATURE

• In addition to rides on the canal boat, the village offers buggy rides and one- and two-hour steam engine excursions on the **Whitewater Valley Railroad.** Longer rail excursions are available from **Connersville**, to the north.

> *Indiana's canal system drove the state into bankruptcy. The experience badly hurt Indiana's reputation and led to legislation that even today prohibits the state from contracting debt.*

WHERE TO STAY

The Grapevine Inn, P. O. Box 207, (317) 647-3738. Quiet country inn, Laura Ashley decorated rooms, private baths, TV, balcony. $$

The Publick House B&B, 28 Duck Creek Crossing, (317) 647-6729. Quiet country atmosphere, private baths, TV, breakfasts "with a gourmet flair." $$ to $$$

Thorpe House Country Inn B&B, P. O. Box 36, (317) 647-5425. 19th-century Greek Revival home, private baths, period furnishings. $$

WHERE TO EAT

The Hearthstone Restaurant, US 52, (317) 647-5204. "Old-fashioned family dining in a warm & casual country setting." $

Hickory Lane at the Depot, US 52, (317) 647-4544. Famous smorgasbord. $

FURTHER INFORMATION

Merchants Association of Metamora, P. O. Box 117, Metamora, IN 47030, Welcome Line: (317) 647-2109.

DIRECTIONS

From Indianapolis, US 52 east (via Rushville) to Metamora.

NASHVILLE, INDIANA

Population: 873

Unlike so many other charming villages, **Nashville** didn't arise from the wealth of lumbermen, cotton planters, bankers or gold miners. Indeed, Nashville and surrounding **Brown County** occupy an area that is relatively poor in natural resources. Nashville's charm originated instead in the backwoods beauty of Brown County, a county with winding country roads, old covered bridges, log cabins and homey stone buildings.

Standing in contrast with the flatness of so much of the Midwest, the mountainous scenery of Brown County began attracting artists over a hundred years ago. One of the earliest and most prominent of the artists was Theodore C. Steele, the Impressionistic artist of Hooser Group fame. Steele's home, studio, gardens and grounds now form the **T. C. Steele State Historic Site,** about eight miles southwest of town. Many of Steele's landscape paintings are on display in the house and studio (1907).

Nashville's center of attraction is the **Brown County Courthouse Historic District** (1873-1937). The district includes a picture-book brick courthouse, the **Historical Society Museum Building,** the **Old Log Jail,** and several other log structures.

Along Nashville's picturesque streets are over 300 art galleries, craft shops, and antique stores. The town is tiny, so park your car and walk. Carriage tours are available for those who wish to add a little romance to their visit.

SPECIAL FEATURE

• Within the borders of Brown County are **Brown County State Park** (the largest in the state), **Yellowwood State Forest** and parts of the **Hoosier National Forest.** In and out of the woods are numerous roads and trails, making the county ideal for nature hikes, horseback rides, and bicycle tours.

One study has ranked Brown County, along with neighboring Bloomington, among the ten most desirable places in the U.S. in which to retire.

In addition to golf courses, country music establishments, and other attractions, Nashville is home to the charming 60-seat outdoor Melchior Marionette Theatre.

WHERE TO STAY

5th Generation Farm, Rt. 4, P. O. Box 90-A, (800) 437-8152. 1848 farmhouse in country, antique furnishings, private baths, recreation room with pool table. $$ to $$$

The Allison House, P. O. Box 546, (812) 988-0814. Country inn, library with fireplace and piano, private baths. $$ to $$$

Mindheims' Inn, Rt. 5, P. O. Box 592, (812) 988-2590. Tucked under an architect-designed home, private entrance, antiques, quilts, TV, private bath, kitchen with groceries. $$ to $$$

The Victoria House, Rt. 5, P. O. Box 117B, (812) 988-6344. Restored Victorian home, TV, antique furnishings. $$ to $$$

Wraylyn Knoll, P. O. Box 481, (812) 988-0733. Guest lounge, swimming pool, pond and creek, fishing, private baths. $$ to $$$

WHERE TO EAT

Nashville House, Main St., (812) 988-4554. Country-fried chicken, baked Hoosier ham, fried biscuits and homemade baked apple butter. $$

FURTHER INFORMATION

Nashville/Brown County Chamber of Commerce, P. O. Box 840, Nashville, IN 47448, (800) 753-3255.

DIRECTIONS

From Indianapolis, I 65 south to exit 68, west on IN 46 to Nashville.

NEW HARMONY, INDIANA

Population: 846

New Harmony was laid out and settled by Harmonists – Lutheran Separatists – in 1814. Ten years later, the village was taken over by a second communal society, this one lasting only a couple of years. Both communities failed, and their utopian ideals never realized, but each stressed intellectual and cultural achievement, and that legacy lives on. For today the quaint little village of New Harmony is alive with musical performances, workshops and conferences, summer theater productions, craft demonstrations and art exhibitions. In addition, many of the tour sites (see below) offer permanent exhibits of art, history and science.

The bridge between New Harmony's past and present is a unique one. Beginning in 1937 various preservation and restoration efforts were undertaken. In the late 1950s construction began on the first of several contemporary structures. In the years since the village has been zoned and its infrastructure upgraded and modernized. New buildings, including a visitors' center, medical clinic and townhouses, have gone up; their architecture has often united modern elements with traditional ones, especially those of the Harmonist tradition. Many of the historic buildings have been restored and converted to museums. The resulting village is a delightful mix of the authentic old with the creative new, of unique shops and good restaurants with history museums and art galleries.

Every visitor should go first to the **Atheneum/Visitors' Center**, a contemporary structure designed by Richard Meier. The center offers an orientation film and exhibits, including a scale model of the village in 1824. All tours begin here. The tours range from a 45-minute orientation tour to a three-hour **New Harmony Story Tour**, which includes escorted entry into 11 sites.

There are 15 tour sites in all, as well as several sites open to the public free of charge. Among the tour sites are **Dormitory #2**, a large residence built for single Harmonists and later the site of a Pestalozzian school; **Thrall's Opera House**, originally a Harmonist dormitory and later remodeled for theatrical performances; and the **Workingmen's Institute**, Indiana's oldest continuously open public library (1838). Another site, the **George Keppler House**, contains exhibits on the life and work of David Dale Owen, Indiana State Geologist and later Chief Geologist for the U.S. Government. The **Maximilian-Bodmer Collection** showcases original artwork from the 1832/1834 expedition of Prince Maximilian and artist Karl Bodmer to the Upper Missouri.

The Labyrinth, a restored maze of hedges, is one of the sites open to the public free of charge. Others include the **Roofless Church** (1960), an interdenominational church that won an award for its designer, and **Tillich Park**, the burial place of theologican Paul Johannes Tillich.

SPECIAL FEATURE

• Nearby **Harmonie State Park** features an Olympic-size pool, 110-ft. water slide, and boat launch on the **Wabash River**. Wildlife, wildflower, and fall foliage viewers have six hiking trails to choose from.

> *New Harmony was one of the country's most important training and research centers for geology between 1830 and 1860.*
> *Congressman Robert Dale Owen, a New Harmony resident, sponsored legislation to establish the Smithsonian Institution.*

WHERE TO STAY

Harmonie B&B, 344 W. Church St., (812) 682-3730. Furnished in fine antiques, full breakfasts. $$

The New Harmony Inn, P. O. Box 581, (812) 682-4491. Fireplaces, balconies, Shaker-type furniture, heated swimming pool, tennis courts, health spa, Jacuzzi. $$ to $$$

The Old Rooming House, 916 Church St., (812) 682-4724. "Lots of reading material, bikes and quiet comfort." $

WHERE TO EAT

Bayou Grill, 504 North St., (812) 682-4431. Diverse menu ranging from omelettes to hearty sandwiches to fried chicken and daily specials. $

Red Geranium Restaurant, 508 North St., (812) 682-4431. Comfortable atmosphere, prime rib, home-made pies, one of Indiana's most popular. $$

FURTHER INFORMATION

Historic New Harmony, P. O. Box 579, New Harmony, IN, 47631, (812) 682-4488.

DIRECTIONS

From Evansville, IN 66 west to New Harmony.

IOWA

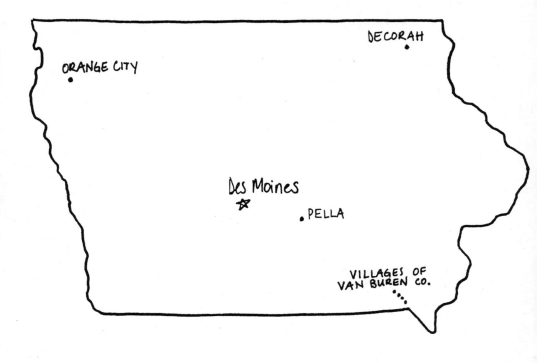

DECORAH

ORANGE CITY

Des Moines

PELLA

VILLAGES OF
VAN BUREN CO.

DECORAH, IOWA

Population: 8,063

Decorah is a very pretty Norwegian-American town nestled among the hills, limestone bluffs and woods of northeastern Iowa's *Little Switzerland*. The town is known for its lovely collection of historic homes and its scenic setting on the **Upper Iowa River**. It's also the seat of **Winneshiek County**, rich in history and cultural tradition (see below).

Decorah's most celebrated point of interest is **Vesterheim**, the Norwegian-American Museum. One of the country's top immigrant museums, the Vesterheim covers nearly a city block and consists of the main building, three buildings acquired in the Decorah business district, and nine authentically furnished structures that have been moved to the site. One of the buildings has been converted to the **Gallery of Pioneer Industry**, with exhibits describing the various crafts of the Norwegian settlers. Among the other buildings are an 18th-century Norwegian home and gristmill and two immigrant log houses from the 1850s and 1860s. The main museum highlights the Norwegian-American immigrant's experience with carved furnishings, decorative arts, traditional costumes and a three-story ship gallery.

The guide for the **Broadway-Phelps Park Historic District** lists over 50 structures. Within the district, entered on the National Register, are houses presenting nearly all major Midwestern architectural styles between the 1850s and 1910. Among those of special note are the 1867 **Ellsworth-Porter House**, now home to the **Winneshiek County Historical Society Museum**; the stucco 1858 **Octagonal House**; the 1862 Gothic Cottage **Grier-Green House**, with elaborate verge board; and the 1867 three-story Gothic Revival **Paine House**.

The natural park-like campus of **Luther College**, a private liberal-arts college (1862), is the result of a 1910 campus landscaping plan. The **Luther College Farm**, acquired by the college in 1929, contains barns, a restored icehouse and other structures dating from the late 1860s to the turn of the century.

Other structures of note in Decorah include the restored 1888 **Milwaukee Road Passenger Depot**, the 1874 **Methodist Church**, and the 1875 **Steyer Bridge**, one of the very few stone-arch bridges in the state. The 1904 **Winneshiek County Courthouse** is known for its intricate stained-glass dome and its **Soldiers Monument** (1886) honoring county residents who served in the Civil War.

Decorah and Winneshiek County offer a wealth of summer and winter recreational opportunities. There are miles of hiking trails in Decorah's 12 parks, and canoeing and tubing are popular on the Upper Iowa River. The area has three golf courses, groomed snowmobile trails and miles of stocked trout-fishing streams. The terrain offers good downhill and cross-country skiing.

SPECIAL FEATURES

• **Palisades Parks** affords an especially beautiful view of the Decorah area.

• **Spillville**, southwest of Decorah, is the home of **St. Wenceslaus Church** (1860), the Old World-style stone church where composer Antonin Dvorak was once guest organist (1893). The building where Dvorak lived, now the **Bily Clock Museum**, houses a collection of unique hand-carved clocks, many animated with mechanical figures. A room on the second floor contains Dvorak memorabilia.

• The **Laura Ingalls Wilder Park and Museum**, a National Historical Site, is located in **Burr Oak**, north of Decorah. The pre-1860 hotel was one of the childhood homes of the famous author.

• The 140-acre **Heritage Farm**, just a few miles north of town, has as its goals the maintenance and display of endangered food crops. Owned by the **Seed Savers Exchange**, the farm maintains 8,000 rare vegetables, 600 varieties of old-time apples, and a small herd of extremely rare **White Park Cattle** (visitors welcome).

Fort Atkinson, south of Decorah, was the only fort ever built in the U.S. to protect a tribe of Indians (the Winnebagos) from other tribes. The reconstructed 1840 fort is today part of the Iowa State Preserves System.

WHERE TO STAY

Broadway B&B, 303 W. Broadway, (319) 382-2329. 1890 Queen Anne home in historic district, full or Continental breakfasts. $ to $$

Knox Landing B&B, R.R. 3 (Box 74), (319) 735-5637. Visits to working farms by appointment, large farm yard. $

Montgomery Mansion, 812 Maple Ave., (800) 892-4955. Restored 1877 home, upstairs sitting room with TV, full breakfasts. $$

Vanaheim Inn, 509 North St., (319) 382-4191. Frame house of Prairie/Craftsman style next to Luther College campus, antiques, piano, reading room. $$

Victoria Cottage B&B Inn, 503 W. Broadway, (319) 382-4897. Restored 1863 brick Gothic Revival home, full breakfasts, refreshments. $$

WHERE TO EAT

Cafe Deluxe, 421 W. Water St., (319) 382-5589. "The Area's Greatest Menu Selection." $

Mabe's Pizza Inc., 110 E. Water St., (319) 382-4297. A Decorah tradition, pasta, broasted chicken. $

Vesterheim Dayton House, 520 W. Water St., (319) 382-9681. Norwegian and American menu, daily specials. $

FURTHER INFORMATION

Decorah Area Chamber of Commerce, 102 E. Water St., Decorah, IA 52101, (319) 382-3990.

DIRECTIONS

From Minneapolis/St. Paul, US 52 south to Decorah.

ORANGE CITY, IOWA

Population: 4,940

Some of the shops of this delightful little town out on the prairies of northwestern Iowa stock Delft pottery, wooden shoes, Dutch dolls, and lace and needlework imported from the Netherlands. Other shops sell Dutch pastries, home-cured dried beef, homemade bologna and bratwurst, and imported Dutch cheese. Among the highlights of the three-day **Tulip Festival** on the third weekend in May are a **Volksparade, Klompen Dancers,** and a **Straatmarkt** – and colorful tulip beds. **Orange City's** founders were obviously Dutch.

Many of the businesses in downtown Orange City have added facades with architectural elements modeled after 17th- and 18th-century Dutch buildings. Every year the number of Dutch storefronts grows. The city has in fact sent a delegation of its citizens to the Netherlands to study that country's architecture.

There are of course replicas of Dutch windmills. Two of them have been built by Orange City businesses: one houses a bank; the other, built by a paint company, is a working mill with authentically furnished living quarters (open to the public).

Although the town was settled by Dutch immigrants in 1870, the Dutch architecture is relatively new. The town's more historic buildings are solidly American. The most imposing of these is the **Sioux County Courthouse** (1904), built in the Richardsonian Romanesque style and listed on the National Register. This grand building has so much to offer, including a 10-foot bronze statue of "Justice" on top of its tower, that a detailed brochure has been prepared for self-guided tours.

Century House is a restored 1900 home decorated and furnished in the manner of the early 1900s (open for tours). Another restored structure, the**Little White Store** (1870s), was moved to its present location in 1880. Typical of its kind, it features a false Western front and upstairs apartment. Although historical items are displayed in its windows, the store is only open on special occasions.

Zwemer Hall (1894), on the campus of **Northwestern College,** is listed on the National Register. The sandstone building is open to the public.

Loyal to its Dutch heritage, Orange City has two Christmas traditions, Welcoming Sinterklaas and Piet into Holland, and the traditional religious holiday of Christmas. The beauty of the lighted religious symbols that decorate the downtown in December is responsible for the town's nickname, "The City of White Lights."

Grasshopper plagues were among the most serious problems facing the early settlers.

WHERE TO STAY
Dutch Colony Inn, IA 10 E., (800) 341-8000. Dutch architecture with Hindeloopen painting on shutters/window boxes, private baths. $$

WHERE TO EAT
Brinkers, IA 10, (712) 737-2322. Dutch bologna, fried potatoes, friedapples, homemade pies. $

The Hatchery, 3rd St. N.W., (712) 737-2889. Quaint eatery housed in small building once used as hatchery. $

FURTHER INFORMATION
Orange City Chamber of Commerce, P. O. Box 36, Orange City, IA 51041, (712) 737-4510.

DIRECTIONS

From Sioux City, US 75 north to IA 10 (just beyond Maurice), IA 10 east to Orange City.

PELLA, IOWA

Population: 9,270

What a delightful contrast! After driving past Iowa cornfields and rolling pastureland, you enter a town whose gardens, streets, even shop windows speak of Holland. Many of the buildings look like their parents could have come from Amsterdam, and during the spring and summer months flowers are everywhere. The town is neat, pretty, unusually clean, prosperous. Old World but also very progressive, **Pella** attributes its good fortune to "old-fashioned virtues like hard work, thrift, honesty and integrity."

The **Dutch Fronts program**, an example of "old-fashioned virtues," is responsible for much of the the charm of Pella's buildings. The program encourages businesses to incorporate stepped gables and other elements of Low Country architecture in their construction and renovation. As a result, even McDonald's has a delightfully Dutch look.

One of the program's most enchanting accomplishments is the **Klokkenspel** (*Glockenspiels* in German), a musical clock that sets animated figures in motion. On one side of the Klokkenspel the figures tell of Pella's history, on the other side they step out of the Tulip Time festival. A computer-driven 147-bell carillon provides the music. The Klokkenspel is one of only two or three animated clock towers in the United States.

The **Pella Historical Village** encompasses some 20 buildings linked by red-brick walkways and, in season, tulips. Among the most interesting of the sites are the **boyhood home of Wyatt Earp**, the **Sterrenberg Library**, the **Scholte Church**, and the **Miniature Dutch Village**.

The picturesque **Scholte House** (1848), built by Pella's founder, features a fine collection of French and Italian antiques. The National Register house may be toured by appointment. The **Scholte Gardens**, behind the house, display over 25,000 tulips and annuals.

Flowering trees and literally hundreds of thousands of tulips and other flowers contribute to Pella's Old World flavor. (Much of this beauty is the result of a comprehensive planting project, another example of the town's energetic planning.) The tulips and everything associated with them are especially colorful during Pella's annual **Tulip Time**, second weekend in May.

Pella is small enough that its beauty and charm can be absorbed on foot. Park your car and enjoy a little bit of Holland.

SPECIAL FEATURE

• **Lake Red Rock**, Iowa's largest lake, is less than four miles from town. The winds make the lake especially popular with sailors, and the over 50,000 acres of diverse habitat attract a variety of nature lovers.

> *Pella shops display Delftware, fine lace and other imports from the Nether-*
> *lands.*
> *Scrubbing the streets before the Tulip Time parade is a Pella tradition.*

WHERE TO STAY

The Clover Leaf B&B, 314 Washington St., (515) 628-9045. Restored 1892 home, antiques, central AC, full breakfasts. $$

Strawtown Inn, 1111 Washington St., (515) 628-2681. Mid-1800s buildings on National Register, private baths, true Dutch breakfasts. $$$

Tulip Tree B&B, 506 E. Liberty St., (515) 628-8224. Century-old house directly behind Historical Village, original oak woodwork. $$

WHERE TO EAT

Strawtown Inn, (see above), (515) 628-4043. Dutch Spiced Beef, Stuffed Porkchop with Apple Dressing, Dutch Apple Bread. $ to $$

FURTHER INFORMATION

Pella Chamber of Commerce, 518 Franklin St., Pella, IA 50219, (515) 628-2626.

DIRECTIONS

From Des Moines, IA 163 southeast to Pella.

THE VILLAGES OF
VAN BUREN COUNTY, IOWA

Populations: from about 20 to 1,020

Here and there in the Midwest and South, usually far from the city, you can still find a little river town where steamboats once stopped, a place that should have died when the boats stopped coming and industry and trains refused to come. Sometimes the town has one or two old brick stores, but not enough to draw many visitors — or merit a listing in a travel book. If **Van Buren County**, tucked away in a remote part of southeastern Iowa, had one town like that, few would care. But Van Buren County has at least *four* such towns, and although most people still don't know about them, they form a collection that more than merits a visit.

The four riverboat towns of Van Buren County lie along the banks of the winding **Des Moines River**. Each is within biking distance of the next. Each has its own personality.

Bentonsport (1839), a National Historic District and the tiniest of the towns, has a number of buildings dating from the 1840s-1860s; it is the only one of the four to boast crafts shops and resident artists. People from Des Moines, Burlington, and elsewhere have renovated some of the houses for use as summer homes.

Bonaparte, founded in 1837, is a National Historic Riverfront District and the smallest Main Street Community in the country. Most of the downtown buildings date from the 1850s-1930s, and many have been restored. Separately listed on the National Register are the **Meek Grist Mill** (1878; see restaurant below), the restored **Des Moines River Lock #5** (1852), and the **Aunty Green Museum** (1844), which houses both a museum and the city library.

Keosauqua is the county seat and largest of the towns. The **courthouse**, listed on the National Register, is the oldest in continuous use in Iowa (tours are available). Another structure on the National Register is the brick and stone **Pearson House** (1847), once part of the Underground Railroad.

Two National Register buildings in **Farmington** are the second oldest church west of the Mississippi (1847), now the **Pioneer Museum**, and a limestone structure (1867) that was once home to a carriage manufacturing company. Farmington is also known for its park on lovely **Indian Lake** and its proximity to **Shimek State Forest** (see below).

Two of the best ways to absord the charm of Van Buren County are by bike and by river. Country roads in most parts of Iowa are good, open and often interesting — in other words, ideal for bicycling. In Van Buren County the cyclist has the added advantage of being unencumbered by traffic lights. The towns can also be seen from a canoe, kayak or tube on the Des Moines River, water conditions permitting.

SPECIAL FEATURES

• **Lacey-Keosauqua State Park**, one of the largest parks in Iowa, features trails that wind along the hills and dales of the Des Moines River. One part of the park contains 19 mounds built by an ancient Indian group.

• The trail system of the **Shimek State Forest**, the largst continuous stand of forest cover in the state, is ideal for hikers and horseback riders in the warmer months, and cross-country skiiers and snowmobilers in the winter.

> *Van Buren County also has eight or so historic towns located away from the river.*

WHERE TO STAY

Note: Perhaps the three most historic and charming buildings in Van Buren County are those listed below as lodgings and restaurants.

Hotel Manning, 100 Van Buren St. (Keosauqua), (800) 728-2718. "A Steamboat Gothic Gem," antique-filled rooms, spacious lobby with 14-ft ceilings and priceless grand piano. $ to $$

Mason House Inn (Bentonsport), Rt. 2 (Box 237) (Keosauqua), (319) 592-3133. Built in 1846 to serve steamboat travelers, full breakfasts served in Keeping Room beside 1880 cookstove. $$ to $$$

WHERE TO EAT

Bonaparte Retreat Restaurant, River St. (Bonaparte), (319) 592-3339. Midwestern cooking served in 1878 grist and flour mill, on National Register. $ to $$

Hotel Manning Restaurant, (see above). Gourmet dining on banks of Des Moines River, beloved Iowa landmark. $ to $$

FURTHER INFORMATION

Villages of Van Buren, P. O. Box 9, Keosauqua, IA 52565, (319) 293-7111.

DIRECTIONS

From Des Moines, I 35 south to exit 12, IA 2 east to Van Buren County (in southeast Iowa).

KANSAS

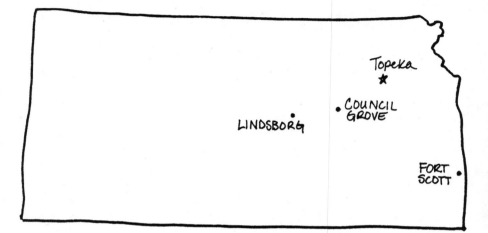

Topeka
★

● COUNCIL
GROVE

LINDSBORG ●

FORT
SCOTT ●

COUNCIL GROVE, KANSAS

Population: 2228

The prairie town of **Council Grove** straddles the old **Santa Fe trail** in the middle of the beautiful Flint Hills of central Kansas. The site of the town once afforded water, and also wood from groves of hardwood trees, for the use of soldiers, explorers and merchant caravans moving west along the Santa Fe trail. The town itself, established in the late 1850s, was for a while the last supply point on the 780-mile trail.

As you walk or drive along **Main Street**, called **Prairie Plaza** today but once part of the Santa Fe trail, you will see buildings that were among the last traces of civilization seen by thousands of homesick settlers in the 1860s as they faced west. Much of the early town survives today as a National Historic Landmark District.

The name of the oldest commercial building in town, the **Last Chance Store** (1857), obviously tells something about the store's history. Another of the town's historic buildings, the **Hays House** (1857), is the oldest continuously operating restaurant west of the Mississippi (see listing below); it has doubled over the decades as a mail distribution center, court room, tavern, meeting place for Sunday morning church services, and printing room for the first local newspaper.

Another important structure from pioneer times, the lovely stone **Kaw Mission State Historic Site/Museum** (1850-51) was built as a boarding school for Native American boys and later served as a school for the children of settlers.

Although Council Grove is out on the prairie, there is probably no other town in the country that lists more trees among its historic sites. **The Council Oak**, from which the name of the town arose, was the site of an 1825 council, attended by U.S. officials and Osage chiefs, that agreed to a treaty giving Whites free passage along the Santa Fe Trail. The tree blew down in a 1958 storm, but the site has been marked by a shrine.

In addition to the Council Oak there was the **Post Office Oak**, a bur oak that is said to have had a cache in its base where people passing along the trail could leave messages. A third tree was the **Custer Elm** under which legend has it George Armstrong Custer camped while patrolling the trail. Check with the visitors bureau for the locations of the trunks of these two trees.

> *Santa Fe Trail ruts can be seen a few miles west of town, just off U.S. 56; they are on private property, so get instructions from the Visitors Bureau on how to visit them.*
>
> *One of the reasons for the health of Main Street is the success of the town in keeping large discount stores away from the outskirts.*

WHERE TO STAY

The Cottage House Hotel, 25 N. Neosho, (800) 727-7903. Once an 1870s boarding house, then an elegant Victorian home and hotel, private baths. $$

Flint Hills B&B, 613 W. Main St., (316) 767-6655. 1913 American Four-Square, boyhood home of former Congressman John Rhodes, antiques, full breakfasts. $$

WHERE TO EAT

Hays House 1857, 112 W. Main St., (316) 767-5911. One of the finest restaurants in Kansas. $$

FURTHER INFORMATION

Council Grove Visitors Bureau, 313 W. Main, Council Grove, KS 66846, (800) 732-9211.

DIRECTIONS

From Wichita, I 35 north to exit 92, north on KS 177 to Council Grove.

FORT SCOTT, KANSAS

Population: 8,362

It seems only fitting that the heartland of America should have one of the country's most beautiful — and beautifully preserved — downtowns. The lawyers, bankers, and socially active women who once moved about these streets in their buggies and carriages must certainly have personified Midwestern middle-class respectability. The setting would have it no other way: brick streets lined by tree-shaded, handsome Victorian homes and awning-shaded, colorfully painted Victorian business blocks. The architecture, while varied, has more depth and age to it than can be dismissed simply as "turn of the century" — some of the buildings go as far back as the Civil War.

At one end of **Main Street** is the **Fort Scott National Historic Site**, a restored 1842 frontier military fort. The only one of its kind in the country, the site comprises 20 buildings, including the hospital, powder magazine, bakery, barracks and officers' row. Within the buildings are 33 historically furnished rooms. During the summer the fort sponsors weapons demonstrations, an Indian encampment and other events. Museum exhibits and an audio-visual presentation introduce the visitor to a relatively unknown, but exciting period in America's history.

Other important restorations in the downtown area include the 1873 Gothic-style **Old Congregational Church**, with antique furnishings, and the **Ralph Richards Museum**, an 1892 home displaying turn-of-the-century wedding dresses, railroad memorabilia, antique tools, an old general store and military artifacts. On the second floor of the museum is a completely furnished Victorian residence with double parlor, library, kitchen and other rooms.

The downtown area is also the site of two notable memorials, the **Twin Trees Monument** (1965), dedicated to the "Bleeding Kansas" turmoil that occurred before and during the Civil War, and the **20th Century Veterans Memorial** (1990), dedicated to all 20th-century veterans of the U.S. Armed Forces.

Fort Scott's sights may be seen by an hour-long trolley ride. Driving tours, antiquing tours and walking tours escorted by costumed townspeople are other options.

SPECIAL FEATURE

• A **U.S. National Cemetery**, one of the 12 such cemeteries designated by President Lincoln, lies on the southeast outskirts of Fort Scott. Established in 1862, and older than the Arlington National Cemetery, the cemetery is the final resting place of Indian soldiers, Civil War veterans and veterans of more recent wars.

> *A Fort Scott brick business provided 50 million bricks used in the construction of the Panama Canal. Fort Scott brick was also used on the first Indianapolis Speedway.*

WHERE TO STAY

The Chenault Mansion, 820 S. National Ave., (316) 223-6800. Elegant 1887 home, ornate woodwork, crystal chandeliers, private baths, full breakfasts. $$ to $$$

Country Quarters, Rt. 5 (Box 80), (316) 223-2889. Old farm house, front porch for Kansas sunsets, hand-carved oak mantle, "great breakfasts." $

The Courtland, 121 E. 1st St., (316) 223-0098. Restored 1906 hotel, sunny Gathering Room, private baths, family heirlooms. $$ to $$$

Huntington House, 324 S. Main St. (316) 223-3644. Renovated 1906 home near historic site, outdoor pool, full or Continental breakfasts. $$

The Lyons' House, 742 S. National St., (316) 223-0779. 1876 mansion, Tiffany tiles around fireplaces, classical millwork, looms and spinning wheels. $$

WHERE TO EAT

Papa Don's Restaurante, 22 N. Main St., (316) 223-4171. Specialty pizzas, pasta, deli sandwiches. $

FURTHER INFORMATION

Visitor Information Center, 231 E. Wall St., Fort Scott, KS 66701, (800) 245-3678.

DIRECTIONS

From Kansas City (KS), US 69 south to Fort Scott.

LINDSBORG, KANSAS

Population: 3076

If you look in one direction, the view is of fields and farms, reminiscent of the Midwest; if you look in another, you see the vast spaces of the West. The countryside is incongruous, and sitting in the middle of it all, and adding to the incongruity, is the delightful little Swedish-American town of **Lindsborg**.

Swedish immigrants settling in the **Smoky Hill River Valley** brought with them a commitment to cooperative farming, but also a love and respect for learning and the arts. The value placed on education led to the founding of **Bethany College**, known today for its liberal arts tradition and beautiful campus.

The love of the arts has manifested itself in many ways, from woodcarving to folk dancing to the establishment of the 400-voice **Bethany College Oratorio Society**. Most obvious to the visitor are the art galleries, one of which is among Lindsborg's top sites: the **Birger Sandzen Memorial Gallery**, on the campus of Bethany College. The gallery displays works by the widely recognized Swedish-American painter and teacher of art, along with works of other artists.

The best way to soak up Lindsborg's charm is to wander the old brick streets. The tidy compactness of the town makes a map unnecessary, although one is available from the CoC. Craft shops are especially prominent, along with the art galleries and studios. The emphasis in the shops and restaurants is of course on things Scandinavian: imports, folk art and contemporary crafts, Swedish pastries.

The **Bethany Lutheran Church**, near downtown, has a hand-crafted altar and collection of large oil paintings that give the interior an appearance suggestive of churches in rural Sweden.

Several blocks from downtown is the **Old Mill Museum**, which features Indian and pioneer-day artifacts as well as natural history displays. The museum complex comprises several historic structures, including the **Smoky Valley Roller Mill** and the **Swedish pavilion** from the 1904 World's Fair.

SPECIAL FEATURES
• The panoramic view from **Coronado Heights**, an elevated park and historic site three miles northwest of town, makes it clear that the West is not far away.

> *The Dala Horse, a popular form of domestic art in Sweden, was selected by Lindsborg as the symbol of its Swedish heritage.*
> *The "little" Old Mill Museum displays over 22,000 items!*

WHERE TO STAY
Swedish Country Inn, 112 W. Lincoln, (913) 227-2985. Swedish pine furniture, full Scandinavian buffet breakfasts. $$

WHERE TO EAT
The City Bakery, 107 N. Main, (913) 227-3908. Swedish pancakes, fresh pastries, ice cream parlor, lunches. $

Swedish Crown, 121 N. Main, (913) 227-2076. Swedish and American menu, smorgasbords, authentic Swedish meat balls and ham loaf. $

FURTHER INFORMATION
Lindsborg Chamber of Commerce, P. O. Box 191, Lindsborg, KS 67456-0191, (913) 227-3706.

DIRECTIONS
From Wichita, I 135 north to exit 72 (Lindsborg exit).

KENTUCKY

BARDSTOWN •

☆ Frankfort

• PLEASANT HILL

• HARRODSBURG

• BEREA

BARDSTOWN, KENTUCKY

Population: 6,801

According to legend, Stephen Collins Foster was inspired by a visit in 1852 to Federal Hill, his cousins' home in **Bardstown**, to write *My Old Kentucky Home*, now the Kentucky state anthem and one of the country's most beloved melodies. It isn't clear whether Foster composed the song while in Kentucky or afterward, or whether in fact Foster ever even visited Bardstown. It doesn't really matter, because both Federal Hill and Bardstown look exactly like what an "old Kentucky home" ought to look like. Foster couldn't have made a better choice.

Kentucky's second oldest town (1780) and a center of bourbon whiskey production, Bardstown has had its ups and downs (Prohibition was one of its downs). But for reasons relating as much to the townspeople's love of home place as anything, Bardstown has gotten more and more beautiful over the years. The old buildings have been spruced up and restored, the trees have grown bigger and the downtown, although certainly much changed over the decades, looks like it hasn't changed in 150 years. This is a lovely little town that may be closer to the ideal Kentucky home than it was even in Foster's time.

Bardstown has about 200 buildings dating back before 1880. A large number of the older homes were built in the late 1700s and early 1800s. Some are brick, some weatherboarded log, a few frame. Georgian, Federal and, to some extent, Greek Revival styles predominate — the Victorian styles never really caught on. Two of the most famous are open to the public. The first, **Wickland** (1813-1830), home of three governors, may be Kentucky's best example of Georgian architecture. The second, the classical brick **Federal Hill** (1800-1820), now the centerpiece of **My Old Kentucky Home State Park**, is shown by guides in antebellum costume.

Running a close second behind Federal Hill on the list of historic landmarks is the venerable **Old Talbott Tavern**. Probably built in the late 1700s, the charming brick and stone structure is believed to be the oldest inn in continuous operation west of the Alleghenies. To mention a few who have passed through its doors: King Louis Philippe, George Rogers Clark, Daniel Boone, Queen Marie of Rumania, Henry Clay, General George Patton, Jesse W. James and John J. Audubon.

St. Joseph Proto-Cathedral, the first Roman Catholic cathedral west of the Alleghenies (1819), is another Bardstown landmark. The restored cathedral has several valuable paintings that were donated by Pope Leo XII and Francis I of the Two Sicilies.

Nearby **Spalding Hall** (1826/rebuilt 1837), once a part of **St. Joseph's College** (for young men), is now home to several businesses and two museums. One of the latter, the **Bardstown Historical Museum**, contains Stephen Foster memorabilia, gifts of Louis Philippe and Charles X of France, Jesse James's hat, and Jenny Lind's velvet cape.

Among the items displayed in the **Oscar Getz Museum of Whiskey History**, also in Spalding Hall, is an 1854 E. G. Booz bottle that gave the world the word "booze," and a copy of the liquor license that Abraham Lincoln and his partners held while running a store in Illinois in 1833.

Other buildings of special note in Bardstown include the **McLean House** (circa 1815), one of Kentucky's finest examples of Georgian-style commercial architecture; the 1827 **Presbyterian Church**; and **Roseland Academy** (1820-1830), noted for its three-flight spiral staircase. The **Old County Jails** (1819/1874) were until 1987 the oldest operating jail complex in Kentucky. Guided tours of the buildings, now a bed and breakfast (see below), are available.

The colorful, costumed cast of the two-hour outdoor musical, *The Stephen Foster Story*, perform more than 50 of Foster's songs.

SPECIAL FEATURES

• Three local distilleries (**Heaven Hill, Jim Beam**, and **Maker's Mark**) offer interesting tours — and good introductions to local history.

• To the northwest of Bardstown is the 10,000-acre **Bernheim Forest**. This lovely area contains trails, ornamental gardens, waterfowl ponds and hundreds of labeled varieties of trees and shrubs.

John Fitch, inventor of the steamboat, died in Bardstown after years of failed efforts to obtain financial and political support for his invention. Ironically, the steamboat and railroad would eventually hurt Bardstown by drawing growth elsewhere.

WHERE TO STAY

The 1790 House, 110 E. Broadway, (502) 348-7072. Antiques, fireplaces, private baths, brick patio overlooking lovely gardens. $$ to $$$

Amber LeAnn, 209 E. Stephen Foster, (800) 828-3330. On almost an acre of ground, private baths, full breakfasts. $$$

Jailer's Inn, 111 W. Stephen Foster, (502) 348-5551. Spacious rooms decorated with heirlooms and antiques, private baths, only one room with resemblance to jail cell. $$ to $$$

The Mansion, 1003 N. Third St., (502) 348-2586. 1851 Greek Revival home on National Register, antiques, hand-crocheted bedspreads. $$ to $$$

Talbott Tavern, Court Square, (502) 348-3494. Oldest western stagecoach stop in America, antiques, private baths, TV, dining room. $$

WHERE TO EAT

Dagwood's, 204 N. Third St., (502) 348-4029. "New York Strip marinated in 12-year-old bourbon and served on white-oak barrel stave with mushrooms." $ to $$

Kurtz Restaurant, 418 E. Stephen Foster, (502) 348-8964. Southern-style meals, skillet-fried chicken, fried cornbread, home-style vegetables. $

My Old Kentucky Dinner Train, 602 N. Third St., (502) 348-7300. Dinner served in restored 1940s dining cars during two-hour trip through central Kentucky countryside. $$$

Talbott Tavern, (see above). In third century of service, fresh farm-raised catfish breaded to a golden brown. $ to $$

FURTHER INFORMATION

Bardstown-Nelson County Tourist & Convention Commission, P. O. Box 867, Bardstown, KY 40004, (800) 638-4877.

DIRECTIONS
From Louisville, US 31E/150 south to Bardstown.

BEREA, KENTUCKY

Population: 9126

Standing in the little park in front of Boone Tavern Hotel in **Berea** is almost guaranteed to bring on feelings of longing and nostalgia. The tulip trees and oaks on the campus across the street have something to do with it; so does the gorgeous white Georgian facade of the hotel, a Kentucky landmark. But it goes beyond that. It is somehow related to what might be called "down home." And Berea has some of the finest of it that our country has to offer.

One of the reasons for this may be that Berea is one of the country's leading centers for the crafting of down-home items. The state in fact has designated Berea the *Folk Arts and Crafts Capital of Kentucky*. It began with the founding in 1855 of the town's centerpiece, **Berea College**, as a place of higher learning for students, chiefly from Appalachia, who could not afford a college education. Tuition was — and still is — provided in exchange for work in various campus departments. Because ceramics, weaving, woodcraft, wrought iron and other crafts formed part of the students' work activities, it was inevitable that Berea College and, more generally, Berea would acquire a reputation for quality crafts.

To appreciate the beauty of Berea's crafts, step into the lobby of the **Boone Tavern Hotel** (1909). Although the sheer quality of the work can hide the fact, most of the furniture and furnishings are handmade. The food is also home-made, of course, and let's face it, things like Boone Tavern Chicken Pie, rhubard conserve, and Southern Black Walnut Pie can only add to the charm.

Around town are shops offering everything from handmade brooms and patchwork quilts to mountain dulcimers and quality furniture. Some of the work is by local craftspeople, some of it is by students in the college's crafts program. The **Log House Sales Room** on Main Street displays student crafts. In addition to focusing on the history and traditional crafts of Appalachia, the **Berea College Appalachian Museum** sponsors exhibits in which regional artists and craftspeople demonstrate their skills.

SPECIAL FEATURE

• A tour of the loomhouse at **Churchill Weavers**, Berea's first non-college industry, provides an opportunity to watch as some of the most beautiful handwoven fabrics anywhere take form on the looms.

Berea College was the first interracial college south of the Mason-Dixon line.
The Draper Building on the Berea College campus is a reproduction of Independence Hall in Philadelphia.

WHERE TO STAY

Boone Tavern Hotel, Main St., (606) 986-9358. One of Kentucky's best-known lodgings. $$

WHERE TO EAT

Boone Tavern Hotel (see above), Main St., (606) 986-9358. Kentucky cooking at its finest, delicious pies. $

FURTHER INFORMATION

Berea Tourist and Convention Commission, P. O. Box 556, Berea, KY 40403 (606) 986-2540.

DIRECTIONS

From Lexington, I 75 south to exit 78 (Berea exit).

HARRODSBURG/PLEASANT HILL, KENTUCKY

Population: 7335

There are no two other towns in the country that in a single day could provide the visitor with a more thorough and delightful introduction to a state than **Harrodsburg** and **Pleasant Hill.** Harrodsburg, the first permanent English settlement west of the Alleghenies, is one of those places where a beautiful setting and collection of historic attractions have blended to produce a town with a truly distinct character — albeit a very Kentucky one. **The Shaker Village of Pleasant Hill,** just seven miles away, provides one of the finest examples of historic restoration in the country. The village is a National Historic Landmark from boundary to boundary.

The **Harrodsburg/Mercer County Tourist Commission** publishes an exceptionally thorough walking/driving tour guides; among other things, the guide begins with a glossary that, with no more than a few minutes' study, is guaranteed to turn the reader into someone with a working knowledge of early American architectural history.

St. Philip's Episcopal Church (1860/61), a Gothic Revival gem, has only one truly centered window, the window back of the altar. For as the designer, the Right Rev. Benjamin Bosworth Smith, taught, "Only Providence is perfect, and man should ever be mindful of such."

Also of note is the Greek Revival **Methodist parsonage** (ca 1840), which has housed more than 60 ministers and their families throughout a century and a half.

Beaumont Inn (1845), a major local landmark, was for over seven decades one of the South's leading female colleges. The building has been owned and operated as a country inn by the same family since 1917 (see below). **Morgan Row** is the oldest rowhouse in Kentucky (1807) and the first one constructed west of the Allegheny Mountains.

Old Fort Harrod State Park features an exact replica of the original fort built in 1774/75. Included on the park grounds are a Federal Monument dedicated to George Rogers Clark (1934), the oldest pioneer cemetery west of the Allghenies, the log cabin in which Abraham Lincoln's parents were married (1806), and the **Mansion Museum**, housed in an 1830 Greek Revival home.

The Shakers were members of the largest communal society in the country during the 19th century, the *United Society of Believers in Christ's Second Appearing*. Called Shakers because of their ritualistic dance, they were celibate, pacifistic, creative and hard-working (and obviously had to recruit from the outside).

Pleasant Hil's 30 original buildings and miles of stone fencing are preserved on 2,700 acres of rolling Bluegrass countryside. Among the village's most notable structures are the **Centre Family Dwelling**, which contains a 40-room exhibit of original Shaker crafts and furniture; the **Trustees Office** (1839), with twin spiral staircases; and the **Meeting House** (1820), where Shaker music is played.

SPECIAL FEATURES

• Excursions along the high limestone cliffs of the historic **Kentucky River** can be taken during the warmer months aboard the sternwheeler *Dixie Belle*. The boat departs a short distance from Pleasant Hill at **Shaker Landing**.

• Filling out the day, evening performances of *The Legend of Daniel Boone*, an outdoor drama adventure, are held in Harrodsburg during the summer months. Among the several events staged in the production is a full-scale **Battle of Boonesborough**.

> *The population of Shakers at Pleasant Hill peaked near 500 in the 1830s.*

WHERE TO STAY

Beaumont Inn, 638 Beaumont Dr., (800) 352-3992. Country Inn on National Register, Kentucky landmark, dining room. $$$

Canaan Land Farm B&B, 4355 Lexington Rd., (606) 734-3984. Ca. 1795 home on working sheep farm, National Register, pool, private baths, full country breakfasts. $$ to $$$

Ms. Jesta Bell's B&B, 367 N. Main St., (606) 734-7834. Elegant 1850s Main Street mansion, near Old Fort Harrod, spacious guest rooms. $$

Shaker Village of Pleasant Hill, 3500 Lexington Rd., (606) 734-5411. Guest rooms throughout village, Shaker reproductions, private baths, TV. $$ to $$$

WHERE TO EAT

Beaumont Inn, 638 Beaumont Dr., (606) 734-3381. "Yellow-legged" Fried Chicken, corn pudding, two-year old Kentucky cured ham. $$

Trustees' Office Inn, 3500 Lexington Rd., (606) 734-5411. Shaker and regional foods served family style, home baking, reservations advised. $$

FURTHER INFORMATION

Harrodsburg/Mercer County Tourist Commission, P. O. Box 283, Harrodsburg, KY 40330, (606) 734-2364.

DIRECTIONS

From Lexington, US 68 southwest to Harrodsburg.

LOUISIANA

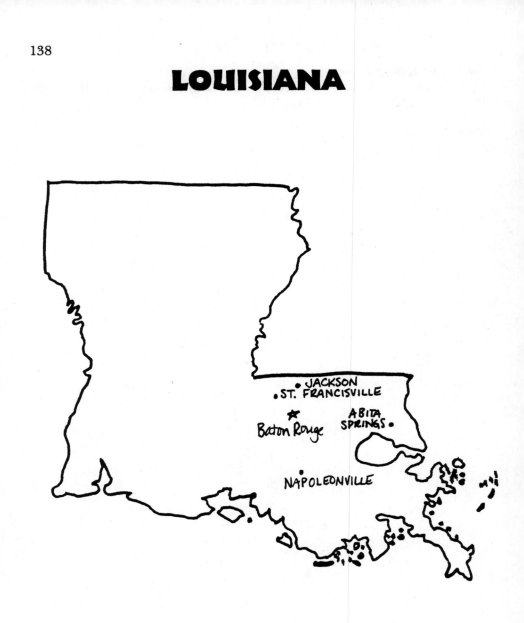

ABITA SPRINGS, LOUISIANA

Population: 1,296

From about 1884 to 1910 New Orleans families used to journey across **Lake Ponchartrain** to escape the city and the yellow fever epidemics. Resorts in **St. Tammany Parish** on the north shore of the lake were attractive because of the clean, fresh ozone-rich air emanating from the thick pine forests there. Although the resort towns are still very much around, and continue to attract visitors, most have been altered by the commercial development that follows heavy automobile traffic. One notable exception is out-of-the-way **Abita Springs**, a town that remains in many ways the delightful little place that it was 100 years ago.

Abita Springs was once an especially popular resort because of its mineral springs. Situated on the banks of the **Abita River**, the **Abita Springs Pavilion** (1888) marks the site of a spring discovered — and enjoyed — by the Choctaw Indians. The town is unique in that its buildings aren't built against one another as in many historic towns. Their wide spacing and location amongst heavy forests give the town a rural, wilderness character. Many of the buildings are turn-of-the-century "shotgun" houses that once served as second homes for New Orleans's middle classes.

There are also "North Shore"-type houses that are variations of the shotguns but that have a projecting section surrounded by galleries on three sides. Adapting to Louisiana's climate, the most dominant features of most of the houses in Abita Springs are their porches.

Abita Springs is for strolling or bicycling — Tammany Parish maintains several good bicycle trails. Here, as elsewhere in the parish, the azalesas, camellias, dogwoods and other flowers are gorgeous. But don't expect much excitement.

The best place for shoppers is **Lee Lane** in nearby **Covington**, itself a lovely town; here, housed in 19th-century Creole cottages, are unique specialty, antique and clothing shops.

SPECIAL FEATURES

• **Honey Island Swamp**, on the eastern edge of St. Tammany Parish, is one of the most pristine river swamps in the country. Nearly 70,000 acres of the swamp make up a protected wildlife area. At least four companies in **Slidell** offer 2- to 4-hour swamp tours, some of them in environmentally safe craft. The tours provide opportunities to observe alligators, snakes, bald eagles, waterfowl, herons, feral hogs, nutria, otters, mink and other animals.

• **Fairview-Riverside State Park** south of Abita Springs offers water-skiing, fishing and crabbing. Under the park's moss-draped oaks is the **Otis House**, built in the 1880s as part of a lumbering camp and renovated in the 1930s to serve as a summer home.

• On the grounds of **Fontainebleau State Park**, also south of town, are the ruins of a brick sugar mill built in 1829 by Bernard de Marigny de Mandeville. The park has a swimming pool and a sailboat ramp for launching directly into **Lake Pontchartrain.**

> *The Lake Pontchartrain Causeway is the longest over-water highway bridge in the world. The causeway was crossed by eight million vehicles in 1992.*
>
> *The Abita spring water is a critical ingredient of a beer now produced by a highly successful local micro-brewery.*
>
> *The conquest of yellow fever was a major factor in bringing Abita Springs's resort era to an end.*

WHERE TO STAY

Riverside Hills Farm B&B, 96 Gardenia Dr. (Covington), (504) 892-1794. Caretaker's cottage on non-working farm, country kitchen, fishing/boating on Tchefuncte River. $$$

Windy Pines (English-style B&B), Old Mandeville, (504) 626-9189. Lovely restored home on north shore of Lake Ponchartrain, guest lounge, swimming pool, TV. $$$

Woods Hole B&B, 78253 Woods Hole Ln. (Folsom), (504) 796-9077. Rustic suite with cathedral ceiling, secluded, fireplace, private entrance, antiques, TV, extended Continental breakfasts. $$$

WHERE TO EAT

La Provence, P. O. Box 805 (Lacombe), (504) 626-9598. French and regional cuisine, outdoor dining, highly rated, reservations advised. $$ to $$$

Red Barn Pub, 501 Lafitte St. (Mandeville), (504) 626-9189. Quaint English pub with bric-a-brac from Old Country, home-cooked lunches, good selection of beers. $

FURTHER INFORMATION

St. Tammany Parish Tourist & Convention Commission, 600 N. US 190, Suite 15, Covington, LA 70433, (800) 634-9443).

DIRECTIONS

From New Orleans, Lake Ponchartrain Causeway north to Covington, La 36 east to Abita Springs.

JACKSON, LOUISIANA

Population: 3,891

Jackson is a gracious old Southern town nestled in the rolling, forested Louisiana countryside east of the Mississippi River and north of Baton Rouge. Established in 1815, the town has over 100 buildings on the National Register of Historic Places, the second largest number in Louisiana. Included are a number of Louisiana raised cottages as well as several excellent examples of provincial Greek Revival and Victorian architecture. As in many small rural Southern towns, the most modest and the most pretentious of the buildings often sit side-by-side, or on the same block. Pamphlets are available for self-guided walking and bicycle tours, and guided group tours may be arranged.

Several of the most beautiful of the houses are old plantation homes that today survive in part as bed and breakfasts (listed below). Two homes of historic importance that are not bed and breakfasts are restored **Centenaria** (ca. 1840), open for tours by appointment, and **Roseneath** (ca. 1832), the town's only full-blown high-style Greek Revival building.

The loveliest buildings from the middle of the 19th-century are churches. The **Methodist Church** (1854) and the **Baptist Church** (ca. 1860) were both built with brick Gothic Revival basilicas. The **Presbyterian Church** (ca. 1852) is of the colonial style and has finely sculptured windows and the old slave gallery. The **Presbyterian Manse** (ca. 1816), now a private residence, was built with wooden pegs rather than nails.

A good overview of the area's rich and exciting history is provided by the **Jackson Museum and Art Gallery**. The exhibits include antique cars and buggies, Civil War relics, historic ship models, and a diorama of **Port Hudson Battlefield** (Civil War). The adjacent **Old Hickory Village** contains a cotton gin, cane press, general store and other structures.

SPECIAL FEATURES

• Thirteen miles to the east of Jackson on scenic LA 10 lies **Clinton**, another charming old Southern town with strong historical connections. One of the town's most important buildings is the lovely **East Feliciana Parish Courthouse** (1840), the oldest courthouse in continuous use in Louisiana. **Lawyers' Row** (ca. 1840 to ca. 1860), which in the 19th century housed some of Louisiana's most skilled lawyers, sits just to the north of the courthouse.

• One of the best ways to learn about the history of this region is to spend some time examining the tombstones in the **Old Jackson Cemetery** and the **Clinton Confederate Cemetery State Commemorative Area**

> *In 1810 the Jackson area became a part of the Republic of West Florida, a country that lasted only 74 days.*
>
> *Jackson was once so well-known for its schools and colleges that it was called the "Athens of Louisiana."*

WHERE TO STAY

Asphodel Inn, Rt. 2 (Box 89), (504) 654-6868. Townhouses and cabins on grounds of old plantation house (1820), full breakfasts, gourmet restaurant, pool, Audubon Society bird sanctuary. $$ to $$$

Brame-Bennett House B&B, 11120 Plank Rd. S. (Clinton), (504) 683-5241. Greek Revival town house, private baths, "plantation breakfasts", wine. $$$

Glencoe PLantation, P. O. Box 178 (Wilson), (504) 629-5387. Magnificent 1890 turreted plantation home with cottages, swimming pool, private baths. $$ to $$$

Milbank, 102 Bank St., (504) 634-5901. Ca.1836 Greek Revival mansion with colorful history, on National Register, house tours. $$ to $$$

WHERE TO EAT

Asphodel Inn, (see above), (504) 654-6868. Plantation dining on the veranda or around the fireplace. $ to $$

Bear Corners Restaurant, next door to Milbank (above), (504) 634-5349. In 1832 building, "Pork Loin with Raisin Glazin'," "Apple Duck." $ to $$

FURTHER INFORMATION

East Feliciana Parish Tourism Commission, P. O. Box 667, Jackson, LA 70748, (504) 634-7155.

DIRECTIONS

From Baton Rouge, US 61 north to LA 10 (at St. Francisville), LA 10 east to Jackson.

NAPOLEONVILLE, LOUISIANA

Population: 802

Napoleonville is a sleepy Southern village on the banks of the meandering **Bayou Lafourche.** Too remote for any kind of commercialization, the place consists only of an old courthouse, school, couple of stores and an assortment of churches and family homes. If travelers stop for anything other than gas or lunch, it's to visit the old **Christ Episcopal Church** (1853). Locals will tell you that people live here "mostly out of habit." The population is probably declining.

Some people pass through the village simply because they enjoy exploring out-of-the-way places, maybe especially places along moss-draped bayous. Most people passing through, though, are on their way to **Madewood Plantation House,** a couple of miles down the bayou.

It is said that lovely Madewood Plantation House took eight years to build, four to cut the lumber and make the bricks and four to erect the house. The Greek Revival house was completed in 1848 and named Madewood because all of the wood used in its construction came from the plantation. The house is on the National Register of Historic Places.

On the plantation grounds are a carriage house, original slave cabins (there were once over 200 slaves) and the Pugh family cemetery. A raised Greek Revival cottage, **Charlet House,** has been moved to the site. Built in the 1820s, the house was once a riverboat captain's home.

Guided tours may be taken of the mansion, furnished with period antiques, and the grounds. Bed-and-breakfast accommodations (see below) are available for those wishing to hang on to the magic of this place a while longer.

> *Madewood Plantation's wealth came from sugar refining. The plantation was once so busy that the sugar house operated 24 hours a day, seven days a week, with only a week's holiday between seasons.*
>
> *The Pugh family, owners of the plantation, got along well, but never inter-married, with their Cajun neighbors. Marriage was restricted to members of English-speaking families.*
>
> *All clothing for the plantation, including that worn by the slaves, was cut and made under the supervision of Mrs. Pugh.*

WHERE TO STAY

Madewood Plantation House, 4250 Hwy. 308, (504) 369-7151. House tours, private baths, wine and cheese, candlelight dinners and full "plantation" breakfasts included in price. $$$

WHERE TO EAT

Politz Restaurant, LA 1 (Napoleonville), (504) 369-7300. Soft-shell crabs, oysters, crawfish, shrimp. $

FURTHER INFORMATION

Madewood Plantation House, 4250 Hwy. 308, Napoleonville, LA 70390, (504) 369-7151.

DIRECTIONS

From New Orleans, US 90 southwest to Raceland, LA 1 north (along bayou) to Napoleonville.

ST. FRANCISVILLE, LOUISIANA

Population: 1,700

A great many of the country's millionnaires in the antebellum 1850s lived on plantations along the **Mississippi River** between Natchez and New Orleans. Quite a number of them had their homes in **St. Francisville** and West Feliciana parish. The interesting thing is that despite the Civil War, the boll weevil, natural disasters and changing times, the situation around St. Francisville hasn't really changed very much: the town and parish are still home to many aristocratic old families, intact working plantations and some of the country's most elegant plantation houses.

St. Francisville sits proudly on bluffs overlooking the Mississippi in the scenic **Tunica Hills** of eastern Louisiana. The area is known as *English Louisiana* because of the ancestry of its settlers (and to distinguish it from *French Louisiana*). The town is steeped in history and has more than 140 structures on the National Register of Historic Places to prove it. Consistent with both the English and Old Southern roots, tradition is important. The old churches and cemeteries are still in use, and dinner is still served with crystal, china and silver. Especially enduring is the hospitality.

In and around St. Francisville are at least 10 grand plantation homes that are open to the public. Seven are open for tours year-round and three may be toured by appointment. Many second as bed and breakfasts (see sample listing below). One of the most gorgeous is **Rosedown Plantation** (1835) with its avenue of moss-draped oaks and magnificent restored gardens. Another is the incredibly beautiful **Greenwood Plantation** house (ca. 1830), a Greek Revival mansion surrounded by 28 columns. Within are silver door knobs and hinges and a 70-foot baronial hall. Although smaller than its pre-Civil War 12,000 acres, Greenwood is still a working plantation.

The Gothic **Grace Episcopal Church** (1858-1860), the second oldest Episcopal church in Louisiana, has an especially beautiful interior with fine plaster work and carved double-rowed pews.

A visit to the exhibits of the **Museum of the West Feliciana Historical Society** provides a good introduction to the town. A wealth of information is available here, including instructions for a mile-long walking or driving loop tour.

Bicycle tours are becoming a popular way to see the region's plantation houses. Conducted bicycle tours and bike rentals are locally available. Another way to enjoy the area is to take a ferry across the Mississippi.

SPECIAL FEATURES

• **Audubon State Commemorative Area**, to the east of St. Francisville, is the site of **Oakley House**, where John James Audubon completed or began 32 of his bird paintings. The simple but beautiful house was built about 1806 and is listed on the National Register. Oakley's rooms have been restored in late Federal Period style. In addition to the house, there is a restored formal garden, large detached plantation kitchen, plantation barn, two slave cabins and other facilities.

• The **Tunica Hills Wildlife Management Area** northwest of St. Francisville is ideal for birdwatching, hiking and horseback riding. The upland hardwood forest area harbors a number of plants classified as rare in Louisiana. Protected animals include the black bear and eastern chipmunk.

> *The builders of Rosedown were among the first Louisiana planters to import camellias.*
>
> *Although cotton is certainly still grown in the Delta, many of today's working plantations, including those of West Feliciana Parish, produce cattle, hay and pecans.*

WHERE TO STAY

The Barrow House, P. O. Box 1461, (504) 635-4791. Ca. 1809 house on National Register, balconies, period antiques, beverages. $$$

Butler Greenwood, 8345 US 61, (504) 635-6312. Working plantation, four dependencies with private baths, swimming pool, guided nature walks, tours of main house. $$$

Cottage Plantation, 10528 Cottage Lane, (504) 635-3674. One of the few remaining complete ante-bellum plantations, original furnishings, private baths, "plantation" breakfasts, pool, Andrew Jackson once a guest. $$$

The Myrtles Plantation B&B, P. O. Box 1100, (504) 635-6277. Ca. 1796 home with 150 live oaks, Baccarat crystal chandeliers, "America's Most Haunted House!" $$$

The St. Francisville Inn B&B, P. O. Drawer 1369, (800) 488-6502. Ca. 1880 Gothic Revival home, New Orleans courtyard, private baths, TV, phones, pool. $$

WHERE TO EAT

D'John's Restaurant, US 61 S., (504) 635-6982. Barbecued ribs the specialty, great family atmosphere. $

Mattie's House Restaurant, the Cottage Plantation (see above). Variety of steak/chicken/seafood specialties, homemade bread. $ to $$

Magnolia Cafe, 121 E. Commerce St., (504) 635-6528. Popular for lunch.

The Myrtles Plantation Restaurant (see above). Baked catfish topped with shrimp and served with new potatoes and vegetables. $$

St. Francisville Inn (see above). Steak Hattie, seafood prepared with a variety of recipes. $ to $$

FURTHER INFORMATION

West Feliciana Parish Tourist Commission, P. O. Box 1548, St. Francisville, LA, 70775, (504) 635-6330.

DIRECTIONS

From Baton Rouge, US 61 north to St. Francisville.

MAINE

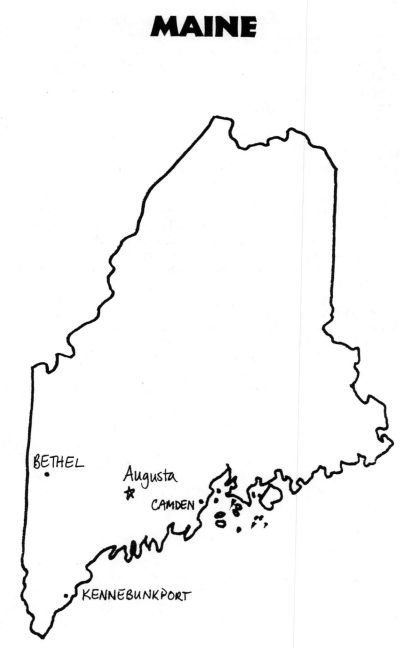

BETHEL, MAINE

Population: 2,375

Bethel is nestled among the scenic **White Mountains** of western Maine. The village has appeared on Christmas cards. **Broad Street,** a National Register historic district, is lined with 19th-century white clapboard houses that are pure New England. Several are now delightful old inns (see listings below).

The oldest house in town, the **Dr. Moses Mason House** (1813), is a museum operated by **The Bethel Historical Society.** On display are period furnishings and early murals; there are also changing exhibits. Another town landmark, the **Gould Academy**, is a highly respected prep school founded in 1836.

Bethel's mountainous setting and proximity to **Sunday River** and other major ski resorts make winter the high season here; the area offers some of the best skiing in the East. The sports calendar is four-season, however. The fishing and hiking are superb, the logging roads are designed for mountain biking, and canoeing opportunities vary from lily-pad paddling to whitewater plunging. The renowned **Bethel Inn & Country Club** has one of the top-ranked golf courses in the Northeast (open to the public).

SPECIAL FEATURES

• About eight miles north of town is the 1870 **Sunday River Bridge,** one of Maine's most picturesque covered bridges. The bridge is sometimes called, for obvious reasons, *Artists' Bridge.*

• **Grafton Notch State Park,** about 14 miles from Bethel, is a mountainous park featuring waterfalls, nature walks and trail heads for five trails, including the **Appalachian Trail.**

> *The NTL Institute, known for its workshops on leadership development, was founded in Bethel in 1947.*
> *The Sunday River Ski Resort offers the only lift-served mountain bike park in the East.*

WHERE TO STAY

Bethel Inn on the Village Common, (207) 824-2175. On 200 acres, golf, skiing, outdoor heated pool, tennis. $$ to $$$

The Chapman Inn, P. O. Box 206, (207) 824-2657. Large sunny rooms, saunas, game room, full breakfasts, access to beach. $$ to $$$

The Hammons House, P. O. Box 16, (207) 824-3170. Ca. 1859 home on National Register, porches and patios, beautiful perennial gardens. $$ to $$$

Norseman Inn, US 2 E., (207) 824-2002. 200-year-old inn, unique fireplaces, breakfasts by the fire. $$ to $$$

Olde Rowley Inn, ME 35 (North Waterford), (800) 568-3466. Colonial accommodations, gourmet dining. $$ to $$$

WHERE TO EAT

Bethel Inn, (see above). Candlelight dining, music on the Steinway. $$

The Moose's Tale, P. O. Box 847, (207) 824-3541. Continental cooking, steaks, seafood, vegetarian dishes. $ to $$

Mothers, Upper Main St., (207) 824-2589. In late 1800s home, popular for lunches, lighter fare. $ to $$

Sudbury Inn, Main St., (800) 395-7837. Gourmet dishes in two dining rooms and tavern, one of best in region. $$

FURTHER INFORMATION

Bethel Area Chamber of Commerce, P. O. Box 439, Bethel, ME 04217, (207) 824-2282.

DIRECTIONS

From Portland, I 495 north to exit 11, ME 26 north to Bethel.

CAMDEN, MAINE

Population: 4,022

Camden is one of those rare places that in real life actually live up to the most romantic of legends. Enticing shops cluster about a picturesque harbor, and time-mellowed New England houses, almost always in white, compete for the prettiest settings along the streets and roads. The grandest or most charming of the houses always seem to have an old sign out front announcing "Antiques" or "Inn." Views of the harbor and bay appear at every turn, and during the warmer months each view includes dozens of white-on-blue sails.

This is sailboat country and to get to know it every visitor should spend at least a couple of hours out on **Penobscot Bay**. Maine needs to be seen from both land and water, weather permitting of course. Camden offers a variety of cruise options on both schooners and motor vessels. Some day trips are as short as an hour, others last all day. For those with more time, overnight, 3-day and 6-day cruises of the Maine coast are available on classic windjammers. Weekend and week-long courses are offered for visitors wishing a "Learned to Sail in Maine" certificate.

Camden's shops, designed as much for the browser as the buyer, tend to shun t-shirts in favor of hand-loomed sweaters and handcrafted jewelry. The restaurants and dining rooms feature some of Maine's most popular products — lobsters, scallops, mussels, clams, haddock, salmon and swordfish. Camden has no fast-food franchies; the general feeling is that they're not needed.

SPECIAL FEATURES

• A road ascends to the top of 900-ft **Mount Battie** in **Camden Hills State Park** just north of town. The views of the bay from the summit are spectacular.

• Just down the coast from Camden is **Rockport**, another picturesque harbor village popular with artists and writers.

In Camden, it is possible to take a "cruise" on a working lobster boat.

WHERE TO STAY

Blackberry Inn, 82 Elm St., (800) 833-6674. Vintage Victorian, spacious rooms, private baths, "scrumptious" breakfasts. $$$

Edgecombe-Coles House, 64 High St., (207) 236-2336. Ocean view, fireplaces, private baths, highly recommended. $$$

Hawthorn Inn, 9 High St., (207) 236-8842. Victorian mansion and carriage house overlooking harbor, private baths, full buffet breakfasts. $$$

Norumbega, 61 High St., (207) 236-4646. Maine's "Castle by the Sea," spectacular ocean views, "exquisite breakfasts," highly rated. $$$

Whitehall Inn, P. O. Box 558, (207) 236-3391. A "landmark for hospitality" since 1901, tennis, restaurant. $$$

WHERE TO EAT

The Belmont, 6 Belmont Ave., (800) 238-8053. Small inn offering array of artfully created New England food. $$

Cappy's Chowder House, 1 Main St., (207) 236-2254. Chowder house plus, raw bar, view from Crows Nest Bakery. $

Peter Ott's, 16 Bayview St., (207) 236-4032. Black Angus beef, fresh local fish and lobster, award-winning desserts. $ to $$

Sail Loft, Public Landing (Rockport, ME), (207) 236-2330. Since 1962, harborside location. $ to $$

Whitehall Inn (see above). Historic country inn, traditional and creative American cuisine. $$

FURTHER INFORMATION

Rockport-Camden-Lincolnville Chamber of Commerce, P. O. Box 919, Camden, ME 04843, (207) 236-4404.

DIRECTIONS

From Portland, US 1 north (along coast) to Camden.

KENNEBUNKPORT, MAINE

Population: 1,100

The booklet distributed by the **Kennebunk/Kennebunkport** CoC is a virtual album of lovely photographs. The scenes are as remarkable for their diversity as their beauty. Here are the sea, broad beaches, harbors, boat yards, rocky coasts, tree-shaded village streets, Victorian gingerbread, historic churches, quaint shops, sleigh rides, flowers and frosty ponds. Some of the most beautiful scenes combine the colors of the sea with the red-violet of the wild rugosa roses that grace the coast.

Kennebunkport is in a sense a collection of colorful places, of images. There's something here for about everyone. But maybe especially for someone who loves the sea and wishes a little seclusion mixed with the charms and comforts of a relaxed old New England town.

Along Kennebunkport's beach, sheltered riverfront and manicured streets stand the magnificent homes of 18th- and 19th-century sea captains, shipbuilders and well-to-do summer residents. Many of the homes are now bed-and-breakfast inns (see below) — few towns can match Kennebunkport in the number, variety and quality of its inns. Few, either, can match the experience of the town's innkeepers. Kennebunkport also boasts several restored seaside hotels cut out of another era.

The **Brick Store Museum** provides a good introduction to the history of the Kennebunks. The museum's shop features quality reproductions and books on local history and crafts. **White Columns** (1851-1853), a gracious Greek Revival mansion with original furnishings, also offers a glimpse at the past. The house, open to the public, is maintained by Kennebunkport's historical society.

The list of activities open to the visitor is as long and varied as the list of views. Many of the historic buildings on **Dock Square** and elsewhere house galleries and artists' studios, as well as a diversity of interesting little shops. For offshore excursions there are whale-watching, sightseeing and sailboat cruises. Fishing-boat charters can also be arranged. More active pursuits include canoeing on the ponds and streams, golfing and cross-country skiing. And, of course, hiking or biking along the coast.

With a collection of over 225 trolleys from around the globe, the **Seashore Trolley Museum** bills itself as the oldest and largest transit museum in the world. Among other attractions, the museum offers its visitors a three-mile ride on an antique electric trolley.

SPECIAL FEATURES

•Just up the coast from Kennebunkport is the picturesque fishing village of **Cape Porpoise**, home port to a fleet of lobster boats. The coastal scenery here is especially beautiful.

• The arrival of Santa Claus by lobster boat and candlelight caroling at the **Franciscan Monastery** are among the events of Kennebunkport's *Christmas Prelude*, celebrated the first weekend in December.

WHERE TO STAY

Captain Jefferds Inn, P. O. Box 691, (207) 967-2311. Antique-appointed Federal home, gourmet breakfasts, afternoon teas, elegant. $$$

Captain Lord Mansion, P. O. Box 800, (207) 967-3141. Restored 1812 country inn, working fireplaces, one of best in country. $$$

The Dock Square Inn, P. O. Box 1123, (207) 967-5773. Classic Victorian decor, canopy beds, private baths, gourmet breakfasts. $$$

Maine Stay Inn & Cottages, P. O. Box 500A, (800) 950-2117. 1860 Victorian inn, garden cottages, private baths and TV, full breakfasts. $$

White Barn Inn, Beach St., (207) 967-2321. Individually-appointed guest rooms, superb restaurant, one of top inns in country. $$

WHERE TO EAT

Note: Kennebunkport is blessed with an unusually large number of fine restaurants. The favorite entree is lobster, of course.

Olde Grist Mill, on Kennebunk River, (800) 274-7478. Fine dining in restored 1794 tidal mill on National Register. $$

Schooners Wharf Inn & Restaurant, P. O. Box 709, (207) 967-5333. Stuffed potato with lobster a delicious specialty. $$

Seascapes, on pier at Cape Porpoise, (207) 967-8500. Unique combination of native seafood and best of American cuisine with a Continental flair. $$

White Barn Inn, (see above). In beautifully restored barn, New England seasonal menu, award-winning. $$$

Windows on the Water, Chase Hill Rd., (207) 967-3313. Wonderful views, fresh seafood, hand-trimmed steaks, "succulent" lobsters. $$

FURTHER INFORMATION

Kennebunk/Kennebunkport Chamber of Commerce, P. O. Box 740, Kennebunk, ME 04043, (207) 967-0857.

DIRECTIONS

From Portland, I 95 south to exit 3 (Kennebunk), east to Kennebunkport.

MARYLAND

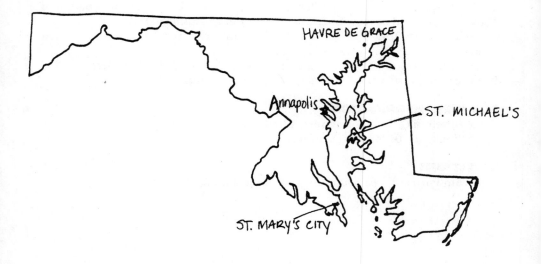

HAVRE DE GRACE

Annapolis

ST. MICHAEL'S

ST. MARY'S CITY

HAVRE DE GRACE, MARYLAND

Population: 8,952

A walk through **Havre de Grace** offers two pleasures in one: a tour of an historic old Chesapeake Bay town and a 1 1/2-mile stroll along or near the coast. Almost all of the town's top sights are on a more-or-less straight 1 1/2-mile line between the **lockhouse** on the north and the **lighthouse** on the south. Not surprisingly, most of the sights (the lockhouse and the lighthouse for beginners) have a direct connection with the water.

About 800 (!) structures contribute to the **Havre de Grace Historic District**. The most interesting were built in the Canal (1830-1850) and Victorian (1880-1910) periods. It was during the former that the town became an important link in the country's growing network of railroads and canals; it was during the latter that the town enjoyed the economic benefits of the late industrial age.

Two mansions of special architectural interest are the **Spencer-Silver Mansion** (1896) and the **Vandiver Inn** (1886), both now bed and breakfasts (see below). George Washington stopped several times at the **Rodgers House**, the oldest structure in town (1787). The oldest church in town is **St. John's Episcopal Church** (1809), noted for its simple early 19th century beauty. Another "oldest" is the **Concord Point Lighthouse** (1827), the oldest lighthouse in the country in continuous use when decommissioned in 1975.

The Susquehanna Museum of Havre de Grace includes the restored locktender's house (1840) and reconstructed pivot bridge adjoining the lock where mule-drawn canal boats once entered the **Susquehanna & Tidewater Canal**. The **Havre de Grace Decoy Museum**, the town's most popular site and home to valuable collections of decoys, celebrates the American folk art of decoy carving.

Today Havre de Grace is in what might be termed a "tourism, recreation, and retirement" era. The waterfront has several marinas, a boardwalk and a chain of lovely parks. Historians will write of this era's buildings, too. Among the newest are waterfront condos, structures that many locals believe only serve to enhance the town's charm.

The annual Duck Fair, held on the grounds of the decoy museum, features a head-whittling contest, punt-gun demonstration and duck-&-goose calling contest.

A $2,000 no-questions-asked reward still awaits the person who returns the original lighthouse lens, missing since 1975 and presumed stolen.

WHERE TO STAY

Susquehanna Trading Company Guest House, c/o 322 N. Union Ave., (410) 939-4252. Turn-of-century house rented as one unit. $$$

Spencer-Silver Mansion, 200 S. Union Ave., (410) 939-1097. 1896 High Victorian stone mansion, large veranda, family plan available, city tours. $$

Vandiver Inn, 301 S. Union Ave., (410) 939-5200. Restored large Queen Anne cottage with five multi-flued chimneys, private baths, gourmet dinners. $$ to $$$

WHERE TO EAT

Bayou Restaurant, 927 Pulaski Hwy., (410) 939-3565. A local favorite for over 40 years, fried oysters. $$ to $$$

Crazy Swede, 400 N. Union Ave., (410) 939-5440. Prime rib and seafood, friendly atmosphere accented by brass and natural wood. $$ to $$$

MacGregor's Restaurant & Tavern, 331 St. John St., (410) 939-3003. All-glass dining room with deck and outside gazebo bar. $$$

Price's Seafood, 654 Water St., (410) 93ª-2782. Homemade crab cakes, crab soup, steamed shrimp, clams, oysters, soft shell crabs. $

Tidewater Grille, 300 Franklin St., (410) 939-3313. Casual dining on water's edge, freshest fish, pastas. $$$

FURTHER INFORMATION

Havre de Grace Chamber of Commerce, 220 N. Washington St., Havre de Grace, MD 21078, (800) 851-7756.

DIRECTIONS

From Baltimore, I 95 north to exit 89, MD 155 east to Havre de Grace.

ST. MARY'S CITY, MARYLAND

Population: 3,200

St. Mary's County, not far south of Washington, D.C., is an agricultural and forested part of Maryland that remains — at least for the present — relatively free of commercial development. Situated on a peninsula bounded by the **Potomac River** on one side and **Chesapeake Bay** on the other, the county is served by highways that go nowhere but the sea. Denied the flocks of tourists that migrate along interstates, the county's restaurants offer seafood at what may be the lowest prices on the Eastern Seaboard north of the Carolinas.

St. Mary's City, in the southern part of the county, was the location of Maryland's first capital (1634-1695) and site of the fourth permanent English settlement in the New World. Although the original town eventually disappeared following the removal of the capital to Annapolis, some of it has been recreated as **Historic St. Mary's City,** a grand 800-acre outdoor history museum.

The museum's Visitors Center complex features an archaeology exhibit hall, orientation materials and museum shop. Guided walking tours begin here.

The various exhibit areas of Historic St. Mary's City are connected by a walking trail system. Scripts highlighting events in the town's history are acted out by costumed interpreters. Included in the re-creation is a 66-acre natural history area that preserves woodland, marsh areas and bluffs along the **St. Mary's River** in much the same state that the settlers found them.

The meticulously reconstructed 1676 brick **State House** is one of the museum's centerpieces. Actual 17th-century court cases, concerning everything from pig stealing to treason, are re-enacted in the first-floor **Assembly Room**.

The re-created **Godiah Spray Tobacco Plantation** is a living history farm. Complete with livestock and crops, the farm portrays the lives of a middle-class planter family in the 1660s. Farm structures include the one-room main **Dwelling House** (even the middle classes had little privacy in Colonial Maryland), tobacco sheds, and animals pens.

The square-rigged *Maryland Dove*, equipped with 17th-century instruments, is a replica of one of the two ships that carried Leonard Calvert, his settlers and colony supplies from England. The tiny size of the ship — which was probably used to carry supplies — nicely underscores the extent of the risks the settlers had to face.

Farthing's Ordinary is a reconstructed 17th-century inn. "Dyett and Drink" are served to modern visitors by **Farthing's Kitchen**, to the rear of the building.

Trinity Episcopal Church, adjacent to Historic St. Mary's City, was constructed in 1829 of bricks from the original State House. **The Leonard Calvert Monument** (1890) stands on the church grounds.

SPECIAL FEATURES

• **Point Lookout State Park** is located to the south of St. Mary's City at the confluence of Chesapeake Bay and the Potomac River. In the park is the site of **Fort Lincoln**, a fort built by Confederate prisoners of war. Two memorials honor the 3,364 Confederate prisoners who died here. A Civil War museum is in the Visitor's Center. Cruises to **Smith Island** depart from the park during the summer.

• **St. Ignatius Church** (1785), in St. Inigoes near St. Mary's City, is a Roman Catholic church with magnificent stained-glass windows and altar. The church has one of the oldest cemeteries in the country. The floor of **St. George's Episcopal** (**"Poplar Hill"**) **Church** (1740), in nearby **Valley Lee**, contains ancient gravestones of four early rectors. Both churches are on the National Register of Historic Places.

> *The Margaret Brent Memorial honors the first woman in America to request the right to vote in a legislative assembly (1648). The request was denied.*

WHERE TO STAY

Camp Merryelande Cottages, P. O. Box 606 (California), (800) 382-1073. Cottages on the beach on St. George's Island, fishing, crabbing, water sports. $$

Old Kirk House, P. O. Box 83 (Scotland), (301) 872-4093. Circa 1800 home overlooking creek, second-story balcony, full breakfasts. $$

St. Michael's Manor, Rt. 5 (Box 17-A) (Scotland), (301) 872-4025. 1805 home overlooking creek, oriental rugs, antiques, full breakfasts, boating/biking available. $$

WHERE TO EAT

Belvedere Motor Inn Restaurant, 60 Main St. (Lexington Pak), (301) 863-6666. Variety of fresh seafood, prime rib the house specialty. $ to $$

Evan's Seafood, Rt. 249 (Box 140) (Piney Point), (301) 994-2299. Crabs, oysters, fish, steak, chicken, waterfront dining. $ to $$

Scheible's Crabpot Restaurant, 23 Wynne Rd. (Ridge), (301) 872-5185. Overlooking Smith Creek, crabcakes, seafood, daily specials, nautical atmosphere. $

Spinnaker's at Point Lookout Marina, Wynne Rd. (Ridge), (301) 872-5145. Fresh seafood, steaks, daily specials. $

Southridge Restaurant, Rt. 5 (Box 91), (301) 872-5151. Crabcakes, steaks. $ to $$

FURTHER INFORMATION

Tourist Information Center, St. Mary's County Chamber of Commerce, 6260 Waldorf–Leonardtown Rd. (MD 5), Mechanicsville, MD 20659, (301) 884-5555.

DIRECTIONS

From Washington (DC), MD 5 south to St. Mary's City.

ST. MICHAELS, MARYLAND

Population: 1,301

There are ideal retirement communities and there are communities ideal for raising families. Although maybe qualifying for either or both of these, the little harbor town of **St. Michaels** clearly sets the standard for yet a third kind of ideal community: the post-family, pre-retirement community, the perfect place for people who, having raised a family and achieved some degree of professional or business success, wish to change careers and pursue second lives.

St. Michaels is in fact home to many people living "second lives," and it's not hard to understand why. The town is picturesque, gently lapped by a delightful harbor, historic to the tune of 350 years, and remote from, but not too much so (maybe two hours), several East Coast metropolises. The natives welcome newcomers, and the shops, restaurants and inns range from the solid to the downright upscale. Biking is a favorite travel mode.

The Chesapeake Bay Maritime Museum, one of the finest in the country, features an outdoor portion with skipjacks, log canoes and a lighthouse; and an indoor portion that traces, among other things, the history of steamboating on the Bay.

Among historic sites is the **Cannonball House** (ca. 1805), a Georgian house whose roof was penetrated by a cannon ball during the War of 1812.

SPECIAL FEATURE

• Sightseeing cruises on **Chesapeake Bay** and the **Miles River** range from the part-day to the overnight, from the narrated historic to the nature-loving.

> *British cannon balls generally overshot the town in the War of 1812 because the forewarned citizens hoisted lanterns to masts of ships and tops of trees.*
>
> *Many visitors to St. Michaels arrive by boat and rent bikes to get around town.*

WHERE TO STAY

Inn at Perry Cabin, 308 Watkins Ln., (410) 745-5178. Quaint English inn, Laura Ashley luxury. $$$

Kemp House Inn, 412 S. Talbot St., (410) 745-2243. 1805 Georgian house, period furnishings, working fireplaces, private baths, Gen. Robert E. Lee slept here. $$$

St. Michaels Harbour Inn & Marina, 101 N. Harbor Rd., (410) 745-9001. Waterfront rooms, restaurant, pool/whirlpool, 60-slip marina, bike/boat rentals. $$$

Victoriana Inn, 205 Cherry St., (410) 745-3368. Antiques, "country" breakfasts, full view of harbor. $$$

Wades Point Inn on the Bay, Wades Point Rd., (410) 745-2500. On 120-acre farm, rooms with views, one-mile jogging/nature trail $$$

WHERE TO EAT

208 Talbot, 208 N. Talbot St., (410) 745-3838. Gourmet cuisine, one of best in region, reservations recommended. $$ to $$$

Carpenter Street Saloon, Talbot St. & Carpenter Alley, (410) 745-5111. Very popular local hangout. $$

Lighthouse Restaurant, 101 N. Harbor Rd., (410) 745-5102. Creative contemporary cooking, lovely view of St. Michaels harbor. $$ to$$$

Morsels, 205 N. Talbot St., (410) 745-2911. Unusual entrees, intimate. $$

St. Michaels Crab House & Bar, 305 Mulberry St., (410) 745-5954. In oldest building on harbor, "All-U-Can-Eat" steamed crabs. $$

FURTHER INFORMATION

Talbot County Chamber of Commerce, P. O. Box 1366, Easton, MD 21601, (410) 822-4606.

DIRECTIONS

From Washington (D.C.), US 50 east (via Chesapeake Bay Toll Bridge) to Easton, MD 33 west to St. Michaels.

MASSACHUSETTS

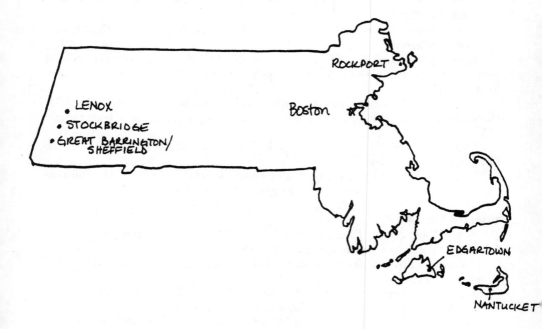

EDGARTOWN, MASSACHUSETTS

Population: 1,138

Located seven miles off the Massachusetts coast, **Martha's Vineyard** is in some ways its own little country. Self-sufficient and independent from the mainland, the islanders refer to the rest of the world as *off island*. Even the climate is different here: bathed by the Gulf Stream, the island enjoys cooler summers and milder winters than the rest of New England. When islanders wish a summer home, they buy or build it on another part of the island. Why travel to the mainland when your own little "country" offers six very different towns and a landscape that varies from beaches and wetlands to hills and forests?

Settled by Europeans over 350 years go, **Edgartown** is Martha's Vineyard's county seat and oldest town. It is best known for its harbor, filled with sailboats and yachts, and its many beautiful old Federal-style whaling captains' homes. Many of the homes can be seen by touring **North** and **South Water streets**; some now serve as inns and restaurants (see listings below).

The 12 rooms of the **Thomas Cooke House** (1765) feature antiques, ship models, costumes and artifacts of the whaling and early farming industries (tours available). The house is just one of several historic exhibits maintained by the **Vineyard Museum.**

The painstakingly restored **Vincent House** (1672), owned by the **Martha's Vineyard Historical Preservation Society,** is the oldest known house on the island (open to the public). Also owned by the Historical Preservation Society, the six-columned Greek Revival **Old Whaling Church** (1843) has been transformed into a performing arts center.

Few places in our country have as many good restaurants and charming inns per capita as Edgartown. There are no fast-food restaurants and discount department stores; they are neither needed nor wanted.

SPECIAL FEATURE

• Each of the towns on Martha's Vineyard has its own character, and no one can agree on which is most charming. In addition to Edgartown, the towns are **Chilmark, Gay Head, Oak Bluffs, Vineyard Haven** and **West Tisbury.**

> *The spreading pagoda tree on South Water Street was brought to Edgartown as a seedling from China in the early 19th century.*
> *Old box pews that are entered through little doors still occupy the Federated Church (1828).*
> *Early 19th-century camp meetings of the Edgartown Methodists helped pave the way for the development of a summer resort industry.*

WHERE TO STAY

The Charlotte Inn, S. Summer St., (508) 627-4751. 1820 home decorated in the English style, European and American antiques, veranda, patios, highly rated. $$$

The Daggett House, 59 N. Water St., (800) 946-3400. Inn comprising several buildings, "country" breakfasts in ca. 1660 dining room overlooking harbor, candlelit dinners. $$ to $$$

The Shiretown Inn, 21 N. Water St., (800) 541-0090. 18th century whaling captains' houses, on National Register, private baths, restaurant, lovely gardens. $$ to $$$

The Shiverick Inn, Pent Ln., (508) 627-3797. Pillared 1840 mansion, antiques and Oriental appointments, private baths, fireplaces, guests "beamed home" by chandelier in cupola. $$$

The Victorian Inn, 24 S. Water St., (508) 627-4784. Ca. 1820 home, on National Register, canopy beds, private baths and balconies, gourmet breakfasts. $$ to $$$

WHERE TO EAT

Andrea's Restaurant, 137 Upper Main St., (508) 627-5850. Northern Italian cuisine, al fresco dining in The Rose Garden. $$$

The Beeftender, Upper Main St., (508) 627-8344. Steak and prime rib, seafood, famous lobster pie. $$

The Navigator Restaurant, Main St., (508) 627-4320. New England fare, fresh seafood, unsurpassed view of harbor. $$$

Starbuck's, N. Water St., (800) 225-6005. In famed Harbor View Hotel, Continental and traditional New England dishes. $$$

The Wharf Pub, Lower Main St., (508) 627-9966. A cozy place popular with islanders, known for its Wharf Chili. $ to $$

FURTHER INFORMATION

Martha's Vineyard Chamber of Commerce, P. O. Box 1698, Vineyard Haven, MA 02568, (508) 693-0085.

DIRECTIONS

Year-round ferries from **Woods Hole** (MA) carry passengers and cars (car reservations recommended). Seasonal passenger ferries sail from **New Bedford, Falmouth,** and **Hyannis** (MA). The island is also connected via regularly scheduled plane service to **Boston, Hyannis, Nantucket,** and **New Bedford.**

GREAT BARRINGTON, MASSACHUSETTS

Population: 2,810

Located 2 1/2 hours north of New York City, New Yorkers often find it unnecessary to travel any farther into the Berkshires than **Great Barrington.** Here there are excellent restaurants, a good collection of historic inns and bed and breakfasts, and many sophisticated shops — especially antique shops. Although the largest town in the southern **Berkshires,** Great Barrington has a small-town atmosphere (it isn't, after all, very big) and a pretty 19th-century brick downtown.

Great Barrington doesn't have the historic sights of its neighbors up the road, including **Lenox** and **Stockbridge** (see selection), but the neighbors are only a few minutes' drive away. So are several delightful little villages —**South Egremont,** for example, with its pretty common. And opportunities for outdoor activities abound. Within a few miles of Great Barrington are golf courses, ski resorts and bicycle touring routes. There's also apple picking in nearby orchards, canoeing on the **Housatonic River** and hiking on **Mount Everett, Monument Mountain,** and the nearby **Appalachian Trail.**

Great Barrington is the home of the **Albert Schweitzer Center,** a museum, library, archives, and wildlife sanctuary dedicated to the life and memory of that great philosopher, physician, musician and missionary. A pleasant and quiet place, the center will appeal more to scholars than to families seeking thrills.

SPECIAL FEATURE
•**Sheffield,** south of Great Barrington, is one of the most delightful and relaxed of the Berkshire villages. Among the village's attractions are the oldest covered bridge in the state, the **Berkshire Choral Festival** and many old homes and fine bed and breakfasts. The village is also an important antique center.

WHERE TO STAY
Baldwin Hill Farm B&B, R.D. 3 (Box 125), (413) 528-4092. Victorian farm home on hill top, spacious lawns, heated pool, full "country" breakfasts. $$ to $$$

Littlejohn Manor B&B, One Newsboy Monument Ln., (413) 528-2882. Turn of-century home on spacious grounds, fine antiques, guest parlor, English breakfasts and afternoon teas. $$ to $$$

Seekonk Pines Inn, 142 Seekonk Cross Rd., (800) 292-4192. 1830s farm house, antique quilts, pool, private baths, full "country" breakfasts. $$$

The Wainwright Inn B&B, 518 S. Main St., (413) 528-2062. 1766 inn and tavern, wrap-around porches, private baths, intimate private dining room. $$ to $$$

Windflower Inn, 684 S. Egremont Rd., (800) 992-1993. Antique-filled country inn, private baths, elegant dining, pool, tennis & golf adjacent. $$$

WHERE TO EAT
Castle Street Cafe, 10 Castle St., (413) 528-5244. Casual cafe and wine bar, pasta, grilled fish and meats, chef-owned. $$

Elm Court Inn, Rt. 71 (Box 95) (N. Egremont), (413) 528-0325. Innovative Continental cuisine served in charming country inn, reservations. $$

The Painted Lady Restaurant, 785 Main St., (413) 528-1662. Northern Italian & Continental cuisine, pasta, fresh seafood. $$

Thornewood Inn & Restaurant, 453 Stockbridge Rd., (413) 528-3828. Romantic country inn, fresh fish, grilled meats, dining on decks. $$

La Tomate, 293 Main St., (413) 528-3003. Bistro setting, Provencial cuisine, chef-owned. $$

FURTHER INFORMATION

Southern Berkshire Chamber of Commerce, 362 Main St., Great Barrington, MA 01230, (413) 528-4006.

DIRECTIONS

From Springfield, I 90 west to Interchange 2, MA 102 south and west to US 7 (at Stockbridge), US 7 south to Great Barrington.

LENOX, MASSACHUSETTS

Population: 1,687

If by November every inn in the village is booked solid for the following summer, the village shouldn't have to worry much about advertizing. And if that village is nestled in a valley in the **Berkshires**, and has a summer performing arts schedule rivaling that of many large cities, it is obvious why the inns are booked solid.

Many of the towns listed in this guide can boast of art galleries, summer stock productions, concerts, and other celebrations of the arts. None, however, possesses the cultural splendor of **Lenox's** billings:

There is first of all the **Tanglewood Music Center**, an estate comprising a mansion, music halls and elegant gardens. And, of course, the **Shed**, the internationally famous summer home of the **Boston Symphony Orchestra**. There is also the 1,200-seat concert hall of the **Performing Arts Center** of the **National Music Center**, where top artists perform. A major music library and a home for retired performers are among the projects planned for the center.

Then there is **The Mount**, Edith Wharton's 1902 summer estate (now the **Edith Wharton Restoration**). The Mount is home to *Shakespeare & Company*, a festival with performances of Edith Wharton, Henry James, and Shakespeare in two indoor and two outdoor theaters.

Lenox also has its off-stage attractions. In addition to one of the finest and most romantic collections of inns in the nation, there are eight or nine art galleries and some of the best shopping in western Massachusetts. Tucked among the woods and hills about Lenox are estates built as summer houses by late 19th- and early 20th-century East Coast millionaires. Most of the houses remain private and their magnificence must therefore be admired from the distance. Some have been converted to inns (see below).

The development of cross-country ski areas is adding winter to the list of Lenox's most popular seasons.

SPECIAL FEATURES

• The grounds and miles of trails of the 1,112-acre **Pleasant Valley Wildlife Sanctuary** north of Lenox provide a beautiful all-season retreat for people as well.

• Among the attractions at the **Berkshire Scenic Railway Museum** are model railroads and a 10-minute train ride.

> *Tea is served between performances staged in the drawing room at The Mount.*

WHERE TO STAY

Apple Tree Inn, 224 West St., (413) 637-4770. Restored 105-year-old inn on 22 hilltop acres, 450 varieties of roses, restaurant, tavern, pool. $$$

Blantyre, P. O. Box 995, (413) 298-3806. Replica of Scottish castle on 85 acres, renowned cuisine, tennis, croquet, swimming, award-winning. $$$

Cliffwood Inn, 25 Cliffwood St., (413) 637-3330. "Belle Epoque" spaciousness, veranda, private baths, fireplaces, evening wine/hors d'oeuvres. $$ to $$$

Cranwell Resort & Golf Course, (800) 272-6935. Tudor mansion, fireplaces, golf course, pool, tennis, marble pub. $$$

Wheatleigh, Hawthorne Rd., (413) 637-0610. Restored mansion on 22 acres, swimming pool, tennis, two restaurants. $$$

WHERE TO EAT

Albion Restaurant at the Village Inn, 16 Church St., (413) 637-0009. Creative American cuisine, afternoon English teas, fine selection of spirits. $$ to $$$

Apple Tree Inn, (see above). Circular dining room with panoramic views, continental cuisine, nightly specials. $$ to $$$

Gateways Inn and Restaurant, 71 Walker St., (413) 637-2532. Top-rated dining room in beautifully restored inn. $$ to $$$

Seven Hills Inn, 100 Plunkett St., (413) 637-0060. Emphasis on freshness, "Heart Healthy or Regular" menus. $$ to $$$

Wheatleigh, (see above). Renowned dining room (prix-fixe), Grill Room (a la carte), lunch in season, reservations advised. $$ to $$$

FURTHER INFORMATION

Lenox Chamber of Commerce, P. O. Box 646, Lenox, MA 01240, (413) 637-3646

DIRECTIONS

From Springfield (MA), I 90 (Massachusetts Turnpike) west to Interchange 2, US 20 north to Lenox.

NANTUCKET TOWN, MASSACHUSETTS

Population: 3,069

Now and then history and nature collaborate to produce an ambience so distinctive and compelling that it has to have a name. The usual practice is to select the name of the town most closely associated with the ambience. **Nantucket** is a good example. For many Americans, Nantucket refers to more than a town or island; it refers to fishing boats and wharves and surf, to old shingled houses with potted flowers, to candlelit dinners in 18th-century dining rooms, to harbors and lighthouses and models of old ships.

Nantucket Town is all of this, and more. The town is also a leading art colony, a major yachting and recreational fishing center, a living museum (the entire island of Nantucket is an historic district). And, the beaches are some of the best in the country, if not the world.

The importance of whaling to Nantucket's history is highlighted by the engaging exhibits of the **Whaling Museum** (1847), one of Nantucket's top sites. The Greek Revival **Hadwen House** (1845), built by a whale-oil merchant, and the elegant decor and furnishings within provide another glimpse of what whaling once meant to Nantucket (open to public).

The **Thomas Macy Warehouse** (1846), the town's **Museum of Nantucket History**, features candle-dipping and other craft demonstrations, and a diorama of Nantucket's waterfront before the fire of 1846.

For a magnificent view of Nantucket Town and Island, climb the tower of the **First Congregational Church** (open to public).

SPECIAL FEATURE

• **The Nantucket Life Saving Museum** is a re-creation of the original station built by the U. S. Life Saving Service in 1874. Picnickers are attracted by the scenic location (open to the public).

> *The Old Mill (1746) still grinds corn during favorable weather. The mill is the sole survivor of four that once served the island.*
> *The two-story Old Gaol (1805), made of logs fastened with iron bolts, may have been the first jail in the U.S. to allow prisoners to go home at night.*

WHERE TO STAY

Anchor Inn, 66 Centre St., (508) 228-0072. 1806 home, once owned by famed Gilbreth family, unspoiled interior, antique paneling, private baths. $$$

The Carriage House, 5 Ray's Ct., (508) 228-0326. Ca. 1865 carriage house, private baths, guest living room with TV, homebaked breakfasts. $$ to $$$

Cliff Lodge, 9 Cliff Rd., (508) 228-9480. 1771 whaling master's home, magical views from roof walk, private baths/TV/phones, patio garden. $$ to $$$

Great Harbor Inn, 31 India St., (800) 377-6609. Lovingly restored 18th-century captain's home, American antiques, handmade quilts, private baths, TV. $$$

Seven Sea Street Inn, 7 Sea St., (508) 228-3577. Post-and-beam inn, widow's walk for sunset views, private baths, Jacuzzi. $$$

WHERE TO EAT

The Atlantic Cafe, 15 S. Water St., (508) 228-0570. "Potent Portables & Gracious Grub," a favorite with islanders and visitors. $ to $$

Boarding House, 12 Federal St., (508) 228-9622. Innovative cuisine, bistro, patio dining, famed chef. $ to $$

Le Languedoc, 24 Broad St., (508) 228-2552. American and Continental cuisine in intimate dining rooms, cafe wine bar. $$

The Seagrille, 45 Sparks Ave., (508) 325-5700. Local fish and shellfish, lobster, steaks, pasta, open year-round. $ to $$

The Woodbox, 29 Fair St., (508) 228-0587. "Nantucket's oldest Dining Room," Beef Wellington, native seafood, hot popovers. $ to $$$

FURTHER INFORMATION

Nantucket Island Chamber of Commerce, Nantucket Island, MA 02554, (508) 228-1700.

DIRECTIONS

Comfortable ships, some operating year-round, serve Nantucket from**Hyannis** (MA). Cars require reservations, but passengers and bicycles do not. (Visitors are discouraged from bringing cars to the tiny island.) Scheduled flights link Nantucket with **Boston, Baltimore,** the **New York** area, **New Bedford, Hyannis** and **Martha's Vineyard.**

ROCKPORT, MASSACHUSETTS

Population: 5,448

Rockport's harbor is one of the most picturesque on the Eastern seaboard. Anyone who enjoys paintings and watercolors of American fishing villages and harbor scenes has seen the harbor in a gallery somewhere. Indeed, an old red shack on Bradley Wharf has been so popular with art students that it has been nicknamed *Motif No. 1.* Many of the famous names in American art, including Winslow Homer and Edward Hopper, placed their easels at or near Rockport harbor at some stage in their lives.

Rockport is designed for walking. The main and back streets of the town are bordered by at least 26 fine homes built between 1692 and 1864, most in the 1700s. Many are adorned with shutters, fan lights and old-fashioned gardens. Also along the streets is a goodly collection of studios and galleries. Of special note (and popularity) are the diverse exhibits in the galleries of the **Rockport Art Association.**

The Headlands and the beaches, including a couple right in town, are ideal for hiking and strolling. Wildflowers abound in the area's waysides, salt marshes, and ponds; birdwatchers spot not only the upland birds of New England, but also a wide selection of shore and sea birds. Island cruises and informative lobstering trips are available for those looking to the water.

SPECIAL FEATURES

• **Halibut Point State Park** affords splendid views of **Ipswich Bay** and, on a clear day, points in New Hampshire and Maine. Closer at hand in the park are tidal pools and a beautiful water-filled granite quarry.

• A house constructed of approximately 100,000 copies of Boston newspapers may be visited at nearby **Pigeon Cove.** The house and its furniture, also made of newspapers, required some 20 years to build.

> *Rockport became the American landfall of the trans-Atlantic cable in 1884. Rockport granite was used in the construction of New York's Woolworth Building, New Orleans's Federal Reserve Bank, Philadelphia's Kensington National Bank and dozens of other structures in the U.S. and elsewhere.*

WHERE TO STAY

The Captain's House, 109 Marmion Way, (508) 546-3825. Restored ocean-front home, attractive yard and patios, private baths. $$$

Eden Pines Inn, Eden Rd., (508) 546-2505. On ocean, large porch and sundeck, private baths. $$$

Ralph Waldo Emerson, Phillips Ave., (508) 546-6321. Inn on the ocean, dining room, heated saltwater pool, whirlpool/sauna. $$$

Linden Tree Inn, 26 King St., (508) 546-2429. 1840 home, gardens, leisurely stroll to beaches, private baths, afternoon treats. $$ to $$$

Seacrest Manor, 131 Marmion Way, (508) 546-2211. "Intentionally quiet," gardens, magnificent views, "famous" full breakfasts, one of finest. $$$

WHERE TO EAT

Note: Rockport has been "dry" since 1856, when some 200 women hatcheted the kegs and poured the contents into the streets. Use a paper bag.

Brackett's Ocean View Restaurant, 27 Main St., (508) 546-2797. "Old-time favorites," seafood, meats and poultry, year-round. $ to $$

Ellen's Harborside, 1 T-Wharf, (508) 546-2512. Three generations of experience specializing in fresh seafood. $ to $$

Folly Cove Pier Restaurant, 325 Granite St., (508) 546-6568. Fresh seafood, steaks, casual atmosphere, sunset dining. $ to $$

The Greenery Cafe/Restaurant, Dock Sq., (508) 546-9593. Fresh seafood, ethnic cuisine, pastas, bakery, overlooking harbor. $ to $$

Peg Leg Restaurant, 18 Beach St., (508) 546-3038. Fresh seafood, "Yankee favorites," on edge of the sea. $ to $$

FURTHER INFORMATION

Rockport Chamber of Commerce, P. O. Box 67, Rockport, MA 01966, (508) 546-6575.

DIRECTIONS

From Boston, US 1 north to MA 128, MA 128 east to exit 9, MA 127 north to Rockport.

STOCKBRIDGE, MASSACHUSETTS

Population: 1,109

The oldest village improvement society in the United States, the Laurel Hill Association, was formed in **Stockbridge** in 1853. The goal of the association, the oldest preservation society in the U.S., was and remains to "glorify God's grandeur by gracefully combining Art and Nature." Stockbridge is also home to the oldest private land trust in the country, The Trustees of Reservations, founded in 1891. The townspeople of Stockbridge were clearly among the first in the nation to draw attention to the beauty of the past, and to the need to protect it.

Given the village's cultural heritage and beauty, the interest in preservation isn't really surprising. For instance, the buildings and architectural styles along Main Street combine to create one of the most picturesque village scenes in the country. The street is the kind of main street that small American towns are supposed to have — which is probably why Norman Rockwell chose to portray it in his famous painting, *Stockbridge Mainstreet at Christmas.*

Among the structures along the street are the famed **Red Lion Inn** (on the far right of Rockwell's painting), the **Cat and Dog Fountain** (1862), the Greek-Revival **Stockbridge Town Hall** and the **Stockbridge Library**, one of the oldest libraries in western Massachusetts (original part built in 1864). On the lower level of the library is a history museum and research center, known as the Historical Room.

Then there are the *Cottages*, summer homes built during the closing years of the 19th and beginning of the 20th centuries by the barons of America's post-Civil War industrialization. Although many of the mansions have since disappeared, enough remain to add color and an Old World sense of aristocracy to Main Street and the other byways in and round the village (see also Lenox). Most are private, but several of the most important — along with a few earlier, colonial houses — are open to the public:

The oldest house is **Mission House** (1739), the home of John Sergeant, first missionary to the Stockbridge Indians. The restored house has period furnishings and a warm colonial garden.

Naumkeag (1885) is one of the village's best-known Cottages. The 26-room gabled mansion, built by an ambassador to England, boasts a collection of Chinese porcelain, elegant furnishings and especially lovely gardens. Although built much earlier (1820s), the Federal-style **Merwin House** displays late 19th- and early 20th-century furnishings. The house and its peaceful grounds also go by the name of *Tranquility.*

Chesterwood is the name of the studio (1898) and Colonial Revival summer home (1901) of sculptor Daniel Chester French. One of the country's foremost artists, it was French who created the *Minute Man* (1875) in Concord, Massachusetts, and the seated *Abraham Lincoln* (1922) in the Lincoln Memorial in Washington, D.C. Chesterwood is home to nearly 500 pieces of sculpture, as well as to gardens and rolling woodlands.

The Norman Rockwell Museum, dedicated to a man unrivalled as a perceiver and illustrator of American charm, contains Rockwell's studio and the world's largest collection of original Rockwell art. Architect Robert A.M. Stern has skillfully fashioned colonial elements to create a new museum building that is itself a masterpiece of American charm. The museum's 36 acres of scenic grounds are available for picnicking and relaxation.

Stockbridge's shops display American and European items ranging from paintings and antiques to gourmet foods, contemporary glass and handknit sweaters. During the summer months the renowned **Berkshire Theatre Festival** presents classic, contemporary and children's theater.

In addition to a booklet for a self-guided walking tour, the CoC distributes instructions for six driving tours of the village and vicinity.

SPECIAL FEATURES

• For a healthy hike leading up to three-state mountain views, ask for directions to the nearby historic **Ice Glen** area.

• The 15-acre **Berkshire Botanical Garden,** northwest of town, features plantings of primroses and conifers, herb garden, rose garden, ponds, woodland walks and, in general, quiet beauty.

• **West Stockbridge**, less frequented than Stockbridge and Lenox, is another charming Berkshires village.

WHERE TO STAY

Arbor Rose B&B, 8 Yale Hill, (413) 298-4744. New England millhouse with pond, antiques and watercolors, home-baked breakfasts. $$ to $$$

Conroy's B&B, P. O. Box 191, (413) 298-4990. 1830 brick Federal-style farmhouse with spacious lawns, home-baked breakfast buffet. $$ to $$$

The Inn at Stockbridge B&B, P. O. Box 618, (413) 298-3337. Georgian colonial inn on 12 secluded acres, baby grand piano, private baths, full breakfasts. $$$

Roeder House B&B, P.O. Box 525, (413) 298-4015. Restored 1856 home with flower gardens, in-ground pool, private baths, full breakfasts. $$$

Tom Carey's Place, 3 Sergeant St., (413) 298-4893. Near town center, antique-filled suites, crackling fireplaces, gardens. $$$

WHERE TO EAT

The Red Lion Inn, Main St., (413) 298-5545. Famed landmark, elegant antique-filled dining room, flower-laden courtyard, reservations. $$$

Shaker Mill Tavern Inn, Rt. 102 (West Stockbridge), (800) 322-8565. Italian specialties, steaks, seafood, chicken, pasta, outside deck cafe. $$

FURTHER INFORMATION

Stockbridge Chamber of Commerce, Stockbridge, MA 01262, (413) 298-5200.

DIRECTIONS

From Springfield, I 90 west to Interchange 2, MA 102 south and west to Stockbridge.

MICHIGAN

FRANKENMUTH, MICHIGAN

Population: 4,408

Frankenmuth, Michigan's *Little Bavaria,* is one of the more unusual of our country's towns. Gabled and towered Bavarian buildings dot the landscape, giving the town a romantic European appearance. At the same time, landscaped parkland and the American love of detached construction put distance among the buildings, giving the town a spacious American appearance. The colorful German architecture of many of the structures, including the glockenspiel tower and covered bridge, is delightful, while many of the tourist attractions along the two-mile business stretch could exist only on this side of Atlantic. A tug of war exists between the authentic and the copied, with charm the sometimes victor.

In 1927, a Frankenmuth restaurant began serving chicken dinners family-style. Word got around and by the 1940s the chicken was attracting people from as far away as Detroit. The use of Bavarian-style architecture made its appearance around 1948. Today, two restaurants (see below) serve over 2,000,000 dinners, mostly chicken, annually. And the architecture is more popular than ever.

Unlike many towns with more natural sources of charm, Frankenmuth has plenty to keep all members of the family busy. Tours of woolen mills, woodcarving shops, a restored grist mill and a brewery inform and entertain at the same time. Among the many interesting shops is one specializing in pewter, another that boasts the world's largest outdoor cuckoo clock, and yet another that displays thousands of dollhouse miniatures in over 100 room settings.

Bronner's Christmas Wonderland, the world's largest Christmas store, offers 500 different styles of Nativity scenes, 260 decorated trees, 200 styles of nutcrackers and over 50,000 unique trims and gifts.

For those tiring of the commercial, there are guided tours of Gothic **St. Lorenz Lutheran Church** (1880). The church has a 167-ft steeple, vivid stained-glass windows, and a carved baptismal font that is a replica of the font in the original St. Lorenz Church in Bavaria.

> *"Franken" refers to the province in Bavaria from which the town's settlers came, and "Muth" means "courage" in German.*
> *Three million people visit Frankenmuth each year.*

WHERE TO STAY

Birch Run's Church Street Manor, 12274 Church St., (517) 624-4920. 19th-century home, individually decorated rooms, full breakfasts. $$

Franklin Haus B&B, 216 S. Franklin St., (517) 652-3383. 1911 home with antiques, private baths, full breakfasts. $$

Keepsake Cottage, 290 S. Haas St., (517) 652-3383. European-style manor of the 1920s, view of Cass River, Sunday "Kaiserschmarren." $$

WHERE TO EAT

Bavarian Inn Restaurant, 1 Covered Bridge Lane, (517) 652-2651. Famous Frankenmuth-style chicken dinners, Bavarian entrees including Sauerbraten and Kasseler Rippchen. $$

Zehnders, 730 S. Main St., (517) 652-9925. Famous family-style chicken and other American dinners served in nine dining rooms. $$

FURTHER INFORMATION

Frankenmuth Convention & Visitors Bureau, 635 S. Main St., Frankenmuth, MI 48734, (517) 652-6106.

DIRECTIONS

From Detroit, I 75 north to exit 136, MI 83 east and north to Frankenmuth.

MACKINAC ISLAND, MICHIGAN

Population: maybe 550 year-round

The stately **Grand Hotel,** white with yellow awnings. The magnificent Victorian *cottages* lining the **West** and **East Bluffs.** The red geraniums against the white clapboards and fence pickets. The purples, lavenders and whites of the lilac trees in the spring. The sound of horses and carriages. The neatness, cleanliness and civility. Above all, the blue waters of **Lake Huron,** everywhere. **Mackinac** (MACK-in-awe) **Island** offers spectacular views and a glorious diversity of images.

Strategically located between **Lakes Huron, Michigan** and **Superior,** Mackinac Island has been a special place for centuries. The Indians, the French, the English and finally the Americans all passed through. The island slipped from beneath one flag to another, but always without bloodshed. The history, the beauty and the pollen-free environment began to attract steamships in the latter half of the 19th century, and Mackinac Island became a resort. Most visitors came to spend a few days; a few, the wealthy, built cottages so that they might spend the summer.

More than 80 percent of the island is now a state park. The island is closed to motor vehicles (except for snowmobiles in the winter, and even these are restricted). All travel is by foot, bicycle or horse. Horse-and-carriage taxi service is available, as are tours and "drive yourself" hourly rentals. There are also private liveries and an abundance of bicycle liveries.

The most important of the historic sites is **Fort Mackinac** (1780), a **Mackinac State Historic Park** and National Historic Landmark. Given by the U.S. Government to the State of Michigan in 1895, the fort is manned by "soldiers" who portray the military life of the very Victorian 1880s. The fort comprises 14 restored buildings, including the Soldiers' Barracks, Post Hospital, the Guardhouse and the Officers' Stone Quarters. The latter was built with 4-foot-thick walls and is one of Michigan's oldest buildings. Each building tells its own special story using exhibits, multi-media programs, costumed reenactments and period craft demonstrations. There are also concerts.

The 1817 **Robert Stuart House,** the home of an Astor Fur Company manager, is now a museum displaying local artifacts, including records of the American Fur Trading Company, and period rooms. The displays of the **Beaumont Memorial** describe the famous 1820s experiments of Dr. William Beaumont, who furthered knowledge of the human digestive system by examining the stomach of a man with a gunshot wound in the abdomen. There's also the 1830 **Mission Church**, the three-story **Indian Dormitory** (now a museum with period furnishings), and the **McGulpin House**, a restored Canadian log residence.

Even visitors staying elsewhere should spend some time at the majestic Grand Hotel. Non-registered guests may stroll the 700-foot veranda, examine the photos in the lower lobby and, after obtaining a special guest pass, explore the Grand Hotel gardens. Luncheon may be taken at any of six restaurants. High tea is served mid-afternoon, and music and demitasse follow dinner in the Parlor. The bar atop the hotel has one of the finest views on the island. An orchestra plays in the evening: there are few experiences so romantic as going by carriage up to the ballroom of the Grand Hotel for an evening of dancing (dress code after 6:00 p.m.).

SPECIAL FEATURE

• A bicycle or carriage tour around the island on MI 185 (8.1 miles) includes such sights as Arch Rock, a natural limestone arch that stands nearly 150 feet above the water; Lover's Leap, a 145-ft. limestone pillar; and Devil's Kitchen, a cave with a spectacular view of the Lower Peninsula and Mackinac Bridge.

> *It should come as no surprise to learn that Mackinac Island's MI 185 is the only state road in Michigan that has never had an automobile accident.*
> *Mackinac Island's beautiful lilacs were introduced in the 1600s by French missionaries.*
> *More than 800,000 people visit Mackinac Island each year.*

WHERE TO STAY

Bay View at Mackinac, P. O. Box 448, (906) 847-3295. Grand 1891 home on waters edge, spectacular seascapes, veranda, private baths. $$$

Cloghaun B&B, P. O. Box 203, (906) 847-3885. Large 1884 home on spacious grounds, antique melodion and square piano. $$ to $$$

Haan's 1830 Inn B&B, P. O. Box 123, (906) 847-6244. Restored Greek Revival home, porches, distinctive rooms, period antiques. $$$

Metivier Inn, P. O. Box 285, (906) 847-6234. Renovated 1877 home, Country French flavor, large porch with wicker, private baths. $$$

Small Point B&B, P. O. Box 427, (906) 847-3758. 1882 home with large veranda, view of Straits. $$

WHERE TO EAT

Note: Mackinac Island is best known for its Great Lakes whitefish and trout. For between meals, try one of the town's famous fudge shops.

The Carriage House, Iroquois on-the-Beach Hotel, (906) 847-3321. Gourmet dining with sweeping view, fresh Lake Superior whitefish. $$

Harbor View Dining Room, Chippewa Hotel, (906) 847-3341. Spectacular view of Straits, lakeside patio, American menu. $$

The Pub Oyster Bar, Main St., (906) 847-3454. Oysters, spiced shrimp, chowders, seafood, pasta, steaks. $ to $$

Village Inn, Hoban St., (906) 847-3542. Special steakburger, VIP Planked Whitefish, specialty soups, lake perch, steaks, chicken. $$

FURTHER INFORMATION

Mackinac Island Chamber of Commerce, Mackinac Island, MI 49757, (906) 847-6418 or 3783.

DIRECTIONS

Commercial air service is available to the island, but most people prefer to go by ferry, departing from either **Mackinaw City** or **St. Ignace**. The ferry ride is itself an experience; among the many spectacular views is that of the five-mile-long Mackinac Bridge that connects Michigan's Lower and Upper Peninsulas.

MANISTEE, MICHIGAN

Population: 6734

The Victorian Port City of Manistee can be reached by land or, if you prefer, by freighter or sailboat or canoe. The shores of Lake Michigan border the town's west side, to the east is **Manistee Lake,** and through the heart of town flows the **Manistee River.**

Manistee's heydey came in the years after the Civil War when, thanks to the vast pine forests, the town became one of Michigan's most important lumbering centers. Seeing no virtue in frugality, the lumber barons built elegant Victorian mansions and a downtown business district that, today, displays what is probably the finest collection of Victorian commercial buildings in Michigan.

The Romanesque **First Congregational Church** (1892), designed by noted Chicago architect William LeBaron Jenney, features 36 stained-glass windows; two of them are Tiffany and two others were displayed at the 1893 Columbian Exposition (tours by reservation).

The Victorian Italianate **Ramsdell Theatre** (1903) boasts, among other things, an act curtain by Walter Burridge, who designed the sets of the original stage production of "The Wizard of Oz" (tours by reservation).

An especially popular place, in part because visitors are always welcome, is Manistee's **Fire Hall** (1889). The structure hasn't undergone usage or design alterations since it was built, and is reputed to be one of the oldest continuously operating firehouses in the state.

There are several ways to explore the Victoriana. Probably the most leisurely and rewarding is a stroll down **River Street,** the main street, followed by a stroll back along the lovely riverwalk. Both parallel the river, and each other, and do what some of the most charming byways in the world do, twist and turn. A tour aboard a 1900s-replica trolley (hourly) is another option.

SPECIAL FEATURES

• But a few blocks from downtown the golden beaches of **Lake Michigan** provide a beautiful backdrop for swimming, picknicking, enjoying nature or just plain lazing.

• Chartering and other marine services are available for those seeking coho and chinook salmon, lake trout, steelhead, brown trout and large, yellow lake perch.

> *Boat watching is a favorite Manistee pastime. Freighters often pass through the center of town on the Manistee River.*

WHERE TO STAY

E.E. Douville House Bed & Breakfast, 111 Pine St., (616) 723-8654. 1879 house, ornate hand-carved wookwork, soaring staircase, antiques. $ to $$

Inn Wick-A-Te-Wah, 3813 Lakeshore Rd, (616) 889-4396. Spacious cottage on Portage Lake. $$

Manistee Country House, 1130 Lakeshore Rd, (616) 723-2367. Pressed tin ceilings, pedestal sinks, potpourri pots on radiators, full breakfasts. $ to $$

The Maples, 435 Fifth St., (616) 723-2904. Large 1905 home with open staircase and oak paneling, wrap-around front porch. $ to $$

WHERE TO EAT

Four Forty West, 440 River St., (616) 723-7902. Overlooking river, excellent whitefish, varied menu. $ to $$.

FURTHER INFORMATION

The Manistee County Chamber of Commerce, 11 Cypress Street, Manistee, MI 49660, (616) 723-2575.

DIRECTIONS

From Grand Rapids, I 96 west to US 31, US 31 north to Manistee.

MARSHALL, MICHIGAN

Population: 6891

Fountain Circle in **Marshall** is without qualification one of our country's grandest circles. Anchored in the center by a Greek Revival Fountain and surrounded by a set of handsome buildings, the circle looks like the product of a marriage between a lovely Continental city and a prosperous Midwestern town. The adjacent streets continue the flavor, except that a little of New England seems to get into the mixture as well.

It was once assumed that Marshall would become the capital of Michigan — moving the capital from Detroit to Marshall was in fact written into the original state constitution. However, when in l847 the state legislature voted on the matter, Marshall lost by just one vote and Lansing was chosen. As a kind of consolation prize, and a considerable one at that, the battle's loser went on to become one of Michigan's most beautiful towns. Today, with 867 designated buildings, Marshall is the largest National Landmark District in the country in the "Small Urban" category.

The CoC's self-guided tour brochure includes no fewer than 130 buildings and 46 historic markers! Several of the houses and sites are open to the public during the **Annual Historic Home Tour** on the first weekend after Labor Day.

The **Honolulu House Museum**, on Fountain Circle, was built by a Chief Justice of the Michigan Supreme Court to resemble the mansion he had occupied in Honolulu as U. S. Consul to the Sandwich (Hawaiian) Islands. A blend of Italianate, Gothic Revival, and Polynesian influences, the house has received a number of awards for the recent restoration of the paint-on-plaster wall and ceiling decorations. Also on Fountain Circle are the lovely stone **Town Hall** (1857), originally built as a stage coach stop and livery stable, and the **National House Inn** (1835), the first brick building in the county and the oldest operating inn in Michigan (see below).

Throughout the historic district, but especially along the streets to the east and north of Fountain Circle, is a virtual museum of 19th and early 20th century American residential architecture. Most of the homes have been restored. The shade trees for which Michigan's towns are well-known make touring the streets especially pleasurable.

SPECIAL FEATURE

• Marshall's **Michigan Avenue** ranks as one of the finest (and healthiest) main streets in the country. A shopping guide is available from the CoC; abundant parking is available behind the shops.

> *The 1839 Greek Revival Governor's Mansion was built on the hopeful assumption that Marshall would become Michigan's capital.*
> *In the 1840s members of Marshall's leading families were sued and heavily fined for their efforts to prevent slave hunters from returning an escaped slave to his former owner in Kentucky.*

WHERE TO STAY

McCarthy's Bear Creek Inn, 15230 C Drive North, (616) 781-8383. In restored home and converted barn overlooking creek, private baths and balconies. $$$

National House Inn, 102 South Parkview (on Fountain Circle), (616) 781-7374. Restored 1835 stagecoach stop, on National Register, massive open-hearth fireplace, upstairs sitting lounge, private baths, mystery weekends. $$$

WHERE TO EAT

Cornwell's Turkey House, 18935 15 1/2 Mile Rd, (616) 781-4293. Turkey served in Michigan's only professional dinner theater. $

Schuler's Restaurant, 115 South Eagle St, (616) 781-0600. Prime rib, seafood, pasta dishes, Schuler's ice cream pies, one of Michigan's best. $$

FURTHER INFORMATION

Marshall Area Chamber of Commerce, 308 East Michigan Avenue, Marshall, MI 49068, (616) 781-5163.

DIRECTIONS

From Detroit, I 94 west to exit 38 (Marshall exit).

ROMEO, MICHIGAN

Population: 3520

Along **Romeo's** tree-lined streets are dozens of gracious old houses, churches and other structures representing architectural styles of the 19th and early 20th centuries. Romeo was part of the underground railroad before and during the Civil war, so many of the homes have secret tunnels and hiding places used by slaves fleeing to freedom in Canada. The town has been designated a National Historical District.

Romeo is surrounded by rolling countryside rich in soil, orchards and roadside markets. There are fruit farms selling farm-fresh apples, peaches, pears and plums. Others sell fresh sweet corn, cauliflower, peppers, tomatoes and other vegetables; yet others sell raspberries, blackberries, blueberries and gooseberries (which make superb pies). Greenhouses offer hanging baskets and potted plants. There are also cider mills and Christmas tree farms and farms offering wagon rides. A map-keyed directory of 40 of the area's roadside markets and greenhouses can be obtained at the CoC.

Romeo is a popular antiquing and golfing center. The town sports no fewer than five golf courses (which nicely help to establish a buffer between Romeo and Detroit's growing northern suburbs.) Other recreations include hayrides and winter sleigh rides.

SPECIAL FEATURES

• A few miles south in Washington is one of Michigan's architectural treasures, the **Loren Andrus Octagon House** (ca 1860). This Italianate structure is surrounded on six sides by a Corinthian-columned porch; in the center of the house is a dramatic spiral staircase that winds all the way up to the third-story cupola (tours by reservation).

• The **Michigan Peach Festival**, held Labor Day weekend, is a Michigan tradition attracting thousands.

The first family orchard in the Romeo area was planted in 1813 and is still in operation!

Between 215 and 221 N. Main Street there's a rare, preserved brickwork pedestrian alley.

WHERE TO STAY

Country Heritage Bed & Breakfast, 64707 Mound Rd., (313) 752-2879. Circa 1840 Greek Revival farmhouse on six acres, fireplaces, swimming pool. $$

Hess Manor B&B, 186 S. Main, (313) 752-4726. Restored 1854 home, Victorian guest parlor, private baths, full breakfasts. $$

WHERE TO EAT

Apple Orchard Inn, Van Dyke at 29 Mile, (313) 752-2188. Classic BBQ Spareribs, Jack Daniel Whiskey Ribs, BBQ Western Beef Ribs. $

FURTHER INFORMATION

Romeo-Washington Chamber of Commerce, P. O. Box 175, Romeo, MI 48065, (313) 752-4436.

DIRECTIONS

From Detroit, MI 53 north to Romeo.

SAUGATUCK/DOUGLAS, MICHIGAN

Population: 954/1,040

With a combined population of less than 2,000, the Lake Michigan harbor villages of **Saugatuck** and **Douglas** boast 26 bed and breakfasts, 14 art galleries, 3 golf courses (including Michigan's second oldest), a Chamber Music Festival and a summer stock theater. They are also home to **Oxbow,** the summer camp of the internationally respected Chicago Institute of Art.

Saugatuck and Douglas are the kinds of places where bed and breakfasts place histories of Great Lakes steamers on coffee tables. The *SS Keewatin,* a 1907 Canadian Pacific Railway passenger liner, is moored here as a museum. Guided tours allow a glimpse of the comfort once enjoyed by steamship travelers on the Great Lakes. The villages share one of the 10 best harbors in the U. S., and that means some world-class Great Lakes sailing.

The two villages also share beautiful unspoiled beaches and, not far away, towering dunes. In the waters outside the harbor, sports fishermen pull in salmon, trout, walleye and perch. Touring options are unusually broad: bicycle, dune buggy, paddlewheeler, cruise boat, ice skates, horse-drawn sleigh, hot-air balloon (etc.).

SPECIAL FEATURE

• The dunes of **Saugatuck Dunes State Park**, just north of the villages, provide beauty and challenge for hikers and, in the winter, trails for cross-country skiiers.

> *The old hand-cranked ferry that connected Saugatuck and Douglas before construction of the bridge is still in operation.*
>
> *The Goose Festival (third weekend in October) in nearby Fennville celebrates the return of 300,000 Canada Geese.*
>
> *Saugatuck and Douglas fought to keep McDonald's out, and won.*

WHERE TO STAY

Beechwood Manor, 736 Pleasant St., (616) 857-1587. Restored 1874 Victorian diplomat's home, on National Register, full breakfasts, croquet. $$$

Fairchild House, 606 Butler St., (616) 857-5985. Sparkling crystal, European featherbeds, champagne breakfasts. $$$

The Park House, 888 Holland St., (800) 321-4535. Saugatuck's oldest residence (1857), private baths, Susan B. Anthony stayed here. $$$

Rosemont Inn, 83 Lakeshore Dr., (616) 857-2637. 1886 Victorian inn across from Douglas Beach, private baths, heated pool. $$$

Wickwood Inn, 510 Butler St., (616) 857-1465. English library-bar, garden room, gazebo, private baths. $$$

WHERE TO EAT

Cafe Sir Douglas, 333 Blue Star Hghw., (616) 857-1401. Daily specials, fresh seafood, filet, art deco setting. $ to $$

Chequers of Saugatuck, 220 Culver St., (616) 857-1868. English pub food and daily specials served among English antiques. $ to $$

Clearbrook Golf Club and Restaurant, 6494 Clearbrook Dr., (616) 857-2000. Creative cuisine in Scottish Golf Club setting. $$

Restaurant Toulouse, 248 Culver St., (616) 857-1561. Country French, wild game, cassoulet, bouillibaisse. $$

Steamboat Lounge, 200 Center St. (Douglas), (616) 857-1441. Continental and American cuisine, seafood. $$

FURTHER INFORMATION

Saugatuck/Douglas Convention and Visitor's Bureau, P. O. Box 28, Saugatuck, MI 49453, (616) 857-1701.

DIRECTIONS

From Chicago, I 94 east to I 196 (near Benton Harbor, MI), I 196 north to exit 36 (Saugatuck/Douglas exit).

MINNESOTA

GRAND
MARAIS.

GRAND
RAPIDS .

STILLWATER
St. Paul ✪ .

RED WING •

GRAND MARAIS, MINNESOTA

Population: 1,171

Grand Marais is a picturesque little harbor town situated on one of the most beautiful shorelines in the United States, the **North Shore of Lake Superior**. Walk along Grand Marais's beach or scan the harbor from the deck of a boat offshore and you can't help but respect the sheer vastness of the northlands.

Beyond the town lie miles of mountains and forests, largely undeveloped, and beyond these is the **Boundary Waters Canoe Area Wilderness**, a natural area that stretches for 150 miles in Minnesota and along the Canadian border. Then there is **Lake Superior**, an inland sea so great that you have to drive 1,026 miles just to get around it! It is uncrowded here.

Start your visit to Grand Marais with a tour of the shops. Then stroll along the harbor and out to the lighthouse and **Artist's Point**. Finally, weather permitting, take to the water. There are boat tours (both launch and sailboat), sailboat rentals, even sailboat charters to magnficent **Isle Royale National Park**. There are bike rentals for those who don't like the water, and places around the harbor to relax for those who would rather watch others doing the moving.

If you have several days to spend in this beautiful area, consider a guided canoe trip, or maybe enrollment in a class at the **Grand Marais Art Colony**. The latter offers week-long classes in watercolor, oils and acrylics, pottery and other media.

One of the best places to turn for indoor entertainment is the **Grand Marais Playhouse**. The playhouse presents plays, concerts and other events and shows during its summer season.

SPECIAL FEATURES

• **MN 61** along the North Shore of Lake Superior is one of the most scenic routes in the country. From Duluth to the Canadian border, and beyond, rugged cliffs and thick forests vie for attention with grand expanses of blue water.

• **The Gunflint Trail** connects Grand Marais with the eastern entrance to the Boundary Waters Wilderness. The black-topped highway winds for 58 miles through and around the wooded hills and glacial lakes of one of the country's great wilderness regions. Check with the CoC in Grand Marais for information on outfitters, lodging and resorts.

> *Northeastern Minnesota's shape has earned it the nickname, "Tip of the Arrowhead."*
>
> *Grand Marais is the ideal place to come for a second spring after the spring flowers of more southern climes have begun to fade.*

WHERE TO STAY

Clearwater Lodge, 355-B Gunflint Trail, (800) 527-0554. 1926 log lodge on secluded Boundary Waters lake, "northwoods" breakfasts. $$

Dreamcatcher B&B, P. O. Box 122, (800) 682-3119. New northwoods-style home overlooking Lake Superior, private baths. $$$

Naniboujou Lodge, P. O. Box 505, (218) 387-2688. Converted 1928 private club, pine-walled guest rooms, hiking to waterfall. $$ to $$$

Pincushion Mountain B&B, 220 Gunflint Trail, (800) 542-1226. Overlooking Lake Superior 1,000 feet below, Finnish sauna, private baths. $$$

The Superior Overlook B&B, P. O. Box 963, (800) 858-7622. New home 200 feet from Lake Superior, Danish "aebleskivers" sometimes on breakfast menu. $$$

WHERE TO EAT

Birth Terrace, P. O. Box 217, (218) 387-2215. In 1898 log mansion overlooking harbor, fresh Lake Superior fish, steaks, famous ribs. $$

East Bay Hotel Family Dining Room, P. O. Box 246, (218) 387-2800. Overlooking Lake Superior, fresh fish, homemade Swedish rye bread. $ to $$

FURTHER INFORMATION

Grand Marais Chamber of Commerce, Grand Marais, MN 55604, (800) 622-4014.

DIRECTIONS

From Duluth, MN 61 northeast (along Lake Superior) to Grand Marais.

GRAND RAPIDS, MINNESOTA

Population: 7,976

The Mississippi River town of **Grand Rapids** is in the heart of the north woods and the *Land of 1,000 Grand Lakes.* What is just as interesting is that some of the north woods and several of the lakes are right in the heart of Grand Rapids. The town is situated on the eastern edge of the **Chippewa National Forest** and boasts four lakes within the city limits and several others just outside. In the summer children jump off docks and fishermen rev up motors. In the fall the "sky-tinted waters" of the lakes and river reflect gold and red as well as blue, and in the winter the town's wooded streets take on that wintry silence.

Naturally, Grand Rapids is geared for those who love the outdoors. There are over 100 resorts on the over 1,000 lakes in town and the **Itasca County area.** There are also nine golf courses, 16 cross-country ski trail systems and 18 snowmobile trail areas. The visitor center distributes maps of bike paths in the city and mountain-biking trails in the county. And of course there are the rivers and lakes for canoeing and for fishing for walleye, muskie, rainbow trout and many others. For the nature lover, the wilderness extends apparently forever.

Grand Rapids serves a large area and maintains an exceptionally busy social and cultural calendar. Many of the events are scheduled downtown at **Central School,** an 1895 schoolhouse listed on the National Register of Historic Places. The schoolhouse is now home to the **Itasca County Historical Society Museum,** the **Judy Garland Museum** (Grand Rapids was Miss Garland's birthplace), and, among other things, a restaurant (see below) and several interesting shops.

SPECIAL FEATURES

• The **Minnesota Forest History Center**, just outside of town, features an authentic reconstruction of an early logging camp and an interpretive center.

• A trolley takes visitors to the base of an enormous open pit at the **Hill Annex Mine State Park** in Calumet, east of town. A sweeping view of the mine is also available from a lookout. The mine is listed on the National Register of Historic Places.

• A tour of the **Blandin Paper Company** and a self-guided auto tour of a company forest management area (south of town) provide enjoyable ways to learn more about Minnesota's paper industry.

> *Over 98% of the shoreline of 69,800-acre Lake Winnibigoshish (Big Winnie) is undeveloped.*
>
> *During the last three weekends in July local entertainers join forces to provide old riverboat entertainment at Showboat Landing on the Mississippi.*

WHERE TO STAY (IN ADDITION TO THE 100-PLUS RESORTS)

Judge Thwing House, 1604 Co. Rd. A, (218) 326-5618. 1910 Colonial-style home in quiet valley near town, full breakfasts. $$

WHERE TO EAT

The First Grade Restaurant, Old Central School, (218) 326-9361. "Scrumptious" lunches in three former schoolrooms. $

Forest Lake Restaurant and Lounge, W US 2, (218) 326-3423. Log setting overlooking Forest Lake, ribs, downstairs steakhouse. $$

Otis's, Sugar Lake Rd., (218) 327-1462. Famous family-recipe roast chicken, family wines, overlooking Sugar Lake. $$

FURTHER INFORMATION

Grand Rapids Depot Visitor Center, 1 NW Third St., Grand Rapids, MN 55744, (800) 472-6366.

DIRECTIONS

From St. Paul, I 35 north to exit 237, MN 33 north to US 2, US 2 northwest to Grand Rapids.

RED WING, MINNESOTA

Population: 15,134

You'd think that having an historic town tucked amongst the scenic bluffs and forests of the upper Mississippi would be enough. Not for the people of **Red Wing**. Apparently believing that everyone wins when nature and humankind work to complement each other, the people of Red Wing have added some 26 parks and hung 220 flowering baskets from the downtown lampposts. The result is a town that, on weekends, has enough beds for only about half of the those who seek them.

It doesn't hurt either that the historic preservation board has the authority to say "no" to about any downtown construction that doesn't remain true to the middle of the 19th century (1858 to be exact). The results of the board's efforts can be enjoyed either by a summer trolley ride or by one of three walking tours — brochures are obtainable at the CoC or front desk of the St. James Hotel (listed below). Twenty-six of the sites along the way are on the National Register of Historic Places.

One of the most visited of the sites is the restored **T. B. Sheldon Auditorium Theatre** (1904), the first municipal theater in the country. The Renaissance Revival theater presents a varied slate of attractions year round. Probably most important to the visitor is a public tour and multi-media program on Red Wing's history.

Boathouse Village is one of Red Wing's most famous attractions. Located on the Mississippi in **Bay Point Park**, the "village" consists of boat storage houses that ride up and down on poles, adjusting to the water's level. The poles are called *gin poles*, because gin bottles were tied to them and hidden in the water during Prohibition. The place is very popular with photographers and artists.

What with the stores downtown, 52 factory outlet and other shops in the **Pottery Place Outlet Center** (itself a National Historic building), and the **St. James Hotel Shopping Court**, Red Wing offers fabulous shopping.

Red Wing has a number of scenic views of the **Mississippi**, and the visitor has an array of sightseeing options. By all means the most time-honored is the 600-foot climb to the top of dramatic **Barn Bluff**. Henry David Thoreau made this climb in 1861 and wrote glowingly of the views. Today there are marked paths and stairways to make the climb easier. Another beautiful view, this time of Red Wing as well as the river, can be reached by driving up to **Sorin's Bluff**. In addition to the views, there are hiking trails and caves to explore. For those who'd rather stay at lower elevations, a river cruise aboard the excursion boat *Schatze* provides a good option. The boat is moored at **Levee Park**.

In 1890, 98 people perished on the excursion boat Sea Wing in a storm on Lake Pepin, down river. The tragedy is marked by a memorial in Levee Park.

WHERE TO STAY

The Candlelight Inn, 818 W. Third St., (612) 388-8034. 1877 Victorian home, library with fireplace, breezy front porch, private baths, full breakfasts. $$ to $$$

Golden Lantern Inn, 721 East Ave., (612) 388-3315. Restored home of three former presidents of Red Wing Shoe Company, private baths, full breakfasts, afternoon snacks. $$ to $$$

Hungry Point Inn, One Olde Deerfield Rd. (Welch, MN), (612) 437-3660. New England-style home, 200-year-old antiques, fireplaces, full candlelight breakfasts. $$ to $$$

Pratt Taber Inn, 706 W. Fourth St., (612) 388-5945. 1876 Italianate mansion, original furniture, porches, bikes. $$ to $$$

St. James Hotel, 406 Main St., (800) 252-1875. Restored 1870s hotel, on National Register, many rooms with view of Mississippi, two restaurants, champagne. $$ to $$$

WHERE TO EAT

Braschler's Bakery & Coffee Shop, 410 W. Third St., (612) 388-1589. Unique "bakery coffee shop," breakfasts, lunches. $

Liberty's Restaurant & Lounge, Third & Plum sts., (612) 388-8877. Red Wing memorabilia, American/Italian/Mexican foods, courtesy car from marinas. $

St. James Hotel's Port of Red Wing, (see above). Riverboat-era dining in authentic period restaurant. $$

FURTHER INFORMATION

Red Wing Area Chamber of Commerce, P. O. Box 133, Red Wing, MN 55066, (800) 762-9516.

DIRECTIONS

From St. Paul, US 61 south to Red Wing.

STILLWATER, MINNESOTA

Population: 13,882

Stillwater is the kind of town you feel you've seen before. The feeling is a warm one, a very positive case of *deja vu.* It's probably because the town is an amalgam of charming old towns everywhere, towns that many of us visited or passed through as children. There's a beautiful river, and up the hill from the river a turn-of-the-century main street; yet farther up steeple spires and hints of old houses rise above the trees. Sets of steps link the steeples and the houses with the downtown below.

A first glance suggests that most of the older buildings are turn-of-the-century. Many of them are, but many, especially those on the National Register of Historic Places, go back much further, to the 1840s-1870s.

Among the structures of special interest are the predominantly Italianate **Washington County Historic Courthouse** (1867-70), the oldest standing courthouse in the state; the early Federal-style **Warden's House** (1853), the residence of 11 wardens for the adjacent **Territorial/State Prison** (1851; only remnants remain); and the **Stillwater-Houlton** (WI) **Lift Bridge** (1931), one of two remaining vertical-lift bridges in Minnesota.

The new (1993) **Stillwater Depot, Logging and Railway Museum** depicts the history of the town and its logging and rail industries. The museum also offers three-hour excursions along the scenic **St. Croix River Valley** on the *Minnesota Zephyr,* a train straight out of the 1940s. In keeping with the earlier era, passengers may have cocktails in the Vista Dome Club cars and enjoy white-linen dinners during the trip.

A brochure containing a map for a self-guided walking or driving tour is distributed by the CoC (allow about 1 1/2 hrs. for walking). A trolley stands ready for a narrated historic tour and a costumed guide is sometimes available to conduct narrated walking tours.

SPECIAL FEATURE

• **The St. Croix River**, a National Wild and Scenic River, is designed for boating. Canoeing and kayaking are popular north of town; to the south sailboats, speedboats, houseboats and yachts navigate the river's to its junction with the Mississippi. Tour boats are available in Stillwater, as are cafes, bars and shops that cater to boaters. And, of course, fishing is great in this part of the world.

> *Believing that a state prison would offer more employment than a state capitol, many Stillwater people back in 1851 sought the prison. And they got it.*

WHERE TO STAY

The Brunswick Inn, 114 E. Chestnut St., (612) 430-2653. Greek Revival Inn built in 1848, fireplaces, private baths, double whirlpools, full breakfasts. $$$

Lowell Inn, 102 N. Second St., (612) 439-1100. "The Mount Vernon of the West," American & European plans, one of best in Midwest. $$$

Outing Lodge at Pine Point, 11661 Myeron Rd. N., (612) 439-9747. Country Inn in 350-acre wooded park, fireplaces, library, Jacuzzi. $$$

Rivertown Inn, 306 W. Olive St., (800) 562-3632. Restored 1882 three-story lumberman's mansion, full breakfasts, overlooking town and St. Croix Valley. $$ to $$$

William Sauntry Mansion, 626 N. Fourth St., (612) 430-2653. Circa 1890 lumber baron's mansion, on National Register, period decor, fireplaces, private baths, three-course breakfasts. $$$

WHERE TO EAT

The Brunswick Inn (see above). Five-course meals served in High Victorian style, fixed price. $$$

Freight House Restaurant, 305 Water St., (612) 439-5718. In historic building with deck overlooking St. Croix River. $ to $$

Gasthaus Bavarian Hunter, 8390 Lofton Ave., (612) 439-7128. Bavarian restaurant in pines serving German cuisine. $ to $$

Lowell Inn (see above). Start with Escargot Bourguigonne, served with a medium-bodied white Chardonnay and Swiss rye; this is an award-winning restaurant. $$$

Vittorio's, 402 S. Main St., (612) 439-3588. Homemade pastas, brewery caves and tours. $ to $$

FURTHER INFORMATION

Stillwater Area Chamber of Commerce, 423 S. Main St., Stillwater, MN 55082, (612) 439-7700.

DIRECTIONS

From St. Paul, I 94 east to MN 95, MN 95 north (along Mississippi River) to Stillwater.

MISSISSIPPI

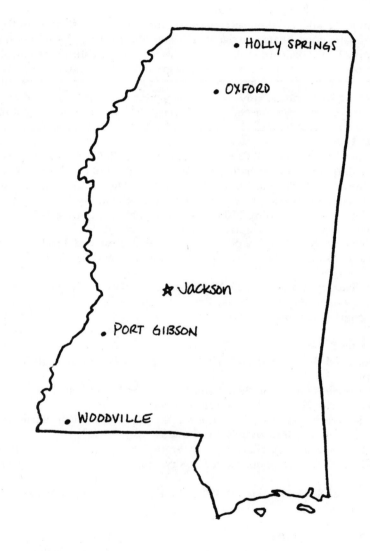

HOLLY SPRINGS

OXFORD

★ Jackson

PORT GIBSON

WOODVILLE

HOLLY SPRINGS, MISSISSIPPI

Population: 7,261

After strolling the sidewalks and viewing what seems to be an endless series of 19th-century mansions, the visitor is going to have three questions, at least. First, where did all the wealth come from? Second, how did so many antebellum mansions get through the Civil War unscathed (especially because Union forces were thick in these parts)? And third, who lives in them?

In answer to the first question, much of the wealth arose from land transactions made during the cotton real-estate boom of antebellum days. Many of those who prospered were (surprisingly) lawyers. Also, the town was settled by a number of well-to-do families from Virginia and the Carolinas.

Second, General Ulysses S. Grant was headquartered here briefly during the Civil War. The story goes that when Confederate General Van Dorn occupied the city, Mrs. Grant pleaded with Van Dorn to respect the privacy of her bedroom — and, incidentally, her husband's private papers. The general obliged and, later returning the favor, General Grant ordered that the town not be torched.

Third, the houses are in demand because many people, often young couples, wish the experience of restoring them. It doesn't hurt either that Holly Springs, just 34 miles from Memphis, attracts families who would rather live away from the big city.

The sheer number and variety of 19th-century mansions make Holly Springs a living museum (although most houses are closed to the public; see below). A brief but representative sampling of the homes includes:

Dunvegan (1845), a one-story Greek Revival home furnished with Empire and Regency antiques and decorated in many rooms with painted murals. Dunvegan's style of architecture is sometimes described as "English basement." Grey Gables (1839-1849), an Italianate house noted for its magnificent spiral stairway and hand-cut Bohemian glass windows.

Montrose (1858), a Greek Revival mansion with a graceful circular stairway, parquetry floors and beautiful cornices (open by appointment). The arboretum on the grounds, with 50 specifimens of native trees, has been designated the Mississippi Statewide Arboretum Walter Place (1859), a magnificent mansion combining Greek Revival and Gothic Revival elements. It was here that General and Mrs. Grant lived during their stay in Holly Springs.

One of the best ways to take in the houses and their grounds is to get a brochure from the CoC and follow green lines painted on the streets. The Green Line Tour may be taken by foot or car. Special group tours of homes, churches and other buildings may also be arranged through the CoC. Many of the homes are open to visitors during the Annual Pilgrimage, the third weekend in April.

The Kate Freeman Clark Art Gallery houses over 1,200 still lifes, portraits and landscapes by the gifted Holly Springs student of William Merritt Chase. Refusing to sell even one painting, Clark willed all of her work to Holly Springs. Only a few of her paintings are on display at any time (open by appointment).

On display at the imposing Marshall County Historical Museum are such diverse items as Chickasaw Indian artifacts, relics from the Civil War and War of 1812, vintage costumes and antique toys.

SPECIAL FEATURE

• An hour or so in the 1837 **Hillcrest Cemetery** can be both an informative and moving experience. Here Victorian cast- and wrought-iron fences enclose old burial plots, and marble and granite obelisks commemorate not only Confederate generals but victims, young and old, of the 1878 yellow-fever epidemic.

> *Federal troops used the basement of the First Presbyterian Church as a stable for their horses.*
>
> *Rust College was established in 1866 to educate newly freed slaves. The college's library is named after the Mississippi-born singer Leontyne Price.*

WHERE TO STAY

Hamilton Place B&B, 105 E. Mason, (601) 252-4368. Circa 1838 home with heirloom antiques, private baths, hot tub and swimming pool. $$$

WHERE TO EAT

Crossroads Fish Shack, Red Banks & Old Hernando rds., (601) 252-7506. "All You Can Eat Catfish," fried oysters, slaw, hushpuppies. $

FURTHER INFORMATION

Holly Springs Chamber of Commerce, 154 South Memphis Street, Holly Springs, MS 38635, (601) 252-2943.

DIRECTIONS

From Memphis (TN), US 78 southeast to Holly Springs.

OXFORD, MISSISSIPPI

Population: 9,984

Oxford is home to several nationally renowned authors. Endowed by the literary heritage of William Faulkner, served by a major state university, and given character by one of the most colorful (and beautiful) squares in small-town America, Oxford seems designed for the writer.

The courthouse and much of the surrounding square were burned by Federal troops in 1864. Some buildings survived in whole or in part, however, and others were rebuilt. Today the magnificently restored and maintained square is home to the "new" **courthouse** (rebuilt 1873), the **city hall** (1885), the **oldest continuing department store in the South** (1897), and a nationally respected **bookstore**, housed in one of the first buildings built after the Civil War. And there's a host of interesting shops and restaurants.

The walking-tour brochure distributed by the tourism council lists four tours, one focusing on the square area and three on Oxford's other historic areas. One of the latter, the area north of the square, embraces a number of structures dating back to the 1830s. One of the oldest and best known is **Isom Place** (1838-

1843), a large planter-style house built of native timber and handcrafted by Indians and slaves. The house, now a bed and breakfast (see below), is furnished with antiques brought to Oxford by mule train (open to non-boarders only by appointment).

The area south of the square contains homes from the mid and late 19th century. By all means the most famous is **Rowan Oak** (1848), the home bought and renovated by William Faulkner. Set in a grove of oak and cedar trees, the house was Faulkner's office, home and quiet refuge from 1930 until his death in 1962. The house, preserved as it was when the Nobel Prize winner died, is open to the public.

The buildings along or near **University Avenue** make up Oxford's fourth historic area. Here are the **University Museums**, a complex of museums boasting excellent collections of 18th- and 19th-century scientific instruments, Southern folk art and Greek and Roman antiquities.

> *The building at 520 N. Lamar, built in 1875, was designed by James and Alexander Stewart, designers of three state capitols and the Savoy Hotel in London.*
>
> *Don't expect to find lodgings in or near Oxford when Ole Miss has a home football game.*

WHERE TO STAY

Isom Place, 1003 Jefferson Ave., (601) 234-3310. Circa 1838 home, on National Register, Oxford antiques and memorabilia. $$

Oliver-Britt House, 512 Van Buren, (601) 234-8043. Restored ca. 1905 Greek Revival manor house, near university and square, private baths. $$

Puddin' Place, 1008 University Ave., (601) 234-1250. 1892 "cottage," screened back porch, antiques, suites with sitting rooms and fireplaces, private baths, unique breakfasts. $$$

WHERE TO EAT

City Grocery, 1118 Van Buren St., (601) 232-8888. Nouvelle, French, Italian, Creole cuisines. $$ to $$$

The Gin, Harrison Ave., (601) 234-0024. Converted cotton gin with patio, college hangout. $

Ruth & Jimmie's Cafe & Sporting Goods, Abbeville (MS), (601) 234-4312. "Mom's cooking," plate lunch served on counter. $

Taylor Grocery, (Taylor, MS), (601) 236-1716. Old grocery with jukebox, catfish served in village known as artists' retreat. $

Yocona River Inn, MS 334, (601) 234-2426. Converted country store and house, catfish, brown bag. $

FURTHER INFORMATION

Oxford Tourism Council, 299 Jackson Ave., Oxford, MS 38655, (601) 234-4651.

DIRECTIONS

From Memphis (TN), I 55 south to exit 243, MS 6 east to Oxford.

PORT GIBSON, MISSISSIPPI

Population: 1,810

According to legend, General Grant proclaimed **Port Gibson** "too beautiful to burn." Whether because of Grant's proclamation or some other reason, the town on **Little Bayou Pierre** was spared. More than a century later it became the first town in Mississippi to be designated a National Historic District. It is one of the South's most beautiful and historic little towns.

Settled around 1788, Port Gibson was chartered as a county seat in 1803. The place was a wide-open frontier town for a spell, but rather quickly succumbed to the advances of civilization. It acquired, for example, the state's first library (1818), second newspaper, and third Masonic Lodge.

Union soldiers crossed the Mississippi River near here in 1863 in what was the largest amphibious landing of troops prior to World War II. The Union victory at the ensuing Battle of Port Gibson, fought a few miles west of town, helped pave the way for the Confederate loss of Vicksburg.

Both within the city and out in the country are a number of lovely historic homes. Four of the most splendid are open for tours — because all four also offer bed-and-breakfast accommodations, they are described below. Several others open their doors during the annual spring pilgrimage. One of these, the 1817 Federal-style cottage named **Englesing**, boasts the state's oldest formal garden. Another, **Gage House** (1830-1850), has a two-story brick dependency that once contained slave quarters and the house's kitchen.

Also known as the *City of Churches*, Port Gibson's **Church Street** is graced by no fewer than eight churches. The **First Presbyterian Church** (1859) is known for the gilded hand that tops its steeple, and also for its chandeliers, originally on the famous Mississippi River steamboat, the *Robert E. Lee*. **Temple Gemiluth Chessed** (1891) is the state's oldest synagogue, and the only one of its architectural style in Mississippi.

Mississippi Cultural Crossroads operates an African-American quilting work-shop and the children's **Peanut Butter and Jelly Theater**. Quilts, and art work by both children and adults, are on display.

SPECIAL FEATURES

• South of Port Gibson is the **Old Country Store**, an 1875 plantation store that's still in operation. The store is one of the area's most popular tourist destinations.

• Southeast of town are the haunting ruins of **Windsor**, the largest antebel-lum house ever built in Mississippi (1859-1861). Spared by the Yankees, the mansion was destroyed by fire from a cigarette in 1890. Only the 23 columns remain.

• **Grand Gulf State Park**, northwest of town, comprises Confederate forts **Coburn** and **Wade**, several restored buildings and a museum containing Civil War memorabilia and a collection of horse-drawn vehicles.

• West of town near the Mississippi River is the ghost town of **Rodney**. Once a busy river town, Rodney was vacated following a shift in the course of the river. The town's **Presbyterian Church** was built in 1829. Do not attempt a visit before checking locally for instructions.

WHERE TO STAY

Canemount Plantation, Rt. 2 (Box 45, Lorman), (800) 423-0684. Restored fine 1855 Italianate home, pool, dinners and breakfasts included in price. $$$

Gibson's Landing, P. O. Box 195, (601) 437-3432. Restored early 1830s home, unusual spiral staircase, faux marble fireplace mantel. $$$

Oak Square Plantation, 1207 Church St., (601) 437-4350. Restored circa 1850 Greek Revival home with 30 rooms, on National Register, massive oak trees. $$$

Rosswood Plantation, (Lorman), (601) 437-4215. Restored 1857 Greek Revival home on 100-acre estate, on National Register, pool. $$$

WHERE TO EAT

The Old Depot Restaurant & Lounge, S. Market St., (601) 437-4711. Southern specialties, seafood, steaks, red beans & rice, po-boys, catfish. $

FURTHER INFORMATION

Port Gibson-Claiborne County Chamber of Commerce, P. O. Box 491, Port Gibson, MS, 39150, (601) 437-4351.

DIRECTIONS

From Vicksburg, US 61 south to Port Gibson.

WOODVILLE, MISSISSIPPI

Population: 1,393

Woodville hasn't changed in 100 years. Not much is happening here today, and people say that not much will be happening tomorrow, either. Many like it that way, and that includes the traveler in search of old out-of-the-way Southern towns that aren't going anywhere.

Woodville is the classic antebellum Southern town. Like most other small Southern towns, but contrary to common knowledge, the homes of the black people, who make up well over half the population, share the streets more or less equitably with the homes of the whites. The old oak and magnolia trees shade a number of beautiful houses and churches built during the first decades of the 19th century. The churches are among the oldest in Mississippi. Several of the antebellum homes bear the columns of classic Greek Revival.

The homes and churches are best toured with the aid of a brochure obtainable at the **Wilkinson County Museum.** The **Woodville Baptist Church** dates from 1809, and the **Woodville Methodist Church** and **St. Paul's Episcopal Church** go back to the 1820s. St. Paul's was the church attended by the family of Jefferson Davis, President of the Confederacy. Many of the historic homes are located on **Church Street;** no house on this or any other street in town, however, is currently open to the public.

Just one mile east of town (on MS 24) is a house that is open to the public —
Rosemont Plantation House, the boyhood home of Jefferson Davis. Built about
1810 by Davis's parents, this lovely house is centered about a large hall that opens
onto front and back galleries. The house was home to five generations of the
Davis family and has many of the family's furnishings.

SPECIAL FEATURES

• About 14 miles west of town on the **Pinckneyville Road** is an old-fashioned
general store, called **Pond Store** (1881), that is straight out of the old rural South.
The adjacent pond, which gave the store its name, was dug generations ago as a
watering hole for animals hauling cotton and other produce to steamboats wait-
ing at **Fort Adams**, just to the west. Tours of the store are available by appointment.

• Next to Pond Store is the **Clark Creek Nature Area**, with over 1,200 acres
of steep bluff woodlands and winding trails. The state park has seven waterfalls,
one of them 50 feet high, and is popular with hikers.

> *Ft. Adams, an old port city, was a Mississippi River entry point into the
> United States prior to the Louisiana Purchase (1803).*
> *Military personnel attached to Ft. Adams built homes in the area of Pond
> Store following the Revolutionary War. Several of these homes, now over 200
> years old, still stand.*

WHERE TO STAY

Southern Gallery Inn, US 61, (601) 888-6301. Country home with galleries/
rocking chairs overlooking gardens, antiques, private baths, TV, pool. $$ to $$$

WHERE TO EAT

Neal's Restaurant and Lounge, US 61, (601) 888-6180. Cajun cooking, mesquite prime rib, Mississippi catfish. $

FURTHER INFORMATION

Wilkinson County Museum, Woodville, MS 39669, (601) 888-3998.

DIRECTIONS

From Jackson, I 20 west to exit 1b (Vicksburg), US 61 south (via Natchez) to
Woodville.

Top: Colonial Williamsburg, Virginia
Bottom: Oldest Bar in Nevada – Genoa, Nevada

The incomparable Grand Hotel, Mackinac Island, Michigan

Top: Gingerbread Mansion, Ferndale, California

Bottom: Amish wagon, Jamesport, Missouri

Top: Lake Placid, New York
Bottom: Leavenworth, Washington

Top: Charming Ohio!
Bottom: Yankton, South Dakota

Top: Waterloo Village, New Jersey
Bottom: Harpers Ferry, West Virginia

Top: Chesapeake Bay Maritime Museum, St. Michaels, Maryland
Bottom: Farmers Hall, Pendleton, South Carolina

Top: Mule Barge, Bucks County, Pennsylvania
Bottom: Craftsbury Common, Vermont

MISSOURI

JAMESPORT

ARROW ROCK

HERMANN

Jefferson City

SAINTE
GENEVIEVE

CARTHAGE

ARROW ROCK, MISSOURI

Population: 70

Arrow Rock and "weekend" are becoming syonymous for many Kansas Cityans. It's all there, enough for two full but restful days: a quiet historic site that can be leisurely toured with or without a guide, interesting shops and craft demonstrations, a top summer repertory theater, good food, a park with an exercise-inviting hiking trail, and a choice of several delightful bed & breakfasts.

It was at Arrow Rock that the **Santa Fe Trail** crossed the **Missouri River**. As such, the village has been catering to travelers since 1829. There are a few Victorian houses, but the early date of settlement means that many buildings are of the Federal style, a style uncommon this far west. Many of the older buildings make up the **Arrow Rock State Historic Site**.

The most prominent building in the historic site is the **Old Tavern** (1834), a two-story Federal-style brick building that houses a visitors center (where guided walking tours begin) and restaurant (see listing below). The most historic of the houses is the small Federal-style dwelling (1837) of **George Caleb Bingham**, the nationally renowned artist. The house is a National Historic Landmark.

Several musicals and a sprinkling of classic dramas are offered in rotating repertory from June into September at the 300-seat **Arrow Rock Lyceum Theater**, Missouri's oldest professional theater.

SPECIAL FEATURE

• The recently restored **Prairie Park**, an 1844 Greek Revival mansion several miles out in the country, is one of Missouri's premier properties. The house was built by the son of Dr. John Sappington, the physician who popularized the use of quinine for treating malaria. Check locally for tour information.

> *Strictly speaking, the Santa Fe Trail didn't begin in Arrow Rock, as is commonly believed, but across the river from Arrow Rock.*

WHERE TO STAY

Borgman's B&B, Van Buren St., (816) 837-3350. 1890s home, family-style breakfasts. $ to $$

Down Over Holdings B&B, Main St., (816) 837-3268. Small lounge, private baths, guest house with kitchen/bath. $$

Miss Nelle's B&B, Main St., (816) 837-3280. Restored ca. 1853 home, fireplace, close to sights. $$

WHERE TO EAT

Evergreen Restaurant, MO 41 one block north of Main St., (816) 837-3251. 1840s home, continental cuisine, homemade breads, gourmet wine selection. $$

The Old Tavern, Main St., (816) 837-3300. 1834 tavern; traditional dishes. $

FURTHER INFORMATION

Arrow Rock Area Merchants Association, P. O. Box 147, Arrow Rock, MO 65320, (816) 837-3268/3231.

DIRECTIONS
From Kansas City, I 70 east to exit 98, MO 41 north to Arrow Rock.

CARTHAGE, MISSOURI
Population: 10,747

Enriched by lead and zinc mines, marble quarries and flour mills, **Carthage** had by the end of the 19th century more millionaires per capita than any other city in the country. Much of the wealth remains, as a drive by the beautifully preserved Victorian homes on **Grand Avenue** and **S. Main Street** will make clear. The town's maple-lined streets are especially lovely in the fall. They're not bad in the spring, either, when the dogwoods are in bloom.

A tour brochure distributed by the CoC provides full architectural histories and color photos for a sample of 20 of the Victorian homes. Dating from the last three decades of the 19th century, the houses represent all major Midwestern Victorian styles. Good examples are the 1870 Italianate **Spencer House**, the magnificent Chateauesque 1887 **Hill House**, and the 1873 **Italian Villa**, known as **Wetzel's Folly**.

Two homes, **Kendrick Place** and the **Phelps House**, offer tours. One of the oldest buildings in the Carthage area, Kendrick Place (1849) has been restored to its pre-Civil War appearance. The 1890s Classical Revival Phelps House has 10 fireplaces and a hand-operated elevator that serves all floors between the base-ment and the third-floor ballroom.

Of interest downtown is the 1894 **Jasper County Courthouse**. Listed on the National Register, the courthouse has several first-floor exhibits of Indian artifacts and mineral specimens from the region's mining days. The building also contains a 1976 mural, *Forged in Fire*, that depicts Carthage's history.

The **Powers Museum** provides a glimpse at local history and the arts; the museum features a variety of changing exhibits. As its name indicates, the **Carthage Civil War Museum** tells the story of the role played by Carthage in the Civil War.

The 5,000-square-foot **Precious Moments Chapel**, southwest of town, was created by artist Samuel Butcher. The nondenominational chapel is noted for its sculptures, carvings and 15 stained-glass windows, all of the Precious Moments motif.

Just outside of town is Lowell Davis's **Red Oak II**, a reconstructed 1930s farming community. Among the restored buildings are a gas station, general store, country school, parsonage, art gallery, feed and seed store, cafe, and child-hood home of Belle Starr. The village is also home to several "bed and baskets" (breakfast comes in a basket).

SPECIAL FEATURE
 • About 10 miles south of Carthage is the **Carver National Monument**, the

birthplace and childhood home of black agronomist George Washington Carver.

> *The first major battle of the Civil War occurred in Carthage on July 5, 1861.*
>
> *A statue of Carthage's Marlin Perkins, host of TV's "Wild Kingdom" series, is located in Central Park.*

WHERE TO STAY

Brewer's Maple Lane Farm B&B, Rt. 1 (417) 358-6312. 20-room home on National Register, original brass light fixtures, barnyard of animals. $$

Grand Avenue Inn B&B, 1615 Grand Ave., (417) 358-7265. Circa 1890 home on National Register, private baths, wine and cheese. $$ to $$$

The Leggett House B&B, 1106 Grand Ave., (417) 358-0683. 1901 Classical Revival home, lace-curtained guest rooms, mosaic-tiled solarium, full breakfasts. $$

WHERE TO EAT

Carthage Deli & Ice Cream, 301 S. Main St., (417) 358-8820. 1950s music and decor, excellent soups, thick sandwiches. $

FURTHER INFORMATION

Carthage Chamber of Commerce, 107 E. Third St., Carthage, MO 64836, (417) 358-2373.

DIRECTIONS

From Springfield, I 44 west to exit 18, US 71 north to Carthage.

HERMANN, MISSOURI

Population: 2,754

Hermann was founded by the German Settlement Society of Philadelphia in 1836 (settled 1837). It's believed that the founders selected this lovely spot on the **Missouri River** because it reminded them of their native Rhine. The original plans called for a large city that would preserve German culture — a kind of home away from home. The city obviously never materialized, but the townspeople's commitment to preserve their German traditions survived. Picturesque little Hermann remains German, consciously so.

Vineyards, part of Hermann's Rhineland heritage, were planted during the town's earliest years, and grape growing eventually became an important part of the area's economy. Today there are four wineries, each offering daily tours. The oldest, **Stone Hill Winery** (1847), has been declared a National Historic District. At the turn of the century Stone Hill was the third largest winery in the world.

Forced by Prohibition to grow mushrooms (in its vast cellars) rather than grapes, the winery was reopened in 1969; in 1989 it became the first Missouri winery since Prohibition to be awarded an international gold medal. The winery has the largest underground arched cellars in the United States.

Another historic winery, the **Hermannhof Winery** (1852), has a magnificent festhalle. The winery's stone wine cellars and winery building are on the National Register of Historic Places.

The streets of the **Hermann Historic District** (the town has two historic districts) are lined with tidy German-American homes and gardens. Several of the houses were built as early as the 1840s. Two of them are preserved as the **Deutscheim State Historic Site**: the German Neoclassical **Pommer-Gentner House** (1842), with furnishings from the 1840s, and the **Strehly House and Winery** (1844), a German Vernacular house furnished in the 1860s-1880s style.

The **German School Building** (1871) **Museums** provide a comprehensive and fascinating look at Hermann's history. Among the museums' exhibits are a hand-made wooden wine press, circa 1835 wood cloth-printing blocks, and boat models and other items depicting the town's river history. One of the museums features dolls and toys from the late 1890s, another displays a handmade Rococo Revival bedroom set of solid walnut.

The White House Hotel (1868) is a three-story brick building, with two-story wing, featuring 15-ft. ceilings, arched hallways and an iron-railed Widow's Walk. The hotel contains 36 rooms with furnishings and decorations from the late 19th century; the kitchen still has its original cook stove. (guided tours)

Hermann abounds with art galleries, antique shops, and quaint craft and gift shops. Crafts include quilts, afghans, handwoven baskets and handcrafted wood items. Black-powder guns, vintage lighting and European giftware are among other items displayed in the shops.

SPECIAL FEATURE

• The rolling **Missouri River Valley** and the foothills of the **Ozarks** to the south combine to make **MO 19**, which passes through Hermann, an especially scenic highway.

> *The Gasconade County Courthouse (1896-1898) was the gift of a local merchant (!)*
>
> *Octoberfest, held the first four weekends in October, features a Showboat Theatre, craft demonstrations, German bands and folk dancing, and lots of food, beer and wine.*

WHERE TO STAY

Alice's Wharf Street B&B, 206 Wharf St., (314) 486-5785. Circa 1840 home with 4-room apartment overlooking Missouri River, full breakfasts. $$

Captain Wohlt Inn, 123 E. Third St., (314) 486-3357. On National Register, antique furnishings, private baths, full breakfasts. $$ to $$$

Schmidt Guesthouse, 300 Market St., (314) 486-2146. Suite with large family room, antiques, full breakfasts, private entrance. $$

Strassner Suites, 132 E. 4th St., (314) 486-2682. Private baths, TV, full breakfasts, courtesy pick-up from Amtrak Station. $$$

William Klinger Inn, 108 E. 2nd St., (314) 486-5930. Historic mansion with

Victorian decor, private baths, full breakfasts, gourmet dinners by reservation. $$$

WHERE TO EAT

The Landing Restaurant and Lounge, 4 Schiller St., (314) 486-2030. German and American dishes. $ to $$

Vintage 47 Restaurant, Stone Hill Winery, (314) 486-3479. In original winery stable and carriage house, German-style Schnitzel, fresh seafood, award-winning chef. $ to $$

FURTHER INFORMATION

Visitor Information Center, 306 Market St., Hermann, MO 65041, (314) 486-2744.

DIRECTIONS

From St. Louis, I 70 west to exit 175, MO 19 south to Hermann.

JAMESPORT, MISSOURI

Population: 570

Jamesport is set in the picturesque rolling countryside of northwestern Missouri. The village is surrounded by beautiful old farms, mature woods and winding rivers. Horses and buggies are common to the roads.

There are really two Jamesports, one complementing the other. The first is the village, a few streets of antique shops and old homes where everyone knows everyone else and no one bothers with street addresses or last names. The second is the surrounding countryside, dotted with Amish farms and country stores.

The village, tiny though it may be, has 16 antique shops and more than 25 craft and specialty shops. There's an old-fashioned soda fountain, of course, and a place that takes "old-time" photos. There are also places to sit and relax, quiet places where in the evening only fireflies and whippoorwills disturb.

Although not settling in Jamesport until the early 1950s, the Amish now farm much of the rich land around the village. Amish families also operate several country stores and greenhouses along the highways. The stores sell everything from fabrics and handmade quilts to homemade noodles, jellies and jams (closed Thursdays and Sundays). Bus tours of the stores and Amish countryside are available.

The Amish maintain seven one-room parochial schools in the Jamesport area.

Visitors need to remember that picture-taking goes against Amish religious beliefs.

WHERE TO STAY

Enchanting Memories Country Cottage, RR. 1 (Box 10), (816) 684-6677. Simple country cottage rented as (romantic) unit. $$$

Country Colonial B&B, Main & East sts., (816) 684-6711. Restored 1894 hotel, double verandas, private baths, study, baby grand piano. $$ to $$$

Richardson House, P. O. Box 105, (816) 684-6677. Restored turn-of-century farmhouse, antiques, rented as unit, "country" breakfasts. $$$

WHERE TO EAT

Gingerich Dutch Pantry and Bakery, South and Broadway sts., (816) 684-6212. Hearty Mennonite cooking, great homemade pies and delicious baked goods.

FURTHER INFORMATION

Jamesport Community Association, Jamesport, MO 64648, (816) 684-6146.

DIRECTIONS

From Kansas City (MO), I 35 north to exit 61, MO 6 east to Jamesport.

STE. GENEVIEVE, MISSOURI

Population: 4,411

The first thing the visitor approaching **Ste. Genevieve** notices is that the town is nestled in a valley (in an old riverbed in fact) near the **Mississippi River**. The second — if not the first — is that the town is dominated by a tall steeple (of the 1876 **Church of Ste. Genevieve**). The third and fourth are that the church and its steeple share the middle of the town's square with a relatively small old courthouse (1821), and that the square is surrounded by 19th-century step-gabled brick storefronts. The most important discovery, however, comes with a stroll down the streets leading off the square. For here lies one of the largest collections of 18th-century houses in the country.

Established between 1725 and 1750 by French settlers, Ste. Genevieve is the oldest town in Missouri. More than 50 of the 18th-century homes built by the settlers survive. Many have been restored; some are private residences and others are house museums (see below). Among them are three of the only four remaining houses in North America of poteaux-en-terre construction (built on poles placed vertically in the ground, with no foundation).

The 19th-century brick buildings on (and off) the square were built by immigrants from southern Germany. These together with the French Colonial buildings form an historic district noted for its craft shops, antique galleries, boutiques and restaurants — as well as its lovely old buildings.

The two logical starting points for a tour of the district are the Tourist

Information Office and the **Ste. Genevieve Museum**. The former provides information for a self-guided walking tour, including cassette tapes. The latter contains collections of local memorabilia; of note are prehistoric Indian relics, Spanish land grants, and artifacts from the **Saline Creek Salt Works**, Missouri's first industry.

Seven structures, six homes and one inn, are of special architectural and/or historic interest:

The **Guibourd-Valle House** (ca. 1784) has elegant furnishings and an attic with hand-hewn oak beams. Outside are a courtyard, rose garden and old stone well (costumed tour guides).

The **Felix Valle House** (1818), a state historic site, is a Federal-style limestone building with early Empire furnishings and original mantels. Inside is an authentically restocked mercantile store; on the grounds are an attractive garden and original brick and frame outbuildings.

The **Bolduc House** (1770), an authentically restored Creole structure, has original 18th-century furnishings, frontier kitchen, and 18th-century culinary and medicinal herb gardens (open to public).

The **Bolduc-LeMeilleur House** (1820), a frame structure with brick nogging, is furnished with early Federal pieces. The house has early 19th-century herb and scented gardens (open to public).

The **Green Tree Inn** (1789) was the first inn and tobacco shop west of the Mississippi. The inn features original walnut shutters and woodwork and a triangular fireplace that opens into three rooms (prearranged group tours only).

The poteaux-en-terre **Amoureaux House** (1770), once the home of a French nobleman, may be the oldest building in Missouri. Among the house's contents is a collection of rare dolls and toys (prearranged group tours only).

The **Bequette-Ribault House** (1778) is another of the four remaining poteaux-en-terre structures in North America (not open to public).

SPECIAL FEATURE

• **Hawn State Park**, southwest of Ste. Genevieve, features pine trees, azaleas and a 10-mile backpacking trail.

A town square divided into two parts by a street (as in Ste. Genevieve), with one part housing a government building and the other a church, indicates Spanish ancestry. (The territory west of the Mississippi was held by Spain from 1762 to 1800.)

According to legend, the posts used for poteaux-en-terre construction were soaked prior to use in arsenic to repel termites.

WHERE TO STAY

Belle Rive B&B, 406 N. 3rd St., (314) 883-3830. Restored 1901 home with two parlors, veranda, 100-year-old ginkgo tree, bicycle, lawn games. $$

Main Street Inn B&B, 221 N. Main St., (314) 883-9199. Restored late 1870s hotel, porch and balcony, private baths, full gourmet breakfasts. $$ to $$$

The Southern Hotel B&B, 146 S.Third St., (314) 883-3493. Renovated circa 1805 Federal-style building, large front parlors, game room, private baths, full French breakfasts. $$ to $$$

Steiger Haus, 1021 Market St., (314) 883-5881. Renovated 1882 farmhouse with 1787 guest cottage, pool, murder mystery weekends, host an 11th-generation native fluent in French. $$

The Inn St. Gemme Beauvais, 78 N. Main St., (314) 883-5744. 1848 country inn in historic district, antiques, full breakfasts. $$

WHERE TO EAT

Old Brick House, Third & Market sts., (314) 883-2724. In oldest brick building west of Mississippi River (1785-1805), fried chicken, liver dumplings. $

Lucretia's Restaurant, 242 Merchant St., (314) 883-5647. In historic Greek Revival home, Continental cuisine, crepes, quiche, dessert tray, classical music. $ to $$

FURTHER INFORMATION

Ste. Genevieve Tourist Information Office, 66 S. Main St., Ste. Genevieve, MO 63670, (314) 883-7097.

DIRECTIONS

From St. Louis, I 55 south to exit 154, US 61 east to Ste. Genevieve.

MONTANA

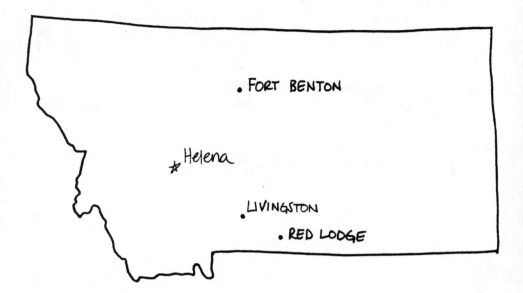

FORT BENTON, MONTANA

Population: 1,660

As the head of navigation on the Missouri River and the West's innermost port, **Fort Benton** was destined to encounter some colorful and rowdy days. And the days came: the town was a fur-trading post, the eastern staging post of the **Mullan Trail** (completed in 1859) connecting with Fort Walla Walla in Washington, a steamboat landing for the Gold Rush of the 1860s, and the southern terminus of the **Whoop-Up Trail** (1870/83), along which flowed whiskey and other goods into western Canada. Only with the 1880s did calm and respectability finally come to town.

Today people drive 150 miles across the sweeping wheat fields of central Montana to spend the day in this historic town. Others select the *Birthplace of Montana* to retire to. All it takes to understand why is a stroll along **Front Street**, now peaceful but once infamous for its "bloodiest block in the West." Separating the street from the Missouri is the steamboat levee, site of the **Lewis and Clark State Memorial** (1976). Staked here and there are signs telling about the days when the levee was crowded with boats, freight, and ox and mule teams. Lovely old cottonwoods and various conifers shade the riverbank and **Old Fort Park**, resting place for the remains of **Old Fort Benton** (1847).

Bordering the street are historic buildings, some of them brick and most from Fort Benton's Golden Years, the early 1880s. The imposing **Grand Union Hotel**, one of Montana's oldest hotels (1882) and now a National Historic Landmark, was once the most luxurious hostelry between Minneapolis and Seattle. **The Old Firehouse**, on the National Register of Historic Places, dates from 1883. The building housed a steam-powered engine and other firefighting equipment shipped from the East by steamboat.

Built about the same time (1880) but located a few blocks from the river is the recently restored Norman Gothic **St. Paul's Episcopal Church** (visitors welcome). The displays of the **Fort Benton Museum of the Upper Missouri** center on the history of the Fort Benton region from the 1840s until 1887. A second museum, the **Museum of the Northern Great Plains**, depicts the history of the homestead era and the region's farming practices.

SPECIAL FEATURES

• The scenery and abundant wildlife of some 150 miles of the unspoiled upper **Missouri River**, designated a Wild and Scenic River, can be seen by canoe (rentals are available) and 3- to 5-day guided boat tours.

• People continue to visit the profile monument and marker over the grave of the dog **Shep**, who spent 5 1/2 years meeting every train at Fort Benton after his master's body was taken away by train in 1936 for burial back East. Although many tried to befriend Shep, the dog faithfully waited for his master's return until killed, ironically, by a train.

> *Another of the sites on Fort Benton's levee is a replica of the Keelboat "Mandan," built for the movie "The Big Sky." Yet another levee site is the hull of the small steamboat, "Baby Rose" (1900).*

WHERE TO STAY

The Sovekammer B&B, 1109 Third Ave. N. (Great Falls), (406) 453-6620. Comfortable old home close to downtown and C.M. Russell Museum, private baths, full breakfasts made with Danish recipes. $$

WHERE TO EAT

Bar-S, 5 mi. east of Great Falls on US 87/89, (406) 761-9550. One of the best steak houses in Montana, seafood, reservations advised. $ to $$.

FURTHER INFORMATION

Fort Benton Visitors Center, P. O. Box 988, Fort Benton, MT 59442, (406) 622-5634.

DIRECTIONS

From Helena, I 15 north to exit 280 (Great Falls), US 87 northeast to Ft. Benton.

LIVINGSTON, MONTANA

Population: 6,701

Robert Redford's selection of **Livingston** as the setting for his movie, *A River Runs Through It*, was entirely appropriate. The beautiful **Yellowstone River**, the longest free-flowing river in the lower 48, runs right through town. And with no fewer than 436 residential and commercial structures listed on the National Register, and the facades of some 20 buildings on **Main Street** restored to their original designs, much of Livingston should and does look like an early 20th-century Montana town.

One of Livingston's principal landmarks is the grand old **Northern Pacific Railroad depot**. The turn-of-the-century depot was designed by the same firm that designed New York's Grand Central Station. Recently restored at a cost of $800,000, the building is now a museum known as the **Livingston Depot Center**.

Lying among four mountain ranges, some of them snow-capped all year, and astride a world-class river, Livingston has attracted artists, writers, actors and musicians. Despite the tiny population, the town and its county boast three resident theater companies. The works of local artists are displayed in more than a dozen fine galleries. Some of the art is traditional, centering on Western, wildlife and angling scenes; much of it, however, is contemporary. Many of the galleries carry pottery, Montana porcelain, basketry, and jewelry.

SPECIAL FEATURE

• **The Yellowstone River** is world-famous for its fishing. The river is also ideal for boating, floating and kayaking. Both whitewater and scenic trips lasting from a half-day up to a week are available through commercial raft companies.

> *The fabulous flyfishing scenes in "A River Runs Through It" were filmed on the nearby Gallatin River.*
> *Livingston is the original and only year-round entry to Yellowstone National Park.*

WHERE TO STAY

Davis Creek B&B, P. O. Box 2179, (406) 222-8319. In rural setting between Livingston and Yellowstone National Park. $$

Greystone Inn B&B, 122 S. Yellowstone St., (406) 222-8319. Spacious home on banks of Yellowstone, full breakfasts. $$

Montana Ranch B&B, P. O. Box 4238, (406) 686-4946. Working family cattle ranch near Yellowstone National Park, fishing. $$

WHERE TO EAT

Calamity Jane's, P. O. Box 648, (406) 222-1071. 1800s atmosphere, steaks, seafood, in downtown historic district. $$

Winchester Cafe, 201 W. Park St., (406) 222-2708. American menu, extensive wine selection, homemade desserts, Western-style breakfasts. $ to $$

FURTHER INFORMATION

Livingston Area Chamber of Commerce, 212 W. Park St., Livingston, MT 59047, (406) 222-0850.

DIRECTIONS

From Billings (MT), I 94 west to exit 332 (Livingston exit).

RED LODGE, MONTANA

Population: 1,958

Winding through the the highest driveable points in both Montana and Wyoming, the 65-mile **Beartooth Scenic Byway** is one of the country's, indeed the world's, most beautiful highways. At one end of the byway is the northeastern gateway to **Yellowstone National Park** At the other end is **Red Lodge**, an old western town tucked Hollywood-style below spectacular mountains and big blue Montana skies.

Nearly all of Red Lodge's downtown district has been added to the National Register of Historic Places. The district includes many stone and brick buildings, their facades restored, dating from the 1880s to 1915. Especially interesting are the original railroad station house (1889) and a group of buildings, known as *Old Town*, that formed the town's business center from 1886-1893.

Among the displays at the **Carbon County Historical Museum** are rodeo memorabilia, the town's first telephone switchboard, and the homestead cabin of

John Johnston, known as "Liver Eatin' Johnson," on whose story the movie *Jeremiah Johnson* was based.

Red Lodge is the site of one of the country's foremost summer festivals, the **Festival of Nations**. The ancestry of the festival can be traced to the 1880s when the discovery of coal attracted hundreds of Finnish, Italian, Scandinavian and other miners to Red Lodge. Later, about 1949, the Festival of Nations was established to help the various cultural groups learn more about each other.

Each day of the 9-day August festival is assigned to a different culture. There are dances, songs, parades and other entertainment along with information on cooking, crafts, customs and languages. On the evening of the day assigned to the Scots, for example, bagpipes, kilts and dancers fill the streets and bars until the last watering hole closes. It's international learning and party time.

As for outdoor forms of recreation, Red Lodge is a four-season paradise. There's downhill skiing at **Red Lodge Mountain Ski Area**, cross-country skiing at **Red Lodge Nordic Center**, white-water rafting trips, bicycling, horseback riding, golfing and fantastic trout fishing.

> *Around 1886 there were four men to every woman in Red Lodge.*
> *Although just 65 miles long, the Beartooth Scenic Byway will demand at least 2 1/2 to 3 hours of your time — you'll simply not want to speed past the views of the glaciers, snow-capped mountains and alpine lakes and plateaus.*

WHERE TO STAY

Pitcher Guest Houses, P. O. Box 3450, (406) 446-2859. Historic 3- and 4-bedroom townhouses, kitchens, woodburning stoves. $$ to $$$

The Pollard Hotel, 2 N. Broadway, (800) 765-5273. Restored historic hotel, TV & phones, racquetball, saunas, hot tubs. $$$

Willows Inn, 224 S. Platt Ave., (406) 446-3913. Renovated 1903 boardinghouse, large sundeck, mountain views, homebaked pastries, two cottages. $$

WHERE TO EAT

Bogart's, 11 S. Broadway, (406) 446-1784. Humphrey Bogart memorabilia, Mexican food, pizzas. $

Old Piney Dell, P. O. Box 212, (406) 446-1111. Steaks, seafood, poultry, catches of the day, rustic atmosphere. $$

17 Broadway "The Restaurant," P. O. Box 1175, (406) 446-1717. Gourmet menu catering to everyone from Montana beef lover to California herbivore. $$

FURTHER INFORMATION

Red Lodge Area Chamber of Commerce, P. O. Box 988, Red Lodge, MT 59068, (406) 446-1718.

DIRECTIONS

From Billings (MT), I 94 west to exit 434 (Laurel exit), US 212 south to Red Lodge.

NEBRASKA

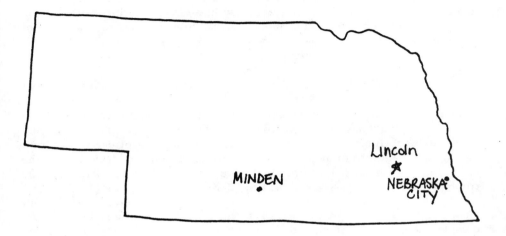

MINDEN

Lincoln

NEBRASKA
CITY

MINDEN, NEBRASKA

Population: 2,749

The cozy little Nebraska prairie town of **Minden** fits about every romantic notion of what a wholesome American hometown ought to be. In the middle of the town square is an old and imposing courthouse with a magnificent white dome. Around the square are prosperous businesses and, bowing to the romantic, no fewer than seven antique shops. Not far from the square is an area of beautiful homes, some with more rooms than really make sense, built by Minden's Victorian-era doctors and lawyers. Finally, there are the farms with their rich irrigated cornfields.

Minden has something else, though, that makes the town just a little different from other prairie towns: Just a few blocks north of the square is the **Harold Warp Pioneer Village**, one of the top museums of its kind in the country. Within the some 26 buildings of this award-winning museum are exhibits employing 50,000 items to trace the development from 1830 onwards of everything from lighting and bath tubs to motorcycles and musical instruments. Included are the oldest internal combustion engine (1876), the oldest jet airplane (1942), an 1890 combine pulled by 30 horses, and the first "Kelvinator" refrigerator (1925).

Among the museum's buildings are several historic structures situated about a *village green*. Included are Minden's first church (1884), an original livery stable complete with harness shop, and an authentic replica of a sod house. The museum also presents daily weaving, broom-making and other craft demonstrations.

Earning Minden the nickname *The Christmas City*, the square and the **Kearney County Courthouse**, especially the dome, are strung every Christmas with 10,000 lights. The lights are turned on as the climax of a Christmas pageant held the last Saturday night in November and the first two Sunday nights in December (the lights are also on every evening from the first production of the pageant until New Year's Day).

SPECIAL FEATURES

• **Fort Kearny State Historical Park** northwest of Minden was once an outpost on the **Oregon Trail**. The park features several re-created structures, including a stockade, along with period artifacts.

• **Fort Kearny State Recreation Area** north of town is the site of the sandhill crane spring migration. Nature lovers will especially enjoy the 5-mile hike-bike trail.

> *Christmas lights were first strung on the courthouse dome in 1915. For many years the bulbs were colored by hand dipping.*

WHERE TO STAY

Prairie View B&B, P. O. Box 137, (308) 832-0123. Afternoon tea served on deck overlooking prairie, bicycles, lawn games, full breakfasts. $ to $$

WHERE TO EAT

City Cafe, 413 N. Colorado Ave., (308) 832-2788. Roast beef, turkey and dressing, ham, baked chicken, solid Midwestern cooking. $

FURTHER INFORMATION

Minden Chamber of Commerce, 509 N. Colorado Street, Minden, NE 68959, (308) 832-1811.

DIRECTIONS

From Omaha, I 80 west to exit 279, NE 10 south to Minden.

NEBRASKA CITY, NEBRASKA

Population: 6,547

The lovely old Missouri River town of **Nebraska City** has a downtown that nicely demonstrates how the old and the new can work together to yield something very charming. It seems that a factory outlet shop established itself on a downtown Nebraska City street and did so well that other small outlet shops followed, interspersing themselves among the town's regular downtown retail establishments. Perceiving the benefits of the new shops, the community proceeded to plant the area with trees and flowers and to add Victorian park benches and period streetlights and trolleys. The result is a beautiful and healthy old-new downtown street.

Set among apple and cherry orchards and heir to over 300 properties on the National Register of Historic Places, Nebraska City was already special long before the arrival of the factory outlets. A good way to see the town is to park your car (free parking) and hop a trolley. The CoC distributes a map of the "trolley trail" and sights along the way.

Among the historic homes served by the trolley is the 10-room **Wildwood Period House**, a Gothic Revival house of 1860s vintage (open to the public), and the **Taylor-Wessel-Nelson House**, considered the finest example of Greek Revival architecture in Nebraska. The latter is now home to the Otoe County Historical Society and may be seen by appointment. Other important sights on the tour are the very Victorian 1880s **Farmers Bank**, winner of the President's National Preservation Award, and the **Old Freighter's Museum**, headquarters of an 1859 freight company and now a history museum (open by appointment).

Best times to visit the town's three orchards are during blossom time, usually the first week of May, and at harvest time, beginning around mid-September. The most famous of the orchards is the **J. Sterling Morton Orchard and Tree Farm** (a National Historic Landmark), named in honor of and forming part of the original estate of the founder of Arbor Day. Barns from the early 1900s, apple sorting and packing, and cider making are among the sights open to visitors.

The elegant 52-room Colonial Revival **Morton mansion** is the central feature of adjacent **Arbor Lodge State Historical Park and Arboretum** A large variety of native trees and shrubs may be seen on the mansion's grounds.

John Brown's Cave and Historical Village features a cabin reputed to be the oldest surviving structure in Nebraska (ca. 1852). Beneath the cabin is a cave that was once a station on the **Underground Railroad**. Also on the property are 18 buildings from various period's in Nebraska City's history.

SPECIAL FEATURES

· The **Meriwether Lewis Steamboat Museum of Missouri River History**, river cruises, and various cultural events add to the charm of **Brownville**, an old steamboat port and one of Nebraska's oldest settlements, downriver from Nebraska City.

> *Nebraska City is a major antique center.*
> *Escaping slaves were fed cornbread and water and allowed to spend the night at John Brown's Cave before resuming their trip north.*

WHERE TO STAY

Thompson House B&B, P. O. Box 162 (Brownville, NE), (402) 825-6551. Restored 1869 house, period antiques, family-style breakfasts. $$ to $$$

Whispering Pines B&B, RR 2, (402) 873-5850. Brick Italianate home with wrap-around veranda, view of pines, full breakfasts. $$

WHERE TO EAT

Lied Conference Center, 2700 Sylvan Rd., (800) 546-5433. "Wholesome American fare" served in rustic Steinhart Lodge. $$

Ulbrick's Cafe, 1513 S. 11th St., (402) 873-5458. Converted filling station with plastic-covered tables, fried chicken, pies homemade with pure lard, a local legend. $

FURTHER INFORMATION

Chamber of Commerce, 806 1st Avenue, Nebraska City, NE, 68410, (402) 873-3000.

DIRECTIONS

From Omaha, US 75 south to Nebraska City.

NEVADA

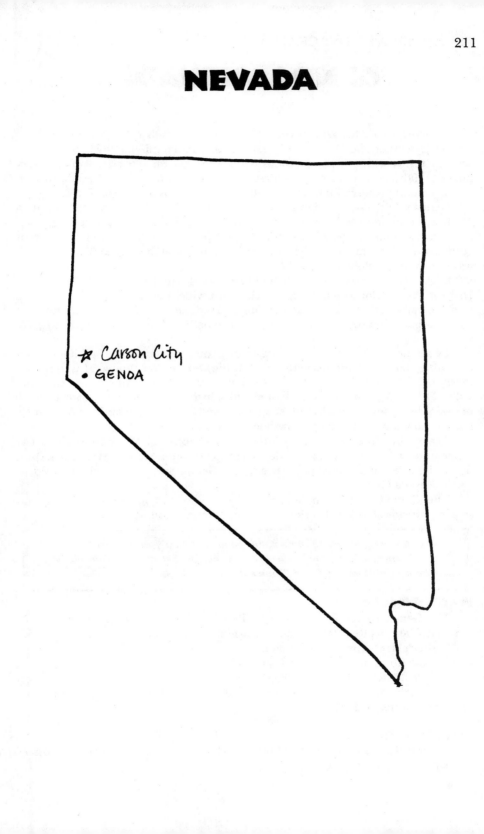

★ Carson City
• GENOA

GENOA, NEVADA

Population: 200

A picturesque Old West town tucked in the foothills of the **Sierra Nevada**, **Genoa** is neither the skeleton of a late 19th-century mining town nor a 20th century resort with glittering casinos. Genoa (accent on second syllable) is very much a 19th century town, the oldest non-Indian settlement in Nevada in fact, but its careful preservation is very much 20th-century, as are its comforts.

Genoa's Old West credentials are impressive. The town was established in 1851 as a trading post, known as **Mormon Station**, that served as a resting place and provisioning station for fur traders and prospectors dreaming of silver or gold. From 1855 until 1916 the town was a county seat, and in 1860 and 1861 it was a stop on the Pony Express.

Today Genoa has nearly 30 buildings listed on the National Register of Historic Places. Construction dates include every decade from the 1850s onward into the early 20th century. The buildings served, and in some cases continue to serve, as guest houses, stores, homes, a dance hall, a Masonic Hall, even a health spa.

By all means the best known and most photographed of the buildings is the charming **Genoa Courthouse** (1865). Now the **Genoa Courthouse Museum**, this lovely brick building served as a courthouse until 1916, then as a school until 1956. The museum has a diversity of exhibits, including the original courtroom, a period schoolroom, a blacksmith shop with hand-forged tools, and antique ranching/farming items, including snowshoes for a horse.

Across the street from the courthouse is a replica of Mormon Station. The replica and historical exhibit inside make up **Mormon Station State Park** Just down the street is another popular site, the **Genoa Saloon**, allegedly the oldest bar in Nevada (1850s).

The Carson Valley can be toured by bicycle, but hot-air ballooning and soaring (world-class) are also exciting ways of getting around.

> *The townspeople make some 3,000 pounds of candy in preparation for the annual "Candy Dance," held the last weekend in September. Now attracting thousands of visitors, the Candy Dance started in 1919.*

WHERE TO STAY

The Genoa House Inn B&B, P. O. Box 141, (702) 782-7075. Restored 1872 home on National Register, antiques, morning coffee at door, refreshments. $$$

Walley's Hot Springs, 2001 Foothill Rd., (702) 782-8155. Historic cottage accommodations, hot mineral springs, pool, fitness center. $$$

The Wild Rose Inn B&B, P. O. Box 256, (702) 782-5697. Reproduction Queen Ane home, antiques, old toys and oak telephones, private baths, full breakfasts, wine. $$$

WHERE TO EAT

Casentini's, 2285 Main St., (702) 782-5414. Italian food, small with lots of atmosphere, locally popular. $$

Inn Cognito, Genoa Ln., (702) 782-8898. Continental cuisine, Cajun and wild game specialties. $$

The Pink House, Main St. & Genoa Ln., (702) 782-3939. Steak and seafood in 1904 guest house. $$

FURTHER INFORMATION

Carson Valley Chamber of Commerce, 1524 Highway 395, Suite 1, Gardnerville, NV 89423, (800) 727-7677.

DIRECTIONS

From Reno, US 395 south (through Carson City) to NV 206, NV 206 southwest to Genoa.

NEW HAMPSHIRE

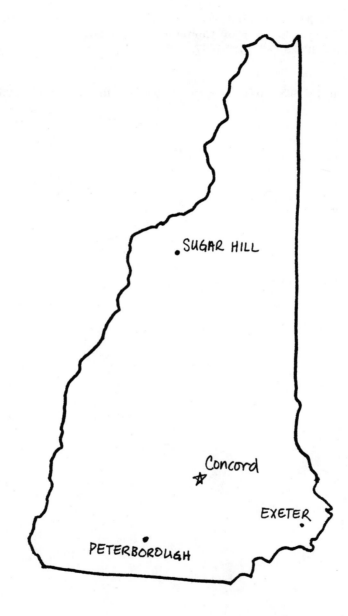

SUGAR HILL

Concord

EXETER

PETERBOROUGH

EXETER, NEW HAMPSHIRE

Population: 9556

Founded in 1638 and located on a tidal river, railroad line, and major highways, **Exeter** possesses the kind of sophistication that comes with centuries of contact and commerce with peoples from other parts. The town not only has a long, but also a rich history, one distinguished by individualism and Revolutionary rebellion and patriotism.

Exeter's architectural diversity gives tangible expression to its wisdom and long history. Buildings from every era line the town's streets. The best way to explore the architecture is by foot (the CoC publishes a brochure for walking tours.) A good starting point for a tour is **Front Street**, bordered by an exceptional collection of handsome Federal-style houses. The 1798 **Congregational Church** is also on this street.

The attractive campus of historic **Phillips Exeter Academy** (1781), also on Front Street, has more than 100 buildings. The 1970 library by Louis Kahn and the ornate 1897 Gothic church are of special architectural interest.

Elsewhere is the **Ladd-Gilman House** (1721), a national landmark that is now the **American Independence Museum**. Included in the museum's collections are one of three Purple Hearts awarded by George Washington, handwritten documents of General and President Washington, and one of the 24 surviving copies of the original Declaration of Independence.

The older part of the **Gilman Garrison House** was built in the mid 1600s of hewn logs. Originally a garrison, the structure was remodeled in the 18th century. Period furnishings include Daniel Webster's desk (open to the public).

Visitors may want to visit some of Exeter's specialty shops. Among the offerings are fine old books, unique gifts for children, and imported foods.

The IOKA Theatre (1915) is one of the oldest movie theaters in the country still in operation.

In 1776 New Hampshire became the first of the colonies to adopt an independent state constitution.

WHERE TO STAY

Inn of Exeter, 90 Front St., (800) 782-8444. Charming Georgian inn on campus of Phillips Exeter Academy, tennis, exercise equipment. $$$

WHERE TO EAT

Inn of Exeter (see above). Creative recipes, gracious dining rooms. $ to $$.

The Starving Chef, 237 Water St., (603) 772-5590. Creative international cuisine, daily seafood specials. $ to $$.

FURTHER INFORMATION

The Exeter Area Chamber of Commerce, 120 Water Street, Exeter, NH 03833, (603) 772-2411.

DIRECTIONS

From Manchester, NH 101 east to NH 108, NH 108 south to Exeter.

PETERBOROUGH, NEW HAMPSHIRE

Population: 5,243

Peterborough is a 19th-century mill town, with old brick buildings that once housed water-powered industries. Unlike many of the New England communities in this guide, which survive largely on tourists and retirees and the past, Peterborough is a working town with business offices, banks, and law firms.

The best introduction to the town is via the **Peterborough Museum**, the intriguing museum of the town's historical society. The museum traces the evolution of Peterborough's economy from a farming community through an Industrial Revolution mill town to a present-day center for magazine publishing. Included in the museum is an old-fashioned country store and restored, furnished houses where girls working in the textile mills once lived.

Long a cultural center, Peterborough is home to one of the best summer theaters in the country, the **Peterborough Players**. The **New England Marionette Theatre**, the country's largest marionette theater devoted primarily to opera, is also here. With the help of skilled puppeteers, the colorful marionettes delight audiences with four performances weekly from May through December.

The galleries of the **Sharon Arts Center**, a few miles south of Peterborough, have shows throughout the year. The center sponsors classes in arts and crafts ranging from painting and weaving to stained glass and printmaking. There is also a shop offering high-quality crafts.

As for the musical arts, the **Monadnock region** offers an impressive series of summer programs. The **MacDowell Colony** is a retreat where composers and other artists can concentrate on their work without outside intrusion. Founded in 1907, the colony evolved from a farm owned by composer Edward MacDowell.

SPECIAL FEATURES

• Peterborough is surrounded by tiny villages of the Christmas-card variety. Some of the prettiest are **Hancock, Dublin, Harrisville,** and **Francestown.**

> *A stay in Peterborough in the 1930s inspired Thornton Wilder to write "Our Town." Peterborough was the site of the play's world premiere.*
>
> *Nearby Mt. Monadnock is the single most climbed mountain in North America.*

WHERE TO STAY

Apple Gate B&B, 199 Upland Farm Rd. (NH 123 S), (603) 924-6543. 1832 home in apple orchards, private baths, candlelight breakfasts. $$

WHERE TO EAT

The Boilerhouse at Noone Falls, US 202 S, (603) 924-9486. Outdoor dining overlooking waterfall, award-winning wine list. $$

Latacarta, 6 School St., (603) 924-6878. Former movie theater, organically grown vegetables, beautiful presentation. $$

FURTHER INFORMATION
The **Greater Peterborough Chamber of Commerce**, P. O. Box 401, Peterborough, NH 03458, (603) 924-7234.

DIRECTIONS
From Manchester, NH 101 southwest to Peterborough.

SUGAR HILL, NEW HAMPSHIRE

Population: 464

Relaxing quietly in the majestic White Mountains, **Sugar Hill** is the quintessential New England village of poet and painter — a place of country auctions, maple sugaring, sleigh rides, old farmhouses, spectacular fall foliage and fields of lupine. The village has changed very little in 100 years, and the villagers work hard to keep it that way. No fast-food, strip-mall, discount-store sprawl spoils the scene.

Once a farming settlement, then an iron-mining community, then a fashionable resort of great hotels, Sugar Hill is today a friendly little village with nothing much more commercial than an old-fashioned store (with excellent cheddar cheese), renowned pancake parlor (see below) and several quaint old inns. The village's **Meeting House** was built in 1831 and the post office has just one room.

The Sugar Hill Historical Museum preserves the village's past with photograhic archives, horse-drawn vehicles and a reproduction of a stagecoach tavern kitchen. An audio-visual show aids in the presentation.

Sugar Hill's tranquil beauty is first and foremost designed for strolling and contemplating and reading. But more active pursuits are also in order. The area boasts many fine hiking trails; inquire locally for trail descriptions and maps. There are also opportunities for fly fishing, golfing, bicycling, skiing, and swimming (at **Echo Lake**). Rock climbing and soaring are available for lovers of heights.

SPECIAL FEATURES
• **Franconia Notch** and **Franconia Notch State Park** are located just a few miles south of Sugar Hill. Franconia Notch is a mountain pass that is traversed for eight miles by a unique interstate parkway. Within the park are the **Old Man of the Mountain** (the famous natural rock formation), the **Flume** (a natural gorge) and the **Basin** (a smooth granite pothole beneath a beautiful waterfall). Other major attractions include the **New England Ski Museum** and the **Cannon Mountain Aerial Tramway**, the latter occupies the site of the first passenger aerial tramway in North America (1938).
• **Frost Place**, Robert Frost's home in nearby Franconia, displays first editions

of Frost's work, photographs and other memorabilia of the great poet. Plaques bearing Frost's poems are placed along the lovely Poetry Trail. (Inquire in advance for hours.)

> *Sugar Hill was the site of the country's first ski school (1929).*
> *Actress Bette Davis was once a summer resident of the village.*

WHERE TO STAY

Blanche's B&B, 351 Easton Valley Rd. (Franconia), (603) 823-7061. Restored 19th-century farmhouse, decorative painting throughout, home-cooked breakfasts. $$

Bungay Jar, P. O. Box 15 (Franconia), (603) 823-7775. Built from 18th-century barn, two-story common area, country antiques, homemade buffet-style breakfasts, afternoon tea/snacks. $$

Foxglove, NH 117 at Lovers Lane, (603) 823-8840. Renovated turn-of-century country home, woodland setting, innkeeper an interior decorator, private baths, North Country-flavored breakfasts. $$$

The Hilltop Inn, NH 117, (603) 823-5695. Victorian inn, English flannel sheets, porch rockers, private baths, country breakfasts, restaurant. $$

Sugar Hill Inn, NH 117, (603) 823-5621. Restored 19th-century inn, mountain views, private baths, country breakfasts, afternoon tea, restaurant. $$$

WHERE TO EAT

Hilltop Inn (see above). Appetizers include Cream of Fiddlehead & Mushroom Soup, Chilled White Gazpacho, Fresh Eggplant Sauteed in a Beer Batter. $$

Polly's Pancake Parlor, NH 117, (603) 823-5575. Home-made buckwheat/cornmeal/oatmeal buttermilk/whole wheat pancakes and waffles, corn-cob smoked bacon and ham, a Sugar Hill tradition. $

Sugar Hill Inn (see above). Chicken Sugar Hill, Beef Tournedos, Spinach Fettucini, fresh seafood, menu changes daily. $$

Sunset Hill House, Sunset Hill Rd., (800) 786-4455. "Pan-seared rainbow trout with herbed hash-brown cakes and walnut sauce." $$

FURTHER INFORMATION

Franconia-Easton-Sugar Hill Chamber of Commerce, P. O. Box 780, Franconia, NH 03580, (800) 237-9007.

DIRECTIONS

From Boston, I 93 north to exit 38 (Franconia), NH 18 north 1/2 mile to NH 117, NH 117 west to Sugar Hill.

NEW JERSEY

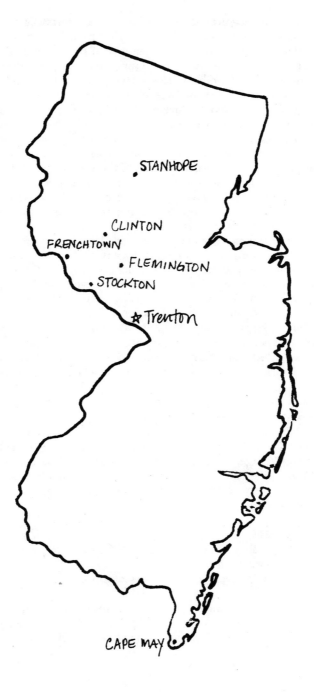

STANHOPE

CLINTON

FRENCHTOWN

FLEMINGTON

STOCKTON

★ Trenton

CAPE MAY

CAPE MAY, NEW JERSEY

Population: 4,668

One of the country's premier Victorian seaside resorts, **Cape May** is among the elite of America's charming towns. If in your mind's eye you can replace the cars with carriages, and the shorts and jeans with bustles and parasols, you can see the town pretty much the way it was. Gorgeous Victorian homes and inns still grace the streets, and visitors still relax on verandas or stroll the sidewalks and seaside promenade. The views and breezes from the sea are timeless, of course.

No one has yet explained the lure of the sea, but Cape May is surviving proof that, whatever its nature, that lure has been around for many generations. The town was known as a resort when New Jersey was still a British colony. Steamship service between Cape May and Philadelphia began in the early 1800s and was soon followed by regular railroad service. Over the years the resort has entertained a number of presidents and other prominent people — including Congressman Abraham Lincoln. Thanks to the growth of Atlantic City in the early 20th century, Cape May stopped developing and became forever fixed in the colorful closing decades of the 19th century.

Cape May's National Historic Landmark District has over 600 preserved Victorian buildings, a number impressive by any standard. The buildings display an unusually wide variety of architectural styles and ornamentation. A stroll among them is a pleasure any time, including after dark, when the streets are lit by gas lamps. There are maps for self-guided walking tours, and visitors wishing guided tours will be dazzled by the number of options.

The **Emlen Physick Estate** (1881), an 18-room Stick-style mansion designed by Frank Furness, is one of the most important of the historic homes. The house and its Eastlake-style furniture may be seen by tour. Many of the most interesting of the other historic houses are now bed-and-breakfast inns (see expanded listing below).

Cape May's attractions are hardly confined to Victorian homes and inns. The **Cape May Point Lighthouse** (1859) guards the shipping lanes between Delaware Bay and the Atlantic Ocean. Now a museum, the lighthouse features displays on its history as well as a 199-step spiral staircase leading to a spectacular view.

Cold Spring Village, north of town, is a re-created 19th-century South Jersey farm village. Included among the restorations are an old jailhouse, an 18th-century inn, a country store and a restaurant. There are also craft shops and demonstrations.

SPECIAL FEATURES

• The **Cape May Bird Observatory** is widely known for its many entertaining programs and bird-watching opportunities.

• The **Cape May Whale Watch and Research Center** offers cruises for whale- and dolphin-watchers.

• Historic **Lewes, Delaware** is only 70 minutes away on the *Cape May-Lewes Ferry*. The ferry offers daily service; during July and August twilight and moonlight cruises are also offered. Passengers may walk, bicycle or drive aboard.

WHERE TO STAY

The Abbey, Columbia Ave. & Gurney St., (609) 884-4506. 1869 Gothic Revival mansion with 60-foot tower, stained-glass windows, beach passes. $$$

Angel of the Sea, 5-7 Trenton Ave., (800) 848-3369. Restored 1850 home, full breakfasts, teas, one of the most elegant anywhere. $$$

Colvmns by the Sea, 1513 Beach Dr., (609) 884-2228. Elegant Victorian home, antiques, gourmet breakfasts, high teas, sherry by the fire. $$$

Sea Holly Inn, 815 Stockton Ave., (609) 884-6294. Ocean-view rooms, private baths, antiques, full breakfasts, afternoon teas. $$$

The Virginia Hotel, 25 Jackson St., (800) 732-4236. Restored 19th-century hotel on charming street, balconies, Victorian and contemporary luxuries. $$$

White Dove Cottage, 619 Hughes St., (800) 321-3683. Restored 1866 home, private baths, air-conditioned, in historic district. $$$

Windward House, 24 Jackson St., (609) 884-3368. Edwardian seaside inn, private baths, full breakfasts, beach passes, bicycles. $$$

WHERE TO EAT

410 Bank Street, 410 Bank St., (609) 884-2127. Quaint and intimate, Creole cuisine. $$

The Lobster House, Fisherman's Wharf, (609) 884-8296. Seafood served on wharf, nautical atmosphere, assorted menu. $$

The Mad Batter, 19 Jackson St., (609) 884-5970. Award-winning restaurant of historic inn, fresh seafood, garden terrace. $$

Washington Inn, 801 Washington St., (609) 884-5697. Lovely 1848 home in heart of town, imaginative Continental/American menu. $$

Watson's Merion Inn, 106 Decatur St., (609) 884-8363. Victorian inn in historic district, several dining rooms, seafood entrees. $$

FURTHER INFORMATION

Cape May Chamber of Commerce, P. O. Box 109, Cape May, NJ 08204, (609) 884-5508.

DIRECTIONS

From Philadephia/Camden, I 76 south to NJ 42, NJ 42 south to Atlantic City Expwy., Atlantic City Expwy to Garden State Pkwy., Garden State Pkwy. south to Cape May.

CLINTON, NEW JERSEY

Population: 2,054

A river lends charm to a town, and if there happens to be an old mill on the river, so much the better. Clinton rests on the banks of *two* rivers, the **Raritan** and **Spruce Run**, and near the confluence of the rivers are *two* picture-book mills.

To get from one mill to the other you must cross a renovated and very sturdy 1870 iron bridge. As if that weren't enough, the mills are separated by a 320-ft. wide waterfall!

The **red mill**, now the **Clinton Historical Museum** and one of the most photographed buildings in New Jersey, was built around 1763. Displayed in the museum are items from the everyday lives of New Jersey's people from 1690 to 1900. On the grounds is a country village with blacksmith shop, 1860 schoolhouse, turn-of-the-century general store and barbershop, and interior of an old post office.

The old stone mill, now the **Hunterdon Art Center**, was built on the other side of the river in 1836. The center sponsors exhibits and classes, concerts and a children's summer theater.

The rivers can be enjoyed by relaxing on the banks (the grounds of the red mill are ideal for this) or launching a canoe. The town's lovely 19th-century homes can be seen by a strolling or driving tour; either way, however, you may have to stop to let the geese and ducks waddle by. There are lots of these birds around, and that means you must also watch where you step.

SPECIAL FEATURE
• Composting toilets, a passive solar heating unit, and other experimental projects coexist with display gardens, nature trails, and an 1890 gazebo in the 63-acre **Hunterdon County Arboretum** six miles south of town.

> *The several owners of the red mill used it to grind flax seeds (for linseed oil), grain, talc and graphite.*

WHERE TO STAY
Leigh Way B&B Inn, 66 Leigh St., (908) 735-4311. Restored 1862 home, antiques, walking distance to Main Street and mills. $$$

WHERE TO EAT
Clinton House, 2 W. Main St., (908) 730-9300. German and American dishes, prime rib, fish. $$

FURTHER INFORMATION
Skylands Region Tourism Council, 330 Route 206 South, Newton, NJ 07860, (201) 579-3933.

DIRECTIONS
From Newark, I 78 west to exit 15 (Clinton exit).

FLEMINGTON, NEW JERSEY

Population: 4,047

Flemington is situated in the pretty rolling countryside of northwestern New Jersey. Sometimes described as a *Victorian town*, Flemington was the second community in New Jersey to be granted an historic district designation. The town has become a medley of beautiful old streets, preserved by careful restoration and stringent building codes, and attractive, up-to-date shopping facilities (see below).

Although much of Flemington is indeed Victorian, some of the town's buildings predate Queen Victoria's reign. For example, the county courthouse, with Greek Revival features, was built in the late 1820s. The town's oldest structure is **Fleming Castle**, built in 1756 by the town's founder, Samuel Fleming. Once an inn, the castle is really a two-story Georgian home (shown by appointment). The **Union Hotel** (1862, altered 1877-1878) is Flemington's most imposing Victorian structure. The ornate, towered structure has hosted a social register of celebrities and is still renowned for its restaurant (see below).

Flemington developed as an agricultural market; joining many other New Jersey communities in the industrial revolution of the 19th century, however, the economy turned to pottery, cut glass (later) and other manufacturing. The newest "industry" is shopping: the town has no fewer than five factory outlet centers, all served in a loop by a trolley. The largest of the centers, **Liberty Village**, is patterned after an early American village, with colonial-style shops, brick walkways and gardens. Many clothing and specialty shops are also located downtown. The town's numerous antique shops are described in a separate CoC brochure, complete with map.

Alternatives — or additions — to shopping include champagne hot-air balloon flights and bicycle tours. Bicycles may be rented for self-guided tours; rentals come with maps showing suggested cycling routes. Another very pleasant activity is to combine a picnic in the countryside with a wine- tasting and vineyard tour.

SPECIAL FEATURE
• The **Black River & Western Railroad** offers an 11-mile round trip between Flemington and Ringoes on a vintage train pulled by a steam engine.

> *Flemington's courthouse was the scene of the 1935 trial of Bruno Hauptmann for kidnapping and murdering Charles Lindbergh's infant son. Reporters at the trial collected at the Union Hotel.*

WHERE TO STAY
The Cabbage Rose Inn B&B, 162 Main St., (908) 788-0247. Queen Anne home crowned with open-air gazebo, antiques, fireplaces, grand piano, "scrumptious" breakfasts. $$$

Jerica Hill, 96 Broad St., (908) 782-8234. Queen Anne home, well-stocked bookcases, screened porch with white wicker, "bountiful" breakfasts, beverages/good sherry. $$$

WHERE TO EAT

Il Rustico, 300 Old Croton Rd., (908) 782-5488. In country setting, Italian cooking, house specialties, reservations recommended. $$

Jake's, US 202 S., (908) 806-3188. American entrees, prime rib, "scrumptious" sandwiches, 12 draught beers on tap. $

Old Vienna Restaurant & Bakery, 26 Main St., (908) 788-2677. Viennese and American cuisine, European pastries, Austrian chefs. $ to $$

Union Hotel, 76 Main St., (908) 788-7474. In historic Union Hotel, fish, prime rib, steaks. $$

FURTHER INFORMATION

Flemington Information Center, 260 US 202, Liberty Court, Suite #900, Flemington, NJ 08822, (908) 806-8165.

DIRECTIONS

From Newark, US 22 west to US 202 (near Bridgewater), US 202 west to NJ 31, NJ 31 north one mile to NJ 523, NJ 523 west to Flemington.

FRENCHTOWN, NEW JERSEY

Population: 1,528

New Yorkers (and others) seeking a picturesque little river town where the days are relaxed and the nights quiet are discovering **Frenchtown** on the Delaware. It isn't everyday that you can find such a place, especially one just 60 minutes out of New York City. But there it is, and let's hope it remains that way.

Frenchtown was on the map, although not necessarily by that name, as far back as the mid-18th century, when a ferry crossed the Delaware at this point. Over the years the town saw a gristmill, a sawmill, the **Delaware Canal**, and railroad, even a poultry industry. But the canal boats stopped and the railroad disappeared, and although the town never died, it did take a long sleep, not really changing much from about 1875 on. Then, 10 years or so ago, charm-loving kinds of people began to rediscover the town, and the restorations, art studios, and antique shops began to appear.

Although Frenchtown remains quiet, there is more to do than admire the setting, charming though it may be. Sophisticated shoppers will find what they're looking for off the cobblestone sidewalks of the antiqued **Main Street**. And sportsmen of all ages can find what they're looking for in or on the waters of the **Delaware River**; the Delaware is a *play river*, meaning that it's great for canoeing, tubing and other river sports.

SPECIAL FEATURE

• The bed of the old railroad has been converted to a first-class hiking/biking path.

WHERE TO STAY

The National Hotel, 31 Race St., (908) 996-4871. Restored 1851 hotel, antique-filled rooms, private baths, suites. $$ to $$$

The Old Hunterdon House, 12 Bridge St., (908) 996-3632. Restored 1864 Italianate mansion, period pieces, shaded sitting porch, private baths, sherry. $$$

WHERE TO EAT

The Frenchtown Inn, 7 Bridge St., (908) 996-3300. Potato Crusted Atlantic Salmon, Rosemary Skewered Gulf Shrimp, Baked Wellington of Pekin Duck. $$$

FURTHER INFORMATION

Skylands Region Tourism Council, 330 Route 206 S., Newton, NJ 07860, (201) 579-3933.

DIRECTIONS

From Newark, I 78 west to exit 15, NJ 513 south to Frenchtown.

STOCKTON, NEW JERSEY

Population: about 600

No more than 3 miles up the Delaware from Lambertville, **Stockton** consists of a couple of historic inns (see below), a wonderful old railroad station, a couple of craft shops, and maybe one grocery store. There are some interesting old homes on the side of the hill, but you won't see much of them from the main road (NJ 29). A narrow, old-fashioned truss bridge connects the little town with Pennsylvania across the Delaware. Situated as it is alongside the Delaware, the old **Delaware and Raritan (D & R) Canal**, and an old railroad bed turned hiking/ biking trail, Stockton is about as likely to be visited today by hikers, bikers and canoeists as by motorists.

Stockton began as a ferry town in the 18th century. The canal and then the railroad came in the 19th century. Now, with the ferry and railroad gone and the canal (actually a feeder for the main canal) long empty of commercial craft, the town survives on its charm and attractiveness as a home for people commuting to New York City and Philadelphia.

On the northern edge of town is the **Prallsville Mills** section of the **D & R Canal State Park**. Here, clustered on the canal, are an 1877 gristmill (open to the public), a 1794 linseed-oil mill, a sawmill, and several other historic structures. The beginning of the canal is a few miles farther north, at a point now occupied by the **Bull's Island** section of the state park. The park offers excellent canoeing, boating, fishing, hiking and birdwatching. Approximately 70 feet wide and 8 feet deep, the canal is ideal for canoeing — and safer than the adjoining **Delaware River**.

SPECIAL FEATURES
• The old railroad-bed trail leads south to **Trenton** and north to **Frenchtown** (see Frenchtown selection). Whether on the trail, canal or river, Stockton is an excellent place to "put into" for food, supplies and rest.

• **Sergeantsville**, four miles northeast of Stockton, is the site of **Green Sergeants Bridge**, New Jersey's last covered bridge.

The Delaware and Raritan Canal was dug by hand by Irish immigrants between 1830 and 1834.

WHERE TO STAY
Note: It was about the following inn that Richard Rodgers and Lorenz Hart wrote the song about "a small hotel, with a wishing well."

Colligan's Stockton Inn, 1 Main St., (609) 397-1250. Originally a 1710 home, wishing well, antiques, private baths, TV. $$ to $$$

The Woolverton Inn, 6 Woolverton Rd., (609) 397-0802. Late 18th-century mansion on magnificent grounds. $$ to $$$

WHERE TO EAT
Colligan's Stockton Inn (see above). American and Continental dishes, lovely historic setting, fireplaces. $$ to $$$

FURTHER INFORMATION
Delaware and Raritan Canal State Park, 643 Canal Rd., Somerset, NJ 08873, (908) 873-3050.

DIRECTIONS
From Trenton, NJ 29 north along Delaware River to Stockton.

WATERLOO VILLAGE, NEW JERSEY

Population: A tiny handful

Situated as it is in a valley alongside a beautiful winding river (the **Musconetcong**) and remains of an old canal, it's hard to believe that picturesque **Waterloo Village** is only minutes from the outer banks of New Jersey's suburbs. But it is, even though the setting is rural, in fact as well as appearance.

Deserted as the railroad, iron furnaces, and history in general moved elsewhere, tiny Waterloo Village (near **Stanhope**) never emerged from the 18th and 19th centuries. The village was an iron town in the 18th century — the forge in fact provided cannonballs for the Revolutionary effort — and then prospered as a canal town in the 19th century. By the 20th century, however, the place was largely forgotten. Then, in the early 1960s, Waterloo Village was "discovered," restored, and opened to the public.

Waterloo Village embraces about 30 structures. Among them are the **Wellington House** (now a museum), general store, **Stagecoach Inn**, and **Methodist Church** (1859). A canal museum, gristmill, blacksmith shop and saw mill provide excellent glimpses at the commercial and industrial life of another day. The village also contains an old farm site and an Indian village. As a general rule, buildings from the 1700s are of stone and those from the 1800s are frame.

As part of its new life, Waterloo Village has become a center for the arts. In the summer the **Waterloo Festival Orchestra** performs in the 2,800-seat concert tent. In addition, top artists perform everything from classical music and opera to jazz and rock during the annual summer music festival. Rounding out the cultural scene, the **Waterloo Festival for the Arts** sponsors a variety of events ranging from antique shows to an Irish festival.

SPECIAL FEATURE

• Like Waterloo Village, nearby **Stanhope** was once a forge town, iron-producing center and port on the **Morris Canal**. The town has many beautiful old houses.

Originally named Andover Forge, Waterloo Village received its present name after Napoleon's celebrated defeat in 1815.

WHERE TO STAY

Whistling Swan Inn, 110 Main St. (Stanhope), (201) 347-6369. Restored 1905 home, period furnishings, circular staircase, private baths, full breakfasts, teas. $$ to $$$

WHERE TO EAT

The Black Forest Inn, 249 US 206 (Stanhope), (201) 347-3344. German food, German decor, German-costumed waitresses, reservations advised. $$

Chequers, 134 NJ 183 (Stanhope), (201) 347-3777. English pub food, steak-and-kidney pie, English beers. $

FURTHER INFORMATION

Waterloo Village, Waterloo Rd., Stanhope, NJ 07874, (201) 347-0900.

DIRECTIONS

From Newark, I 280 west to I 80, I 80 west to exit 27, US 206 north to Stanhope.

NEW MEXICO

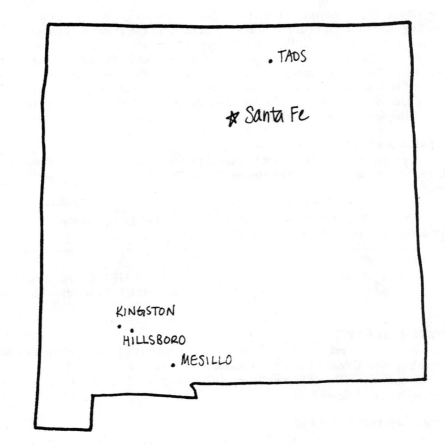

HILLSBORO/KINGSTON, NEW MEXICO

Population: 200/30

The old mining towns of **Hillsboro** (gold) and **Kingston** (silver) are two of the major finds of this guide. Few Americans have heard of these tiny spots. Indeed, many New Mexicans have never heard of them.

Both villages are tucked away far out on the rolling high desert of southwestern New Mexico. Neither is really on the way to anywhere. The road that leads to them eventually winds its way through the **Black Range** to the west, but there's nothing in particular on the other side of the mountains — except more spectacular scenery. Overhead the skies are true blue, and the waters coming down from the mountain are sparkling.

Although Hillsboro is on the desert, its **Main Street** passes through a natural grove of old cottonwood trees. Among the trees are several quaint shops, two art galleries and a bed and breakfast (see below). It's easy to see why movies and commercials have been filmed here. The town also has an old church (1882) that's still in use, the ruins of the old courthouse (the county seat was moved elsewhere in the early 1940s) and, on its outskirts, apple orchards, the reason for the town's annual **Apple Festival**. There's also a small museum, the **Black Range Museum**, that displays gold-mining artifacts dating from about 1875 to 1900.

Nothing much remains of tiny Kingston, nine miles down the road, but a few historic buildings and a lovely setting. There's an old brick assay office, the **Victorio Hotel** (now a private residence) and the **Percha Valley Bank Museum**, with its collection of mining artifacts and antiques (open by appointment).

SPECIAL FEATURE

• Although virtually in the middle of nowhere themselves, Hillsboro and Kingston are within excursion distance of the beautiful Black Range, the **Gila Cliff Dwellings National Monument**, the **City of Rocks State Park** and **Elephant Butte Lake State Park**.

> *Jane Fonda and Ted Turner's Ladder Ranch is located between Hillsboro and Truth or Consequences (to the east).*
>
> *Corpses used to be kept in the basement of the Victorio Hotel in Kingston until the spring thaw made burial possible.*

WHERE TO STAY

Black Range Lodge B&B, Kingston, (505) 895-5652. Late 1800s rock lodge, private baths. $$

The Enchanted Villa B&B Inn, Hillsboro, (505) 895-5686. Historic two-story adobe home built for British nobleman, full breakfasts, restaurant. $$

WHERE TO EAT

Enchanted Villa B&B Inn (see above). Home-cooked meals by appointment. $

Hillsboro Orchard & Sweetwood Bar-B-Que, Hillsboro, (505) 895-5642. Only brisket in the world smoked over apple wood, under-orchard dining. $

FURTHER INFORMATION

Black Range Business Association, P. O. Box 152, Hillsboro, NM 88042, (505) 895-5686.

DIRECTIONS

From Albuquerque, I 25 south to exit 63, NM 152 west to Hillsboro/Kingston.

MESILLA, NEW MEXICO

Population: 1,975

The Mexican-American town of **Mesilla** nicely fits the romantic stereotype of the Old Southwest: a plaza, a mission-style church and, of course, old one-story adobe buildings that front directly on the street. Many of the buildings are the same that lined the streets nearly a century and a half ago. Thanks to a zoning ordinance, the original scale of the town and the architectural character of the buildings are carefully preserved.

Also known as **La Mesilla** and **Old Mesilla,** Mesilla has a history that even Hollywood would have difficulty matching: Apache attacks, shootings, the trial of Billy the Kid, cockfights, caravans on the **Chihuahua Trail,** the signing of the **Gadsden Purchase** (1854), and arrivals and departures of the **Butterfield Overland Mail and Stage Line.** Prospering as a transportation center on a major route to the West Coast, and as a supply center for ranching and mining operations, Mesilla grew from a small settlement in the late 1840s to the largest town between San Antonio and San Diego in the 1880s. Then the inevitable happened: the railroad went to Las Cruces instead of Mesilla. Mesilla was left to wither.

San Albino Church, originally built in 1855 and rebuilt in 1906, overlooks the plaza. The church offers masses in Spanish as well as English. Many of the historic adobe buildings about the plaza now house galleries, boutiques, unique shops and restaurants (see below). The plaza area is the kind of place where strolling, shopping and sightseeing all blend together. The shops offer an excellent selection of Indian and Southwestern handmade jewelry, Kachinas, and Southwestern art and fashions.

About three blocks off the plaza is the **Gadsden Museum,** a house museum shown by guided tour. The museum features possessions, including the famous Gadsden Purchase painting, of the Albert Jennings Fountain family, a family prominent in Mesilla Valley history.

SPECIAL FEATURES

• During harvest time, chiles, melons, tomatoes and other produce can be bought at roadside stands along **NM 28** (south) and other highways in the **Rio Grande Valley.**

•Nearby **Las Cruces** has two interesting historic districts of its own. The streets of the **Mesquite Street Historic District** are lined with traditional adobe houses tinted with pastels or left in natural shades of beige. Turn-of-the-century houses and other buildings displaying a range of architectural styles, including Spanish-Pueblo Revival and Mission Revival, occupy the **Alameda Depot Historic District.**

> *The Mesilla Valley is known throughout New Mexico for its chiles. Strings of red chiles, called "ristras," are often hung for decoration.*
> *The wooden beams that support the roofs of adobe buildings are "vigas." The vigas, exposed on the ceiling, are an important element in New Mexican interior decoration.*

WHERE TO STAY

Hilltop Hacienda B&B, 2520 Westmoreland (Las Cruces), (505) 382-3556. On 18 acres with panoramic views, spacious verandas/patios, "delicious" breakfasts. $$

Lundeen's Inn of the Arts, 618 S. Alameda Blvd. (Las Cruces), (505) 526-3327. 1890 Mexican-Territorial inn adjoining art gallery, antiques, library, beverages. $$ to $$$

Meson de Mesilla, P. O. Box 1212, (800) 732-6025. Peaceful setting, private baths, gourmet breakfasts, bicycles, pool. $$ to $$$

WHERE TO EAT

Double Eagle Restaurant, on the plaza, (505) 523-6700. Dining "amidst the splendor of beautiful antiques." $ to $$

El Patio Restaurante y Cantina, on the plaza, (505) 524-0982. Mexican entrees and steaks, outdoor patio dining. $

Meson de Mesilla (see above). Continental cuisine, seafood and meat entrees. $$

La Posta Restaurant, just off plaza, (505) 524-3524. In old Butterfield Stage Building, "serving Mexican food since 1939." $

FURTHER INFORMATION

Las Cruces Convention & Visitors Bureau, 311 North Downtown Mall, Las Cruces, NM 88001, (800) 343-7827.

DIRECTIONS

From El Paso (TX), I 10 north to exit 140 (Las Cruces), NM 28 south to La Mesilla.

TAOS, NEW MEXICO

Population: 4065

Taos is a delightful alternation between ambience and art. The alternation is almost literal, with attention swinging between strolls along adobe streets and visits to world-class galleries. The ambience is itself only one step away from art. The walled gardens with their hollyhocks, arched entries and antique wooden doors have been the subjects of thousands of paintings and watercolors. An old adobe house with blue window frames and sashes and potted pink geraniums can bring out the artist in anyone.

There's more even than the ambience to induce the artist, however. There are the mountains, always changing in hue and brightness, and mesas, rivers and forests whose beauty seems only to increase with each change in season. Then there's that New Mexico light, with its special purity. Mix all of this together with the creative traditions of New Mexico's three principal cultures — Native American, Hispanic, and Anglo — and you have one of the world's major art centers.

Taos has 100 plus art galleries! Work varies from traditional to contemporary, and from the pure to the blended and interbred. In one shop you'll find pottery with intricate geometrical decoration from the Acoma pueblo, in the next will be handcrafted contemporary jewelry with shapes and colors defying any description beyond 'Southwestern" and "spectacular."

Top exhibits of Taos's art history can be found in the **Millicent Rogers Museum**, rich in variety of folk art, and the **Harwood Foundation Museum**, operated by the University of New Mexico and featuring works by Taos artists from 1898 to the present. Two other superb art collections are displayed in the **Fechin Institute**, the historic home of Russian emigre artist Nicolai Fechin, and the **Ernest Blumenschein Home and Museum**, built in the 1700s and furnished as it was when the artist lived there (1919 to 1960).

The massive adobe buttresses of the **San Francisco de Asis Church** (early 1700s) have made the church a popular subject for many artists, including Georgia O'Keeffe. The beautiful interior is famous for its Spanish religious carvings.

Nearby **Taos Ski Valley**, **Red River**, and **Angel Fire** offer some of the finest skiing in the U.S.

SPECIAL FEATURES

• The period rooms of the **Martinez Hacienda**, open to the public, provide a glimpse into Spanish Colonial life. The haciendas were self-sufficient villages that had to contend with the constant threat of Comanche and Apache raids.

• The **Taos Pueblo** is one of Taos's, and indeed New Mexico's, top sites. Composed of multi-story adobe buildings, the pueblo is the finest example of Pueblo architecture anywhere and has inspired the Pueblo Revival style now popular throughout the Southwest. Centuries old, the pueblo is still inhabited.

> *Contemporary Taos cooking is a creative blend of Mexican, Southwestern Spanish, Continental and California cuisines.*

WHERE TO STAY

Brooks Street Inn, P. O. Box 4954, (505) 758-1489. Adobe houses, shady walled garden, fireplaces, private baths, full breakfasts. $$$

Casa de la Chimeneas B&B Inn, P. O. Box 5303, (505) 758-4777. Adobe home in lush garden setting, fireplaces, TV, phones, gourmet breakfasts, hor d'oeuvres, highly rated. $$$

Orinda, P. O. Box 4451, (505) 758-8581. Old hacienda with spectacular mountain views, suites, kiva fireplaces, private entrances, "healthy" breakfasts. $$$

Salsa del Salto, P. O. Box 1468, (505) 776-2422. Two-story stone fireplace, down comforters, tennis, heated pool, gourmet breakfasts, convenient to Taos Ski Valley. $$$

Taos Hacienda Inn, P. O. Box 4159, (800) 530-3040. Walled hacienda on National Register, patios, fountains, original art, hand-crafted furniture, fireplaces, gourmet breakfasts. $$$

WHERE TO EAT

Apple Tree Restaurant, 123 Bent St., (505) 758-1900. Old adobe house with courtyard, guitarist, New Mexican and New American cooking. $$

Doc Martin's at the Taos Inn, 125 Pueblo Norte, (505) 758-1977. Southwest cuisine in historic building with courtyard, fireplaces. $$

Lambert's Restaurant, Pueblo Sur, (505) 758-1009. Historic building in land-scaped setting, contemporary American menu, famed dessert sampler. $$

Roberto's Restaurant, Kit Carson Rd., (505) 758-2434. New Mexican Spanish cooking. $

Tapas de Taos Cafe, 136 Bent St., (505) 758-9670. Eclectic tastes from around the world, unique and changing menu. $

FURTHER INFORMATION

Taos County Chamber of Commerce, P. O. Drawer I, Taos, NM 87571, (800) 732-8267.

DIRECTIONS

From Albuquerque, I 25 north to exit 282 (Santa Fe), US 84 north to Espanola, NM 68 north to Taos.

NEW YORK

LAKE PLACID

SKANEATELES

CAZENOVIA

Albany

COOPERSTOWN

CHAUTAUQUA

CORNING

COLD SPRING

SOUTHAMPT

CAZENOVIA, NEW YORK
Population: 3,007

The similarity of **Cazenovia** to a New England village is something visitors frequently note, especially as they drive down the hill and into town. Dating as far back as the early 1800s, the buildings downtown are of brick with quaint contrasting white door and window surrounds, and sometimes colonial-style shutters. Listed as an Historic District on the National Register, the downtown area is pure picture-postcard. The rest of the village, primarily residential, consists of stately old homes, tree-lined streets and lovingly maintained lawns and gardens.

Of special interest downtown is **Lincklaen House** (ca. 1835), one of the most gracious of the country's old inns (see listing below). Inside are high ceilings, carved moldings, colonial chandeliers and large fireplaces; visitors are welcome.

Lorenzo, just south of town, is a stately full front-gabled Adam mansion built in 1807. Preserved as the **Lorenzo State Historic Site**, the house has original furnishings, arboretum and magnificent views of the lake and surrounding hills.

Cazenovia's rolling setting is also very reminiscent of New England. The village is nestled at the foot of lovely **Cazenovia Lake**, popular with sailboaters. Country inns and cider mills dot the landscape. With winter comes cross-country skiing (there are numerous groomed trails), and a little later, maple sugaring.

SPECIAL FEATURES
• At **Chittenango Falls State Park**, just four miles from town, the water plunges 167 feet over ledges and boulders.
• One of the best ways to take in the local scenery is to make the ten-mile drive around Cazenovia Lake.

> *Many of Cazenovia's residents work in Syracuse, 25 hilly minutes away.*

WHERE TO STAY
The Apple Farm B&B, E. Pompey Hollow Rd., (315) 655-8466. Restored 1835 Greek Revival farmhouse in apple orchard, private baths, full breakfasts, tennis, trout fishing. $$ to $$$

The Brewster Inn, US 20, (315) 655-9232. 1890 summer home overlooking lake, antiques, library, lovely grounds, dockage. $$$

Edgewater Hollow B&B, 4880 W. Lake Rd., (315) 655-8407. Quiet wooded waterfront setting, deck, porch, private baths, wine, boat tours. $$ to $$$

Lincklaen House, 79 Albany St., (315) 655-3461. Hospitality for more than 150 years, individually stenciled rooms, private baths, phones, TV, President and Mrs. Cleveland among famous guests. $$$

Willowbank B& B, 21 Forman St., (315) 655-9868. 1810 home of Cazenovia's founder, on lake, full breakfasts, park & swimming adjacent. $$ to $$$

WHERE TO EAT
Brewster Inn (see above). On the water, Continental cuisine, award-winning chef and wine list. $$

Lincklaen House (see above). Elegant Main Dining Room and flowered Courtyard, American cuisine. $$

Wheatberry of Cazenovia, 63 Albany St., (315) 655-2102. Interesting dishes, acclaimed desserts. $ to $$

FURTHER INFORMATION

Central Leatherstocking Country, NY, 327 N. Main St., Herkimer, NY 13350, (800) 233-8778.

DIRECTIONS

From Syracuse, NY 92 southeast to Cazenovia.

CHAUTAUQUA, NEW YORK

Population: 350 to 10,000

The Chautauqua Institution was founded on the shores of **Chautauqua Lake** in 1874 as a summer school for Sunday-school teachers. A pioneer in adult education, the institution soon expanded to include other summer schools. Along the way lodgings ranging from cottages to grand hotels were built to house the students. Today Chautauqua Institution, a National Historic Landmark, is a self-contained Victorian village on the shores of an enchanting lake. The beautifully restored 1881 **Athenaeum Hotel** (see listing below) is one of the many Victorian buildings that in and of themselves would justify a visit here.

During the 9-week session, extending from late June to late August, admission is by gate ticket. In addition to the lodgings, the grounds are sprinkled with restaurants, shops, art galleries, a library and a broad array of educational and recreational facilities. Many of the activities are designed for children as well as adults. The gate ticket is good for all events and activities except opera and theater performances (for which separate tickets must be purchased). Special 3-, 4-, and 7-night vacation and cultural packages that combine lodgings (American or European plan) and gate tickets are available by reservation.

The arts are represented by a symphony orchestra; opera, dance, and theater companies; chamber music concerts; art exhibits; film festivals and concerts by popular entertainers. Dozens of 1-day, 1-week, 9-week and other courses offer instruction in everything from sailing and investment to writing and piano. Also, distinguished speakers deliver lectures on philosophy, politics and religion.

> *Admission to the grounds is open when the institution is not in session; many — but not all — of the hotels, restaurants and other facilities are closed, however.*

WHERE TO STAY

Note: The visitor may choose among a variety of accommodation options on Chautauqua's grounds — call or write for information.

The Athenaeum, P.O. Box 66, (800) 821-1881. Restored Victorian hotel facing Chautauqua Lake, tennis, golf. $$$

Plumbush B&B, (P. O. Box 332, RD 2, Mayville, 14757), (716) 789-5309. Circa 1865 restored home, music room with piano and organ, less than one mile to Chautauqua. $$$

WHERE TO EAT

Athenaeum Hotel (see above). Classic American cuisine, coat and tie, elegant. $$$

Hot Rock Cafe, on institution grounds, (716) 357-5383. Meals served on heated rocks. $

(**Tally Ho** and the **Festival Market** are two more of the several restaurants serving Chautauqua's grounds.)

FURTHER INFORMATION

Chautauqua Institution, Chautauqua, NY 14722, (800) 836-2787.

DIRECTIONS

From Buffalo, I 90 south to exit 60, NY 394 south to Chautauqua.

COLD SPRING, NEW YORK

Population: 1,998

If you take the Hudson Railroad north from New York City along the Hudson River, you'll soon enter a region where the river and the Appalachian Mountains meet. Along an especially beautiful stretch of the river in this region, about 50 miles from New York City, the train stops at **Cold Spring**, one of the most picturesque little towns in the Hudson Valley.

Main Street is flanked by shade trees and an array of charming 19th-century storefronts. There are more more than a dozen shops catering to collectors and lovers of antiques and memorabilia. There are also shops selling books, chocolates, nautical gifts, handcrafted jewelry, hand-knitted Irish sweaters, dried flowers, gourmet foods and unique clothing. There are also some good pubs. And Cold Spring, neighboring **Garrison**, and the surrounding region are renowned for their excellent restaurants (see sample below).

Cold Spring was a foundry town during the Revolutionary and Civil Wars. A variety of exhibits from those and other days in the town's history are on display in the **Foundry School Museum** — an 1850s schoolhouse and museum of the **Putnam County Historical Society**.

Just south of town and with a sweeping view of the Hudson is **Boscobel** (1804), a fully restored and outstanding example of New York Federal domestic architecture. Inside the house is a superb collection of Federal furniture and decorations (guided tours); on the grounds are an herb garden, orangerie, and rose garden.

Nature enthusiasts are drawn to Cold Spring for several reasons. One of them is the **Constitution Marsh Wildlife Sanctuary,** operated by the National Audubon Society, south of town (canoe tours available). Another is the**Manitoga Nature Preserve,** an 80-acre nature center with beautiful woodlands and water-falls (self-guided tours). Hikes along country roads and cruises on the **Hudson** (from **West Point**) are also great ways to enjoy the area's natural attractions.

SPECIAL FEATURES

• Four miles south of Cold Spring is **Garrison,** another charming Hudson River town — and one also served by the Hudson Railroad. The **Garrison Art Center** houses a gallery and schedules a variety of art classes.

• The **United States Military Academy** at West Point is south of town across the river. West Point's Visitors Center offers tours of and information on the academy. The best way to reach West Point is via the **Bear Mountain Bridge,** 9 miles south of Cold Spring.

> *Cold Spring's name is believed to have originated with a reference to the local spring by General George Washington.*

WHERE TO STAY

3 Rock Street B&B, 3 Rock St., (914) 265-2330. Spacious rooms, on bluff overlooking Hudson, private baths, Jacuzzis. $$ to $$$

Hudson House, 2 Main St., (914) 265-9355. Historic landmark on banks of Hudson, balconies, private baths, seasonal cuisine. $$ to $$$

Pig Hill B&B, 73 Main St., (914) 265-9247. In heart of village, beautifully decorated rooms, antiques, quaint. $$ to $$$

WHERE TO EAT

Cold Spring Depot, foot of Main St., (914) 265-2305. Steaks, ribs, seafood, specials, clams, steamers & mussels, Dixieland Jazz on lawn weekends. $ to $$

Hudson House (see above). Boneless breast of Long Island duck, oven-roasted Rock Cornish game hen. $$

Plumbush Restaurant & Inn, Rt. 9D, (914) 265-3904. Continental cuisine, shrimp in beer batter, live brook trout, reservations required. $$$

Riverview Restaurant, 45 Fair St., (914) 265-4778. Italian cuisine, fresh pasta and seafood, brick-oven pizza. $ to $$

Vintage Cafe, 91 Main St., (914) 265-4726. Fettucine Escargot with sundried tomatoes, Roast Boneless Duckling with cassis; reservations suggested. $$

FURTHER INFORMATION

The Putnam County News & Recorder, 86 Main St., Cold Spring, NY 10516, (914) 265-2468. **Note:** *Don't confuse with the town of Cold Spring Harbor on Long Island!*

DIRECTIONS

From New York City, US 9 north to Cold Spring (across from West Point).

COOPERSTOWN, NEW YORK

Population: 2,180

At latest count the **Cooperstown** area had about 80 bed-and-breakfast inns, possibly the largest number per capita in the country. Some overlook the shores of beautiful **Otsego Lake**, others grace the streets of the historic district, and yet others are tucked along the winding roads and creeks of the surrounding countryside. They cater to every budget, mood and personality, and vary from quaint cottages to working farms to Victorian mansions. And they exist for good reason, for even without its lake, rolling hills, forests and lovely old farms, Cooperstown's arts calendar and world-class sights would make the little town one of the most charming and interesting resorts in the United States.

As with the bed and breakfasts, Cooperstown probably has the largest number of museums per capita in the country. The Big Three are the **National Baseball Hall of Fame and Museum**, the **Farmers' Museum**, and the **Fenimore House Museum**.

The **National Baseball Hall of Fame** was founded in 1939 to honor the game's heroes and to serve as the game's historian by assembling, preserving and displaying information and memorabilia. Among the over 6,000 items currently on display are wood carvings of Babe Ruth and Ted Williams. A multi-media show is presented continuously in the museums's new two-hundred-seat theater.

The **Fenimore House**, a grand, columned mansion on the shore of Lake Otsego, has three floors of galleries featuring outstanding collections of folk, academic and decorative arts. There is also a gallery displaying memorabilia associated with novelist and social critic James Fenimore Cooper. The building is home to the museum and offices of the **New York State Historical Association**.

Life in rural upstate New York between the Revolutionary and Civil Wars is recalled by the buildings, artifacts, and craft demonstrations of the **Farmers' Museum**. Included on the picturesque grounds of the museum complex are the **Main Barn** and the **Village Crossroads**, a collection of buildings comprising a general store, druggist, church, tavern, working farm and other historic structures.

Coopertown's other museums include the **Larry Fritsch Baseball Card Museum**, the imaginative **Corvette Americana Hall of Fame**, and the **Fly Creek Cider Mill** (1956), a water-powered mill that uses equipment dating from the late 19th and early 20th centuries.

Everything from jazz to chamber music is performed by top artists during the winter season (ending in December) of the **Cooperstown Concert Series**. In the summer there is the renowned **Glimmerglass Opera**. The visual arts are represented by shows at **Gallery 53 Artworks** and the **Smithy-Pioneer Gallery** (in Cooperstown's oldest building, 1786), as well as at numerous fine craft, antique and gift shops on Main Street.

Coopertown's recreational options include bicycle tours, water sports on Lake Otsego and, of course, practice at one of the baseball batting ranges.

Because parking in Cooperstown is limited, consider parking in a perimeter parking area (free) and riding the trolley about town.

SPECIAL FEATURES

• At **Glimmerglass State Park** on the north side of the lake is **Hyde Hall** (1817/1835), a 50-room mansion with two grand public rooms, two libraries, two kitchens and several dozen other rooms. Although undergoing restoration, the mansion is open weekends and by special tour at other times.

• The **Cherry Valley Museum** (1832) in the historic village of **Cherry Valley** northeast of Cooperstown features a unique collection of local memorabilia.

Cooperstown was founded by and named after the father of James Fenimore Cooper.

Almost 400,000 visit the National Baseball Hall of Fame each year.

WHERE TO STAY

Angelholm B&B, 14 Elm St., (607) 547-2483. On quiet side street in heart of town, sumptuous breakfasts, afternoon teas. $$$

The Bassett House Inn, 32 Fair St., (607) 547-7001. Restored inn, clock collection, 1894 billiard table, private baths. $$$

The J. P. Sill House B&B, 63 Chestnut St., (607) 547-2633. 1864 Italianate home, spacious grounds, down comforters, "lavish" breakfasts. $$$

Thistlebrook B&B, R.D. 1 (Box 26), (607) 547-6093. Overlooking lovely valley, European and Oriental antiques, heated pool in garden room, private baths. $$$

Toad Hall, the B&B, R.D. 1 (Box 120) (607) 547-5774. Restored 1820s stone farmhouse on 80 acres, antiques, art, "hearty" breakfasts. $$$

WHERE TO EAT

The Hawkeye Bar & Grill (in Otesaga Hotel), P.O. Box 311, (607) 547-9931. English pub atmosphere, American entrees from grill. $$

Rose & Kettle Restaurant, 4 Lancaster St. (Cherry Valley), (607) 264-3078. In circa 1810 family home, all choices prepared on premises, chef-owned, reservations recommended. $ to $$

Terrace Cafe, 10 Hoffman Ln., (607) 547-8938. Three dining rooms, outdoor terrace, American cuisine, fresh fish, chef-owned. $ to $$

FURTHER INFORMATION

Cooperstown Chamber of Commerce, 31 Chestnut St., Cooperstown, NY 13326, (607) 547-9983.

DIRECTIONS

From Albany, US 20 west to NY 80, NY 80 south to Cooperstown.

CORNING, NEW YORK

Population: 11,938

Corning receives high points on the ideal-American-hometown dimension. First, nestled on the banks of the **Chemung River** and surrounded by the rolling woodland of southwestern New York, the town has a scenic setting. Second, home to the headquarters of two Fortune 500 companies, it also has a sound economic base. And third, Corning has an active downtown/historic district and a town plan that encourages walking. The car is often left home, and sidewalk visiting and old-fashioned friendliness are the beneficiaries.

The **Market Street Historic District** is a four-block area of fine old commercial buildings that have been restored to a late 19th-century appearance. The district's brick sidewalks are lined with shade trees and a colorful collection of specialty shops, restaurants, antique stores and — in case the visitor forgets this is Corning — glass-blowing shops. There's also a restored 1880 ice cream parlor and the beautiful new **Riverfront Park** (a gift of Corning, Inc.).

One of Corning's (and New York's) top attractions is the **Corning Glass Center**. The center depicts all aspects of glass, including its history, uses, manufacture and service as an art form. The center comprises the **Corning Museum of Glass**, the **Hall of Science and Industry**, the **Steuben Glass Factory**, and several retail shops (tours available).

The **Rockwell Museum**, another top attraction, is housed in an historic Romanesque Revival building. The museum has superb collections of American Western art, Carder Steuben glass, and antique toys. Films and changing exhibitions are also featured.

Centering more on local and regional history, the **Benjamin Patterson Inn Museum Complex** boasts an impressive collection of restored structures. Foremost among them is the furnished 1796 **Benjamin Patterson Inn**, a former stagecoach stop. Others include the log **DeMonstoy Cabin** (1784), the authentically furnished one-room **Browntown School** (1878) and a replica of the **Starr Barn** (1868).

The **One Seventy One Cedar Arts Center** features art exhibits, classes and, in its **Studio Access to Glass**, glass-blowing instructions (visitors may make their own paperweights).

In the summer months daily performances of the **Mark Twain Musical Drama** are held just a few minutes away. The spectacular production's music and dancing celebrate the life and writings of the much-loved author. (Twain wrote *Adventures of Huckleberry Finn* and several other works while residing at a nearby farm.)

SPECIAL FEATURE

• The **National Soaring Museum**, located between Corning and Elmira, focuses on aviation history. Featured are the country's largest glider and sailplane collection, a cockpit mockup, and films on soaring. A glider field and scenic overlook are adjacent.

The Corning area is one of the best in the country for soaring.
Much of today's Corning is the result of a major reconstruction effort undertaken after devastating floods in 1972.

WHERE TO STAY

"1865" White Birch B&B, 69 E. First St., (607) 962-6355. 1865 home, full home-baked breakfasts, short walk to Market Street. $$

Delevan House, 188 Delevan Ave., (607) 962-2347. Southern colonial home in quiet surroundings, full breakfasts, cold summer drinks. $$ to $$$

Rosewood Inn, 134 E. First St., (607) 962-3253. Restored 1855 home, fine antiques, private baths, Victorian wood-paneled dining room, gourmet breakfasts. $$$

WHERE TO EAT

Blossom's, P. O. Box 150 (Painted Post), (607) 962-2456. American cuisine served in beautiful setting. $$

London Underground Cafe, 69 E. Market St., (607) 962-2345. Unique three-level setting, creative menu, fresh-baked desserts, tea andscones. $$

Rojo's, 36 Bridge St., (607) 936-9683. Pub atmosphere, steaks, chops, pasta, seafood. $ to $$

Sorge's Restaurant, 66-68 W. Market St., (607) 937-5422. A Corning tradition for over 40 years, Italian-American menu. $

Upstate Tuna Company, 73 E. Market St., (607) 936-8862. Grilled fresh seafood/meat/ poultry, historic bar. $$

FURTHER INFORMATION

Corning Chamber of Commerce, 42 E. Market St., Corning, NY 14830, (607) 936-4686.

DIRECTIONS

From Rochester, I 390 south to exit 43 (Corning exit).

LAKE PLACID, NEW YORK

Population: 2,485

Host to the Olympic Winter Games of 1932 and 1980, and situated among the hills and lakes of the lovely **Adirondacks**, **Lake Placid** is a place of scenery and spectacular sports facilities. **Main Street's** sophisticated shops and restaurants add a cosmopolitan air.

Yet the charm of Lake Placid only begins with the setting. For arising from the sports complexes, and echoed by the hillsides, is the nostalgic kind of charm that comes with grand memories, memories of gold-medal achievements and cheers and national anthems.

Lake Placid is as complex as its charm. There are many Lake Placids, and all have to be sampled if the town is to be known. Each sports facility is its own village. Even the lake is too complex to be grasped by a glance. Unless you have time to spare, take some kind of organized tour. The bus tours are good, the 1-hr.

narrated boat cruise wins raves from visitors, and the **Lake Placid Olympic Site Tour** (sponsored by Eastman Kodak Company) offers a convenient, comprehensive self-guided motor tour of the sports complexes. For a geographical overview, scan the region from a scenic flight.

One of the most active of the sports complexes is the **U.S. Olympic Training Center**, where visitors are free to watch as athletes from all over the country train. **The Olympic Center**, another complex open to visitors, is the largest indoor ice facility in the world. Figure skaters, hockey players and speed skaters train on the center's rinks. At the **Olympic Jumping Complex** even watching can be breathtaking as athletes train on the 70- and 90-meter ski jumps. Training takes place all year, with plastic matting replacing snow in the warmer months.

The **Lake Placid Sinfonietta** concerts, held weekly during the summer, are among the most popular of Lake Placid's many cultural events.

SPECIAL FEATURE

• On a clear day the summit of **Whiteface Mountain** offers one of the most spectacular panoramic views in the country. Drive the 6-mile **Whiteface Mountain Veterans Memorial Highway** (near **Wilmington, NY**) to the parking area near the summit, then complete the climb by a short hike or by a unique elevator ride through the heart of the mountain.

> *The internationally famous figure skater Sonya Henie won a gold medal in 1932 for her performance in the Olympic Center.*

WHERE TO STAY

Adirondak Loj, Adirondak Loj Rd., (518) 523-3441. Lodge in wilderness setting at trail head, since 1890. $ to $$

Highland House Inn, 3 Highland Place, (518) 523-2377. Adirondack decor throughout, blueberry pancakes, private baths. $$

Mountain Hearth Inn, 338 Old Military Rd., (518) 523-1114. Renovated 19th century farmhouse, wonderful mountain views, "bountiful" breakfasts. $$ to $$$

Stage Coach Inn, 370 Old Militlary Rd., (518) 523-9474. Guests welcomed since 1833, antiques, full breakfasts. $$ to $$$

Willkommen Hof, Rt. 86, (800) 541-9119. European-style guesthouse, German cooking, sitting room with fireplace and piano. $ to $$

WHERE TO EAT

Alpine Cellar, E on NY 86, (518) 523-2180. Authentic Swiss and German dishes, imported beers. $$

Averill Conwell Dining Room, 5 Mirror Lake Dr., (518) 523-2544. Fine candlelight dining, overlooking lake, dress code. $$ to $$$

Lake Placid Manor, Whiteface Inn Rd., (518) 523-2573. On the lake, one of region's favorites, reservations advised. $$ to $$$

La Veranda, 1 Olympic Dr., (518) 523-3339. Restored home, French cuisine in attractive setting, summer months only. $$

FURTHER INFORMATION

Lake Placid Convention & Visitors Bureau, Olympic Center, Lake Placid, NY 12946, (800) 447-5224.

DIRECTIONS

From Albany, I 87 north to exit 30, NY 73 northwest to Lake Placid.

SKANEATELES, NEW YORK

Population: 2,724

Skaneateles (pronounced something like "scan ee AT las") lies at the top of a gorgeous lake by the same name. The village and the lake complement each another, the one enhancing the beauty of the other.

Skaneateles's downtown is an historic district containing numerous brick buildings constructed in 1835 to replace wooden structures destroyed in a fire. Brick-lined sidewalks and cast-iron lampposts complete the scene to produce something out of an old photo album. Trees, hanging floral arrangements and hand-painted storefronts give the photo color. Proud of the beauty and vitality of the downton, the village has been successful so far in keeping shopping malls at bay.

In the surrounding neighborhoods are faithfully restored and landscaped homes dating from the early 1800s onward. Here as well as downtown, the streets are notable for the attention given to maintenance, cleanliness and historic authenticity.

Skaneateles Lake is one of the most beautiful and popular of New York's **Finger Lakes**. The 16 x 1 1/2 mile lake has crystal-clear water, with a through-the-water visibility of 25 feet (the lake has New York's highest water-quality rating). The lake is ideal for virtually all water sports, including scuba diving. The village has two waterfront parks, one for swimming and one for enjoying the scenery.

SPECIAL FEATURE

• Sightseeing, lunch, Sunday brunch and dinner **cruises** offer one way to tour the lake. Driving tours around the lake offer another — check with the CoC for itinerary suggestions.

> *Friday-evening gazebo concerts and Sunday-afternoon polo matches form part of Scaneateles's entertainment calendar.*

WHERE TO STAY

Earll Manor B&B, 986 Old Seneca Tnpk., (315) 685-3041. In country close to village, lots of windows, antiques. $$ to $$$

Evergreen Manor B&B, 98 W. Genesee St., (315) 685-6829. Once home on the Underground Railroad, sweeping lawns, near shops and lake. $$ to $$$

The Gray House B&B, 47 Jordan St., (315) 685-5224. Victorian home, walking distance to shops and lake. $$ to $$$

Millard's at the Summit B&B, 1715 E. Lake Rd., (315) 673-2254. Old home with panoramic view of lake, full breakfasts, restaurant/tavern downstairs. $$ to $$$

Sherwood Inn, 26 W. Genesee St., (315) 685-3405. 1860s stagecoach stop, antiques, restaurant, opposite beach. $$ to $$$

WHERE TO EAT

Krebs, 53 W. Genesee St., (315) 685-5714. Regionally renowned, selections served family style, no printed menus, all-you-can-eat. $$$

Sherwood Inn, (see above). American menu, seafood, steaks. $$

FURTHER INFORMATION

Skaneateles Chamber of Commerce, P. O. Box 199, Skaneateles, NY 13152, (315) 685-0552.

DIRECTIONS

From Syracuse, I 81 south to exit 15, US 20 west to Skaneateles.

SOUTHAMPTON, NEW YORK

Population: 3,980

For many decades a resort of the celebrated and wealthy, **Southampton** is renowned for its grand beachfront estates. It's true that relatively modest beach houses can also be found here, and bordering the streets and lanes of the village are all kinds of houses, plain as well as fancy. It's also true that the town's year-round residents include a variety of people of very ordinary wealth, among them some who are very talented but who have yet to make it or who have chosen to withdraw from the race. But in the summer and on weekends Southampton's mood remains trendy, affluent, arty; the seaside town is still — and may always be — a favorite flocking ground for New York City's successful and near-successful.

Southampton's oldest surviving house, and indeed the oldest English-type saltbox house in New York, is the restored **Halsey Homestead** (1648). The house, open to the public, contains authentic 17th- and 18th-century furnishings. In the back is a colonial herb garden.

The **Parrish Art Museum** (1898), housed in a handsome Italianate structure, features 19th- and 20th-century American art; collections by William Merritt Chase and Fairfield Porter, two renowned artist-residents of Southampton; Renaissance pieces; and other works. The permanent collection holds more than 2,000 pieces.

Another fine museum, the **Southampton Historical Museum,** is housed in a grand two-story whaling captain's house (1843). The museum's exhibits include colonial relics, local Indian artifacts, and antique toys. Among the displays on the grounds are a furnished one-room schoolhouse, blacksmith shop, cobbler's shop, and a country store housed in a pre-Revolutionary barn.

St. Andrew's Dune Church was originally a Life Saving Station built by the Government in 1851. A church since 1879, the walls and windows have beautifully inscribed Biblical passages. On the grounds are remnants of old shipwrecks.

Southampton boasts many sophisticated boutiques, art and craft galleries, and gourmet food shops. The southeastern coast of Long Island is blessed with miles of beautiful beaches and dunes; beach access can be a problem, however, so check in advance with an innkeeper or the CoC. Because Long Island's east end is (fortunately!) beyond commuting distance to New York City, the Southampton area still harbors beautiful farms — and well-stocked farm stands. The region is ideal for hiking and biking (bike rentals are available).

Lodging and restaurant reservations are a must during the summer months. Bed and breakfasts may be booked solid months in advance.

SPECIAL FEATURES

• **Westhampton Beach, Sag Harbor, East Hampton,** and other picturesque coastal towns are just a few miles away.

• Several oceanside state parks are located at the eastern tip of Long Island, among them **Montauk Point State Park,** site of the 1795 **Montauk Lighthouse.**

> *Suffolk County is dotted with 18th- and 19th-century windmills. All are of English design.*

WHERE TO STAY

Louise Beckman, 124 Burnett St., (516) 283-0732. Homey Cape Cod home, antiques, walking distance to village. $$$

Carol Conover, P. O. Box 98 (Water Mill), (516) 726-7618. Secluded wooded setting, fireplace, private baths, full breakfasts, pool and deck. $$$

Little White House on Hill Street, Hill St., (516) 283-2596. Turn-of-century farmhouse, beautifully furnished, antiques, short stroll to village. $$$

The Old Post House Inn, 136 Main St., (516) 283-1717. In center of village, original part from 1684, on National Register, private baths, restaurant. $$$

WHERE TO EAT

American Hotel Dining Room, Main St. (Sag Harbor), (516) 725-3535. In 1846 inn, French cuisine, reservations required, highly recommended. $$ to $$$

John Duck, Jr., Prospect St., (516) 283-0311. German-American cooking, steaks, seafood. $$ to $$$

Maidstone Arms, 207 Main St. (East Hampton), (516) 324-2004. In early 1800s inn, creative American cuisine, excellent wine list, reservations suggested, highly recommended. $$ to $$$

Post House Restaurant (see above). Continental cuisine, famed Sunday brunch, patio dining. $$ to $$$

Starr Boggs, 23 Sunset Ave. (Westhampton Beach), (516) 288-5250. Local fish the specialty, one of Long Island's finest. $$ to $$$

FURTHER INFORMATION

Southampton Chamber of Commerce, 76 Main St., Southampton, NY 11968, (516) 283-0402.

DIRECTIONS

From New York City, I 495 (Long Island Expwy.) to exit 71, NY 24 southeast to Hampton Bays, NY 27 to Southampton.

NORTH CAROLINA

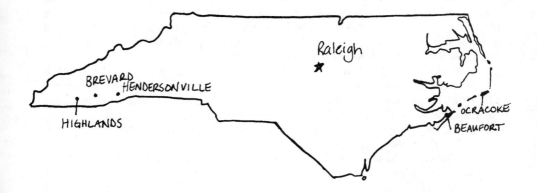

BEAUFORT,
NORTH CAROLINA

Population: 3808

Sometimes the sights are themselves active, and then sightseers need only linger passively by to enjoy them. And so it is along the old waterfront of the picturesque port and county seat of **Beaufort**. Sailboats bob at anchor or dock, dingies and harbor cruise boats come and go, sailors talk of shrimping, restaurants smell of fresh seafood and street musicians entertain.

Settled around 1710, and once the target of attack by pirates, Beaufort is North Carolina's third oldest town. Aware and proud of their history, the people of the town have done much to preserve and restore their architectural heritage. As with the waterfront, much of the town's history can be enjoyed with little effort: the harbor area from the deck of a cruise boat, the streets from the seat of an English double-decker bus.

The **Beaufort Historical Association** has been responsible for the restoration of many important structures. One of the most prominent, the **Joseph Bell House** (ca. 1767), provides an excellent example of early Beaufort architecture. The house has 18th-century furnishings. The **Josiah Bell House** (ca. 1825), another restoration and the association's welcome center, has a beautiful side garden maintained by the Garden Club.

The oldest surviving public building in the county, the **Carteret County Courthouse** (1796) has authentic furnishings and boasts among its possessions an original thirteen-star American flag. Ask about guided tours of these and other restorations.

Among the graves of the **Old Burying Grounds**, which date to 1731, are those of victims of the Indian Wars.

The **N. C. Maritime Museum**, one of Beaufort's top sites, displays boats and boat models, outstanding shell collections and other exhibits concerned with the maritime and natural history of the North Carolina coastal region. The museum also offers field trips, lectures and other programs.

SPECIAL FEATURE

• Wild herds of ponies, with ancestors dating back to Colonial times, are Beaufort's most novel attraction. **Carrot Island** and **Bird Shoals**, which form part of a nature reserve system and are visible from Beaufort's waterfront, are home to many species of birds, some endangered, as well as to the ponies. Check locally for information on ferry service to the sites.

Ann and Queen Streets were named for Queen Anne, who ruled at the time the town was surveyed in 1713.

Hurricanes in the late 19th century eventually drove as many as 600 people from nearby Shackleford Banks, a now-unoccupied shoal under review as a possible wilderness area.

WHERE TO STAY

Beaufort Inn, 101 Ann St., (800) 726-0321. Contemporary inn on waterfront, famous breakfasts, bicycle and boat slip rentals. $$ to $$$

Captains' Quarters, 315 Ann St., (919) 728-7711. Restored turn-of-the-century home in quiet location, family heirlooms, private baths, one block from waterfront. $$ to $$$

Delamar Inn B&B, 217 Turner St., (919) 728-4300. Restored 1866 home, antiques, private baths, "delightful" breakfasts, upper porch, on historic homes tour. $$ to $$$

Inlet B&B, 601 Front at Queen Streets, (919) 728-3600. Contemporary inn on harbor, private porches, ceiling fans, unsurpassed views of Cape Lookout and Beaufort harbor. $$ to $$$

WHERE TO EAT

Beaufort Grocery Co., 117 Queen St., (919) 728-3899. Cozy French cafe atmosphere with flowered tablecloths and "Beaufort Green" decor, own baking. $$

The Beaufort House, 502 Front St., (919) 728-7541. Fresh local seafood, prime rib, original salads and varied pastas. $ to $$

The Spouter Inn, 218 Front St., (919) 728-5190. Scallops Parmesan, Maryland-style crab cakes, bouillabaisse, paella. $ to $$

FURTHER INFORMATION

Carteret County Tourism Development Bureau, P. O. Box 1406, Morehead City, NC 28557, (800) 786-6962.

DIRECTIONS

From Raleigh, US 70 southeast to Beaufort.

BREVARD, NORTH CAROLINA

Population: 5,388

Brevard (accent on second syllable) is the seat of **Transylvania County**, a county covered by thick forests and boasting some of the highest elevations in the **Appalachian Mountains**. The mountains and forests give rise to trout-filled streams, and the streams tumble over waterfalls with names like **Looking Glass**, **Slippery Witch**, **Turtleback**, **Horsepasture** and **Rainbow**. The county is home to more than 250 waterfalls!

A major cultural center, Brevard adds its own kinds of beauty. The **Brevard Music Center** attacts talented musicians from around the world to its stage. Spotlighting the center's summer season are operas, operettas, musicals, pops concerts, chamber music and performances by renowned soloists.

On Thursday evenings the sounds of bluegrass and original mountain music can be heard at **Silvermont,** an historic mansion. Contributing to the cultural calendar during the winter, spring and fall are the **Brevard Little Theatre** and the **Brevard Chamber Orchestra** Brevard is also home to **Brevard College,** which, as might be expected, has a respected music department.

In or near downtown are the 1851 brick courthouse (site of a summer art show) and a number of 19th-century homes, some of which offer lodging (see below). **Main Street** is known for its thriving specialty, antique, and craft shops. All sorts of crafts are practiced in the Brevard area, including weaving and quilt making. The hand-crafted furniture is especially sought after.

Not far from town are more than 450 miles of hiking trails that wind through mountains and along rivers and streams. The **French Broad River** is popular with canoers and kayakers. In the winter, the **Blue Ridge Parkway** offers good cross-county skiing, and glorious scenery.

SPECIAL FEATURES

• One of the county's most popular waterfalls, **Sliding Rock,** is a 150-ft natural water slide. About 11,000 gallons of cold water flow down the slide every minute.

• Situated in the **Pisgah National Forest** is the **Cradle of Forestry,** the country's first forestry school. The restored turn-of-the-century campus is now a hands-on museum.

• **US 276** north of Brevard has been designated a Scenic Byway.

> *Pisgah Forest, once owned by George Vanderbilt, was the country's first managed woodland.*
> *Rare white squirrels may be seen scampering about in Brevard's city parks.*

WHERE TO STAY

Inn at Brevard, E. Main St., (704) 884-2105. Turn-of-the-century inn listed on National Register, full breakfasts, public dining room. $$ to $$$

Key Falls Inn, Everett Rd. (7 miles from town), (704) 884-7559. 1860s farmhouse, waterfall, porches, "sumptuous" breakfasts. $$ to $$$

Red Lion Inn, US 178 (10 miles south of town), (704) 884-6868. Veranda by mountain stream, big open fireplace, restaurant, hiking, fishing. $$ to $$$

Sassy Goose, (US 276 12 miles from town), (704) 966-9493. On 50 wooded acres, 6-acre lake, private baths, swimming, croquet. $$ to $$$

Womble Inn, 301 Main St., (704) 884-4770. Large and comfortable parlor, 18th- and 19th-century antiques, private baths. $$ to $$$

WHERE TO EAT

Chianti's, NC 280 and US 276 and US 64, (704) 862-5683. Highly recommended Italian cuisine. $ to $$

Falls Landing, 23 E. Main St., (704) 884-2835. Fresh seafood, conch fritters, pasta. $ to $$

Oh Susanna's, 230 W. Main St., (704) 883-3289. Soups, salads, sandwiches, daily dinner specials. $ to $$

FURTHER INFORMATION
    Brevard Chamber of Commerce, 35 West Main Street, Brevard, NC 28712, (800) 648-4523.

DIRECTIONS
    From Asheville, I 26 south to exit 9, NC 280 southwest to Brevard.

HENDERSONVILLE, NORTH CAROLINA

Population: 7,284

With its mild and healthful climate and glorious mountain scenery, **Hendersonville** is a retreat, and it has been for close to 200 years. Maybe longer, because the Cherokees are believed to have come here to seek solitude long before the arrival of any Europeans.

Rice and indigo plantation owners from Charleston and other lowland towns once built summer homes in the Flat Rock area just south of here so that their families could escape the heat, humidity and malaria of the coastal region (see also Pendleton, SC). The plantation families were followed by Georgians and Floridians seeking to escape the yellow fever epidemics. Later, victims of tuberculosis and other chest ailments were attracted by the region's altitude. Maintaining the tradition, retirees from the East and Midwest wishing to escape the cities and cold winters began settling here in the 1940s and 1950s.

Hendersonville is today as popular as ever as a place to escape to. The air and water are pure, crime is low and the pace of life easy. The town is one our grandparents or great grandparents could have lived in. The country is rural, a place where people watch birds or go on wildflower walks.

There are two historic districts, one in **Flat Rock**, 3 miles south, and the other in Hendersonville. The Flat Rock historic district is older, dating back to the summer days of antebellum planters. Hendersonville grew as businesses developed to serve those retreating to the area, and so its district dates to a later stage of the 19th century.

Many of the summer homes built by privileged Charlestonians and others from the coastal region remain in private hands as estates and can only be seen from the distance, if at all. There is one most notable exception to this rule, however: **Connemara** (ca. 1838), the farm where Carl Sandburg and his family lived for 22 years. Now the **Carl Sandburg Home National Historic Site**, the home and grounds of the beloved American poet are open to the public. The house is kept very much like it was when Sandburg lived there, and numerous hiking trails lead to the goat farm and to panoramic views of lakes, rolling hills and, in the distance, the **Blue Ridge Mountains**.

Another structure from the days of the Southern aristocracy open to the public is the Episcopal **Church of St. John in the Wilderness**, in Flat Rock. The church was built in 1833 as a chapel for the estate of an English-born family. The chapel was later turned over to the Episcopal Diocese and, in 1852, doubled in length. The church has been entered in the National Register.

Ten blocks long, Hendersonville's **Main Street** has 194 businesses. The late 19th-century buildings, many with restored storefronts, house antique shops, upscale clothing shops, bakeries and coffee shops. An alternative form of shopping is offered at the **Henderson County Farmer's Curb Market**, in operation for more than 60 years. Here there are garden-fresh vegetables, baked goods, apghans and aprons, all home-grown or homemade.

There are several well-known golf courses, each unique, and others are being built (many are open to the public). Comedy, classic, musical, whodunnit and other kinds of hits from the Broadway and London stages are presented each summer at the **Flat Rock Playhouse**, one of the ten best summer stock theaters in the country. Other productions are offered by the **Hendersonville Little Theater** and the **Belfry Players**. Inquire at the visitors center for information on these and other events, including performances of mountain music.

SPECIAL FEATURE

• **Chimney Rock Park**, 20 minutes east of Hendersonville, offers an eye-dazzling 75-mile view of the rugged western North Carolina landscape. Within the park is a 400-foot waterfall, rock formations and nature trails.

> *The Hendersonville area ranks as the seventh largest apple producer in the country. And, yes, there's an annual apple festival (September).*

WHERE TO STAY

Claddagh Inn, 755 N. Main St., (800) 225-4700. Turn-of-century inn on National Register, private baths, TV and telephones, full breakfasts. $$ to $$$

Flat Rock Inn, 2810 Greenville Hwy. (Flat Rock), (800) 323-3273. Renovated 1888 summer retreat on National Register, croquet, horseshoes, family-style breakfasts, refreshments. $$ to $$$

Stillwell House B&B, 1300 Pinecrest Dr., (704) 693-6475. Restored 1920s home of Europoean design, private baths, artwork, beautiful grounds. $$

The Waverly Inn, 783 N. Main St., (800) 537-8195. Renovated 1898 inn on National Register, rocking chairs on veranda, private baths, full breakfasts, refreshments. $$ to $$$

Woodfield Inn, US 25 S 2 miles, (800) 533-6016. Originally the Farmer Hotel (1850), antebellum atmosphere, antiques, Civil War reenactments, restaurant. $$ to $$$

WHERE TO EAT

Expressions, 114 N. Main St., (704) 693-8516. Creative upscale dining. $$ to $$$

Highland Lake Inn, Highland Lake Rd., (704) 696-9094. Continental cuisine, one of best in region. $$ to $$$

Hubert's, Laurel Park Vilage, US 64 W, (704) 693-0856. International menu, beautiful presentation. $$

The Park Deli Cafe, 437 N. Main St., (704) 696-3663. Unique park setting, 15 pasta dinners, barbecued ribs, full-meal salads. $

FURTHER INFORMATION
Visitors Information Center, 739 N. Main Street, Hendersonville, NC 28792, (800) 828-4244.

DIRECTIONS
From Asheville,I 26 south to exit 18 (Hendersonville exit).

HIGHLANDS, NORTH CAROLINA

Population: 948 (village only)

Tucked in the middle of a national forest in western North Carolina's Blue Ridge Mountains, **Highlands** is a place of mountain streams, dogwood and rhododendron, autumn brilliance, snow-capped mountains, waterfalls and craft shows. There are no theme parks, chain restaurants, factory outlets or video arcades. Highlands is a place for lovers of nature.

Established in the 1870s, Highlands was known by the 1880s as a health resort and refuge from the heat of Southern summers. (Several of the inns of those days have been renovated and once again greet visitors; see below). With a cool average altitude of 4,118 feet, the little town became a summer hideaway for the affluent from the South, especially Atlanta. For Atlanta's privileged, Highlands became synonymous with summer mountain retreat. Many built second homes here, expensive second homes. They still do.

The wealth of Highlands's summer residents is reflected in the merchandise in the shops, the restaurant menus and the many fine country clubs. It's indeed possible that Highlands has the largest number of excellent restaurants per capita in the United States. The town boasts a multitude of boutiques and quaint shops. Some offer art, others antiques, and yet others handmade items of wood, iron, fabric, etc. Shop windows display music boxes, custom-designed jewelry, porcelain, Oriental rugs, bird and even bat (!) houses.

The cultural scene is similarly rich. The **Highlands Playhouse** stages professional productions in its hilltop theater, and each year music lovers make their way here to attend the highly respected month-long **Highlands Chamber Music Festival**. Local artists display their works in the **Bascom-Louise Gallery**, located in the Hudson Library, as well as in private galleries.

It is nature, however, that dominates Highlands. The **Highlands Nature Center** features indoor wildlife exhibits, botanical gardens, and seminars and lectures. The area around Highlands is known for its mountain trails, challenging golf courses, and trout-fishing streams. There are excellent campgrounds and scenic highways. Of very special note are the waterfalls (see also Brevard); at least seven sizable falls are located within a few miles of town. Visitors are cautioned to view the falls from a distance and not to climb them.

SPECIAL FEATURE

• **Franklin**, 16 or so miles northwest of town, is famous for its gem mining. Visitors are invited to mine for rubies, sapphires and other stones. The drive to Franklin (**US 64**) is one of the most scenic in North Carolina.

WHERE TO STAY

Highlands Inn, P. O. Box I030, (704) 526-9380. Historically renovated 1880 inn on National Register, antique furnishings, colonial stenciling. $$$

Innisfree Inn, P. O. Box 2464 (Cashiers), (704) 743-2946. Victorian estate overlooking Lake Glenville, veranda, terraced gardens, game room and library, private dock, private baths, phones. $$$

Lakeside B&B, US 64 W., (704) 526-4498. On Lake Sequoyah, private canoe, private baths, full breakfasts. $$

The Old Edwards Inn, P. O. Box I030, (704) 526-5036. Authentically restored 1878 Inn on National Register, antiques, colonial wallcoverings, restaurant. $$$

The Phelps House B&B Inn, Rt. 1 (Box 55), (704) 526-2590. 1885 inn, antiques, porch, private baths, hearty breakfasts, lunches and dinners available. $$

WHERE TO EAT

Frog & Owl Cafe, Buck Creek Rd., (704) 526-5500. In old mill, French cuisine, reservations required, one of best in North Carolina. $$ to $$$

Lakeside Restaurant, Smallwood Ave., (704) 526-9419. Overlooking lake, Continental tradition, fresh seafood, Trout Almondine. $$

Nick's Calico Cottage, NC 28 S., (704) 526-2706. Cooking "with an Italian flair," steaks, prime rib, seafood. $$

On the Verandah, US 64/NC 28 W., (704) 526-2338. On Lake Sequoyah, Continental menu, seafood, pasta, excellent wine selection. $$

Paoletti's Restaurant, E. Main St., (704) 526-4906. Classic northern Italian cuisine. $ to $$

FURTHER INFORMATION

Highlands Chamber of Commerce, P. O. Box 404, Highlands, NC 28741, (704) 526-2112.

DIRECTIONS

From Asheville, I 26 south to exit 9, NC 280 southwest to US 64 (near Brevard), US 64 west to Highlands.

OCRACOKE, NORTH CAROLINA

Population: 700

A quiet and relaxed way of life continues among the picturesque **Outer Banks** houses and live-oak trees that cluster about the pretty little harbor. Unless there's a rush on to catch the next ferry, there's no reason to hurry. The bicycle is the best way to get around town. This is one of the Atlantic Coast's true treasures!

Located on **Ocracoke Island** in the middle of **Cape Hatteras National Seashore, Ocracoke Village** relaxes next to 17 miles of unobstructed oceanfront. Because buildings may not be built near the ocean, the shops and restaurants stick close to the village. Just down the beach is the **Ocracoke Lighthouse** (1823), the oldest lighthouse still in operation in North Carolina. The site is popular with artists and photographers.

One of the most popular ways to tour Ocracoke Island's beaches is by horseback.

SPECIAL FEATURE

• Day trips are available to **Portsmouth**, an abandoned village on nearby **Portsmouth Island**. Some of the village has been restored under the supervision of the National Park Service.

The waters and coves hereabouts were once the haunt of Edward Teach, otherwise known as Blackbeard, and other pirates.

Four Royal Navy sailors killed near here in 1942 are buried in the village's British Cemetery.

WHERE TO STAY

The Berkley Center Country Inn, P. O. Box 220, (919) 928-5911. On the harbor, plenty of character and atmosphere. $$ to $$$

Crews Inn, Ocracoke, (919) 928-7011. Wrap-around porch, antique furnishings, secluded location. $$

Eugenia's B&B, P. O. Box 611, (919) 928-1411. 1907/08 Ocracoke home brimming with antiques, full breakfasts. $$

The Island Inn, P. O. Box 9, (919) 928-4351. "With a flavor of yesterday," heated pool, TV, restaurant, open year-round. $ to $$$

WHERE TO EAT

The Back Porch Restaurant, Ocracoke, (919) 928-6401. Publishes own cookbook, homemade breads and desserts. $ to $$

Cafe Atlantic, P. O. Box 123, (919) 928-4861. Grilled seafood, homemade desserts. $ to $$

Captain Ben's, Ocracoke, (919) 928-4741. Old high school gym coverted to attractive restaurant, clam chowder, prime rib. $ to $$

FURTHER INFORMATION

Outer Banks Chamber of Commerce, P. O. Box 1757, Kill Devil Hills, NC 27948, (919) 995-4213.

DIRECTIONS

Toll ferries connect **Ocracoke** with the mainland at **Cedar Island** (crossing time approximately 2 1/4 hours) and **Swan Quarter** (approximately 2 1/2 hours). Reservations for the toll ferries are strongly recommended. The ferry to **Hatteras Inlet** (approximately 40 minutes) is free. Call (919) 928-3841 for reservation and schedule information.

NORTH DAKOTA

FORT RANSOM, NORTH DAKOTA

Population: 111

Fort Ransom is a quaint little Norwegian-American village nestled in the scenic **Sheyenne River Valley** of southeastern North Dakota. Along its recently paved main street are buildings with rosemaling, inside as well as out, and on the wooded slopes of the valley above the main street, houses climb apparently without pattern. This is the kind of place that yearns to be painted and photographed. It is the site of a major arts and crafts festival.

Of special interest in the village is the **Ransom County Historical Museum**, which houses exhibits and artifacts from Fort Ransom's pioneer years. Nearby is a newly restored country schoolhouse.

Fort Ransom is remote from the interstates and beaten tourist routes — it may be the only community in this guide that isn't served by at least one state highway. Yet the village is literally surrounded by scenic and recreational attractions: one mile south, in **Fort Ransom Historic Site**, are the archealogical remains of a log fort that was used from 1867 to 1872 to guard a settlement trail and the **Northern Pacific Railroad**, then under construction.

One mile north is **Fort Ransom Ski Area**, popular with downhill skiers. Two miles north is beautiful **Fort Ransom State Park** (see below). Three miles southeast is the 509-acre **Sheyenne State Forest**, great for canoeing and snowshoeing. And traversing the village is the 46-mile-long **Sheyenne Valley Snowmobile Trail**

As if all of this weren't enough, the area is rich with old farmsteads, reminders of the Norwegian farm families who settled here in the 1870s and 1880s.

SPECIAL FEATURE

• **Fort Ransom State Park** features cross-country ski trails, canoe rentals and canoe campsites. There is also a scenic overlook that provides spectacular views of the Sheyenne River Valley. The park is best know, however, for its **Fort Ransom Sodbusters Days**, a July get-together that attracts thousands with turn-of-the-century plowing and threshing demonstrations, displays of antique farm equipment, quilting, ice-cream making, farm-style cooking and other early farming and household re-creations.

> *The original buildings of two early homesteads have been incorporated as part of Fort Ransom State Park.*
> *The Sheyenne Valley Snowmobile Trail is maintained with funds from snowmobile registrations, required in North Dakota.*

WHERE TO STAY

Bonhus House Guest Inn, 341 Third Ave. NW (Valley City), (701) 845-2229. 1908 home, near antique shops, full breakfasts when requested, scenic drive to Fort Ransom. $$

WHERE TO EAT

Fort Cafe, Main Street, (701) 973-2301. Daily specials served in grocery store. $

FURTHER INFORMATION

Fort Ransom State Park, P. O. Box 67, Fort Ransom, ND 58033, (701) 973-4331.

DIRECTIONS

From Fargo, I 29 south to exit 48, ND 46 west to Ransom County 58, Ransom County 58 south — look for signs.

MEDORA, NORTH DAKOTA

Population: ca. 101

There are few better ways to recapture the spell of a small 1800s cattle town than to stroll along **Medora's** boardwalks. Along the way are restored buildings like the **Rough Riders Hotel** (1884; see below) and **St. Mary's Catholic Church** (1884). The spell isn't hurt by the awesome beauty of one of the country's finest Western settings — the **North Dakota Badlands.** Nor the knowledge that Theodore Roosevelt once rode these parts. In the evening the gas street lights are turned on and the quiet stirred by the sounds of a vaudeville show (the *4M Review* in the old town hall).

Medora was named for the wife of the Marquis de Mores, a French aristocrat who in 1883 founded the town. De Mores came to Dakota Territory to seek his fortune in the cattle and meat-packing industry. The fortune was never made and the family was seldom seen here after 1886, but during his stay the marquis built a town and a legacy.

De Mores is best remembered today through his 26-room frame summer home, or *chateau,* which overlooks Medora. The house, along with the stables and several other outbuildings, is now the **Chateau de Mores State Historic Site.** Most of the furnishings are European and American antiques, some of them summer-cottage rustic, original to the family.

The **Medora Musical** is a grand spectacle of music, dancing, comedy and variety acts that pay patriotic tribute to Theodore Roosevelt's "Bully Spirit." The show, performed by professional entertainers, is presented in a 2,750-seat amphitheater reached by a large outdoor escalator. The amphitheater is positioned to offer a breathtaking view of the Badlands. While here, inquire about tickets to one of North Dakota's major eating events, the **Pitchfork Steak Fondue.**

SPECIAL FEATURES

• Medora is the entrance to the **South Unit** of the **Theodore Roosevelt Na-**

tional Park, a park known for its Badlands scenery and wildlife, including buffalo, wild horses and elk. A visitors center, museum and Roosevelt's **Maltese Cross Ranch cabin** are near the entrance.

 • Several miles north in the park is the **Peaceful Valley Ranch,** an old dude ranch and now a park concession that offers a variety of horse-back trail rides. The rides vary in length from 1 hour to overnight. Several, lasting from 4 to 5 1/2 hours, journey to the park's **Petrified Forest** and **Painted Canyon.** A trail ride is a must for those who have the time.

> *In addition to Theodore Roosevelt and the Marquis de Mores, Medora has attracted such notables as silent-screen star Tom Mix and Marie, Queen of the Rumanians.*
>
> *General George Armstrong Custer camped just a few miles south of Medora's site in 1876 on his way to Little Big Horn.*

WHERE TO STAY

 Rough Riders Hotel, Downtown Medora, (701) 623-4422. Restored 1880s hotel, TV, restaurant, summer months only. $$

WHERE TO EAT

 Rough Riders Hotel (see above). Rustic dining room in historic hotel, steaks, buffalo burgers, good wine selection. $ to $$

FURTHER INFORMATION

 Site Supervisor, Chateau de Mores State Historic Site, Medora, ND 58645, (701) 623-4355.

DIRECTIONS

 From Bismarck, I 94 west to exit 24 (Medora exit).

OHIO

KELLEY'S
ISLAND

PORT
CLINTON

VERMILION

ZOAR

BERLIN

GRANVILLE

Columbus

BERLIN, OHIO

Population: 1,000

Perhaps half of all Amish people in the world have their farms in the rolling countryside around **Berlin** (accent on first syllable) and other towns and villages in this part of east central Ohio. It goes without saying that the countryside is picturesque: Amish farms are traditional American farms, with big barns and proper farmhouses.

Shunning the modern, the Amish drive buggies rather than cars and favor kerosene lamps over electric lights. They love the handmade and the home-baked. It's no coincidence that at least three other towns in this guide lie in or close to Amish areas (Lewisburg and Lititz, Pennsylvania, and Jamesport, Missouri).

People from Berlin have been heard to claim that "Lancaster County, Pennsylvania is like the Disneyworld of Amish; Berlin is the real thing." And it's true that the some 70 businesses in and around the town are locally owned, and that the area's volume of business is still too small to pose much danger to the countryside. Still, beginning to loom along the highways are the Country Malls, Country Markets, Country Stores and other Country Businesses that capitalize on country charm while at the same time marring the country landscape.

A guided tour of **Behalt**, a 10-ft. by 265-ft. cyclorama, offers a good and very enjoyable introduction to the Amish and Mennonite peoples. The enormous painting traces the history of these people from their beginning in 1525, in Zurich, Switzerland, to the present.

Another way to learn about the Amish is to visit an Amish farm that's open to the public. One choice is **Yoder's Amish Home** east of town. Here visitors may tour two Amish homes, pet farm animals, have a buggy ride and otherwise take a somewhat romantic look at the Amish lifestyle.

An usually large number of Berlin stores sell locally crafted furniture, often of oak. The town is also a good place to shop for fine quilts. Food shops offer delicious locally made cheeses, ice creams and pastries. Another way to shop for local foods and crafts is to travel the back roads. Many Amish farms have shops. This is also a good way to meet the Amish and to learn more about their farms.

SPECIAL FEATURE

• **Baltic** and **Winesburg** are among the most charming and unspoiled of the area's towns and villages.

> *Remember that the Amish regard the photograph as a sign of vanity, something forbidden by the Bible.*
> *Founded in 1816, Berlin had a population of 75 by the time of the 1830 census.*

WHERE TO STAY

Charm Countryview Inn B&B, OH 557 (near Charm), (216) 893-3003. Spacious porch with view of Amish countryside, private baths, full "country" breakfasts. $$$

Donna's B&B, East St., (216) 893-3068. Country decor, kitchenettes, private baths, TV, freshly baked evening snacks. $$

Overnite Getaway, P. O. Box 416, (216) 893-2529. Pleasant view, peaceful, close to shops, porch swing. $$

Pomerene House Accommodations, P. O. Box 185, (216) 893-2842. National Register home, two-room Victorian suites rented as units. $$

WHERE TO EAT

Boyd and Wurthmann Restaurant, P. O. Box 140, (216) 893-3287. Home-style cooking, homemade desserts, a local favorite. $

Chalet in the Valley, OH 557, (216) 893-2550. Swiss/Austrian/Amish cooking, schnitzels, bratwurst, steaks, fondues. $ to $$

FURTHER INFORMATION

Berlin Area Visitors Bureau, P. O. Box 177, Berlin, OH 44610, (216) 893-3467.

DIRECTIONS

From Akron, I 77 south to exit 83, OH 39 west to Berlin.

GRANVILLE, OHIO

Population: 4,353

Granville's settlers came from Massachusetts and Connecticut in the opening years of the 19th century. They brought with them their New England ways, including some of their architecture. Even today their heritage can be seen — and felt — in Granville. But there are also strong Midwestern elements here, and the fusion of the New England with the Midwestern has produced a lovely town.

Granville is a place to relax, to stroll, to think or read. It's also the place for the Midwesterner seeking a meal in a gorgious old inn. The restored facades and beautiful landscaping along **Broadway**, Granville's main street, maintain a New England flavor, with maybe a little Continental color thrown in. As is true of central Ohio in general, Granville's trees and shrubs seem especially lush.

The **Robbins Hunter Museum**, housed in an 1842 Greek Revival mansion, displays furniture, oriental rugs and other decorative arts from the mid-1800s. Hand tools and other artifacts from settlement days are on exhibit at a second museum, the **Granville Historical Society Museum**. The museum is the oldest (1816) of more than 100 buildings on the National Register of Historic Places.

The chapel and 11 other campus buildings of **Denison University**, an attractive private liberal arts college, are listed on the National Register. **Licking County** has paved old railroad routes to construct trails for walkers, bikers, skaters and skateboarders.

> *The Columbus Polo Club plays at Bryn Du east of town on Sunday after-noons during the warmer months (public admitted).*

WHERE TO STAY

The Buxton Inn, 313 E. Broadway, (614) 587-0001. Restored stagecoach tavern, antique-furnished rooms. $$ to $$$

Follet-Wright House B&B, 403 E. Broadway, (614) 587-0941. 1860 village home, private baths, homemade Danish rolls a breakfast specialty. $$

The George T. Jones House B&B, 221 E. Elm St., (614) 587-1122. 1861 home on National Register, period furnishings, private baths. $$

The Granville Inn, 314 E. Broadway, (614) 587-3333. In tradition of an English country house, "plump" comforters, private baths, public dining room. $$

Granville Manor B&B, 4058 Columbus Rd., (614) 587-4677. 1850s home on three rolling acres, private baths, hot tub, 3 mins to Granville. $$

WHERE TO EAT

Aladdin Restaurant, 122 E. Broadway, (614) 587-0253. Local favorite, home-cooked food. $

The Buxton Inn (see above). American-French cuisine. $$

The Granville Inn, (see above). Fresh seafood, prime rib, Chicken Oscar, famous raisin bread, elegant Sunday buffet. $$

Victoria's Olde Tyme Deli and Ice Creams, 134 E. Broadway, (614) 587-0322. Light dining in one of Ohio's favorite places. $

FURTHER INFORMATION

The Licking County Convention and Visitors Bureau, P. O. Box 702, Newark, OH 43058-0702, (800) 589-8224.

DIRECTIONS

From Columbus, OH 16 east to Granville.

KELLEYS ISLAND, OHIO

Population: 200

For many years, even before the Civil War, excursion steamers plied the waters of the Great Lakes. One of the ports of call was the **Village of Kelleys Island** on the shores of the largest American island in Lake Erie. Today the boats are smaller, but Kelleys Island is still a port of call, and an especially pleasant one at that.

Following a common scenario, the charm of Kelley's Island and its village is due in part to "undevelopment." At the turn of the century the island was home to numerous wineries, a fishing industry and farming as well as to tourism. The population was four times what it is today. Then the industry began to disappear, and the 2,800-acre island became relatively undeveloped (a big chunk now belongs to the state). Rich in flora and fauna as well as reminders of another day, the island is today known for its quiet and relaxed atmosphere and is listed in its entirety on the National Register of Historic Places.

The island has two unique state memorials. The first, the **Glacial Grooves**, discovered back when there was blasting in the quarries, has been described as the most spectacular example of glacial carvings in the country. The second, **Inscription Rock**, contains well-preserved pictographs inscribed by Erie Indians hundreds of years ago.

Cars are permitted here, but most visitors rent bikes or golf carts and tour the island at a pace more befitting the setting. Hiking is also popular, and the island has nature trails that boast fossils (very popular these days) and abandoned quarries as well as cedar trees and a diversity of bird species. Other activities include summer swimming, winter ice fishing, and year-round wine-tasting.

SPECIAL FEATURE

• The 352-foot **Perry's Victory and International Peace Memorial**, commemorating Commodore Perry's victory over the British fleet in the War of 1812, is located in nearby **Put-in-Bay**. There is daily summer boat service to Put-in-Bay from Kelleys Island.

Datus and Irad Kelley purchased the island for $1.50 an acre in the 1830s.

WHERE TO STAY

Cricket Lodge B&B, P. O. Box 323, (419) 746-2263. 1905 lakefront home on National Register, "leisurely" breakfast served on screened porch. $$$

Eagles Nest, P. O. Box 762, (419) 746-2708. Surrounded by trees and lawn, private baths, studio & efficiency suites available. $$$

Fly Inn, P. O. Box 471, (419) 746-2525. Modern home, private baths, Jacuzzi, pool, pool table. $$$

Inn on Kelleys Island, P. O. Box 11, (419) 746-2258. 1876 home with private beach, beautiful views. $$

Sweet Valley Inn, P. O. Box 733, (419) 746-2750. Restored Victorian home, spacious antique-filled rooms, open year-round. $$$.

WHERE TO EAT

Fresch's, 1 block north on Division St.,(419) 746-2304. Quaint Victorian home serving Italian and Continental cuisine. $$

Kelley's Island Wine Co., Woodford Rd., (419) 746-2537. Wine-tasting room and gourmet deli in 19th century winery. $

Village Pump, W. Lakeshore Dr., (419) 746-2281. Fresh Lake Erie perch, home-prepared food, famed Brandy Alexanders. $ to $$

FURTHER INFORMATION

Kelleys Island Chamber of Commerce, P. O. Box 783, Kelleys Island, OH 43438, (419) 746-2360.

DIRECTIONS

You can get to **Kelleys Island** by island-hopping cruisers out of **Sandusky** (OH), by ferryboats and cruisers from **Marblehead** (OH), and by air from Sandusky and **Port Clinton** (see selection). And, of course, you can get there by private boat. Check with the CoC for schedules. No matter how you get there, do allow at least four or five hours, preferably several days.

PORT CLINTON, OHIO

Population: 7,106

Port Clinton is an old port town, a gateway town, a place on the way to **Catawba Island**, to **Kelleys** and **South Bass** islands way out in Lake Erie, and to anywhere else in or on Lake Erie where boats can go. Port Clinton is where sightseeing and fishing trips begin. It is one of those towns whose appeal is based in part on anticipation.

Nicknamed the *Walleye Capital of the World*, the port was once a center for commercial fishing, boatbuilding and various industries related to the water. Although commercial fishing remains, the water-based industries have given way to water-based recreations.

Foremost among the recreations are fishing and boating. Charters are available for the pursuit of smallmouth black bass, walleye, perch and other lake fish. There are also marinas and outfitters for private boaters; for sightseers in general, there are excursion boats serving the resort and "party" village of Put-in-Bay on South Bass Island.

Sailors and other visitors will find Port Clinton's downtown well-stocked with shops and restaurants. There are several structures of historic interest here as well. One is the venerable **Island House Hotel**, now restored (listed below). Another is the sandstone Romanesque Revival courthouse, listed on the National Register of Historic Places; of special interest are the murals on the upper floors depicting Ottawa County's history.

The **Portage River Lift Bridge**, linking downtown to western **Ottawa County**, was designed by a female engineer in the late 1920s. It seems that the program printed for the bridge's dedication listed the engineer only by first initial and last name, whereas all men involved with the project were listed by their first as well as last names. The bridge, carefully preserved, still operates to allow boats to pass out to Lake Erie.

SPECIAL FEATURE

• Adjoining Port Clinton to the east is **Catawba Island**, now a peninsula. This is an area of beautiful homes, shops, orchards and farm markets. Peaches have been long associated with the region and are still grown there. Trolley tours that include Catawba Island on their itinerary originate in Port Clinton.

> *The National Rifle and Pistol Matches have been held each July and August at Camp Perry, west of Port Clinton, since the turn of the century.*
> *Movie stars used to stay at the Island House Hotel while outfitting their classic wooden Matthews yachts, built in Port Clinton.*

WHERE TO STAY

The Island House, 102 Madison St., (800) 233-7307. "Lake Erie's Centennial Hotel," established 1886, restored 1986. $$ to $$$

WHERE TO EAT

The Garden at the Lighthouse, 226 E. Perry, (419) 732-2151. In old home of lighthouse keeper, Fish Market Salad popular. $$

Island House (see above). American cuisine with fresh Lake Erie perch and walleye specialties. $$

Mon Ami, 2845 East Wine Cellar Rd., (800) 777-4266. In historic winery, outdoor dining and BBQs, own baking, weekend entertainment. $$

FURTHER INFORMATION

Ottawa County Visitors Bureau, 109 Madison St., Port Clinton, OH 43452, (800) 441-1271.

DIRECTIONS

From Toledo, OH 2 east to Port Clinton.

ROSCOE VILLAGE, OHIO

Population: about 500

Roscoe Village is a little canal community cut from the 1830s. The village, near **Coshocton**, is an authentic restoration, not a reconstruction; a living community, not a museum. The sidewalks are brick and the lampposts and signs antique. Guides wear 1830s clothing. Period crafts are demonstrated and the products sold in quaint shops. There's an old inn (which happens to have one of the finest dining rooms in Ohio) and lovely perennial gardens. Some of the restorations are private homes. The population is almost exactly what it was in the 1830s.

Adding to the realism is a 1 1/2-mile restored section of the old **Ohio and Erie Canal**. Tours of the canal aboard a horse-drawn replica of an 1800s canal boat are one of the village's most popular attractions (45 minutes).

Founded in 1816, Roscoe Village was from the 1830s to the 1860s a busy canal port. The railroad and, terminally, a disastrous flood in 1913, drove the little vilage into oblivion. Following a scenario almost exactly that of Waterloo

Village in New Jersey (see selection), the town was rediscovered in 1968 and restoration of its buildings begun. The village was to become Ohio's — and one of the country's — premier restored villages.

The newly opened **Visitor Center & Exhibit Hall** features miniature dioramas and a wide-screen high-tech theater presentation on early transportation. Within the village are seven historical museums, including a working 19th-century print shop, an 1825 working man's home and the **Toll House**, whose exhibits demonstrate 19th-century building techniques as well as modern restoration techniques. The separately administered **Johnson-Humrickhouse Museum** is noted for its collections of Native American, Eskimo, and Asian artifacts.

SPECIAL FEATURES

• **Coshocton**, one mile away across the **Muskingum River**, has a beautifully restored downtown area.

• South of Roscoe Village in Muskingum County is **The Wilds**, the largest private land preserve in the world. Built on 9,154 acres of reclaimed land, the preserve is designed to protect rare wildlife. The land may be toured by car or tram.

> *Roscoe Village's Whitewoman Street got its name from a white captive, Mary Harris, who was married to an Indian and lived in the area in 1750.*
> *The Muskingum River is the only river that both begins and ends within Ohio.*

WHERE TO STAY

1890 B&B, 663 N. Whitewoman St. (Coshocton), (614) 622-1890. Victorian home next to scenic towpath, antiques, home-baked breads. **$$ to $$$**

Apple Butter Inn B&B, 455 Hill St. (Coshocton), (614) 622-1329. Circa 1840s Greek-Revival home overlooking village, lazy-day rockers, private baths. **$$ to $$$**

Katy McCourt's Guest House, P. O. Box 1397 (Coshocton), (614) 622-7236. Restored 1856 home on National Register, fireplaces, antique ballroom chandelier, art gallery. **$$$**

Log House B&B, P. O. Box 30 (Conesville), (614) 829-2757. Restored 1840s log house, antiques, common room, "hearty" breakfasts. **$$**

Mary Harris House B&B, 42768 US 36 (Warsaw), (614) 824-4141. Ancient shade trees, stone garden, porch swing, private baths. **$$ to $$$**

WHERE TO EAT

Andy's Restaurant, 1167 Walnut St. (Coschocton), (614) 622-2753. Traditional American cooking, locally popular. **$**

King Charlie's Tavern (in Roscoe Village Inn), 200 N. Whitewoman St., (614) 622-2222. Rustic tavern serving light meals. **$**

Old Warehouse Restaurant, 400 N. Whitewoman St., (614) 622-4001. Restored 1838 warehouse, family-style dining, "historic entrees." **$ to $$**

Robson's, 442 Main St. (Coshocton), (614) 622-8262. 22 seafood choices, 12 chicken, 15 beef and pork, 12 Italian, 7 cheese cakes. **$**

Roscoe Village Inn Dining Room, 200 N. Whitewoman St., (614) 622-2222. Traditional American and international repertoire prepared by award-winning chef. **$$**

FURTHER INFORMATION

Roscoe Village Foundation, 381 Hill St., Coshocton, OH 43812, (614) 622-9310.

DIRECTIONS

From Cleveland, I 77 south to exit 65, US 36 west to Coshocton (Roscoe Village).

VERMILION, OHIO

Population: 11,127

Vermilion is sometimes described as a "New England seaside community" and a home of steamship captains. The reference to New England is given in quotes because Vermilion isn't of course in New England, but no qualification is needed for the reference to the steamship captains: more than 50 Great Lakes captains made their homes here in the latter part of the 19th century.

An active Lake Erie port as far back as the early 1800s, many of Vermilion's people — and their homes — had New England roots. The roots can still be seen in a part of the downtown waterfront area that has been restored as **Harbour Town 1837**. Here are gracious captains' homes, the old **Town Hall**, the old **Opera House**, and numerous specialty shops and unique restaurants. Further evidence of the New England roots can be see in the white Cape Cod homes nestled on the lagoons of the **Vermilion River**.

The **Inland Seas Maritime Museum** tell the fascinating story of the Great Lakes using paintings, photographs, models and artifacts. The museum features a simulated ship's bridge and a replica of the **Vermilion Lighthouse**.

Reflecting its popularity with fishing and recreational craft, Vermilion has an excellent small-boat harbor. The town also has several fine beaches. Sail and power boat rentals, fishing charters and bicycle rentals provide good ways to enjoy this charming "New England" port city and summer resort.

> *The floors of the Great Lakes contain the remains of thousands of shipwrecks.*
> *Schwensen's, still very much in business, is a century-old family bakery.*

WHERE TO STAY

Capt. Gilchrist Guesthouse, 5662 Huron St., (216) 967-1237. Restored 1885 home on National Register, majestic buckeye trees, antiques, private baths. $$ to $$$

WHERE TO EAT

Chez Francois, 555 Main St., (216) 967-0630. "That French Restaurant & Riverfront Cafe in Vermilion." $$$

McGarvey's, 5150 Liberty Ave., (216) 967-8000. Riverfront restaurant serving fresh seafood and Lake Erie fish. $ to $$

FURTHER INFORMATION

Vermilion Chamber of Commerce, 5495 Liberty Ave., Vermilion, OH 44089, (216) 967-4477.

DIRECTIONS

From Cleveland, US 6 west to Vermilion.

ZOAR VILLAGE, OHIO

Population: 177

The streets of the picturesque little village of **Zoar** are entering the 21st century looking in good measure like they did in the first half of the 19th century. Just how this happened is a little piece of classic American history.

Persecuted for their religious beliefs in Germany, a group known as German Separatists immigrated to the United States and founded the town of Zoar — named for Lot's Biblical town of refuge — in 1817. Finding themselves unable to provide for themselves and to pay for their new land, the Zoarites chose to pool their individual properties and operate as a commune. The commune prospered, and by the middle of the century the *Society of Separatists of Zoar* had acquired assets valued at more than $1 million. Among their holdings at one point were four boats on the Ohio & Eric Canal (see "Roscoe Village" selection).

Economic and social factors were eventually to plague the group, however, and in 1898 the Society disbanded. During the years following, members of the younger generations left to seek brighter futures elsewhere, and outsiders bought and restored the buildings as members of the older generations died. Ten of the buildings have been restored, or are being restored, by the Ohio Historical Society. Prominent among the other restorers have been families from Canton, just a few miles to the north.

Five of the historic buildings are log cabins; the rest are two-floor structures, some brick and some frame (but filled with brick masonry, or nogging). The solid Old World construction of the buildings has added to their value and encouraged restoration efforts.

Visitors should first stop by the **Zoar Store** (1833) to purchase tour tickets and to see an introductory video. Reproductions of 19th-century wares are also sold here. (Note: tours are only offered seasonally.)

The historic district comprises 12 blocks. The most imposing of the buildings maintained by the **Ohio Historical Society**, and therefore open to the public, is the **Number One House** (1835-1845), a Georgian-style house that was the home of Zoar Society leader Joseph Baumeler and several other families. Among the historical society's other properties are the bakery (1845), tin shop (1825), blacksmith shop (1834), wagon shop (1840) and garden and greenhouse (1835). Zoar may be best known for the beauty of the formal **community garden**. The garden occupies an entire village square and is arranged with geometric precision according to a Biblically-inspired pattern.

The old **Town Hall**, now a museum maintained by the **Zoar Community Association**, displays old photos, tinware, furniture and other Zoar memorabilia (by appointment). The majority of buildings are private residences, shops, restaurants and bed and breakfasts (see below). The 1868 schoolhouse (usually closed) and 1853 **Meeting House** (now United Church of Christ) are among the village's most handsome buildings.

> *Because there is no home delivery, Zoarites treat the post office as a common meeting place.*
>
> *Men and women possessed equal political rights in The Society of Separatists of Zoar.*

WHERE TO STAY

The Cobbler Shop Inn B&B, 2nd & Main strs., (216) 874-2600. Restored 1828 shop/home, rooms carefully restored and furnished to period, "sumptuous" breakfasts. $$

The Zoar Tavern, 1 Main St., (216) 874-2170. 1831 home of village doctor, hand-hewn beams, antiques, private baths, telephones and TV. $$$

WHERE TO EAT

Inn on the River, P. O. Box 452, (216) 874-3770. Dinners served in 1830 canal inn, outdoor gazebo/patio area with grill. $$

The Zoar Tavern (see above). Fresh seafood, steaks, casual oaken atmosphere, "sumptuous" desserts. $$

FURTHER INFORMATION

Zoar Village, P. O. Box 404, Zoar, Ohio 44697, (216) 874-3011.

DIRECTIONS

From Cleveland, I 77 south to exit 93 (Bolivar), OH 212 south to Zoar.

OKLAHOMA

FREEDOM

PAWHUSKA

GUTHRIE

Oklahoma
City

FREEDOM, OKLAHOMA

Population: 264

Freedom is a little cowtown out on the plains of western Oklahoma. The population hasn't changed much since about 1918, when the town moved by wagon from another site to be near the new railroad. The thing to be grateful for is that Freedom has survived at all, because countless other small rural towns haven't. The major reasons for the survival have been the foresight, determination and cohesion of the town's "straight-shooting" and "down-to-earth" citizens.

Freedom is nestled on the north bank of the historic **Cimarron River**. To the south can be seen towering red bluffs that almost demand the company of a cowtown. In response to that demand, the saloon, bank and other buildings along Freedom's main street have been fronted with rough cedar to give the appearance — and mood — of an Old Western town.

Displayed in one of these buildings, the **Freedom Museum**, are early-day household items, antique tools and machines, and a prehistoric elephant tusk unearthed on a local farm.

Every once in a while a little Western color is added by a shootout on **Main Street** staged by local townspeople. The big event of the year, however, is the **Annual Freedom Rodeo and Old Cowhand Reunion** Held the third weekend of August and billed as *The Biggest Open Rodeo in the West*, the three-day event features a full rodeo, country dances each night, a Chuckwagon Feed, Western Art Show and other events befitting a major cowtown event. The rodeo has been a Freedom tradition since 1939.

SPECIAL FEATURES

• **Alabaster Caverns State Park**, 6 miles south of town, includes the largest gypsum cave open to the public in the country. Within the 3/4-mile long cave are two forms of gypsum: alabaster, which comes in pink, white, and mixed colors, and selenite, which comes in sparkling crystals. Guided tours are conducted daily.

• Also in the park are hiking trails and, at the bottom of **Cedar Canyon**, a beautiful swimming pool.

On the Cimarron just a few miles west are hundreds of acres of salt flats. Salt Haulers Grave, north of Freedom, is where the bodies of salt haulers massacred by Indians were buried by local cowhands.

WHERE TO STAY

Heritage Manor, Rt. 1 (Box 33) (Aline, OK), (405) 463-2563. 1903 home filled with antiques, pump organ, 5,000-volume library, full breakfasts. $ to $$ (**Note:** Aline is about 60 miles southeast of Freedom, but a visit there is worth the drive.)

WHERE TO EAT

Cattleman's Cafe, P. O. Box 182, (405) 621-3289. The name says it all. $

FURTHER INFORMATION

Freedom Chamber of Commerce, P. O. Box 125, Freedom, OK 73842, (405) 621-3276.

DIRECTIONS

From Oklahoma City, I 40 west to exit 101, US 281 north (via Watonga) to Seiling, US 183 west to OK 50, OK 50 north to Freedom.

GUTHRIE, OKLAHOMA

Population: 10,518

At high noon on April 22, 1889, a pistol was shot and thousands dashed across the border into Oklahoma to claim free land in the central part of the state. Some went by train, others by horseback, wagon or foot. In the morning **Guthrie** consisted of not much more than a train depot; by evening there was a tent and a wagon city of some 10,000 *Boomers.* From 1890 until 1907, Guthrie was the territorial capital of Oklahoma, and from 1907 to 1910 the state capital. Then the capital was moved to Oklahoma City, and Victorian Guthrie stood still.

Embracing 400 city blocks and more than 1,300 pre-1910 buildings, Guthrie today has one of the largest urban historic districts in the United States. Virtually every building from the 19th century survives. Much more than a museum, the beautifully restored downtown is alive with shops, restaurants, an original saloon, and turn-of-the-century trolleys. A carriage can frequently be seen conveying newlyweds to the **Harrison House** (see below).

Guthrie is home to several quite unique museums. Site of Oklahoma's first daily newspaper, the **State Capital Publishing Museum** features turn-of-the-century printing equipment. The **Oklahoma Frontier Drug Store Museum**, a turn-of-the-century pharmacy, is furnished with wooden drug-store fixtures and antique wall cabinets with pharmacy memorabilia. Among the displays is a 1910 wooden telephone booth. Yet another museum, the **Oklahoma Territorial Museum**, is a showcase of territorial and early statehood artifacts.

Dominating Guthrie's skyline, the **Scottish Rite Masonic Temple** boasts stained-glass windows, an elegant marble atrium, two theaters, a ballroom, reading salons and a Gothic library. The structure is the largest Scottish Rite temple in the world (open to the public).

A cultural center today as it was in territorial days, Guthrie has the only full-time professional theater in Oklahoma. The **Pollard Resident Theatre Company** performs classic and contemporary plays and musicals in two theaters 11 months each year. As for music, one of the lovely theaters of the Masonic Temple hosts a first-class concert series.

SPECIAL FEATURE

• The **National Cowboy Hall of Fame and Western Heritage Center** is located about 25 miles south of Guthrie in Oklahoma City. The museum commemorates those who settled the West with paintings, statuary, portraits of TV and film stars, life-size settings, stagecoaches and other exhibits.

> *When the "89ers" reached Guthrie, they found that many of the choicest properties had been claimed by people who had sneaked in before the rush. These, and eventually all Oklahomans, came to be known as "Sooners."*
>
> *A Guthrie city directory published several months after the rush listed 39 doctors and surgeons, 40 restaurants and 46 grocery stores.*

WHERE TO STAY

The Caretakers Cottage Guest House, 1016 W. Warner St., (405) 282-0012. Victorian cottage, oriental rugs, private sitting roms, private baths, full gourmet breakfasts. $$$

Harrison House, 124 W. Harrison St., (800) 375-1001. In five restored turn-of-the-century buildings, antiques, period wallpapers and curtains, private baths. $$ to $$$

The Redstone Country Inn B&B, 1016 W. Warner St., (405) 282-0012. English-style country inn, suites with antiques, private baths, full gourmet breakfasts, beverages. $$$

The Stone Lion Inn, 1016 W. Warner St., (405) 282-0012. Restored 1907 mansion, pecan trees, private baths, full gourmet breakfasts, dining room, murder mystery weekends. $$ to $$$

Victorian Rose B&B, 415 E. Cleveland St., (800) 767 3015. Circa 1894 Queen Anne home, antiques, wrap-around porch with wicker swing, full breakfasts, coffee/tea. $$ to $$$

WHERE TO EAT

The Blue Belle, 224 W. Harrison St., (405) 282-6660. Western saloon where Tom Mix bartended (1902-1904), steaks, crab legs, sandwiches. $

Granny Had One, 113 W. Harrison St., (405) 282-4482. Evening buffets, barbecued brisket, beef pot roast, chicken, homemade pastries. $

The Sand Plum, in Harrison House (see above), (405) 282-7771. Continental cuisine, ribeye, grilled swordfish, roast duck, one of Oklahoma's best. $$

FURTHER INFORMATION

Guthrie Convention & Visitors Bureau, P. O. Box 995, Guthrie, OK 73044, (800) 299-1889.

DIRECTIONS

From Oklahoma City, I 35 north to exit 157 (Guthrie exit).

PAWHUSKA, OKLAHOMA

Population: 3,825

Up in northern Oklahoma and far from the interstates stretches a region of grassland hills known as the **Osage**. The landscape is reminiscent of the High Plains, although these don't begin for more than another 100 miles to the west. Home to a few ranchers and a sprinkling of little towns, the area hasn't been known to many since the oil-boom days of the 1920s.

Although small, **Pawhuska** is the seat of **Osage County**, capital of the **Osage Indian Nation** and the largest town for miles. Part of the town's charm is that it doesn't seem to belong. A downtown filled with mostly brick turn-of-the-century and 1920s buildings (89 of them on the National Register) might belong in many places, but not in a valley among the vast expanses of the **Osage Hills**.

The best way to see Pawhuska is to park your car and, as with most charming towns, explore **Main Street** by foot. Unlike most charming towns, however, Main Street here is still being discovered by outsiders. It's the original. Art galleries, antique and curio shops and the rest haven't yet imposed their own versions of charm. The most historic of the buildings include the **Immaculate Conception Catholic Church** (1887), noted for its beautifully colored stained-glass windows, and the **Constantine Theatre**, built in the 1880s as a grand playhouse with outstanding acoustics. Both structures may be toured by appointment.

The **Osage Tribal Museum** is the oldest continually operated tribal museum in the country. Located on the **Osage Agency Campus**, the museum boasts a collection of over 2,000 rare photographs of early Osage Indians and the town of Pawhuska.

Exhibits of the **Osage County Historical Museum** include a monument to the country's first Boy Scout Troop (established in 1909), two Santa Fe Railroad cars that once served Pawhuska, and a restored one-room schoolhouse

Just 7 miles north of town starts Pawhuska's (and Oklahoma's) most important old-new attraction, the Nature Conservancy's recently established **Tallgrass Prairie Preserve**. The purpose of the preserve is to restore a native American tallgrass prairie ecosystem. The preserve, which now totals over 36,000 acres, may be visited by following a marked drive. Along the way are scenic overlooks where visitors may step out of their cars and take a closer look at the flora and fauna, including perhaps some of the recently reintroduced bison.

SPECIAL FEATURES

• Taking a nature walk at **Osage Hills State Park** northeast of Pawhuska offers an especially enjoyable way to become acquainted with the starkly beautiful Osage.

• One of the finest Western museums in the country, the **Woolaroc Museum and Wildlife Preserve**, is just a 30-minute drive east of Pawhuska. The museum and preserve are the legacy of a 3,600-acre ranch built by the founder of the Phillips Petroleum Company in the 1920s. The museum is celebrated for its artwork, including paintings by Frederic Remington and Charles Russell, and its outstanding collections of Navajo blankets, Colt Paterson firearms and other Indian and Western art and artifacts.

Until the Allotment Act of 1906 the Osage Indians roamed the prairies as they wished and held the land in common.

Under President Ulysses S. Grant's "Church Policy," the Quakers were given charge of the country to which the Osage Indians were assigned. However, many of the Indians were (and are) members of the Roman Catholic Church because of an earlier contact with that church.

WHERE TO STAY

Inn at Woodyard Farms, Rt. 2 (Box 190), (918) 287-2699. 1880s-style farmhouse on 74 rolling acres, private baths, full Oklahoma-style breakfasts. $$

WHERE TO EAT

Bad Brad's Bar-B-Q, 1215 W. Main St., (918) 287-1212. "Best Bar-B-Q in Oklahoma, Kansas AND Texas!" $

FURTHER INFORMATION

Pawhuska Chamber of Commerce, 114 W. Main Street, Pawhuska, OK 74056, (918) 287-1208.

DIRECTIONS

From Tulsa, OK 11 north to OK 99, OK 99 north to US 60, US 60 west to Pawhuska.

OREGON

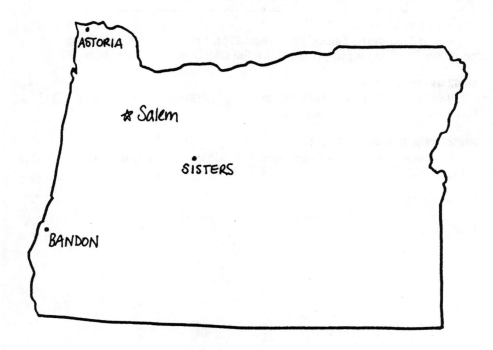

ASTORIA

✳ Salem

SISTERS

BANDON

ASTORIA, OREGON
Population: 10,069

Astoria is in many ways a small American edition of a Scottish port city. In the background are hazy, brooding mountains; closer in are patches of rich green and, in the foreground, the waters of a large estuary, or firth. Astoria has a long maritime history and boasts a nice collection of proud Victorian houses, just as do Scottish cities.

The **Astoria Column** up on **Coxcomb Hill** is especially reminiscent of Edinburgh, a city known for its classical hilltop memorials. The 125-foot column makes an ideal first stop on a visit to Astoria. Dedicated in 1926 and patterned after the Trajan Column in Rome (erected in 114 A.D.), the column bears a pictorial frieze commemorating landmark events in Astoria's history. Inside is a 164-step circular staircase leading to a breathtaking view of the lower **Columbia River** and the **Pacific Ocean**.

Salmon canneries and forest and shipping industries turned Astoria into a lively boom town in the late 1800s (the town was apparently also a notorious shanghaiing port), and Astoria's many ornate Victorian homes remain a tangible reminder of those times. Many of the homes are now bed & breakfast inns (a few are listed below).

Perhaps the best known of the houses is the 1885 **Capt. George Flavel Mansion**, now a museum of the **Clatsop County Historical Society**. Among the house's many outstanding features are six handcrafted fireplace mantels, each carved from a different hardwood and accented by a different imported tile surround.

Astoria is blessed with one of the finest marine museums in the world, **The Columbia River Maritime Museum**. In the Great Hall, designed with a soaring waveform, and in seven exhibit galleries are displays on fishing and whaling, steamboating and sailing, history and adventure. Some of the exhibits are real-life vessels, including the West Coast's last seagoing lighthouse, now a floating National Historic Landmark.

> *Known as the "Graveyard of the Pacific," the region around the mouth of the Columbia River has seen the loss of more than 100 ships and 2,000 small craft.*
>
> *Nearby Fort Stevens, now a state park, was the only military installation in the continental U.S. to be fired on by the Japanese in World War II (June 21, 1942).*

WHERE TO STAY

Astoria Inn B&B, 3391 Irving Ave., (503) 325-8153. Restored 1890s farmhouse on hillside overlooking river, private baths, full "country" breakfasts, snacks. $$$

Columbia River Inn B&B, 1681 Franklin Ave., (800) 847-2475. Beautiful 1870 "Painted Lady," quiet and convenient. $$ to $$$

Franklin Street Station B&B, 1140 Franklin St., (800) 448-1098. Ornate 1900 home of shipbuilder, private baths, full breakfasts. $$ to $$$

Grandview B&B, 1574 Grand Ave., (800) 574-1574. Three-story Victorian home with river view, close to sights, suites available. $ to $$$

Rosebriar Hotel, 636 14th St., (503) 325-7427. Restored 1902 home, vintage rugs, brass chandeliers, full breakfasts. $$ to $$$

WHERE TO EAT

Cafe Uniontown, 218 W. Marine Dr., (503) 325-8708. In historic 1907 building, beef, fresh seafood. $$

Pier 11 Feedstore & Deli, 77 11th St., (503) 325-0279. Converted freight depot, unique atmosphere. $ to $$

Seafare Restaurant, 400 Industry, (503) 325-3551. Overlooking marina and river, live entertainment. $$

Ship Inn, 1 2nd St., (503) 325-0033. A true fish and chips house, one of best seafood restaurants in Oregon. $

FURTHER INFORMATION

Greater Astoria Chamber of Commerce & Visitor Center, P. O. Box 176, Astoria, OR 97103, (503) 325-6311.

DIRECTIONS

From Portland, US 30 northwest to Astoria.

BANDON, OREGON

Population :2,215

Within the city limits of **Bandon** (or **Bandon-by-the-Sea**) you'll find one of the most beautiful beaches on the West Coast. Rock-studded and with smooth white sand, it may be the most beautiful between Alaska and Acapulco; at least the locals think so. Offshore are spectacular rocks, or *seastacks*, home to seals and other animals. Bandon also has a river, the **Coquille**, and two national wildlife refuges within its limits.

Bandon's **Old Town** is home to a colorful collection of art galleries and craft shops. Not only do visitors admire and/or shop for arts and crafts, they watch the works take shape as weavers, silversmiths, woodworkers and others display their skills. Many of the shops are in historic buildings that were fortunate enough to escape devastating fires in 1914 and 1936. Cranberry sweets are among the items unique to Bandon's shops (try a free sample).

Even considering its marine location, Bandon offers the visitor an unusually wide variety of activities. Seal watching and, in season, whale watching are popular. (Don't disturb seal pups resting on the shore — their mothers may reject them.) Birdwatching is also popular — puffins, for example, can be seen in the spring on **Elephant** and **Table Rocks**. Fishing, both dockside and deep-water, is excellent. So are clamming and crabbing. Crab rings as well as fishing gear can be rented.

Among the many other beach activites are kite-flying, horseback riding and tidepooling. Beachcombing is rewarded with finds of driftwood, petrified wood, agate and jasper. Windsurfing is popular on the river and local lakes; there's a windsurfing school south of town.

SPECIAL FEATURES

• Three tempting suggestions for the beach- and shopping-weary: a sternwheeler cruise on the **Coquille River**, a visit to a cheese factory, a cranberry bog tour. Check with the CoC for details.

• Hundreds of free-roaming birds and animals may be met, petted, filmed and talked to at **West Coast Game Park** south of town.

> *Proud of its fame as a major kite flying center, Bandon offers kite-flyers information and instruction.*

WHERE TO STAY

Floras Lake House B&B, 928701 Boice Cope Rd., (503) 348-2573. Over sand dune from ocean/beach, common room with wood stove, private baths, decks, continental plus breakfasts. $$$

Lighthouse B&B, 650 Jetty Rd., (503) 374-9316. On the beach, private baths, "heart-healthy" breakfasts. $$$

Sea Star Guesthouse, 370 1st St., (503) 347-9632. In heart of Old Town, harbor and beachland views, private baths, TV, full breakfasts. $$ to $$$

WHERE TO EAT

Andrea's, 160 Baltimore, (503) 347-3022. Changing seasonal menu, local seafood, international flavors, "sinful" cheesecakes. $ to $$

Bandon Boatworks, S. Jetty Rd., (503) 347-2111. Ocean-view dining, seafood entrees. $ to $$

Lord Bennett's, 1695 Beach Loop Dr., (503) 347-3663. Seafood entrees, broiled steaks, panoramic views of coastline. $ to $$

Sea Star Bistro, 2nd St., (503) 347-9632. Mediterraneuan entrees, paella, ragouts, Fish Nicosia, Smoked Game Hen. $ to $$

The Station, Highway 101, (503) 347-9615. Oysters, squid, shrimp, scallops, sole, halibut, salmon. $

FURTHER INFORMATION

Bandon Chamber of Commerce, P. O. Box 1515, Bandon, OR 97411, (503) 347-9616.

DIRECTIONS

From Portland, I 5 south to exit 120, OR 42 west to Coquille, 42S to Bandon.

SISTERS, OREGON

Population: 820

Sisters is a tribute to what can happen when a spectacular setting is complemented with human planning and imagination. Overlooked by the snow-capped peaks — including those of the **Three Sisters** — of central Oregon's **Cascade Range**, and bordered by forests of towering ponderosa pines, Sisters's setting would itself guarantee the town high marks.

But what makes the little town so special is its Old West flavor. Originally due to special incentives, and more recently a building code, buildings in the downtown area conform to an 1880s' architectural style. The building code also restricts elevations to 30 feet or less, thereby preserving the panoramic views of the Cascades. The result is a business district with charm and character — the kind of place where people linger even when they've got nothing particular to buy.

The range of goods in the shops is impressive for a small town (although Sisters serves an area of several thousand). Bordering the Western streets are galleries, boutiques and an especially interesting and diverse array of gift and specialty shops.

Sisters opens onto an outdoor paradise. There are no fewer than nine public and private golf courses within 25 miles of town. The region's many unspoiled rivers, lakes and streams provide opportunities for sailing, boating, swimming, rafting and fishing. The mountains and forests beckon horseback riders, hikers and climbers. For the winter months there are two major downhill ski areas and hundreds of trails for cross-country skiing, snowshoeing and snowmobiling. The snowmobile trails rank among the best in the country.

The Sisters area is dotted with resorts and campgrounds. Several outfitters cater to those planning trips into the wilderness.

SPECIAL FEATURES

• The approximately 100-mile loop of a National Scenic Byway begins just west of town. One part of it, **McKenzie Highway (OR 242)**, is closed in the winter. Check locally for routing and road conditions.

• The crystal-clear **Metolius River** emerges from the ground at the base of **Black Butte** in **Camp Sherman**, a community northwest of Sisters. The 42-degree water forms one of the largest spring-fed rivers in the country.

> *Many of the peaks in the nearby Cascades are potentially active volcanos, especially South Sister and Mt. Bachelor.*

WHERE TO STAY

Conklin Guest House, 69013 Camp Polk Rd., (503) 549-0123. Old ranch house with panoramic views of mountains and forests. $$$

Lake Creek Lodge (in Camp Sherman), Star Route (Sisters), (503) 595-6331. Since 1935, rustic cabins, mod. American plan (in summers). $$$

WHERE TO EAT

The Gallery Restaurant, 230 W. Cascade St., (503) 549-2631. "Old-Fashioned Family Restaurant." $ to $$

Hotel Sisters Restaurant, 105 W. Cascade St., (503) 549-7427. Western saloon and restaurant in renovated 1914 hotel. $$

FURTHER INFORMATION

Sisters Area Chamber of Commerce, P. O. Box 430, Sisters, OR 97759, (503) 549-0251.

DIRECTIONS

From Portland, I 5 south to exit 233 (Corvallis), US 20 east to Sisters.

PENNSYLVANIA

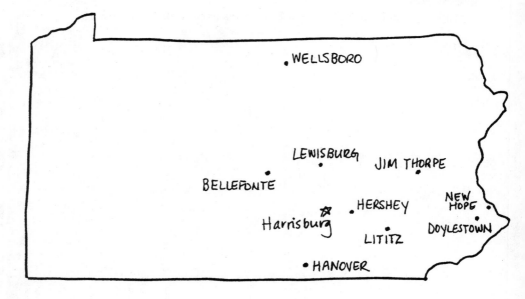

BELLEFONTE, PENNSYLVANIA

Population: 6,358

Visitors sometime arrive expecting the **Big Spring** in **Bellefonte** to be another Old Faithful. They shouldn't. The Big Spring doesn't gush, or do anything else very dramatic, although it does produce 11,500,000 gallons a day, enough for Bellefonte's water supply. The Big Spring is a looking pond, a peaceful place to be. Adjacent is **Talleyrand Park**, with gazebo and foot bridges, where people stroll on Sundays and listen to concerts by local musicians. A nice place to relax awhile.

Bellefonte is a relaxed kind of town in general. Maybe it's because the town's growth leveled off around the turn of the century and a little of the way of life of another century still lingers. The old residential streets as well as downtown share in the attitude.

The walking-tour brochure distributed by the CoC is in fact an 1874 city map with 45 little numbers superimposed to show the more important sites. The map's message is clear: a lot of what was Bellefonte in 1874 is still around.

Throughout the town are fine old buildlings, with the accent on fine as much as old. Especially noteworthy are the early Georgian buildings. A beautiful example is the the gray-stone, white-shuttered 1815 **Potter Home**. This lovely building now houses an interesting historical museum. Visitors who enjoy strolling shaded streets should include Linn, Curtin, and N. Allegheny streets in their tour.

SPECIAL FEATURE

• At the old brick **Train Station** the **Bellefonte Historical Railroad** offers seasonal excursions aboard its two rail diesel cars. The excursion to **Curtin Village**, a 19th-century ironworks village with restored furnace and 1831 ironmaster's mansion, is particularly recommended.

> *Bellefonte ("beautiful fountain") started out as Big Spring, but was renamed after "Big Spring" was visited by the French statesman, Talleyrand, who was in exile in America from 1794 to 1796.*
>
> *Bellefonte was one of the first towns in the world to have electricity (1884).*

WHERE TO STAY

The Dartt House B&B, 251 N. Allegheny St., (814) 353-0408. Restored 1879 doctor's home, 12-ft. ceilings, claw-foot tubs, guest den and kitchen. $$

Garrett B&B, 217 W. Linn St., (814) 355-3093. Restored 1860 home with 16 rooms, guest sitting room, stocked refrigerator. $$.

WHERE TO EAT

The Gamble Mill Tavern, Lamb St. Bridge, (814) 355-7764. Parts date from 1786, fresh seafood, duck, extensive beer and wine selection. $ to $$

FURTHER INFORMATION

Bellefonte Area Chamber of Commerce, Train Station, Bellefonte, PA 16823, (814) 355-2761.

DIRECTIONS

From Scranton/Wilkes-Barre, I 81 south to I 80, west to exit 23, PA 150 south to Bellefonte.

DOYLESTOWN, PENNSYLVANIA

Population: 8,575

Doylestown is not a suburb, but neither is it a gossipy small town. It isn't a tourist spot, but it *is* a spot that many tourists like to visit. Philadelphia isn't far away, but neither is the famed **Bucks County** countryside with its time-mellowed stone farmhouses. Doylestown is charming, but the charm is that of a real town, of a town where families are raised and groceries bought. The charm was never designed to cater.

Doylestown's 250 years of history, its selection as the county seat of Bucks County, its location and interesting architectural admixture, these and other factors have contributed to an unusually rich cultural heritage and diversity. James A. Michener, Pearl S. Buck, and Oscar Hammerstein II are a few of the creative and accomplished who over the years have chosen to make their homes here.

The town is probably best known for the three unique concrete structures that make up the **Mercer Mile**. The first, **Fonthill Museum**, was the 44-room home built by eccentric millionaire Henry Chapman Mercer to display his 900 prints and eye-dazzling tile collection. The building was inspired by European castles and aided in its design by a good dose of imagination. Fonthill is a National Historic Landmark (guided tour).

The **Mercer Museum**, the second member of the Mercer Mile, displays a fabulous collection of more than 50,000 early American tools and other objects. The third building, the **Moravian Pottery and Tile Works** (1912), is a living history museum where decorative tiles and mosaics are produced just as they were 90 years ago (self-guided and guided tours).

The **James A. Michener Art Museum of Bucks County**, located in reconstructed buildings of the Bucks County prison, houses a superb collection of 19th and 20th century regional American art.

SPECIAL FEATURE

•Just 15 minutes away is **Green Hills Farm**, the 1835 stone farmhouse and 60-acre estate of Nobel and Pulitzer prize-winner Pearl S. Buck (tours).

> Concern over the possiblity of fire led Henry Mercer to construct the buildings of the Mercer Mile of reinforced concrete.
>
> The 60-acre Henry Schmieder Arboretum at Delaware Valley College is little-publicized but well worth a visit.

WHERE TO STAY

Doylestown Inn, 18 W. State St., (215) 345-6610. Turn-of-century hotel in heart of town, designer-decorated rooms, private baths, dining room. $$$

Highland Farms, 70 East Rd., (215) 340-1354. Former estate of lyricist Oscar Hammerstein II, pool, tennis court. $$$

The Inn at Fordhook Farm, 105 New Britain Rd., (215) 345-1766. 18th-century fieldstone house on National Register, antique-filled, full "farm" breakfasts, afternoon teas. $$$

Pine Tree Farm, 2155 Lower State Rd., (215) 348-0632. 1730 stone farmhouse, fireplaces, antiques, pool, tennis, full breakfasts. $$$

WHERE TO EAT

Cafe Arielle, 100 S. Main St., (215) 345-5930. French bistro, seafood, duck, reservations required weekends. $$

Conti Cross Keys Inn, Rts. 313 & 611, (215) 348-9600. 1758 inn, five dining rooms, one of finest in region. $$

Doylestown Inn, (see above). Local specialties, outdoor dining in season. $$

FURTHER INFORMATION

Bucks County Tourist Commission, Inc., P. O. Box 912, Doylestown, PA 18901, (800) 836-2825.

DIRECTIONS

From Philadelphia, PA 611 north to Doylestown.

HANOVER, PENNSYLVANIA

Population: 14,399

Hanover is in many ways a model of small-town America. It has been a manufacturing and trade center since Colonial days, but there was never an economic heyday; growth has been gradual. The townspeople continue to take pride in the values of their German ancestors — hard work, thrift, cleanliness. And it shows. There are no slums. Many families have prospered over the years, and as with so many charming Pennsylvania towns, the money has found its way into handsome homes and solid public buildings. As a result, Hanover is a town with fine buildings representing virtually every decade of American history.

A regional retail center, Hanover has many specialty and factory-outlet shops; but the shops do not sprawl forever on the town's outskirts. Many are located downtown, on the busy **Center Square**. And while growth is important to Hanover, the word is modified by "managed." Lying at the foot of the lovely **Pigeon Hills**, boasting one of the country's largest horse farms and prospering from the rich agricultural land that surrounds them, Hanoverians do not seek sprawl. They are contained, hidden, tucked away from major highways — and they like it that way.

Laid out in 1763, and witness to such events as a visit by President Washington and the first Civil War battle on Northern soil, the town has a long and interesting history. Perhaps the most notable of the historic buildings is the **Neas House**, a circa 1783 Georgian mansion with double-end chimneys. The house is owned by the **Hanover Area Historical Society** and serves as a museum focusing on local culture during the late 18th and early 19th centuries (closed during the winter months). (The historical society distributes brochures for self-guided tours of the downtown area.) Another interesting site is the **Wirt Park Fire Station Museum**, where you'll find 18th-century hand-pump engines and an 1882 Silsby Steam Engine.

Hanover is also home to two especially noteworthy churches. One, **St. Matthew Lutheran Church**, has one of the largest pipe organs in the world. The second, **Conewago Chapel**, just northwest of town, is the oldest stone Catholic church building in the nation (ca. 1787).

SPECIAL FEATURES

• The **Hanover Shoe Farms**, three miles southwest of town, is the world's largest standardbred horse farm. Founded in 1926, the farm is famous for its many record-breaking trotters and pacers (self-guiding tours).

• Two miles southeast of Hanover is **Codorus State Park**, with woodland, one of the country's largest swimming pools and a lake with 26 miles of shoreline.

> *On the day before the Battle of Gettysburg in 1863, Confederate troops under Gen. J.E.B. Stuart were engaged by Union forces in a running battle on the streets of Hanover. The encounter prevented Stuart from arriving at Gettysburg until the second day of the battle and therefore contributed to the eventual Union victory.*

WHERE TO STAY

Beechmont Inn, 315 Broadway, (800) 553-7009. Elegant 1834 Federal-period inn, antiques, fireplaces, private baths, gourmet breakfasts, picnic baskets. $$$

WHERE TO EAT

The Altland House, Center Square (Abbottstown), (717) 259-9535. "Contemporary dining in an historic atmosphere." $$

Patty & John's Restaurant, Westminster Ave., (717) 637-2200. In beautiful country setting overlooking golf course. $$

FURTHER INFORMATION

Hanover Area Chamber of Commerce, 146 Broadway, Hanover, PA 17331, (717) 637-6130.

DIRECTIONS

From Baltimore, I 795 north to terminus (Reistertown), MD 30 north to PA border, PA 94 north to Hanover.

HERSHEY, PENNSYLVANIA

Population: 11,860

Hershey's ancestry is very different from that of other towns in this guide. For one thing, almost all of the town is less than 100 years old. For another, the town is a company town, a *planned* company town.

This is where Milton Hershey built the world's largest chocolate manufacturing plant between 1903 and 1905. Hershey also built a new community around his factory; deliberately avoiding the usual anonymous company town, however, he chose instead to create a "real home town." And somewhere along the line — 1900 is as good a year as any — Hershey was born.

It's hardly surprising that the major sites all bear the name Hershey. What is more surprising is that some of the most impressive sites were built during the Depression as part of Milton Hershey's attempt to provide jobs.

A 45-minute trolley-type bus tour of Hershey's sites is offered during the summer months:

At **Hershey's Chocolate World**, cars take passengers on a 12-minute Disney-style tour that explains the chocolate-making process. A dessert cafe and Chocolate Fantasies food stand ensure that not only the brain gets nourished here.

Hersheypark is an attractive 87-acre theme park that really does have something to please everyone. There are more than 50 rides, some of them state-of-the-art. For those uninterested in mechanical thrills, the park offers shows, strolling performers, theme areas that include 17th- and 18th-century English and German villages, restaurants and the 11-acre **ZooAmerica North American Wildlife Park**. The zoo features five environments, including an indoor collection of animals and plants native to the Sonoran Desert.

The **Hershey Museum** (est.1933) has three major themes: the history of Milton Hershey and the town he founded, an outstanding Pennsylvania German collection, and collections of objects representing several native American cultures. A Victorian house stands in the main gallery.

The lovely 23-acre **Hershey Gardens** (est. 1937) features collections of unusual plants, an All-America Rose Selections display garden, old-fashioned roses, a Japanese garden and many other plantings.

Hershey also has one of the country's grand old cinemas, the **Hershey Theatre** (1933). Clouds appear to move among the stars on the elaborate ceiling.

> *The Hershey Rose Gardens attracted more than 20,000 visitors on opening day in 1937.*
>
> *Founders Hall, on the Milton Hershey School campus, is capped by the largest unsupported dome in the Western Hemisphere.*

WHERE TO STAY

The Hotel Hershey, Hotel Rd., (717) 533-2171. Listed in Historic Hotels of America Registry, Spanish-influenced Fountain Lobby, full resort. $$$

WHERE TO EAT

The Circular Dining Room, in Hotel Hershey (see above). Original stained-glass windows, overlooking formal gardens, legendary. $$$

FURTHER INFORMATION
Capital Region Chamber of Commerce, 114 Walnut St., P. O. Box 969, Harrisburg, PA 17108-0969, (800) 995-0969.

DIRECTIONS
From Harrisburg, US 322 east to Hershey.

JIM THORPE, PENNSYLVANIA
Population: 5,048

The brick and stone towers, steeples and gables peering from the mountain valley look almost Old World. The narrow Victorian streets reinforce the impression. But it isn't clear what part of the Old World the town might belong to, and besides, some of the architecture is certainly American. What is clear is that for people who love charming towns, **Jim Thorpe** is a real find.

With roots deep in anthracite coal, canals, the railroad, county government and, later, tourism, **Mauch Chunk** (now Jim Thorpe) prospered throughout the 19th century, especially between the 1850s and 1890s. Much of the prosperity was converted directly into grand homes and public buildings. The town declined, however, in the early 20th century, in parallel with the decline of the coal industry. In an act of hope and a desire to win publicity and tourists, the town in 1954 offered the widow of the famous 1912 Olympic athlete Jim Thorpe a proper burial and memorial for her husband in exchange for the use of his name.

The visitor's first order of business should be by all means a walking tour of the historic district. A good starting point is the **Jersey Central Railroad Station** (1888), which now houses the **Tourist Welcoming Center**. The station has a unique end tower that helps contribute to the town's quaint appearance.

A more prominent tower highlights the rough-faced sandstone **Carbon County Courthouse** (1893). The building's main courtroom is noted for its oak paneling and stained-glass skylight. Yet another prominent tower belongs to the Gothic Revival **St. Mark's Episcopal Church** (1869). The church's stunning interior, open for tours, is distinguished by Tiffany windows, an ornate baptismal font and an English Minton tile floor.

Millionaires Row and **Stone Row** are picturesque old residential structures. The former, built between 1860 and 1890, consists of homes built by families made wealthy by old Mauch Chunk's industries. The latter (also mid 1800s) consists of 16 individualized three-story rowhouses built for employees of the Lehigh Valley Railroad. Renovated or undergoing renovation, many of the homes in both rows now house art galleries and studios, antique and specialty shops, apartments, cafes and bed and breakfasts.

Overlooking downtown and by all means the most imposing of the 19th-century homes is the 20-room **Asa Packer Mansion** (1860). The rooms of the

Italianate mansion, open to the public, are furnished with such items as an ancient Egyptian chair and a solid ebony Steinway grand piano.

There are several ways to enjoy the surrounding **Pocono Mountains**: hiking or biking the 16-mile old **Switchback Railroad bed**, rafting down the **Lehigh River** (guided tours), and taking a scenic train excursion along the Lehigh River. When the mountains are snow-covered, they can be enjoyed by downhill and cross-country skiing, tobogganing and snowmobiling.

SPECIAL FEATURES

• **Flagstaff Park** offers a panoramic view of Jim Thorpe and the Pocono Mountains.

• The 20-ton granite **Jim Thorpe Mausoleum** is just east of town on **PA 903**.

> *Also among the furnishings of the Asa Packer Mansion is a chair that belonged to Robert E. Lee and a chandelier that was copied for use in the movie "Gone with the Wind."*

WHERE TO STAY

Hotel Switzerland, PA 209 & Hazard Sq., (717) 325-4563. Renovated 1830s hotel, antiques, magnificent Victorian barroom. $$

The Inn at Jim Thorpe, 24 Broadway, (717) 325-2599. Restored Victorian hotel, private baths, TV, restaurant and tavern. $$ to $$$

Tiffany's B&B, 218 Center St., (717) 325-8260. 1846 home, fireplaces, mahogany-beam ceiling, grape arbor, huge front veranda. $$

Victoria Ann's B&B, 68 Broadway, (717) 325-8107. On Millionaire's Row, crystal and silver on breakfast table. $$

WHERE TO EAT

Black Bread Cafe, 47 Race St., (717) 325-8957. First floor of unique Victorian townhouse, gourmet sandwiches, homemade soups, weekend dinners. $ to $$

FURTHER INFORMATION

Carbon County Office, Pocono Mountain Vacation Bureau, P. O. Box 27, Jim Thorpe, PA 18229, (717) 325-3673.

DIRECTIONS

From Philadelphia, PA 9 (Pennsylvania Tpk. N.E. Ext.) north to Interchange 34, US 209 west to Jim Thorpe.

LEWISBURG, PENNSYLVANIA

Population:5,785

The streets of historic **Lewisburg** are bordered by beautiful old buildings that open directly onto the sidewalks. The buildings are generally brick and display a diversity of Victorian decorations and facades that were added, according to the fashion of the period, subsequent to their construction. Between the sidewalks and the streets are period street lamps. Various little gardens, sometimes planted between buildings and sometimes in windowboxes and elsewhere, add color. Many of the buildings, especially those along **Market Street**, house businesses and, upstairs, apartments. The area is so lively — and at the same time charming — that space is in demand.

An old canal and **Susquehanna River** town, with roots in the 18th century, Lewisburg flourished first in the 1820s and 1830s, then again in the middle of the 19th century, and yet again in the 1920s. A number of Federal-style buildings were constructed during the first period of growth; during the second and even more prosperous period, the architecture was Federal Revival, a style similar to but more spacious than the original. The growth of the 1920s occurred largely in what were then the outskirts of town, and so the older buildings were largely protected. Today, 54 19th-century structures, and groups of structures, of special architectural and/or historic interest line the streets.

Two of the most important have been converted to history museums. The first, the **Packwood House Museum**, was a late 18th-century log tavern that evolved into a three-story Victorian hotel. The rooms now display a wide variety of early Pennsylvania and American decorations and other artifacts. The second museum is the **Slifer House Museum**, a restored 20-room Italianate mansion (1861) with a wrap-around veranda and gracious lawn (tours).

Bucknell University, a private liberal arts college, has long been a part of Lewisburg — in fact, the first commencement was held in 1851. One of the buildings on the beautiful hillside campus is the state-of-the-art, 1200-seat **Weis Center for the Performance Arts**. The center presents top artists in the fields of music, theater and dance.

Lewisburg is a major center in central Pennsylvania for the arts and crafts. Of special interest is an 1883 mill that has been restored and converted to an antique and crafts marketplace. Here over 200 dealers and 35 artisans display their antiques and hand-crafted wares.

SPECIAL FEATURE

• Rail excursions through Lewisburg and the river and farming country about the town are offered by the **West Shore Railroad**. The trips last 1 1/2 or 2 1/2 hours; inquire locally for schedules.

> *The original name of Lewisburg was Derrstown, after the town's founder, Ludwig Derr. It's not completely clear why the name was later changed; it probably had something to do with the fact that in English "Ludwig" is "Lewis." Lewisburg has one of the lowest crime rates in the country.*

WHERE TO STAY

Brookpark Farm B&B, PA 45 W., (717) 523-0220. "Down on the Farm Hospitality," gallery and unique shops on farm. $$

The Inn at Olde New Berlin, 321 Market St. (New Berlin), (717) 966-0321. Victorian full-service country inn, small-town setting. $$$

Pineapple Inn, 439 Market St., (717) 524-6200. 1857 Federal-style home with Greek Revival trim, antiques, full "country" breakfasts. $$

Teneriff Farm B&B, PA 45 E. (Susquehanna Valley), (717) 742-9061. Working farm, country atmosphere, "choice" breakfasts. $$

WHERE TO EAT

Gabriel's, in The Inn at Olde New Berlin (see above). Continental and American cuisine with a Pennsylvania touch. $$

Lewisburg Inn, 101 Market St., (717) 523-8200. French cuisine, excellent wine cellar. $$

Yoders Family Restaurant, R.D. 1 (Millmont), (717) 922-4688. Pennsylvania Dutch cooking, own bakery. $

FURTHER INFORMATION

Lewisburg Area Chamber of Commerce, 418 Market St., Lewisburg, PA 17837, (717) 524-2815; and **Susquehanna Valley Visitors Bureau**, P. O. Box 268, Lewisburg, PA 17837, (800) 458-4748.

DIRECTIONS

From New York City, I 80 west to exit 30 (just across Susquehanna River), US 15 south to Lewisburg.

LITITZ, PENNSYLVANIA

Population: 8,280

The old Moravian town of **Lititz** nicely illustrates what is turning out to be the next stage in the evolution of many of our country's charming towns — the home away from the city. Blessed with a well-preserved 18th century historic district (and many fine homes from the next two centuries, too), and located not many country miles from several urban centers, Lititz has become a popular place to live for people who work in Lancaster, Harrisburg, even Philadelphia. As is so often true of adopted towns, newcomers to Lititz like to restore old houses and attend crafts shows and weekend band concerts in the park.

Lititz was founded in 1756 by members of the Moravian Church and remained a closed religious community until the mid-1800s. Then, in the mid-1900s, a major preservation effort began as people realized that a priceless 18th-century treasure lay along East Main Street. Now a stroll down **Main Street** is a stroll into the past, but because the splendidly preserved buildings are still in use, the stroll is into a past that is still very much a part of the present.

Two buildings open to the public are the **Johannes Mueller House** (1792), a living museum of a Moravian home and workplace, and the **Schropp House** (1793) next door, now the **Lititz Museum**. Also on Main Street is the restored house (original from 1871) where General John A. Sutter, of California Gold Rush fame, spent the last seven years of his life. Sutter is buried in the church cemetery behind **Moravian Church Square**.

Linden Hall, the oldest girls' boarding school in the country, is also in the historic district. The school's Sisters' House and Linden Hall were built in 1758 and 1767, respectively.

SPECIAL FEATURES

• An entertaining history of American candy-making is on display at the **Wilbur Chocolate Company's Candy Americana Museum** There is also a candy shop.

• **Marietta** and **Strasburg** are two other very charming Lancaster County towns.

> *The country's first commercial pretzels were made in the bakery adjoining the Peter Kreider House, known as the "Pretzel House."*
>
> *Lititz Springs Park is the site of one of the oldest annual 4th of July celebrations in the country.*

WHERE TO STAY

Alden House B&B, 62 E. Main St., (800) 584-0743. Restored 1850s home, three porches, private baths, walking distance to attractions, continental-plus breakfasts. $$

Sleepy Mill Farm B&B, 470 Snavely Mill Rd., (717) 626-6629. Restored 1802 stone farmhouse, private baths, full "country" breakfasts. $$

Swiss Woods B&B, Blantz Rd., (800) 594-8018. Swiss chalet, common room, gardens, private baths, goosedown comforters, Swiss breads and pastries. $$

Spahr's Century Farm B&B, 192 Green Acre Rd., (717) 627-2185. House on peaceful 70-acre farm. $$

WHERE TO EAT

General Sutter Inn, 14 E. Main St., (717) 626-2115. Five-course meals served in historic building. $$

Log Cabin, 11 Lehoy Forest Dr. (Leola), (717) 626-1181. Prime sirloin, broiled flounder, shrimp scampi. $$ to $$$.

FURTHER INFORMATION

Pennsylvania Dutch Convention & Visitors Bureau, 501 Greenfield Rd., Lancaster, PA 17601, (717) 299-8901.

DIRECTIONS

From Harrisburg, I 76 east to exit 20, PA 72 south to Manheim, PA 772 to Lititz.

NEW HOPE, PENNSYLVANIA

Population: 1,400

If a good measure of a town's charm is the number of years that the town's beauty, history and art have attracted large numbers of visitors, then **New Hope** is a grandmaster of charm: For fifty years — at the very least — Philadelphians and others in the region have been treating themselves and out-of-town guests to excursions to New Hope.

And with good reason. The setting is the scenic **Delaware River**. The history is tangible and everywhere — even if Washington did choose to cross the river a few miles to the south. Many of the buildings are 18th century and built of that incredibly beautiful Bucks County fieldstone. The shopping, lodging, dining and entertaining are discriminating and overseen by people with decades of experience making them that way. You know that a town's got something going for it when even New Yorkers are willing to venture across the Hudson (and Delaware) to visit it.

For those wanting to know more about the region's history, there's the **Parry Mansion** (1784), which displays decorative arts dating from the period between 1775 to 1900 (guided tours). There's also the old **Delaware Canal**, now a state park and National Historic Landmark. The canal can be seen the way it was seen by people 150 years ago — by mule-drawn barge!

New Hope's prime pastimes tend to be dining and simple old-fashisoned window shopping. For evening entertainment, guest stars of the Bucks County Playhouse perform musicals and dramas from Broadway's past and present.

Bike tours provide an excellent, maybe the best, way to tour Bucks County.

SPECIAL FEATURES

• The **New Hope & Ivyland Rail Road** offers a 9-mile trip on early 20-th century coaches and dining car pulled by an original steam locomotive.
• **Vineyards** in Bucks County produce award-winning wines. Several wineries offer cellar tours and free wine-tasting.

WHERE TO STAY

Ash Mill Farm, P. O. Box 202, (215) 794-5373. 1790 manor house filled with antiques, "country breakfast and tea to music of Mozart & Brahms." $$$

The Fox & Hound of New Hope, 246 W. Bridge St., (215) 862-5082. Restored 1850 home on two acres, private baths, "gourmet" breakfasts. $$$

Hotel du Village, Phillips Mill & N. River rds., (215) 862-9911. Secluded setting, private baths, pool, tennis courts. $$$

Wedgwood Inn of New Hope, 111 W. Bridge St., (215) 862-2570. Fireplaces, carriage rides, croquet, gazebos, tea/refreshments. $$$

The Whitehall Inn, P. O. Box 250, (215) 598-7945. Fireplaces, heirloom sterling, high teas, rose garden, pool, four-course candlelight breakfasts. $$$

WHERE TO EAT

Gerenser's Exotic Ice Cream, 22 S. Main St., (215) 862-2050. Sit-down ice cream parlor, ice cream made on site. $

Havana Restaurant, 105 S. Main St., (215) 862-9897. American regional cuisine, live music on weekends. $ to $$

Karla's Restaurant, 5 W. Mechanic St., (215) 862-2612. International cuisine, terrace dining and bistro. $$

La Bonne Auberge, Village 2 (off Mechanic St.), (215) 862-2462. Historic stone farmhouse, beautiful gardens, outdoor terrace, award-winning. $$ to $$$

Odette's Restaurant, S. River Rd., (215) 862-2432. 1794 home on banks of the Delaware, alfresco dining. $$ to $$$

FURTHER INFORMATION

Bucks County Tourist Commission, P. O. Box 912, Doylestown, PA 18901, (215) 345-4552.

DIRECTIONS

From Philadelphia, PA 611 north to PA 263 (at Willow Grove), PA 263 north to US 202, US 202 east to New Hope.

WELLSBORO, PENNSYLVANIA

Population:3,430

The **Allegheny Plateau** of north central Pennsylvania is one of the most rugged and scenic areas of the eastern United States. It is also one of the least populated — and least known. Its most dramatic geographic feature is the spectacular *Grand Canyon of Pennsylvania,* a winding 50-mile-long, 1,000-foot-deep gorge. Its most beautiful little town is **Wellsboro.**

Wellsboro is a community of wide boulevards, gas lights, lovely large homes and stately old elms and maples. The town is sometimes described as New England-like. The mood is decidedly relaxed and friendly, the kind of place where a shopping trip becomes a social event.

The townspeople are openly proud of their **Main Street,** a beautifully manicured boulevard lined with nicely preserved Victorian buildings. One of the elms along the way dates back to the 1700s. On the public square, called **The Green,** is another object of pride — a fountain with the delightful bronze statue *Wynken, Blynken and Nod* (1938). Next to the fountain is a plaque bearing Eugene Field's famous poem.

Two of Wellsboro's most handsome buildings are the 1835 **county courthouse,** facing the Green, and the 1894 **First Presbyterian Church.** The "Lincoln Door House" has a front door that was an 1858 gift from Abraham Lincoln to the owners; the door came from a building in Springfield, Illinois. The **Wellsboro Cemetery** (1855) has many historic tombs and a beautiful setting.

The **Tioga County Historical Society Museum** is located in the **Robinson House** (circa 1820, with 1840s' additions), listed on the National Register. Originally a tavern, the museum features an 1892 Estey organ and items associated with the life of author George Washington Sears, known by the Indian name of Nessmuk. In the Museum Annex, a replica of the Greek Revival 1864 First National Bank, are a 1923 Model T Ford truck and various military, home-making, dressmaking and millinery exhibits.

The seat of a county with 100 miles of stocked streams, seven lakes and abundant state forests and parks, Wellsboro is one of Pennsylvania's most popular sporting centers. Summer sports include boating, fishing, golfing and horseback riding. With the winter come downhill and cross-country skiing, snowmobiling, ice fishing and skating. The canyon is perfect for white-water rafting and canoeing when the spring waters are up.

SPECIAL FEATURE
• The streams and lookout points of the **Pennsylvania Grand Canyon** begin just a few miles out of town. Self-guided driving tours through the area are aided by a series of directional arrows of different colors.

> *The statue of Wynken, Blynken and Nod was the work of Mabel Landrum Torrey. A marble version of the work may be seen in Denver's Washington Park.*

WHERE TO STAY
Auntie M's B&B, 3 Sherwood St., (717) 724-5771. Elegant home, the governor's choice when visiting town, "gourmet" breakfasts. $$

Coach Stop Inn, R.D. #4 (Box 137), (717) 724-5361. Old stagecoach stop on 100 acres, colonial charm, modern rooms, TV, private baths, restaurant. $$

Four Winds B&B, 58 West Ave., (800) 368-7963. Restored Victorian home in town, "excellent" breakfasts. $$

Foxfire B&B, R.D. #2 (Box 439), (717) 724-5175. Country farmhouse, full breakfasts, owner a gourmet chef specializing in vegetarian meals. $ to $$

Wind Rush Farm B&B, R.D. #5 (Box 18), (717) 724-1525. Country setting near PA Grand Canyon, home-baking, horseback riding available. $$

WHERE TO EAT
Penn Wells Hotel Dining Room, Main St., (800) 545-2446. In restored 1869 hotel, Victorian atmosphere, daily specials, international buffet luncheons. $ to $$

The Steak House, Main St., (717) 724-9092. Variety of steaks, roast turkey & stuffing, chicken, seafood, daily specials. $ to $$

The Wellsboro Diner, Main St., (717) 724-3992. In continuous operation since 1939, fine example of 1930s diner, unique atmosphere. $

FURTHER INFORMATION
Wellsboro Area Chamber of Commerce, P. O. Box 733, Wellsboro, PA 16901, (717) 724-1926.

DIRECTIONS
From Rochester (NY), I 390 south to NY 17, NY 17 south to US 15 (near Corning), US 15 south to US 6 (Mansfield), US 6 west to Wellsboro.

RHODE ISLAND

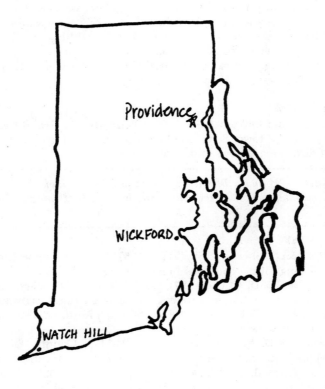

WATCH HILL, RHODE ISLAND

Population: 500

Watch Hill, an Historic Landmark Community, is really three villages in one, and there are plenty of breathtaking views of the Atlantic for all of them. The first is a seaside resort, a place where families have been coming for beach-side holidays since the 1840s. The second is a charming little harbor village where Westerly people come to shop for a special gift or enjoy a lunch by the sea. The third is a colony, founded in the late 1800s, of summer homes owned by a tightly-knit group of American aristocrats.

The great Victorian homes, or *cottages*, are elegant but sprawl more casually than their cousins in nearby Newport. Although the occupants and the interiors of the mansions are usually inaccessible, the grand exteriors, the winding roads linking them, and the magnficent ocean views are there for everyone to enjoy.

One of Watch Hill's logos is a bronze statue of **Ninigret**, chief of Rhode Island's branch of the **Niantics**, the tribe that once occupied this area. The statue, sculpted in Paris in 1914, overlooks the harbor. Watch Hill's most unique attraction is the **flying-horse carousel**, the oldest merry-go-round in the country (built prior to 1879). The still-operating steeds, once water-powered but now motor-driven, are suspended by chains from a large turning wheel and "fly" out when in motion. The **lighthouse**, of brick with a granite tower, was built in 1858 to replace an earlier structure (exterior viewing only).

> *Every year dozens of people get married in the lovely non-denominational Watch Hill Chapel (1875).*
>
> *The nearby Misquamicut Golf Club is one of the oldest in the country (1895; private).*

WHERE TO STAY

The Inn at Watch Hill, Bay St., (401) 596-0665. Spacious rooms with ocean views, private baths, balconies. $$$

Shelter Harbor Inn, 10 Wagner Rd. (Rt. 1, Westerly, RI), (800) 468-8883. Surrounded by fields with rustic stone walls, own beach, full breakfasts. $$$

Watch Hill Inn, 50 Bay St., (800) 356-9314. Originally built 1890, on hill with cool summer ocean breezes, tennis, private baths. $$$

WHERE TO EAT

The Olympia Tea Room, Bay St., (401) 348-8211. Seafood specialties. $$

The Positano Restaurant (Watch Hill Inn), (see above). Italian cuisine in elegant surroundings, overlooking bay. $$ to $$$

FURTHER INFORMATION

Greater Westerly-Pawcatuck Area Chamber of Commerce, Rt. 1, Post Rd., Westerly, RI 02891, (800) 732-7636.

DIRECTIONS

From Providence, I 95 south to exit 92 (Connecticut), CT 2 south to RI 78, RI 78 south (crossing US 1) to RI 1A, RI 1A south to Watch Hill.

WICKFORD, RHODE ISLAND

Population: 2,750

Located on a harbor stirred by colorful fishing boats, private yachts, and quahog skiffs (the *quahog* is a type of clam), **Wickford Village's** shops would make a perfect setting for a TV commercial showing people loading a station wagon with a just acquired antique or work of art.

Wickford is an unspoiled New England fishing village with tree-lined streets and memories going back to colonial times. Many of the village's late 18th- and early 19th-century houses survive. A few are bed and breakfasts (see below); some house shops and other businesses. There are also a number of 19th-century summer houses.

One of the most venerated of Wickford's possessions is the **Old Narragansett Church** (1707, moved 1800), the oldest Episcopal church in the northern United States. The church has box pews, a slave gallery, a silver communion set that was a gift from Queen Anne, and the oldest church organ (1680) in North America. The Romanesque Revival **St. Paul's** was built in 1847.

Although not far from Providence, Wickford remains essentially rural, in character as well as setting. The age of the village can be appreciated by noting that several generations of English settlers had lived here before the word "Revolution" was even spoken. There were once even grand plantations in the area that were worked by slaves and indentured servants (although in 1774 Rhode Island became the first colony to outlaw the importation of slaves).

SPECIAL FEATURES

• **Smith's Castle,** just north of Wickford, is one of the oldest plantation houses in the country (1678; with 18th- and 19th-century additions). The furnished house and its lovely colonial, waterfront and cutting gardens may be seen by guided tour.

• The birthplace of **Gilbert Stuart,** famous for his portraits of George Washington (and many others), is five miles south of Wickford. Among the features of the restored house (1751) are corner fireplaces and hand-blown window panes. The house is also the site of the country's first snuff mill, still operative (guided tours).

> *The Wickford Art Festival is one of the oldest art shows in the country. Many visitors choose to visit Wickford by boat.*

WHERE TO STAY

1773 Narragansett House, 71 Main St., (401) 294-3593. Once a colonial tavern, apartment suite with private entrance, TV, private terrace. $$$

John Updike House, 19 Pleasant St., (401) 294-4905. Elegant 1745 Georgian house on waterfront, period decor, fireplaces, deck and common room. $$ to $$$

Meadowland B&B, 765 Old Baptist Rd., (401) 294-4168. Victorian country home, "sumptious" candlelight breakfasts. $$

The Moran's, 130 W. Main St., (401) 294-3497. Cottage near village center, family-style breakfasts, picnic area. $$

Wickford House B&B, 68 Main St., (401) 294-6479. Guest suite in historic inn, period antiques, overlooking gardens. $$$

WHERE TO EAT

The Carriage Inn, Tower Hill Rd., (800) 270-2466. Jonnycakes, clam cakes, old tavern atmosphere. $$

FURTHER INFORMATION

Wickford Chamber of Commerce, Wickford, RI 02852, (401) 295-5566.

DIRECTIONS

From Providence, US 1 south to Wickford.

SOUTH CAROLINA

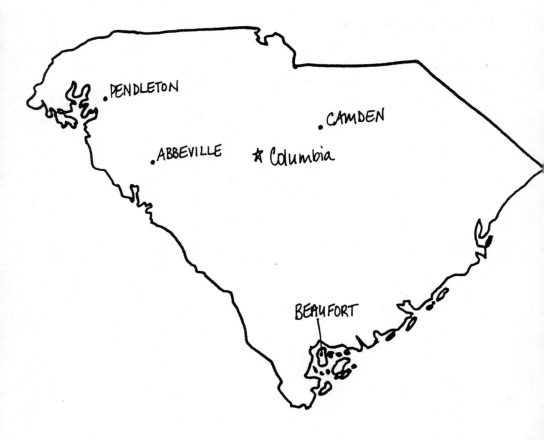

ABBEVILLE, SOUTH CAROLINA

Population: 5,778

Abbeville is a beautiful old Southern town (founded 1758) situated in the rolling countryside of Upcountry South Carolina. The townspeople successfully cling to a traditional small-town life style. Visiting is in, hurrying is out, and many businesses close on Wednesday afternoons (and Sundays, of course). In recent years Mennonite families from the North have been acquiring area farms; the inevitable result has been an increasingly prosperous and beautiful countryside.

At the center of the **Abbeville Historic District** is a picture-postcard town square. The square is bordered by brick-paved streets and businesses with facades carefully restored to their turn-of-the-century appearance. Traditional hardware and farm-supply stores sit cheek by jowl with antique and chic specialty shops.

Among the buildings on the square is the magnificently restored **Opera House** (1908), pride of the town. Early in the 20th century, when Abbeville was a railroad stopover for road shows, the three-balconied Opera House hosted such vaudeville stars as Fanny Brice, Jimmy Durante, and Groucho Marx. Now in the second chapter of its life, the elegant theater is home to the year-round productions of the professional Opera House Players.

A wonderful walking town, Abbeville boasts many gracious 19th-century homes, both antebellum and postbellum, and no fewer than 36 churches. The most historic of the homes is the **Burt-Stark House** (circa 1840), a plantation house where Confederate President Jefferson Davis stayed on his retreat from Richmond at the end of the Civil War. (The house may be toured by appointment.) The lovely Gothic Revival **Trinity Episcopal Church** (1860) has hand-carved woodwork and a stained-glass chancel window that was made in England.

Abbeville has two interesting museums. The **Abbeville County Museum**, housed in the three-story county jail (1850s), features artifacts from the town's more than two centuries of history. The **Abbeville County Library** is home to the **Poliakoff Collection of Western Art**, an excellent collection of contemporary Native American ceramics, weavings and other art objects.

Abbeville may be seen by a self-guided tour or by one of three guided tours — check with the CoC.

SPECIAL FEATURES

• The nearby town of **Due West** is home to beautiful **Erskine College**, the oldest denominational liberal arts college in South Carolina (1839). Much of this charming little town is on the National Register of Historic Places.

• Located on **Richard B. Russell Lake** 13 miles away, **Calhoun Falls State Park** offers water sports and, in the spring, spectacular displays of redbuds and dogwoods.

> *Site of the first organized meeting to adopt an Ordinance of Secession, and the final meeting place of the Confederate Council of War, Abbeville was "the birthplace and the deathbed of the Confederacy."*
>
> *The chancel window of Trinity Episcopal Church made it safely through the Union blockade of Charleston.*

WHERE TO STAY

Belmont Inn, 106 Court Sq., (803) 459-9625. Renovated turn-of-century hotel, elegant lobby, period furnishings. $$ to $$$

Somewhere In Time B&B, P. O. Box 746 (Due West), (803) 379-8671. Restored 1897 home on National Register, antiques, wrap-around porch, fish pond, candlelight breakfasts. $$

WHERE TO EAT

Belmont Inn (see above). American and Continental cooking, steaks, swordfish. $ to $$

The Village Grill, 114 Trinity St., (803) 459-2500. "Simple, Fresh and Good," rotisserie chicken, ribs, gourmet sandwiches. $

FURTHER INFORMATION

Greater Abbeville Chamber of Commerce, 104 Pickens St., Abbeville, SC 29620, (803) 459-2181.

DIRECTIONS

From Columbia, I 26 north to exit 54 (near Clinton), SC 72 south (via Greenwood) to Abbeville.

BEAUFORT, SOUTH CAROLINA

Population: 9,576

Sometimes described as an "undeveloped Charleston," **Beaufort** (pronounced BYOU fert) has become a favorite retirement spot for corporation presidents, prominent writers and artists, and senior military personnel. It's not difficult to understand why. The picturesque coastal town is blessed with one of the lovliest historic districts in the country, excellent restaurants, seven naturally beautiful golf courses, a variety of cultural opportunities, great fishing, bountiful sunshine and access to miles of unspoiled beaches.

Early in the 19th century indigo and, later, long staple sea-island cotton, brought wealth to area planters, and magnificent homes to Beaufort's streets. Many of the homes and plantations still survive because Beaufort was occupied by Union forces early in the Civil War and the town and nearby plantations were spared.

Old Point, part of the **Beaufort Historic District,** contains over 150 antebellum homes, many with lovely landscaped gardens. A setting for several films, the enchanting area is made to order for leisurely walking or bicycling. The verandaed white homes, the moss-draped live oaks and the splashes of color added by the roses, camellias, azaleas and other flowers produce at times an almost impressionistic effect.

Two of Beaufort's historic houses are open to the public: the Greek Revival **George Parsons Elliott House** (1844), furnished with priceless antiques, and the Federal-style **John Mark Verdier House** (circa 1790), noted for its fine interior details. The Marquis de Lafayette was a guest in the Verdier house in 1825. Other beautiful old homes (private) include the Greek Revival **Joseph Johnson House** (1859), the early 19th-century frame **Henry Farmer House**, and the double-verandaed **Tidalholm** (circa 1853).

St. Helena's Episcopal Church is one of the oldest churches (1724) still in use in the United States. The building was used as a hospital during the Civil War. The **Beaufort Museum**, once an arsenal, was constructed of brick and tabby in 1798 (rebuilt 1852). The Gothic Revival structure features prehistoric shark teeth, fossils, early Indian pottery, and Civil War and plantation memorabilia.

Both local tradition and retiree interest have fostered a number of cultural organizations. Among them, the **Beaufort Orchestra Guild**, the **Beaufort Little Theatre**, the **University of South Carolina at Beaufort's seasonal music program**, and the **Byrne Miller Dance Theatre**.

There are many ways to enjoy the natural beauty of Beaufort's southern coastal setting. Fishing (offshore, surf, or pier) is a favorite pastime; boat rentals and private charters are available. Nearby beaches offer swimming and shelling. The **Beaufort River** can be viewed by a stroll or jog along the seawall promenade of the **Henry C. Chambers Waterfront Park**. The area boasts many tennis courts and, as noted, beautiful golf courses.

SPECIAL FEATURES

• The 5,000-acre **Hunting Island State Park**, 16 miles from Beaufort, offers over three miles of unspoiled beaches. Park visitors may survey the scene from an abandoned lighthouse.

• Nearby **Port Royal**, one of the state's earliest settlements, has a 1,260-ft. boardwalk.

> *Legend has it that the flat tombstones of St. Helena's Episcopal Church were used as operating tables during the Civil War.*

WHERE TO STAY

Bay Street Inn, 601 Bay St., (803) 524-7720. Circa 1850 planter's mansion overlooking river, antiques and art, beautiful library, garden, full breakfasts, bikes. $$$

Old Point Inn, 212 New St., (803) 524-3177. 1898 home in historic district, close to river, private baths. $$ to $$$

Rhett House Inn, 1009 Craven St., (803) 524-9030. Antebellum home, antique-filled rooms, antique pool table, private baths, full breakfasts, sherry, bikes. $$$

Twosuns Inn B&B, 1705 Bay St., (803) 522-1122. Colonial Revival home in historic district, panoramic bay view, private baths, full breakfasts, tea/sherry. $$$

WHERE TO EAT

The Anchorage House, 1103 Bay St., (803) 524-9392. In 18th-century mansion, water views, Lowcountry cooking, seafood, chicken, daily specials. $$

Emily's, 906 Port Republic St., (803) 522-1866. Continental cuisine, intimate atmosphere, prix-fixe menu, dinner reservations required. $$

Plum's, 904 1/2 Bay St., (803) 525-1946. Casual waterfront dining, pasta, soups, salads, homemade ice cream. $

Wilkop's White Hall Inn, US 21 (on Lady's Island), (803) 524-0382. Fresh local seafood, gorgeous sunsets over Beaufort River. $$

FURTHER INFORMATION

The Greater Beaufort Chamber of Commerce, P. O. Box 910, Beaufort, SC 29901, (803) 524-3163.

DIRECTIONS

From Charleston, US 17 west to US 21 (Gardens Corner), US 21 south to Beaufort.

CAMDEN, SOUTH CAROLINA

Population: 6,696

Rare indeed is the town, especially a Deep Southern town, whose beauty and charm can be discussed with little mention of the 19th century and the War Between the States. Created by order of King George II in 1733, **Camden** was a Revolutionary War town. And the town's fame as a horse-training and breeding center belongs more to the 20th century.

The original Camden was a British stronghold during part of the Revolutionary War, fortified with a stockade wall and six small surrounding forts. Although they won the nearby **Battles of Camden** and **Hobkirk Hill**, the British took heavy losses at the latter and evacuated Camden, setting fire to the fortifications as they left. In recent years excavations at the site have uncovered the remains of the old town, its fortifications, a large powder magazine and the **Kershaw-Cornwallis House**, headquarters for General Cornwallis and other officers during the 1780-81 British occupation (see below).

The excavations provided the basis for **Historic Camden**, a 92-acre partial reconstruction and park. In addition to several reconstructed fort sites, this unique Revolutionary War park features miniature dioramas, a model of the original town, a narrated slide presentation, and nature trails.

The park also has a number of interesting historic buildings that have been moved to the site from other locations. The jewel of the park, however, is the reconstructed Kershaw-Cornwallis House. The exterior of this house is an exact replica of the original 1780 Georgian-style mansion; the inside, with period furniture, is modeled after the interiors of Charleston houses of the same period.

The **Camden Historic District**, not to be confused with Historic Camden, is an oak-shaded area of more than 60 lovely houses and other buildings. Many of the houses are beautifully-maintained, privately-owned mansions that date from the 19th century (although much of Camden was burned by Sherman in 1865). The CoC has information on walking, driving, and special guided tours of the district.

SPECIAL FEATURES

•Horses are second only to textiles in importance to Camden's economy. There are two major training centers for horses, one for steeplechase training and the other for flat-race training. There are also two major equestrian events, the **Carolina Cup Steeplechase** and the **Colonial Cup International Steeplechase**. Both take place at the **Springdale Race Course**.

Many of the roads around Camden are dirt rather than paved in deference to the unprotected feet of the horses.

The horse industry was started in large part by well-to-do Northerners who were attracted by the area's beautiful homes and mild winter climate.

WHERE TO STAY

Carolina Oaks, 127 Union St., (803) 432-2366. Fireplaces, antiques, full breakfasts, one traveling party accommodated at a time. $$

The Carriage House B&B, 1413 Lyttleton St., (803) 432-2430. Circa 1840 cottage, antiques, hostess an interior designer, full breakfasts. $$

Greenleaf Inn, 1308/10 N. Broad St., (803) 425-1806. Restored ca.1810 and 1890 houses, "traditional flavor with contemporary convenience." $$ to $$$

WHERE TO EAT

Lilfred's, 11 Main St., (803) 432-7063. Soft-shell crayfish a specialty. $ to $$

Mill Pond Restaurant, 84 Boykin Mill Road (Boykin, SC), (803) 424-0261. Breast of Duck with Lingonberry Sauce served in old mill. $$

The Paddock, 514 Rutledge St., (803) 432-3222. Continental cuisine with Southern specialties. $ to $$$

FURTHER INFORMATION

Kershaw County Chamber of Commerce, P. O. Box 604, Camden, SC 29020, (803) 432-2525.

DIRECTIONS

From Columbia, I 20 northeast to exit 98, US 521 north to Camden.

PENDLETON, SOUTH CAROLINA

Population: 3,314

The wealthy of the Old South tended to divide their lives between two beautiful worlds: the pillared plantation of novel and screen and the less familiar summer retreat. In South Carolina the former was usually *Lowcountry*, meaning coastal and often not far from Charleston. The latter was usually *Upcountry*, in the higher and cooler elevations of the western part of the state. **Pendleton**, in the foothills of the **Blue Ridge Mountains**, was a favorite Upcountry summer retreat (see also Hendersonville, NC).

The town, listed in its entirety on the National Register of Historic Places, is centered about a delightful village green set with period streetlamps and shaded park benches. On the streets about the green stand many lovely homes from the late 18th and early 19th centuries. Some of the finest restaurants in this part of South Carolina are also here.

The first stop for the visitor should be **Hunter's Store** (1850), headquarters for the **Pendleton District Historical, Recreational and Tourism Commission** The center offers everything from cassette tape tours in English and French to art exhibits, local crafts, and a book shop.

Fronting on the village green, across from Hunter's Store, is the peaceful old **Farmers Society Hall** (1826), town landmark and the oldest continuously used farmers hall in the country. Perhaps the most prominent members of the **Pendleton Farmers Society** (in essence an agricultural club) was U.S. vice president and statesman John C. Calhoun.

St. Paul's Episcopal Church (1822) has most of its original furnishings. Few of the region's early settlers were in fact Episcopalians — but many of the coastal families summering in the town were. The gravestones in the churchyard read like a South Carolina history book. Many famous South Carolinians are also buried near the **Old Stone Church**, an early Presbyterian church (1802) on the road between Pendleton and Clemson.

In the country just outside town are several old plantation homes; some of them have also served as summer homes. Two of them, **Ashtabula** (1820s) and four-story **Woodburn** (ca. 1830), are now house museums.

SPECIAL FEATURES

• **Fort Hill plantation house** (ca. 1806), home of John C. Calhoun, and Hanover House (1716), a transplanted Lowcountry French Huguenot home, are on the campus of **Clemson University**, just 3 1/2 miles away. Both houses are open to the public.

> *Several of the streets in Pendleton's historic district bear the names of blacks who have contributed with special distinction to the town and region's heritage.*
>
> *The presence of an Episcopal church in non-Episcopal Upcountry is usually a good sign that the area was once a summer refuge for (Episcopal) Lowcountry planters.*

WHERE TO STAY

Liberty Hall Inn, 621 S. Mechanic St., (803) 646-7500. Circa 1840 home, antiques, high ceilings, wide verandas. $$

WHERE TO EAT

Farmers Hall Restaurant & Tea Room, Village Green, (803) 646-7024. Classic cuisine served in Farmers Hall, reservations appreciated. $ to $$

Liberty Hall Inn (see above). Tonight's Chicken, Orange Roughy Mediterranean, Carolina Crab Cakes. $ to $$

Pendleton House, 203 E. Main St., (803) 646-7795. Restaurant and pub in cozy 1880 home. $$

FURTHER INFORMATION

Pendleton District Historical, Recreational & Tourism Commission, P. O. Box 565, Pendleton, SC 29670, (803) 646-3782.

DIRECTIONS

From Atlanta, I 85 northeast to exit 14 (in South Carolina), SC 187 north to Pendleton.

SOUTH DAKOTA

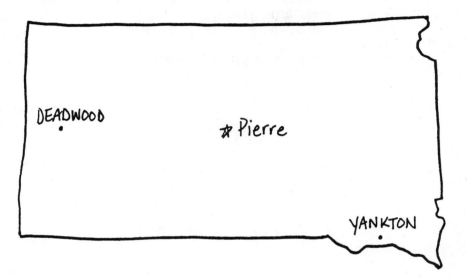

DEADWOOD, SOUTH DAKOTA

Population: 1,830

A heated nightlife, Old West saloons, and busy gambling parlors have been especially prominent during two periods in **Deadwood's** history. The first, the wild period of the 1870s and 1880s, was triggered by the discovery of gold in the **Black Hills**. Prospectors, claim jumpers, prostitutes, gunfighters, gamblers, hell-raisers and opportunists breathed fire in **Deadwood Gulch**. Law and Order amounted to an occasional vigilante court. Those were the days when a Jim McCall could kill a Wild Bill Hickok and get by with it (at least for a while), and a Calamity Jane could boast that she captured the killer when in fact she never did.

The second of the colorful periods began in the 1980s and is in full swing at this moment. In the 1980s Deadwood decided to legalize gambling (maximum wager $5.00) and use 4% of the profits for historic restoration. The town also decided that all restoration, whether funded by gaming or private monies, would be closely supervised by **Deadwood's Historic Preservation Commission**.

The result is a National Historic Landmark with a cobblestoned **Main Street**, period street lights, trolleys, buried utilities — and more than 80 Old-West-style gaming halls! The best of the first wild period is back, and the worst is buried with Wild Bill Hickok, Calamity Jane, Potato Creek Johnny, and the rest up in **Mount Moriah Cemetery**.

Not that the gambling halls offer the only game in town. The **Adams Memorial Museum**, or "Deadwood's attic," offers a good glimpse of the old Deadwood, including the biggest gold nugget ever found in the Black Hills. Some 72 life-size figures in 19 settings offer another kind of glimpse of Deadwood's history at the **Ghosts of Deadwood Gulch Wax Museum**.

Farther afield, several golf courses and ski resorts offer their own varieties of recreation.

SPECIAL FEATURES

• Tours of the **Broken Boot Gold Mine** (operated by the Deadwood-Lead Chamber of Commerce) include a guided trip through timbered tunnels and hugh underground "rooms" (or stopes) of an historic mine.

• Just a few winding miles up the road is mile-high **Lead** (pronounced Leed), another charming town and also on the National Register. Here there's a narrow turn-of-the-century Main Street and Victorian houses, modest to mansion, clinging to steep hillsides. One of the top sights is the **Black Hills Mining Museum**, with interesting displays and a walk-through replica of a gold mine.

> *Deadwood was destroyed three times, twice by fires and once by a flash flood, during its earliest years.*
> *Founded in 1876, the Homestake Gold Mine in Lead is the oldest continuously operated gold mine in the world.*

WHERE TO STAY

Adams House B&B, 22 Van Buren St., (605) 578-3877. Fine 1892 residence, family's original antiques, "delicious" breakfasts. $$ to $$$

Bullock Hotel, 633 Main St., (800) 336-1876. 1895 city landmark, elegant gaming parlors and polished staircases, luxurious Victorian lodging. $ to $$$

Deer Mountain B&B, HC 37, P. O. Box 1214 (Lead), (605) 584-2473. Unique log home, fireplace, pool table, family-style full breakfasts, hors d'oeuvres. $$ to $$$

Historic Franklin Hotel, 700 Main St., (800) 688-1876. 1903 hotel on National Register, columned porch and sun veranda, gaming halls. $$ to $$$

WHERE TO EAT

Cousin Jack's Restaurant, 605 Main St., (605) 578-2036. Casual family dining in English pub atmosphere. $

The Depot, 155 Sherman St., (605) 578-2699. "The Best Prime Rib and Shrimp Scampi west of the Missouri." $

Jakes Restaurant, 677 Main St., (800) 999-6482. Grilled walleye, Cajun Seafood Tortellini, one of best in South Dakota. $$

Silverado Restaurant, 709 Main St., (800) 584-7005. "Complete gaming and dining experience," prime rib, seafood, homemade desserts. $

Sophie's Slots & Sodas, 672 Main St., (605) 578-1515. Ice cream treats on longest marble soda fountain west of Mississippi. $

FURTHER INFORMATION

Deadwood-Lead Chamber of Commerce, 735 Main St., Deadwood, SD 57732, (800) 999-1876.

DIRECTIONS

From Rapid City, I 90 west to exit 30, US Alt.14 west to Deadwood.

YANKTON, SOUTH DAKOTA

Population: 12,703

Yankton has clean air, no traffic jams, low crime, arts programs and excellent schools, in other words, it's a model American hometown. Another part of the town's appeal lies in its success in blending the old with the new. For while Yankton works to mold a town that will be as proud of its 21st-century heritage as its 19th-century, this descendant of an old riverboat town and capital of **Dakota Territory** (1861 to 1883) also respects and preserves its historical heritage.

Third Street, Yankton's main street, is protected as part of a National Register Historic District, but the size of the town demands more business space, and so there is also a modern shopping mall. New houses are built, but the town maintains guard over the many lovely homes from the 1870s and 1880s that grace the historic district. New industry is courted, but people point with pride to the oldest continuing industry, the **Gurney Seed and Nursery Co.,** established in 1894.

The same blending of old and new can be seen — and heard — in **Riverside Park**. Here passengers cruise the Missouri on a half-scale replica of an 1870s paddlewheeler, *The Far West*, while music from a choral group, or maybe a blues or rock concert, in the amphitheater echoes off the walls of a nearby replica of the **Dakota Territorial Capitol**.

Yankton's premier tourist attraction, the **Dakota Territorial Museum**, is quite literally jammed with reminders and artifacts of Yankton's territorial days. Included in the museum complex are a rural schoolhouse, **Great Northern Railway Depot** (1892-1893), blacksmith shop, an 1870 parlor, and an office replica of Dakota Territory's first governor.

SPECIAL FEATURES

• Just 4 or so miles down the Missouri is the beautifully developed **Lewis and Clark Recreation Area**. The area is located on the banks of **Lewis and Clark Lake**, a 33,000-acre reservoir that stretches for 30 scenic miles along the **Missouri River**. The lake and recreation area boast a marina, boat rentals, sandy beaches, biking trails, fishing, everything.

> *French fur traders were in the Yankton area as early as the 1780s and 1790s, several years before Lewis and Clark came through in the early 1800s. The original "Far West" broke a speed record carrying wounded soldiers from the Little Big Horn to Bismarck.*

WHERE TO STAY

The Mulberry Inn B&B, 512 Mulberry St., (605) 665-7116. 1873 home on National Register, walnut paneling, two parlors with marble fireplaces, "sumptious" breakfasts, wine/cheese. $ to $$

WHERE TO EAT

The Library Restaurant, 401 Capitol St., (605) 665-0186. Dining in beautiful surroundings of historic Carnegie Library. $ to $$

Happy Jack's Supper Club, E. SD 50, (605) 665-7626. Great steaks, a Yankton tradition. $

FURTHER INFORMATION

Yankton Area Chamber of Commerce, P. O. Box 588, Yankton, SD 57078, (605) 665-3636.

DIRECTIONS

From Sioux Falls, I 29 south to exit 26, SD 50 west to Yankton.

TENNESSEE

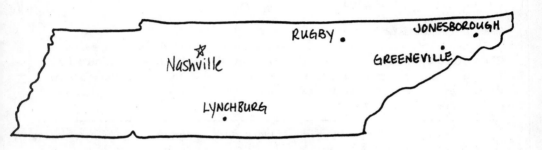

GREENEVILLE, TENNESSEE

Population: 13,532

Greeneville — and east Tennessee in general — has an ambience that doesn't quite seem to belong to most of the rest of Tennessee, nor to North Carolina just across the border. It is partly mountain, partly Southern and partly something else, something rooted in pride and self-determination.

Greeneville has always had a mind of its own. The town was once the capital of the **State of Franklin**, a state that because of a complex piece of history existed for a few years in the 1780s but was never recognized by the U.S. Congress. Less than a century later, Greeneville sided with the Union in the Civil War, even though the region was geographically in the South.

Greeneville's downtown historic district has tree-lined streets bordered by lovely antebellum homes and churches of the Federal and Greek Revival styles. The brick sidewalks and absence of power lines (buried) contribute to the beauty. The district embraces more than 35 structures. One of them is an authentic reconstruction of the capitol of the *Lost State of Franklin*. Others include the **Greene County Stone Jail** (1838/1882), the Federal-style **Valentine-Sevier House** (1820) and the **Sevier-Lowry House** (1790s), the oldest structure in Greeneville.

Several of the structures make up the **Andrew Johnson National Historic Site** (Johnson was the 17th president of the United States): The **Visitor Center Complex**, which includes Johnson's tailor shop, a museum and the president's 1830s house; the **Homestead**, Johnson's home from 1851 until his death in 1875; and the **national cemetery** where Johnson and his family are buried.

Probably the grandest of the homes is the restored **Dickson-Williams Mansion** (1815-1821), known as the *Showplace of East Tennessee*. The circular staircase, which rises three full flights, provides elegant tribute to the craftsmanship of the two Irishmen who designed and built the house. Davy Crockett, Andrew Jackson, the Marquis de LaFayette, and Henry Clay were all guests here.

The historic district includes three churches of special beauty: the 1860s Greek-Revival **Greeneville Cumberland Presbyterian Church**, the 1850 white-frame **St. James Episcopal Church** (which has the oldest organ in Tennessee) and the 1848 Federal-style **First Presbyterian Church.**

SPECIAL FEATURES

• The **Andrew Johnson Presidential Library and Birthplace Replica** are on the campus of **Tusculum College**, the oldest college west of the Alleghenies (1794), located just a few miles east of Greeneville (check locally for directions). Nine of the college's structures have been established as the **Tusculum College Historic District.** Campus tours are available.

• **Davy Crockett's Birthplace State Historic Area** is east of town on **TN 351**, near Limestone, TN.

> *Andrew Johnson was the only senator of a Southern state to reject secession from the Union.*

WHERE TO STAY

Big Spring Inn, 315 N. Main St., (615) 638-2917. Guest library, spacious porches, beautiful antiques, full breakfasts. $$ to $$$

Harmony Hill Inn, P. O. Box 1937 (Chuckey, TN), (615) 257-3893. 150-year-old farmhouse, panoramic mountain views. $$ to $$$

Hilltop House B&B Inn, P. O. Box 180, (615) 639-8202. 1920s manor house, English antiques, mountain views. $$ to $$$

Oak Hill Farm B&B, P. O. Box 342A, (615) 639-2331/5253. Modern farm house with views of Appalachians and Cumberlands, fishing tours. $$ to $$$

Snapp Inn B&B, P. O. Box 102 (Limestone), (615) 257-2482. 1815 Federal home with antiques, private baths, country setting, full breakfasts. $$ to $$$

WHERE TO EAT

Augustino's Restaurant & Lounge, 2679 US 11E Bypass, (615) 639-1231. Continental and Italian cuisines, reservations recommended. $$

FURTHER INFORMATION

Greeneville/Greene County Tourism Council, 207 N. Main St., Greeneville, TN 37743, (615) 638-4111.

DIRECTIONS

From Knoxville, I 40 east to I 81, I 81 northeast to exit 23, TN 34 east to Greeneville.

JONESBOROUGH, TENNESSEE

Population: 3,091

Many charming towns can transport the visitor to another era, but they do so with varying degrees of believability and authenticity. **Jonesborough** is among those that do it most believably and authentically. The sidewalks are brick, there are no stoplights, even the power and telephone lines are hidden underground. Here you enter another time, and a beautiful time it is. At night the street lights, which look like gaslights, illuminate with a rare softness. Drive down **Main Street** after dark and you'll know that Jonesborough takes its history seriously.

Jonesborough was founded in 1779 and is Tennessee's oldest town. Its historic district, with over 150 structures, was the first in Tennessee to be listed on the National Register. The town's history is closely linked with the lives of many notable Americans, including three presidents — Andrew Jackson, James Polk, and Andrew Johnson. Records indicate that Andrew Jackson fought several duels here.

The **Jonesborough-Washington County History Museum** has over 30 professionally designed exhibits. Check here for guided walking tours, brochures for self-guided tours, and information on horse-drawn carriage tours. The **Discover Jonesborough's Times and Tales Tour**, which brings the town to life through stories and anecdotes, has been honored with two prestigious awards (reservations a must).

The place where the presidents stayed, and often conducted official business, was the **Chester Inn** (1797), now restored and painted in authentic (of course) shades of cream and russet. The inn was built on the **Great Stage Road** from Washington, D.C. and is Jonesborough's second oldest building.

The oldest building is the **Hawley House** (1790, with 1818 additions), a log home that today is also a bed and breakfast (see listing below). Among the many other historic homes are the three brick row houses making up **Sisters Row** (ca. 1820), built by Samuel Jackson for his three daughters. The brick was handmade on site, and although the houses are very similar, each has a distinctive fanlight and other features.

Jonesborough has several interesting antebellum churches. One of them is the Greek Revival **Presbyterian Church** (1840s), with a slave gallery and original pews and pulpit. Another is the **Baptist Church** (1850), a church with exceptionally rare and beautiful hand-painted etched-glass windows.

> *Each October Jonesborough's National Association for the Preservation and Perpetuation of Storytelling sponsors the highly respected National Storytelling Festival.*
>
> *The country's first abolistionist paper, "The Emancipator," was published in Jonesborough in 1820. Jonesborough was later a Union stronghold.*

WHERE TO STAY

Hawley House B&B, 114 E. Woodrow Ave., (615) 753-8869. An 18th century log and frame dwelling, antiques, folk art, private baths. $$

Jonesborough B&B, P. O. Box 722, (615) 753-9223. Lovely restored 1848 home in historic district, antiques, fireplaces, secluded terrace, "delightful" breakfasts. $$

Jonesborough's Bugaboo B&B, 211 Semore Dr., (615) 753-9345. On quiet wooded hilltop, private baths, home-grown fruits and vegetables, full breakfasts. $$

Sheppard Springs B&B, 1208 TN 81 North, (615) 753-6471. Ca. 1863 farmhouse, 1700s springhouse, private baths, "truly hearty" breakfasts. $$

WHERE TO EAT

Main Street Cafe, 117 W. Main St., (615) 753-2460. A "Fresh Market Cafe" in Old Post Office across from Chester Inn. $

The Parson's Table Restaurant, 102 Woodrow Ave., (615) 753-8002. Continental dining and "Victorian romance" in 1870s church. $$

FURTHER INFORMATION

Jonesborough Visitors Center, P. O. Box 375, Jonesborough, TN 37659, (615) 753-5961.

DIRECTIONS

From Knoxville, I 40 east to I 81, I 81 to exit 23, east on TN 11.

LYNCHBURG, TENNESSEE

Population: 4,721

Nestled among the hills, hollows and springs of south central Tennessee, **Lynchburg** is virtually synonymous with the **Jack Daniel Distillery**, the oldest registered distillery in the United States (1866). Regular tours include visits to the **Barrelhouse**, the original 19th-century office and **Cave Spring** (responsible for a major ingredient of the whiskey). The steps in whiskey-making, including the distillery's famous charcoal-mellowing process, are explained.

The itinerary for Lynchburg is relatively short, but very pleasant. After making reservations for mid-day dinner at **Miss Mary Bobo's Boarding House** (see below), walk over to the visitors center of the distillery for a tour. After the tour, it's Miss Mary Bobo's for "dinner." The afternoon can be spent napping, browsing through the shops, and relaxing on a bench in the town square. Whittling is still a favorite pastime in the square, and visitors are welcome to take a seat and watch (this may be one of the few places in the country where it's perfectly safe to sit next to a stranger with a knife).

The **Moore County Courthouse** (1884), on the square, was built of bricks made by the people of Lynchburg. On the lawn is a monument (1927) honoring the county's Confederate soldiers.

About the square are little shops that sell white-oak barrels, art, Jack Daniel memorabilia, needlework, antiques. There's even a hardware where locals — and visitors — can pass the time with a game of checkers. One of Lynchburg's most popular products (after the whiskey) is the **Tipsy Cake** (made with the whiskey, of course).

The **Ledford Mill & Tool Museum**, east of town, is home to an old gristmill (1884) and collection of 18th- and 19th-century wood-working tools.

> *The water produced by Cave Spring is pure limestone water, always 56 degrees cool and virtually iron-free.*

WHERE TO STAY

Lynchburg B&B, P. O. Box 34, (615) 759-7158. Restored circa 1877 home close to town square, antiques, shady front porch, private baths, TV. $$

WHERE TO EAT

Miss Mary Bobo's Boarding House, just off square, (615) 759-7394. Mid-day dinner served family-style in lovely old home, eight or ten different dishes, home-grown vegetables, homemade pies or cobblers, reservations a must. $

FURTHER INFORMATION

Lynchburg & Metro Moore County Chamber of Commerce, P. O. Box 421, Lynchburg, TN 37352, (615) 759-4111.

DIRECTIONS

From Nashville, I 24 south to 111 (Manchester), TN 55 southwest to Lynchburg.

RUGBY, TENNESSEE

Population: about 75

Although residing in the rough-and-ready wilderness of Tennessee's **Cumberland Mountains, Rugby's** settlers formed literary and theatrical groups, played tennis and dressed for afternoon tea. Their English village had as many as 70 buildings and a population of around 450 (in 1884). Today only 22 of the gabled buildings survive, but they form what the National Trust calls one of the "most authentically preserved historic villages in America." Nestled among tall trees near a river gorge, it is also one of the prettiest.

It all began in 1880 when English author and social reformer Thomas Hughes established the community as an experiment in cooperative agrarian living. Part of the purpose of the community was to provide a place for the landless younger sons of Britain's landed gentry to learn and practice manual and agricultural tradaes. The community wasn't designed to be exclusively English, however; some of the settlers were American.

The experiment was not to succeed (tennis and tea drinking don't build cities); many of the colonists left and in a decade or two the village drifted into a small farming community. Revival of the village began in 1966, when **Historic Rugby, Inc.**, set about preserving, restoring and exhibiting some of the colony's remaining buildings. The village is now listed on the National Register of Historic Places.

Several of the buildings, all painted in their original Victorian colors, may be toured. One of them, the **Schoolhouse Visitors Center**, contains exhibits that chronicle the history of the village. Another, the Gothic Revival **Christ Church Episcopal** (1887), has the original hanging lamps and 1849 rosewood organ. The organ is still used for the church's services. The **Thomas Hughes Library** (1882) has some 7,000 original volumes of Victorian fiction and non-fiction; the library hasn't changed since the 1880s. **Kingstone Lisle** (1884), the delightful rural Gothic Revival cottage built for Rugby's founder, contains original Rugby furnishings.

Most of the surviving homes, now private residences, are normally closed. However, many are open during the **Rugby Pilgrimage**, the first weekend in October.

Rugby has two shops, both truly unique. One carries traditional crafts and British foods, among other items; the other specializes in Victorian gifts and area history books.

SPECIAL FEATURE

• In the Rugby vicinity are the **Big South Fork National River & Recreation Area, Frozen Head** and **Pickett** state parks, and the **Obed Wild & Scenic River** area. These and other facilities offer hiking, biking, horseback riding, seasonal rafting, remote river canoeing, fishing and camping.

Thomas Hughes, author of "Tom Brown's Schooldays," devoted much of his time to helping the English working classes.
The trails built by the colonists down to the river are still in use.

WHERE TO STAY

Newbury House B&B, Historic Rugby, (615) 628-2441. Restored mansard-roofed boarding house, front veranda, full breakfasts, tea/coffee. $$

Victorian Cottages, Historic Rugby, (615) 628-2441. Restored 1879 house (Pioneer Cottage) and reconstructed Gothic Revival cottage (Percy Cottage). $$

WHERE TO EAT

The Harrow Road Cafe, Historic Rugby, (615) 628-2441. Cumberland Plateau home cooking and British Isles specialties. $ to $$

FURTHER INFORMATION

Historic Rugby, Inc., P. O. Box 8, Rugby, TN 37733, (615) 628-2441/2430.

DIRECTIONS

From Knoxville, I 75 north to exit 141, TN 63 west to US 27, US 27 south to TN 52 (Elgin), TN 52 west to Rugby.

TEXAS

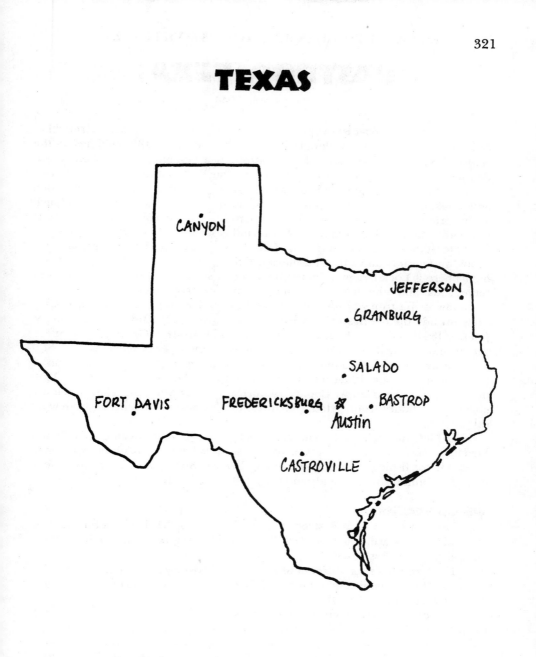

CANYON

JEFFERSON

GRANBURG

SALADO

FORT DAVIS

FREDERICKSBURG

BASTROP

Austin

CASTROVILLE

BASTROP, TEXAS

Population: 4,044

Established in 1832, **Bastrop** was here before Texas even became a republic. Built on the banks of the Colorado River and boasting over 130 buildings on the National Register of Historic Places, Bastrop is a peaceful, gracious old town. People who live here report a certain "magical quality" to it. It's the kind of place where a town tour begins with the arrival of a horse-drawn carriage at the bed and breakfast. And yet Bastrop is relatively uncommercialized — unusual for such an historic and attractive (and cosmopolitan) little Texas community, especially one within easy driving distance of Austin and Houston.

Late 19th-century buildings on **Main Street** house specialty stores, antique shops, restaurants and other businesses. One of the most interesting establishments here is **Lock Drugs**, a 19th-century doctor's office and drug store that still serves sodas and other treats in an old-fashioned ice cream parlor.

Many of Bastrop's historic structures lie in and around the downtown area. They include the the **Bastrop Christian Church** (ca. 1895), **Old Bastrop County Jail** (ca. 1891) and **Courthouse** (ca. 1883). The 1889 **Bastrop Opera House** offers year-round dinner-theater productions, as well as other special activities.

The streets in and around downtown also contain an interesting collection of antebellum and late 19th-century homes and churches. One, a restored 1850 home, houses the **Bastrop County Historical Society Museum**. The museum's collection includes frontier tools, pictures, furnishings, documents and other local artifacts.

The CoC maintains information for self-guided driving, walking, bicycle and Medallion Homes tours. With two city parks on its banks, the **Colorado River** is accessible for fishing, canoeing and tubing. **Bastrop State Park** (see below) offers fishing, swimming, nature study and hiking. Bastrop has two fine golf courses.

SPECIAL FEATURES

• Just east of town, in **Bastrop State Park**, is an especially beautiful stand of pines. The trees are called the *Lost Pines* because they occur so far from their normal range in East Texas.

• The **Central Texas Museum of Automotive History** is about 12 miles south of town. The museum displays some 85 beautiful vintage cars, including Model T's, a Duesenberg, and a 1911 Napier.

• The Bastrop area offers a number of beautiful drives, including **TX 71** east to Smithville. Inquire locally concerning scenic county roads.

The "Bastrop Advertiser" is the oldest weekly newspaper in Texas (est. 1853).

Bastrop was named after a Dutch nobleman, Felipe Enrique Neri, Baron de Bastrop, an important figure in Texas's settlement days. Unknown to the people of the day, Bastrop was an imposter, wanted in Holland for embezzlement.

WHERE TO STAY

The Historic Pfeiffer House, 1802 Main St., (512) 321-2100. 1901 "Carpenter Gothic" home on National Register, high ceilings and antiques, collection of old quilts, full breakfasts. $$

WHERE TO EAT

Gin-U-Wine Oyster Bar/Restaurant, 707 Chestnut St., (512) 321-9864. Tiny New Orleans-style bistro, seafood, enchilada plate. $

La Fuente's Uptown Grill, 905 Main St., (512) 321-9585. A local favorite for Mexican food. $

FURTHER INFORMATION

Bastrop Chamber of Commerce, P. O. Box 681, Bastrop, TX 78602, (512) 321-2419.

DIRECTIONS

From Austin, TX 71 east to Bastrop.

CANYON, TEXAS

Population: 11,365

One of the charming things about Texans is that they want to believe that their state is much farther west than in fact is geographically true. (This does not of course include East Texans, who place themselves somewhere deep in the heart of the Old South). One consequence of this romantic inclination is the existence of Texas towns, especially in the western part of the state, that have more of the character of the Old West than do many towns in more westerly states. **Canyon** is a wonderful example of an Old West Texas town.

Sitting proudly out on the plains of the Panhandle, Canyon is ranch country. The town isn't far from beautiful **Palo Duro Canyon** (see below), something that doesn't hurt its Old West flavor. Like other Panhandle towns, the trees and buildings, especially the older houses, stand in picturesque contrast to the starkness of the surrounding plains.

The **Randall County Courthouse**, on the square in the center of town, was built in 1908/1909 in the Beaux-Arts style. The structure has suffered over the years from several unfortunate modernization efforts and is now the target of an active restoration effort. Various specialty shops, galleries and art studios are among the businesses that surround the square.

The **Panhandle Plains Museum**, located on the campus of **West Texas A & M University**, is the oldest and largest state museum in Texas; it is also one of the finest Western museums in the world. One of its many exhibits is a small Panhandle community of the early 1900s complete with reconstructed log cabins and shops filled with authentic memorabilia. Other exhibits include the restored T-

Anchor Ranch House (late 1870s), a transportation exhibit with early 19th-century automobiles, a filling station (with Model-T Ford) straight from the 1930s, and, among the skeletons, a life-size Allosaurus. Distributed among the museums's five galleries is one of the Southwest's finest art collections.

There are several ways to enjoy the surrounding Old West country. Two nearby ranches offer wagon rides to the rim of a canyon where dinner (or maybe breakfast) is served chuckwagon-style and entertainment cowpoke-style. There are also guided trail rides and horse-drawn wagon rides in the canyon area. Inquire at the CoC for details.

SPECIAL FEATURES
• About 12 miles east of Canyon is **Palo Duro Canyon State Park**, site of a gorgeous 800-foot canyon with spires and other rugged geological features. The three most popular ways to take in the scenic views are hiking, horseback riding and hopping aboard the **Sad Monkey Railroad**, a miniature railroad.
• Palo Duro Canyon State Park is the site of Paul Green's musical drama, *Texas*, performed in the 1742-seat **Pioneer Amphitheater**. The colorful outdoor drama features a professional cast of 80 along with spectacular sound and light creations presented against the backdrop of a 600-foot cliff (reserved seats).

Palo Duro Canyon State Park was the site of the last Indian battle in Texas (1874).

WHERE TO STAY
Country Home B&B, Rt. 1 (Box 447), (806) 655-7636. New/old country house with beautiful view, hot tub. $$ to $$$

Hudspeth House, 1905 4th Ave., (806) 655-9800. Restored 1909 Canyon landmark, Victorian antiques, spa, full breakfasts, beverages. $$ to $$$

WHERE TO EAT
Note: Expect Texas Panhandle menus to feature Mexican-American dishes, Texas-sized steaks, Texas Toast or sourdough biscuits, hot pinto beans, pies and cobblers, and lots of fresh coffee.

The Canyon Grill, 419 16th St., (806) 655-1124. Prime T-bone steak, chicken-fried steak, home-style meatloaf. $

Cope's Coney Island, 2201 4th Ave., (806) 655-1184. Everything from steaks to hot dogs to stew, known for good cooking. $

Pepitos Mexican Restaurante, 408 23rd St., (806) 655-4736. Stuffed jalapenos, tamales, chili rellenos, fajitas. $ to $$

Railroad Crossing Steakhouse, 14th Ave. and Lubbock Hwy., (806) 655-7701. Steaks and seafood, popular salad bar. $ to $$.

FURTHER INFORMATION
Canyon Chamber of Commerce, P. O. Box 8, Canyon, TX 79015, (806) 655-1183.

DIRECTIONS
From Amarillo, I 27 south to exit 110, US 87 south to Canyon.

CASTROVILLE, TEXAS
Population:2,159

Settled in 1844 by immigrants from the French-German provinces of Alsace and Lorraine, **Castroville** was by the 1850s a picturesque little Alsatian village. *The Little Alsace of Texas* looks a little more like Texas these days, but the Alsatian flavor is still very much in evidence: nearly 100 stone buildings from the original Alsatian village remain, Alsatian (a Germanic dialect) is spoken by some of the older townspeople, local kitchens and menus feature Alsatian dishes, and Alsatian folk music is preserved by the **Alsatian Dancers of Texas.**

There was a time when Castroville was one of Texas's largest cities, but in the 1880s the railroad bypassed the town, allowing the picturesque architectural heritage to survive. The historic district, encircled in part by one of those lazy Texas rivers, the **Medina**, contains 97 structures. Most were constructed of limestone and cypress timbers and finished with white plaster. Many go as far back as the 1840s and 1850s. The majority, one-story cottages with the asymmetric rooflines of their Alsatian ancestors, are private residences or homes to businesses, including some of Castroville's dozen or so antique and craft shops.

Among the most imposing of the multi-story buildings are the **Carle House and Store** (1865), the porticoed **Tarde Hotel** (1852; now a private residence) and the striking Gothic-style **St. Louis Catholic Church** (1870). The largest structure is the galleried **Moye Center**, now a retreat but built originally (1873) as a convent and motherhouse.

Castroville's most famous building is the **Landmark Inn**, begun in 1849 and established as an inn in 1854. Now a part of the **Landmark Inn State Historical Park**, the inn still offers overnight accommodations (see below). Other structures in the historical park include a residence, stone grist mill and arched stone waterway, all dating from the 1850s.

A guide for a walking tour of the historic district is distributed by the CoC. Guided tours are also available, as are tours of homes conducted by the **Castroville Garden Club** (by appointment).

SPECIAL FEATURE
· One of the country's most charming cities, **San Antonio**, is 20 miles to the east of Castroville. Top sights in San Antonio include the **Paseo del Rio**, several historic missions, the **Alamo**, and the **Institute of Texan Cultures.**

> *Only Stephen F. Austin brought more settlers to Texas than the founder of Castroville, Henri Castro.*
> *Castroville was the first Texas town to be established west of San Antonio.*

WHERE TO STAY
Castro House, 209 US 90 W., (210) 538-3588. Restored 1800s cottage rented as unit, claw-foot bathtub, turn-of-century antiques, fully equipped kitchen, TV. $$$

The Haby Settlement Inn B&B, H.C. Box 35A (Rio Medina), (210) 538-2441. 1890s farmhouse rented as unit, 11-ft. ceilings, antiques, "country" breakfasts, lawn chairs. $$ to $$$

Landmark Inn, 402 Florence St., (210) 538-2133. Historic 1850s inn, no air conditioning/telephones/meals, posted with Alsatian motto "He who values his own tranquility, knows to respect that of others," old rockers on second-floor gallery. $

Mary M B&B, 1306 Fiorella St., (210) 538-9602. Cottage rented as unit, antiques, fully equipped kitchen, TV. $$$

The Swan and Railway Country Inn, P. O. Box 446 (LaCoste), (210) 762-3742. Restored circa 1910 small hotel, health resort with pool/sauna/exercise room and classes, antiques, long porches, three meals. $$$

WHERE TO EAT

Note: Castroville is famous for its Alsatian sausage and pastries.

The Alsatian, 403 Angelo St., (210) 538-3260. Quaint 1800s cottage setting, Jagerschnitzel, Chicken Poivrade, Grilled Shrimp a Quatre Epices. $ to $$

Chantilly Restaurant, 309 La Fayette St., (210) 538-9531. Dining in Victorian atmosphere, daily specials, homemade rolls and desserts. $

La Normandie Restaurant, 1302 Fiorella St., (210) 538-3070. Traditional French cuisine, entrees from Normandy to Alsace. $ to $$

FURTHER INFORMATION

Castroville Chamber of Commerce, P. O. Box 572, Castroville, TX 78009, (210) 538-3142.

DIRECTIONS

From San Antonio, US 90 west to Castroville.

FORT DAVIS, TEXAS

Population:1,100

Fort Davis is truly a town of the Old West, the Old West of history as well as of the movies. Throughout much of the 19th century wagon trains and stage-coaches passed through the area on their way west on the old San Antonio—El Paso road. Fort Davis (1854 to 1891) was one of several forts built to guard the road. Almost by Hollywood script, Apaches and Comanches attacked travelers on the road, and troops rode out of the fort to pursue the raiders (although with only modest success). Infantry men from the fort also escorted mail and freight trains and patrolled the region's vast spaces. Sometimes the calvary rode out to attack the Indians. And all of this took place in the foothills of the Davis Moun-tains, a made-to-order Western backdrop.

The town of Fort Davis grew up alongside the fort during the latter part of the century. In addition to serving the fort, the town was a center for ranchers and a kind of resort for Texans wishing to escape the heat and humidity of the coastal summers. The elevation, low humidity and cool climate also attracted people suffering from tuberculosis.

It would be an exaggeration to say that the town's life style hasn't changed in 100 years, but there are those who claim that it hasn't changed much in 50 years. Crime is virtually non-existent, and the water remains clear and the air fresh. Nobody uses street names, and everybody knows everyone else. There are many small old adobe houses, and there's a town square surrounded by limestone and adobe buildings from the late 19th and early 20th centuries. The gift shops and art galleries weren't here 50 years ago, but the old soda fountain was.

Many of the town's buildings lie next to or among large volcanic boulders. Of special note are the 1904 **First Presbyterian Church** and the 1898 **St. Joseph's Catholic Church.** The 1884 **Methodist Church** is the oldest Protestant Church building between San Antonio and El Paso. The **Union Mercantile,** on the east end of the square, is the town's oldest building (1873).

According to the National Park Service, the old fort — now the **Fort Davis National Historic Site** — is "considered the best surviving example of a frontier Indian Wars post in the Southwest." Half of the more than 50 original structures of the fort survive. The site includes a visitor center and museum, a picnic grove and a nature trail system. Costumed interpreters conduct tours and present demonstrations during the summer months.

The **Overland Trail Museum,** owned and operated by the **Fort Davis Historical Society** (open by appointment), was once a grocery store (1883). It features a large collection of county photos, a restored frontier kitchen, and a barber shop. The **Chihuahuan Desert Visitor Center,** just south of town, has gardens and walking trails that introduce the visitor to native flowers, cacti, and trees.

SPECIAL FEATURES

• The **Scenic Loop** is a 75-mile road that ascends into the **Davis Mountains**; at one point it reaches the highest point in the Texas highway system (6,791 feet). Along the way are the **Fort Davis Historic Site,** the **McDonald Observatory** (see below), the **Barrel Springs Stage Stop,** the **Point of Rocks** picnic area, and other scenic and historic points. Most of the land fronting the Scenic loop is private property, usually a working ranch, and travelers are advised not to trespass. Flash floods are possible, as are native animals and cattle on the road.

• The **McDonald Observatory,** 17 miles north of town (and on the Scenic Loop), is the third largest viewing complex in the United States. Check at the visitor center for information on tours of the dome, solar viewing, star parties, and other public programs.

Fort Davis was one of the first posts in the West where black troops, called "Buffalo Soldiers," served (1867 to 1885).

WHERE TO STAY

Hotel Limpia, P. O. Box 822 (on the square), (800) 662-5517. Restored 1912 pink limestone hotel, 12-ft. ceilings with ornamental tin, glassed-in veranda, porches, private club. $$ to $$$

Indian Lodge, P. O. Box 1458 (Davis Mountain State Park), (915) 426-3254. Older part a picturesque pueblo-style hotel built in 1930s by C.C.C., handmade furniture, pool, restaurant. $$ to $$$

Neill Doll Museum, edge of town, (915) 426-3969. Restored 1898 home, large doll collection, antique furnishings. $$

Wayside Inn B&B, edge of town, (800) 582-7510. Down-home lodging for entire family, full "cowboy" breakfasts. $$

WHERE TO EAT

Hotel Limpia Dining Room (see above). Burgundy-marinated Roast Beef, Rio Grande Chicken, Adobe Spaghetti, vegetable plate, steaks. $ to $$

FURTHER INFORMATION

Fort Davis Chamber of Commerce, P. O. Box 378, Fort Davis, TX 79734, (915) 426-3015.

DIRECTIONS

From El Paso, I 10 east to exit 206, TX 17 south to Fort Davis.

FREDERICKSBURG, TEXAS

Population: 6,934

Fredericksburg's considerable charm doesn't fit neatly into any category. The very wide straight streets and their limestone and frame houses, some with Victorian gingerbread trim, don't belong to a German town. Yet some of the buildings do reveal a German ancestry, and these and the biergartens and general European ambience hardly describe a typical Texas town. Fredericksburg is unique — and belongs on the itinerary of anyone touring Texas.

One of the first things that will strike the visitor as unique are the smallish homes dotting the back streets. These were once *Sunday Houses*, weekend houses where farming and ranching families stayed when they were in town to buy supplies, sell produce, dance and party — and attend church services. In the era of the horse and buggy, simply getting to and from town took such a large chunk of the day that staying over was often necessary.

By all means the most incongruous, yet enchanting of Fredericksburg's historic sites, is the restored **Nimitz Steamboat Hotel** (1852). Looking very much like an old steamboat getting ready to plough across the Texas Hill Country, the hotel was built and managed by the grandparents of Admiral Nimitz, five-star admiral and hero of the Pacific in WW II. The hotel is today the **Admiral Nimitz State Historical Park** and houses a three-floor **Museum of the Pacific War**, with audiovisual exhibits and hands-on displays. The ballroom and four of the hotel's original guest rooms are also on view. Behind the hotel is the restful **Japanese Garden of Peace**, a gift from the people of Japan.

The **Vereins Kirche Museum** is a replica (1935/36) of an octagonal building (1847) that was, among other things, a school and a fort during the latter half of the 19th century. The landmark building, now owned and operated by the **Gillespie County Historical Society**, is a local history museum and archives. James Michener is one of several researchers who have used the archives.

A good glimpse of an earlier Fredericksburg is provided by the **Pioneer Museum Complex**. The complex includes the 1849 stone **Kammlah House**, a National Historic Trust Site, which has on display eight furnished rooms, a wine cellar, and stone-covered yard (*hof*). Among other structures in the complex is the Victorian **Fassel House**, an old schoolhouse, and the authentic **Weber Sunday House**.

If you're like most people, it's only a matter of time before you head for one of Fredericksburg's biergartens. Here the tastes and smells are very much like those of the Old Country, but the lovely old limestone walls and the live oaks shielding the tables from the Texas sun are uniquely Fredericksburg. This is Texas German at its delightful best! (Some biergartens are open year round.)

SPECIAL FEATURE

• **Fort Martin Scott**, two miles east of town, was the first U.S. Army frontier fort in Texas. The reconstructed fort is now a state historic site.

> *More than 3,000 antique toys from the 1875-1950 period are on display at the Bauer Toy Museum.*

WHERE TO STAY

Country Cottage Inn, 249 E. Main, (210) 997-8549. Inn includes the 1850 Kiehne House and 1866 Chester Nimitz birthplace, private baths, private entrances, TV, phones, Laura Ashley fabarics. $$$

The Delforge Place, 710 Ettie, (210) 997-5612. Restored 1898 home,12-foot ceilings, antique chandeliers, private baths, TV, phones, "world-class gourmet" breakfasts, beverages. $$$

The Herb Haus, 402 Whitney St., (800) 259-4372. Turn-of-century cottage, private courtyard, antiques, TV, phones, "herbal continental" breakfast, wine. $$$

Magnolia House, 101 E. Hackberry, (800) 880-4374. 1925 house, European antiques, fireplaces, patio with fish pond/waterfall, TV, suites, "gourmet seven-course breakfast" on antique china. $$$

Schmidt Barn B&B, 231 W. Main, (210) 997-5612. 130-year-old limestone barn converted to guest cottage, antiques, sunken tub, phone, "German-style" breakfasts, herb/flower garden. $$$

WHERE TO EAT

Der Lindenbaum, 312 E. Main, (210) 997-9126. Rhineland-style cuisine, schnitzels, sauerbraten, bratwurst, steaks. $ to $$

Engel's Deli & Patio, 320 E. Main, (210) 997-3176. Luncheon specials with homemade bread, desserts, strudel. $

The Gallery Restaurant, 210 E. Main, (800) 737-2524. German & Italian entrees, steaks, seafood, full-service bar. $$ to $$$

Mamacita's Restaurant & Cantina, 506 E. Main, (210) 997-9546. Fajitas, enchiladas, top-shelf margaritas, full-service bar. $

The Plateau Cafe, 312 W. Main, (210) 997-1853. Texas/German cooking in "true early Texas environment," biergarten. $

FURTHER INFORMATION

Fredericksburg Convention & Visitor Bureau, 106 N. Adams, Fredericksburg, TX 78624, (210) 997-6523.

DIRECTIONS

From San Antonio, I 10 north to exit 523, US 87 north to Fredericksburg.

GRANBURY, TEXAS

Population: 4,045

True to its Texas heritage, **Granbury** isn't content to be just one thing. Granbury is an historic 19th-century town, an antique and crafts center, a place for Ft. Worthians and Dallasites to go for dinner and a play or musical, a country resort nestled along the shores of 30-mile-long **Lake Granbury.**

Granbury's town square was the first in Texas to be listed on the National Register of Historic Places. On the square is the Second Empire-style **Hood County Courthouse** (1891). A Seth Thomas town clock was installed when the courthouse, built of native limestone, was completed. Around the square are beautifully restored late 19th-century and turn-of-the-century commercial structures. One of the handsomest is the 1886 **Granbury Opera House,** a two-story Italianate theater that still stages musicals, plays, original productions, and melodramas.

Also of note are the limestone **Old Hood County Jail** (1885), which now houses the **Granbury Visitor Center,** and the 1893 **Nutt House,** originally and currently a hotel (see below). The buildings on the square are home to more than 50 antique and specialty shops, art galleries, boutiques and restaurants.

On the streets off the square is a collection of fine Victorian homes, many of them of the Queen Anne style. Granbury's historic buildings may be seen on a tram ride (with narrated tour) and by guided group tours, self-guided tours and historic home tours.

Lake Granbury, lined with vacation homes and condominiums, offers a variety of water sports and the setting for some scenic golf. Sightseeing excursions and dinner cruises are available on two Mississippi-style riverboats. Lest the visitor forget that this is Texas, Granbury also boasts the world's largest 18-hole miniature golf course.

The **Texas Amphitheater** in nearby **Glen Rose** presents a musical drama, *The Promise,* that portrays the life of Christ. For those preferring their entertainment on the screen, Granbury boasts a 1950s **drive-in theater.**

SPECIAL FEATURES

• **Dinosaur Valley State Park,** west of Glen Rose, features the best-preserved dinosaur tracks in the state. The park also has nature trails and a visitor center.

• Also west of Glen Rose, the **Fossil Rim Wildlife Center** offers a 9-mile drive through a 2,900-acre conservation area containing over 1,000 endangered and exotic animals.

> *Granbury has a rich folklore. Among the legends is that the real John Wilkes Booth, President Lincoln's assassin, was never captured and that he once resided in the town under the name of John St. Helen. Another legend is that Jesse James is buried here rather than in Missouri.*

WHERE TO STAY

The Doyle House B&B, 205 W. Doyle, (817) 573-6492. Individually appointed rooms, private entrances, TV, full breakfasts on weekends. $$$

The Iron Horse Inn B&B, 616 N. Thorp Springs Rd., (817) 579-5535. Restored Craftsman-style home, ornate millwork, private baths, library, full breakfasts, wine. $$$

The Nutt House, Town Square, (817) 573-5612. 1893 hotel with air-conditioned guest rooms, dining room, sweet shop. $ to $$

Pearl Street Inn B&B, 319 W. Pearl St., (817) 579-7465. 1912 Prairie-style home, antiques, individually appointed rooms. $$$

WHERE TO EAT

The Merry Heart Tearoom, 109 N. Houston St., (817) 573-3800. "Fresh and delightful fare served in an authentic Victorian atmosphere." $

The Nutt House (see above). Country cooking, homemade light breads and hot-water cornbread. $

FURTHER INFORMATION

Granbury Convention & Visitors Bureau, 100 N. Crockett, Granbury, TX 76048, (800) 950-2212.

DIRECTIONS

From Ft. Worth, US 377 southwest to Granbury.

JEFFERSON, TEXAS

Population: 2,199

Jefferson has one of the most beautiful collections of mid-19th century homes in Texas, but the collection might not be there if it hadn't been for the earnest labors of the U. S. Corps of Engineers. It happens that Jefferson, on **Big Cypress Bayou**, was once a major Texas riverport, second only to Galveston in tonnage shipped. The town was also the Gateway to Texas for settlers, a home to wealthy planters, and a Confederate ammunition and food supply center.

Then came the *Great Decline*:

In 1873, while removing a major log jam on the **Red River** below Shreveport, Louisiana, U.S. Corps of Engineers dredgers unwittingly lowered the water level on the Big Cypress so much that shipping to Jefferson was no longer feasible. Jefferson went dormant, along with its treasure of lovely homes.

Jefferson's shady streets can be toured by foot, motorized trolley, horse-drawn carriage and probably several other ways. Many of the historic homes may be seen by appointment, several by regularly scheduled tour. Among those in the latter category are the single-story neoclassic **Beard House** (1860), the four-columned Greek Revival **Freeman Plantation** (1850), and the lovely transitional **House of Seasons** (1872), identified by its unique cupola.

The **Excelsior House Hotel** (see listing below), one of Jefferson's top sights, has been in continuous operation since the 1850s. Include the hotel and its New Orleans-style courtyard in your tour whether or not you're staying there. Another Jefferson treasure is the *Atalanta*, a private railroad car built in 1888 for railroad tycoon, Jay Gould. There is no better way to apprehend the extravagance of late 19th-century millionaire life than to tour this car.

Jefferson boasts a number of impressive collections, some public and some private. The **Jefferson Historical Museum** displays many of the public ones: Civil War artifacts, old Bibles, pioneer doctors' instruments, ironstone, old Jefferson bottles, etc. Another public collection, the new **Texas Heritage Archives and Library**, might just as well be called the *Museum of the Republic of Texas,* so extensive and valuable are its holdings from the 1836-1845 period. Private collections of antiques and artifacts may be seen in Jefferson's some 49 arts and crafts and collectibles shops.

> *The final resting place and artifacts from the Jefferson-bound steamboat, the "Mittie Stephens," were finally located in 1993. The boat took the lives of 64 people when it burned and sank on Caddo Lake in 1869.*

WHERE TO STAY

The Captain's Castle, 403 E. Walker, (903) 665-2330. Main House & nearby Carriage House and Cottage, on National Register, private baths, "gourmet" breakfasts. $$$

Excelsior House, 211 W. Austin, (903) 665-2513. A Texas landmark, antiques throughout, "plantation" breakfasts. $$ to $$$

Hale House B&B, 702 S. Line St., (903) 665-8877. 1880 home, antiques, breakfasts served with silver and crystal. $$ to $$$

Pride House B&B, 409 E. Broadway, (903) 665-2675. 1888 home with 12-ft ceilings, wrap-around porch, private baths, Praline Pears/Eggs Galveston/Raspberry Butter part of full breakfasts. $$$

Roseville Manor, 217 W. Lafayette, (903) 665-2528. Antique furnishings, private baths, individual climate control, TV, phones. $$$

WHERE TO EAT

Galley Restaurant and Lounge, 121 W. Austin St., (903) 665-3641. In historic building, steaks, seafoods, charbroiled chicken, rated one of best "down-home" restaurants in Texas. $$

Black Swan, 210 W. Austin St., (903) 665-8922. In restored home, Southern and Creole cooking, "country dining with a touch of elegance." $$

The Grove, 405 Moseley, (903) 665-2638. Chef-owned historic home, "eclectic bill of fare," Old South surroundings. $$

Stillwater Inn, 203 E. Broadway, (903) 665-8415. Restored 1893 home with antiques, French and American cooking, grilled seafoods, steaks. $$ to $$$

FURTHER INFORMATION

Marion County Chamber of Commerce, 116 W. Austin, Jefferson, TX 75657, (903) 665-2672.

DIRECTIONS

From Shreveport (LA), I 20 west to US 59, US 59 north to Jefferson.

SALADO, TEXAS

Population: 1,200

Sitting near the tree-shaded banks of spring-fed **Salado Creek** in central Texas is what may be Texas's most charming little town. Although blessed with a lovely setting and a long and genteel history, **Salado** (pronounced sa LAY doh) is so little known that it is sometimes called the "undiscovered jewel of Texas." Many people who regularly travel the nearby interstate have never heard of it, and there are people living just a few miles away who have never been there.

Salado Creek once nourished a stage stop and later a branch of the **Chisholm Trail**. But Salado came into being because of the generosity of plantation owner Colonel Sterling C. Robertson, who in 1859 gave the land for the town. Once born, the town's character was molded by respected **Salado College** (1860 to about 1885), whose students and educators brought to Salado a level of culture and prestige foreign to most other Texas frontier towns.

Following the usual scenario, the railroads bypassed Salado, and the town was destined to become a small, quiet village. The village has undergone a recent revitalization as many of the old homes and other buildings have been restored to house bed and breakfasts (see below), some of the finest restaurants in central Texas (see below), and a very inviting collection of art galleries, potteries, antique and craft shops, boutiques and book shops.

Eighteen of the village's buildings are listed on the National Register. Tapes for a driving tour may be rented at the **Stagecoach Inn** (see below). Also, several of the houses are open during an historic homes tour held every December.

One of the houses is the **Baines home**, an 1866 saltbox built by the great-grandfather of President Lyndon Baines Johnson. Two other interesting houses include the 1868 Greek Revival **Armstrong-Adams House**, once occupied by a series of doctors as well as student boarders, and the old rock **Barton House**, built in 1866 by a Dr. and Mrs. Barton who wished to educate their 10 children at Salado College.

Salado Creek is the first Natural Landmark in Texas. The town is so proud of the creek that a committee has been established to monitor the quality of the water. One of the best places to enjoy the beauty of the crystal-clear waters is at **Pace Park**, once an Indian campground. A bronze statue of **Sirena**, a beautiful Indian maiden who by legend was transformed into a mermaid by a magical fish, graces a bubbling spring of the creek.

SPECIAL FEATURE

• In the country south of town stands the 22-room plantation home (1852/ 1857) and stone slave quarters built by Col. Robertson. The house remains in the hands of the Robertson family. Occasional tours are available; check with the CoC for information.

> *The ruins of Salado College have been stabilized preliminary to reconstruction efforts.*
> *Salado hosts the Texas Scottish Games and Gathering of the Clans every November.*
> *Dr. Barton, builder of Barton House, is believed to have introduced watercress to Salado Creek. The plant fourishes there today.*

WHERE TO STAY

Country Place B&B, Rt. 1 (Box 19VA), (817) 947-9683. Old Texas country house, fields of bluebonnets, full "country" breakfasts. $$$

Halley House B&B, P. O. Box 125, (817) 947-1000. 1860 home with antiques, oak trees, "gourmet" buffet breakfasts. $$$

Inn on the Creek, P. O. Box 858. Three lovely historic houses and a cottage, porches, full "country" breakfasts. $$ to $$$

Inn at Salado, P. O. Box 500, (817) 947-8200. Renovated 1872 home on National Register, tree-covered brick terraces, private baths. $$$

The Rose Mansion, P. O. Box 500, (817) 947-8200. 1870 Greek Revival mansion, grand parlor, acres of landscaped grounds. $$$

WHERE TO EAT

Inn on the Creek (see above). "Romantic" five-course meals served on weekends, by reservation. $$

Stagecoach Inn, Old Chisholm Trail, (800) 732-8994. Traditional Texas dining in historic 1861 stage stop, fixed-price menu. $ to $$

Tyler House Restaurant, Main St., (817) 947-5157. French and Continental cuisine served in 1857 home, extensive wine list, afternoon teas. $ to $$

Young-Williams Manor, 400 N. Main St., (817) 947-0306. Special entrees served in classic dining room, murder-mystery dinner theater on Friday nights. $ to $$ ($$$ for dinner theater)

FURTHER INFORMATION

Salado Chamber of Commerce, P. O. Box 81, Salado, TX 76571, (817) 947-5040.

DIRECTIONS

From Austin, I 35 north to exit 283 (Salado exit).

UTAH

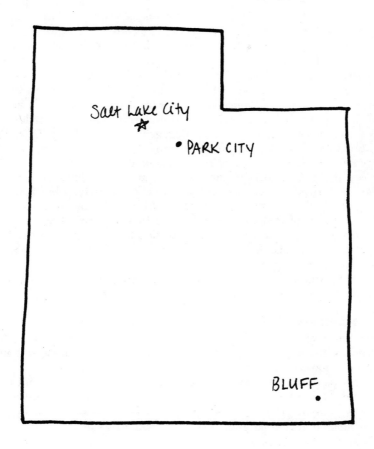

Salt Lake City
☆

• PARK CITY

BLUFF
•

BLUFF, UTAH

Population :about 250

Guarded by the towering **Navajo Twin Rocks, Bluff** lies in a canyon along the **San Juan River** in southeastern Utah. The town is one of those legendary little Western settlements that combine the vestiges of Victoriana with some of the most spectacular scenery in the country.

Bluff was settled by Mormons in 1880. At first the settlers were compelled to group their cabins in a defensive fort, but as the region became safer, the cabins were moved to individual lots. There they provided shelter while larger stone houses were erected. Bluff's growth was to be short-lived, however, for in 1893 the county seat moved to Monticello and the town was progressively abandoned. Many of the houses were eventually torn down, and the remainder lost much of their Victorian ornamentation through negligence or rebuilding. Of the original 30 or so buildings, only about 14 survived; most of these are being preserved, and in many cases restored to their original appearance.

Explore the tiny historic district on foot, and then climb up on **Cemetery Hill**. The memorials here remind of a time that was anything but romantic. For example, James Decker, one of the original settlers, and four of his children died of diptheria during a two-month period in late 1900 and early 1901.

The area around Bluff is rich in prehistoric sites. Within short driving, if not walking, distance are six or seven **Pueblo Anasazi** and **Navajo rock art** panels composed of various representational images and abstract motifs. There are also several Pueblo Anasazi sites. One, situated on Cemetery Hill, consists of a Great House, a Great Kiva, and remnants of a prehistoric road.

SPECIAL FEATURES

• Nine national parks and monuments are within a two-hour drive. The vast **Navajo Indian Reservation** is adjacent, and the spectacular **Valley of the Gods** is only a few miles away. Inquire locally concerning guided tours.

• River trips down the wild and archaeologically rich **San Juan** and **Colorado** rivers can be arranged locally. The trips vary in length from one to several days.

> *A unique black-on-red pottery was collected in 1936 at one of the local Pueblo Anasazi village sites. The pottery is now known to Southwest archaeologists as Bluff Black-on-red.*
>
> *At one time the Navajos crossed the river by means of a swinging bridge, still in place.*

WHERE TO STAY

Bluff B&B, P. O. Box 158, (801) 672-2220. Frank Lloyd Wright-style home on 17 desert acres, private canyon, private baths. $$

Calabre B&B, P. O. Box 85, (801) 672-2252. In town, slide show on request, swimming privileges, full breakfasts. $

WHERE TO EAT

Cow Canyon Trading Post & Restaurant, 163 Mission Rd., (801) 672-2208. Traditional Navajo dishes, TexMex and Italian fare, reservations recommended. $

The Sunbonnet Cafe, Historic Loop, (801) 672-2201. "Home of the Navajo Taco," beef stew and fry bread, Sheepherder Sandwiches. $

The Thai House, Historic Loop, (801) 672-2355. Traditional Thai cuisine served in historic home. $

FURTHER INFORMATION

Bluff Town Board, P. O. Box 85, Bluff, UT 84512, (801) 672-2252.

DIRECTIONS

From Flagstaff (AZ), US 89 north to US 160, US 160 east to US 163 (at Kayenta), US 163 north to Bluff.

PARK CITY, UTAH

Population: 4,468

Named after its park-like setting, **Park City** is a unique and engaging mixture of the old and the new. The old can be seen in the Victorian buildings and various mementos from the town's mining past. The new is seen in the many condos, modern ski resorts, and numerous shops and boutiques. But the old and the new don't coexist, they blend.

Many of the shops are housed in restored historic buildings, and transportation on **Main Street** is provided by an old-fashioned trolley. The blend is most beautiful in the winter, when people in colorful ski gear stroll through a wonderland of snow-covered Victorian buildings and inviting inns, restaurants and pubs.

One of the few Utah towns not founded by Mormons, Park City boasted some 27 saloons at one point early in its history. The silver in the surrounding **Wasatch Mountains** helped turn 23 people into millionnaires, including George Hearst, father of William Randolph Hearst. By the 1930s, however, it was clear that silver was becoming part of the town's past and the people began to look toward the snow for their future.

And what a future it turned out to be! Park City now has three major ski resorts, three shopping centers (including Main Street), around 15 art galleries and a free bus system. There are also 80 restaurants, and the apres-ski and nightlife scenes are among the most highly rated in the country.

Park City has had 64 buildings placed on the National Register of Historic Places. Many are on Main Street. One of special interest to those wishing to know the town is the **Visitor Information Center/Museum.** Once the **City Hall,** the museum tells the story of Park City's mining past and transition to a major resort. In the basement is **Utah's Territorial Jail,** used longer than any other territorial jail in the West.

Park City is both a summer and winter resort. The summer tourist will find six distinctive golf courses, hiking and horseback riding trails and more than 80 miles of mountain-bike trails. A ski lift serves hikers and bikers. In addition to the ski resorts, winter sports fans will find opportunities and facilities for snowmobiling, cross-country skiing and ice skating. Hot-air balloons color the skies in both summer and winter.

SPECIAL FEATURE

• Four Nordic ski jumps, a freestyle jump and a snowboard half-pipe have been recently constructed at **Utah Winter Sports Park**. For the summer jumper there is a unique freestyle aerial splash pool, with four aerial ramps, and the 90-meter jump is equipped with high-tech materials for use in warm weather. Ski-jump lessons are available.

> *Park City's ski resorts reported 970,000 skier days during the 1992/93 season.*
> *More than 1,000 miles of tunnels, remnants of the mining area, lace through the surrounding mountains.*

WHERE TO STAY

The Blue Church Lodge, P. O. Box 1720, (800) 626-5467. Remodeled 1897 church, on National Register, antique country charm, fireplaces. $$ to $$$

Imperial Hotel, P. O. Box 1628, (800) 669-8824. 1904 hotel on National Register, lace curtains and antiques, hot tub. $$ to $$$

The Old Miners' Lodge, P. O. Box 2639, (800) 648-8068. Renovated 1893 building in historic district, "hearty country" breakfasts. $$ to $$$

The Snowed Inn, 3770 N. UT 224, (800) 545-7669. Victorian mansion, European antiques, restaurant, transportation to slopes. $$ to $$$

The Washington School Inn, P. O. Box 536, (800) 824-1672. 1889 school refurbished as four-story inn, on National Register, indoor hot tub, sauna, full breakfasts. $$$

WHERE TO EAT

Adolph's, 1541 Thaynes Canyon Dr., (801) 649-7177. European and American cuisine, "Swiss hospitality," entertainment. $$

The Barking Frog, 368 Main St., (801) 649-6222. Innovative Southwestern cuisine, sweet & spicy chilies, outdoor dining. $$

Cafe Terigo, 424 Main St., (801) 645-9555. Pesto pizza and fresh pastas, seafood, daily specials, outdoor dining. $$

The Glitretind Restaurant at Stein Eriksen Lodge, (800) 534-1302. Seafood specialties, alpine setting, dining on deck. $$ to $$$

The Riverhorse Cafe, 540 Main St., (801) 649-3536. New American innovative cuisine, fresh seafood, regional specialties. $$

FURTHER INFORMATION

Park City Chamber of Commerce/Convention & Visitors Bureau, P. O. Box 1630, Park City, UT 84060, (800) 453-1360.

DIRECTIONS

From Salt Lake City, I 80 east to exit 145, UT 224 south to Park City.

VERMONT

CRAFTSBURY COMMON

GREENSBORO

STOWE

Montepelier

MIDDLEBURY

DORSET

MANCHESTER

GREENSBORO/CRAFTSBURY, VERMONT

Population (Village): 717/994

Greensboro and **Craftsbury** are up in the Northeast Kingdom of Vermont, a region that looks like what much of our country looked like — or should have looked like — 100 years ago. The setting is strictly rural. The roads, mostly dirt and often tree-lined, wind Currier & Ives-style over rivers, through woods and past farmsteads. Every turn in the road brings a new and delightful view. There is little traffic, leaving the driver free to watch for moose, blue herons and wildflowers.

Greensboro and Craftsbury don't have many stores or other businesses. Both are little collections of white-painted homes, churches and a general store or two. Villagers seeking anything more than bread, gasoline and a few other necessities must make a 30- or 45-minute drive. Craftsbury boasts two libraries and evening concerts on the large **Common** (lovely). There's a charming British woolen shop in **East Craftsbury**. Tucked at the southern end of **Caspian Lake**, Greensboro has an especially well-stocked old general store, **Willey's**.

The gently sloping countryside, the shaded backroads, the deep forests, the lakes and rivers are tailor-made for camping, hiking, biking, fishing and water sports. There's an extensive trail network for cross-country skiing. Naturalists and others who prefer their countryside totally undeveloped will find true wilderness not far away in **Essex County**.

WHERE TO STAY

Brassknocker Inn B&B, R.R. 1 (Box 89A) (East Craftsbury), (802) 586-2814. Spacious guest rooms, antique cookstove, large country kitchen. $$ to $$$

Craftsbury B&B on Wylie Hill, Craftsbury Common, (802) 586-2206. 1860s hilltop home, spectacular views, full breakfasts. $$

Finchingfield Farm B&B, R.R. 1 (Box 1195) (East Craftsbury), (802) 586-7763. Turn-of-century country house, English antiques, library, down comforters, full breakfasts, adjoining farmland perpetually protected. $$ to $$$

Highland Lodge, R.R. 1 (Box 1290) (Greensboro), (802) 533-2647. Small 1860s inn & cottages on lake, water sports, hiking paths, cross-country skiing, children's playhouse, modified American plan. $$$

Inn on the Common, Main St. (Craftsbury Common), (800) 521-2233. Famous gardens, great views, pool, English croquet, modified American plan. $$$

WHERE TO EAT

Craftsbury Inn, Main St. (Craftsbury), (800) 336-2848. Chef-owned 1850 country inn, full bar. $$

Highland Lodge (see above). "Truly imaginative meals . . . with creative tastes and textures." $$

FURTHER INFORMATION
Lamoille Valley Chamber of Commerce, P. O. Box 445, Morrisville, VT 05661, (802) 888-7607.

DIRECTIONS
From Springfield (MA), I 91 north to exit 25, VT 16 south to Greensboro Bend, county road west to Greensboro and Craftsbury.

MANCHESTER/DORSET, VERMONT

Population (Village): 561/550

Manchester and **Dorset** have 19th-century church steeples and houses, most of them white and *big*, many with green shutters, clustered about village greens and framed by hills and forests. The predominant colors are green and white, the particular proportions of each dependent on the season. Giant shade trees — including of course maples — and winding roads complete the foreground. The scene is perfect for gracious old inns, colonial dining rooms and crackling fireplaces.

Manchester and Dorset are not places where people typically go to seek work. They are places to retreat from work. The interesting thing is that this has been true since the middle of the 19th century, at least. In the 1850s, as today, these villages were places of holiday or retirement. Indeed, the history of Manchester is virtually inseparable from the history of its centerpiece, the **Equinox**, Vermont's premier inn (listed below).

While benefiting from the past, Manchester and Dorset do not ignore the present and future: Their buildings are beautifully restored, Manchester's downtown thrives, Dorset's rural charm persists, and development rights for many of the nearby farms are held by land trusts. A lot of work, time and love have gone to make this true.

Manchester is home to **Hildene** (1905), the 24-room Georgian Revival mansion built by Robert Todd Lincoln, the only son of Abraham and Mary Todd Lincoln to survive to maturity. The house's original furnishings and Lincoln family effects may be seen by daily tours (and candlelight tours during the Christmas season). The formal gardens have been restored. Of the estate's 412 acres, 200 have been set aside as "forever wild."

The **Southern Vermont Art Center** is housed in another colonial revival mansion, **Yester House** (1917), in Manchester. Paintings, sculptures, photographs and other works of art are exhibited in 11 of the house's 28 rooms. Classical and chamber music, jazz, and voice and instrumental solos and duets are performed in the adjacent **Louise Ryals Arkell Pavilion**. Also on the grounds are the Sculpture Garden and the lovely **Boswell Botany Trail,** managed by the **Manchester Garden Club.**

The **American Musem of Fly Fishing,** also in Manchester, boasts a collection of more than 1,000 rods and 400 reels. The collection includes fly rods used by Dwight D. Eisenhower, Daniel Webster, Ernest Hemingway, Winslow Homer, Bing Crosby and other famous Americans.

The **Dorset Playhouse,** noted for good theater, offers a range of performances in both summer and winter. A resident professional group performs in the summer as the **Dorset Theatre Festival;** the **Dorset Players** present periodic shows during the winter.

Manchester is a gateway to several well-known Vermont ski areas. The region also offers groomed as well as ungroomed trails for cross-country skiing. Twenty-one groomed trails are on the grounds of Hildene (see above), along with a warming hut.

SPECIAL FEATURE

• From May through October a 5.2-mile winding toll road can be driven to the top of **Mt. Equinox.** Several states, and even Mount Royal in Montreal, can be seen from the top of the mountain on clear days. Picknicking is available on the grounds of the **Monastery of the Carthusian Order** on the side of the mountain.

> *Among the summer residents in Manchester during the Civil War year of 1863 were Mary Todd Lincoln and her son, Robert Todd.*
> *Mary Lincoln Beckwith, Abraham Lincoln's great granddaughter, was the last member of the Lincoln family to live at Hildene. Beckwith died in 1975.*

WHERE TO STAY AND EAT

Note: In the following listing, five inns are described as lodgings and five as restaurants. Because many inns in Manchester and Dorset offer superb dining as well as lodging, the assignment to one or the other category was in most cases random. The price codes are appropriate to the category described.

The 1811 House, VT 7A (Manchester), (802) 362-1811. 1770s Federal-style home on seven acres, fine paintings, canopy beds. $$$

Barrows House, VT 30 (Dorset), (802) 867-4455. American regional cuisine, country dining with an "elegant flair." $$ to $$$

The Black Swan, VT 7A (Manchester), (802) 362-3807. Continental cuisine "with a California flair," fresh fish, game, daily specialties, fresh flowers. $$ to $$$

The Chantecleer, VT 7A (Manchester), (802) 362-1616. Continental cuisine, tableside service, chef-owned, reservations required. $$ to $$$

Cornucopia of Dorset, P. O. Box 307 (Dorset), (802) 867-5751. 1880 country village home, fireplaces, private baths, full "gourmet" breakfasts. $$$

The Dorset Inn, VT 30 (Dorset), (802) 867-5500. Oldest continuously operating inn in Vermont, "gourmet American food with subtle French overtones," reservations requested. $$ to $$$

The Equinox, Vt. 7A (Manchester), (800) 362-4747. Vermont landmark on National Register, pools, tennis courts, golf course. $$$

Inn at West View Farm, VT 30 (Dorset), (802) 867-5715. Beautiful country inn, "interesting variety of dishes expertly prepared." $$ to $$$

Reluctant Panther, just off VT 7A (Manchester Village), (802) 362-2568. 1850s landmark, private baths, TV, "country hospitality for the sophisticated traveler." $$$

The Wilburton Inn, off VT 7A (Manchester Village), (800) 648-4944. 20-acre Victorian estate overlooking valley, spacious rooms, pool, tennis, golf. $$$

FURTHER INFORMATION

Manchester and the Mountains Chamber of Commerce, P. O. Box 928, Manchester Center, VT 05255, (802) 362-2100; (Other Zips: Dorset, 05251, and Manchester Village, 05254).

DIRECTIONS

From Burlington, US 7 south (via Rutland) to Dorset and Manchester.

MIDDLEBURY, VERMONT

Population: 6,007 (excluding students)

With a village green, shuttered colonial houses, church steeples, museums, beautiful old inns, and nearby skiing, **Middlebury** is a resume of New England's charms. The countryside is pastoral. Visible to the east are the **Green Mountains**, to the west across **Lake Champlain,** the **Adirondacks.** Other New England towns may also have this; what separates Middlebury is that its livelihood depends on a college campus rather than tourist promotion. College towns seem to offer a gentler way of life and a setting more appealing to retirees and others seeking quality in their lives.

Middlebury College is one of the oldest (1800) and most prestigious colleges in the United States. Its beautiful 1,200-acre main campus is dotted with colonial buildings of gray limestone or white marble. Three of the oldest, **Painter Hall** (1816), **Old Chapel** (1836), and **Starr Hall** (1860) make up lovely **Old Stone Row.**

The **Middlebury College Center for the Arts** includes an award-winning concert hall, theater, and library. One of the center's five components, the **Middlebury College Museum of Art,** houses traveling exhibitions as well as a permanent collection. The latter is noted for its Cypriot pottery, 19th-century sculpture and contemporary prints.

About the village green and along the tree-shaded streets are a number of lovely town landmarks. Of special note are the Federal-style **Painter House** and the much-photographed 1809 **Congregational Church,** with a many-faceted steeple designed to give a little in the wind. The **Community House,** an 1815 home, has hand-carved fireplaces and a spiral staircase; the house is in constant use for art and crafts classes and other community events.

Middlebury is one of the three locations of the **Vermont State Craft Center at Frog Hollow.** A non-profit visual arts organization, the center displays the works of over 300 Vermont craftspeople in its galleries. The wood, fabric, painting and other wares are for sale, but visitors are welcome to browse. The Middlebury site also has studios, demonstrations and classes — and good views of **Otter Creek**. Vermont arts and crafts may also be seen at the **Vermont Folklife Center**. In addition to displaying folk art, the center uses video tapes to illustrate the state's folk traditions

The **Sheldon Museum**, the first incorporated village museum in the country, contains one of Vermont's foremost collections of antiques and curios. Housed in an 1829 tavern, later a home, the museum's rooms display furniture, guns, newspapers and countless other items. In the library are bound copies of everything published in Middlebury since 1801.

The **Historic Marble Works** makes shopping an historic experience. Here on the courtyards of 1890s buildings are restaurants and little shops. A scenic river footbridge leads to **Frog Hollow Mill**, an old three-story stone mill housing yet more shops and another restaurant.

Middlebury College's **Snow Bowl** offers excellent alpine skiing (open to the public). The Middlebury area also has a good selection of groomed cross-country trails.

SPECIAL FEATURE

· The **Morgan Horse Farm**, the *Home of the Morgans*, is located just outside of town. A breeding farm since the 1800s, its mission is to preserve and promote the country's first breed of horses. The farm is operated by the University of Vermont (guided tours).

The Pulp Mill Bridge (1806) is Vermont's only two-lane separated covered bridge still open to traffic.
Otters can often be seen playing in Otter Creek, which flows through town.

WHERE TO STAY

Middlebury Inn, Court House Square, (800) 842-4666. An 1827 inn now comprising three buildings, private baths, TV, phones, highly recommended dining room. $$ to $$$

The Swift House Inn, US 7 & Stewart Ln., (802) 388-9925. Three historic buildings on spacious lawns, antiques, carved marble fireplaces, private baths, phones, steam room/sauna, award-winning cuisine. $$$

Waybury Inn, VT 125, (800) 348-1810. Quiet old inn with individually furnished rooms, antiques, private baths, full breakfasts, dining room respected for its traditional New England fare. $$$

WHERE TO EAT

Note: The three inns listed above are also known for their fine dining.

Dog Team Tavern, Dog Team Rd., (802) 388-7651. Prime rib, swordfish steak, home-style vegetables, Dog Team Sticky Buns, Maple Oatmeal Pie. $$

Fire & Ice Restaurant, 26 Seymour St., (802) 388-7166. "Steak Rockport—half pound Filet Mignon stuffed with lobster and finished with hollandaise sauce." $$

Mill Street Coffee & News, in Frog Hollow Mill, (802) 388-1063. Specialty coffee shop, bagels, croissants, brioche, light lunches. $

Mister Up's, Bakery Ln., (802) 388-6724. Fresh Norwegian Salmon, New England Lobster & Salmon Cakes, Zuppa de Pesce, lighter fare. $ to $$

Woody's, 5 Bakery Ln., (802) 388-4182. Overlooking Otter Creek, fresh seafood and Vermont lamb are the specialties. $ to $$

FURTHER INFORMATION

Addison County Chamber of Commerce, 2 Court St., Middlebury, VT 05753, (802) 388-7951.

DIRECTIONS

From Burlington, US 7 south to Middlebury.

STOWE, VERMONT

Population: 3,433

Stowe is a white-steepled, picture-book New England village nestled in the **Green Mountains** beneath **Mt. Mansfield**, Vermont's highest peak. One of the first ski resorts in the East, Stowe is second to none in the East in its number — and variety — of fine runs. What is less well-known is that Stowe is also second to none in its number — and variety — of bed-and-breakfast inns. Although the village population is only about 450, the number of bed and breakfasts is somewhere between 30 and 40! B&B inns and guest houses vary from private home to stately inn, from rustic to Laura Ashley, from Tyrolean Austrian, to Colonial American.

The beauty of Stowe Village is in part due to its age (200 years in 1994) and the charming old buildings, including a covered bridge, that come with age; it's also in part due to a very strict zoning code that governs even the size and shape of signs (neon not allowed). The village is popular as both a summer and winter resort. Because of Stowe's unique climate, flowers do especially well; indeed, the gardens themselves merit a summer visit.

The village is noted for the beautiful crafts and other items displayed in its shops. The arts are well represented. The **Helen Day Art Center** has changing art exhibits and maintains an active calendar of programs and classes. Among the evening options are summer performances of the **Stowe Playhouse** and beckoning tables in one of the village's cozy pubs.

The Stowe area offers about every outdoor recreation but sponging and deep-sea fishing. Included among the summer offerings are rollerblading, wildlife-watching on Mt. Mansfield, speeding down a 2,300-ft. alpine slide, trout fishing, and sightseeing from an enclosed gondola. In addition to fabulous downhill skiing, winter activities include snowmobiling, ice skating and — thanks to miles of groomed trails — superb cross-country skiing.

SPECIAL FEATURES

•**VT 108** north from Stowe through **Smugglers Notch** offers a particularly scenic drive during the summer months (closed winters). Along the way are waterfalls, hiking trails and parking areas. Magnificent views can also be enjoyed from an auto toll road that climbs to the top of Mt. Mansfield.

•Visitors may watch milking or purchase wool yarns or fresh vegetables at some of the area's working farms. Check locally for instructions, and always call the farm in advance.

•There are at least six covered bridges in the Stowe vicinity. Check locally for locations and routing.

> *During Prohibition liquor was smuggled from Canada through the mountain gorge that was named, subsequently and consequently, "Smugglers Notch."*

WHERE TO STAY

Note: Many of Stowe's inns, including several listed here and in the dining section below, are noted for both their lodgings and meals.

The 1860 House B&B Inn, P. O. Box 276, (802) 253-7351. Historic home on National Register, in village, private baths, trout pond. $$$

The Inn at the Brass Lantern, 717 Maple St., (800) 729-2980. Circa 1800 farmhouse, antiques, private baths, fireplace rooms. $$ to $$$

Butternut Inn at Stowe, 2309 Mountain Rd., (800) 328-8837. Eight acres of gardens, private baths, pool, antiques, afternoon teas. $$ to $$$

The Gables Inn, 1457 Mountain Rd., (800) 422-5371. 1850s farmhouse, private baths, antiques, pool and hot tub, colorful gardens, famed "hearty Vermont" breakfasts. $$ to $$$

Green Mountain Inn, Main St., (800) 445-6629. Restored 1833 inn on National Register, antiques, central location, two restaurants. $$$

WHERE TO EAT

Edson Hill Manor, 1500 Edson Hill Rd., (800) 621-0284. On secluded 225-acre estate, innovative American cuisine, reservations. $$

Gracie's Restaurant, Main St., (802) 253-8741. Steaks, salmon, swordfish, scallops, shrimp, vegetarian dishes. $ to $$

Hob Knob Inn, 2364 Mountain Rd., (800) 245-8540. Fireside dining, fresh fish, Black Angus steaks. $$

Whiskers, 1652 Mountain Rd., (800) 649-8996. 5 antique-filled dining rooms, famous prime rib, lobster, seafood, chicken, pasta. $$

Ye Old England Inn, 433 Mountain Rd., (800) 477-3771. "Gourmet dining in a soft romantic candlelit atmosphere," rare cognacs, vintage ports. $$

FURTHER INFORMATION

Stowe Area Association, P. O. Box 1320, Stowe, VT 05672, (802) 253-7321.

DIRECTIONS

From Burlington, I 89 east to exit 10, VT 100 north to Stowe.

VIRGINIA

CHINCOTEAGUE

LEXINGTON

Richmond ★

BEDFORD

WILLIAMSBURG

• ABINGDON

ABINGDON, VIRGINIA

Population: 7,003

Abingdon's two "A" words are Ambience and Arts. Chartered in 1776, Abingdon is the oldest town of British ancestry west of the Blue Ridge Mountains. Bordering the brick sidewalks of the 20-square-block historic district are stately but warm old houses displaying Georgian, Adam, and other traditional architectural styles. Some of the finest now open their doors as bed-and-breakfast inns (see below). Perhaps the most imposing — and renowned — is the **Martha Washington Inn** (1832), originally a private residence but variously a college and hospital since. Now an elegant hotel, the Martha Washington has one of the most respected restaurants in this corner of the world (see below).

As for the arts, Abingdon bills itself as the "cultural center of southwest Virginia." And with excellent reason. For beginners, the town is home to the oldest professional resident theater in the United States, the **Barter Theatre**. Earning its name from the Depression-era practice of bartering for tickets with home-grown produce, the theater's two stages present quality performances of classic and contemporary works. Actors appearing at the Barter have included Hume Cronyn, Gregory Peck, Patricia Neal, and Ernest Borgnine.

The visual arts are represented by an almost endless array of shops and galleries. The works represent a nice mix of the old and the new and range from contemporary paintings to centuries-old Appalachian crafts. Among the regional crafts are woodcarving, quilting, weaving, dried flowers and corn shuckery.

Rotating exhibits are held at the **William King Regional Arts Center**, an affiliate of the **Virginia State Museum of Fine Arts**. The center houses studios and classrooms as well as galleries. Arts and crafts are also displayed in the **Cave House**, an 1858 Victorian landmark sitting on top of limestone grottos. The building, listed on the National Register, has three-story walnut stair railings and other features that complement the various displays. Yet another setting for the display of art is the **Arts Depot**, a restored 1890 freight station.

In a delightful setting just outside of town is **White's Mill**, the only water-powered commercial mill in southwest Virginia. Across from the mill is an old general store with long counters and a pot-bellied stove. The mill is listed on the National Register of Historic Places (guided tours).

SPECIAL FEATURES

• The **Virginia Creeper Trail**, a National Recreation Trail, originates just off **Main Street** and travels 34 miles to the foot of **Whitetop Mountain** near the Virginia/North Carolina border. Once a railroad, the pathway is popular with hikers, bikers, horseback riders and cross-country skiers.

• The 115,000-acre **Mount Rogers National Recreation Area** to the east of Abingdon boasts more than 300 miles of trails, including 60 miles of the great **Appalachian Trail**. Some of the trails form circuits. Included in the recreation area are the three highest mountains in Virginia.

Abingdonians like to brag that their first visitor was Daniel Boone.

WHERE TO STAY

Inn on Town Creek, 445 E. Valley St., (703) 628-4560. Landscaped with brick patios and rock gardens, antiques, private baths. $$$

Litchfield Hall, 247 Valley St., NE, (703) 676-2971. Renovated historic home, antiques, mementos from world travels, full breakfasts. $$$

Silversmith Inn, 102 E. Main St., (703) 676-3924. 1871 brick home in historic district, private baths, full breakfasts. $$$

Summerfield Inn, 101 W. Valley St., (703) 628-5905. 1920s brick home in convenient downtown location, private baths. $$$

Victoria & Albert Inn, 224 Oak Hill St., (703) 676-2797. Small Victorian inn, fireplaces, silver-service breakfasts. $$$

WHERE TO EAT

Abingdon General Store & Gallery, 301 E. Main St., (703) 628-8382. Unique store and gallery, two restaurants "with gourmet flair." $ to $$

The Hardware Company, 260 W. Main St., (703) 628-1111. Dining in a renovated hardware store. $ to $$

The First Lady's Table, in Martha Washington Inn, (703) 628-3161. Traditional Southern dishes, elegant Victorian setting. $$

P. J. Brown & Company, 414 E. Main St., (703) 628-4111. Contemporary flavor, steaks, prime rib, seafood, daily specials. $ to $$

The Starving Artist Cafe, 134 Wall St., (703) 628-8445. Cafe doubling as a local art gallery. $ to $$

FURTHER INFORMATION

Abingdon Convention and Visitors Bureau, Fields-Penn 1860 House Museum, 208 West Main St., Abingdon, VA 24210, (800) 435-3440.

DIRECTIONS

From Roanoke, I 81 west to exits 17 or 19 (Abingdon exits).

BEDFORD, VIRGINIA

Population: 6,073

If points representing central Virginia's various historic and scenic attractions were connected by lines on a map, the lines might very well intersect in **Bedford**. To the north beckon the beautiful **Blue Ridge Mountains**. To the south lies **Smith Mountain Lake**, one of the loveliest spots in the Southeast. To the east and west are two of Virginia's most historic cities, **Lynchburg** and **Roanoke**. Many more interesting sites lie at other compass points.

Bedford's rolling, tree-lined streets bring to the map another pretty town and another historic district. Charming, revitalized **Main Street** is lined with commercial buildings straight out of the 1890s. It is the busiest street in town (Bedford was one of Virginia's first Main Street cities). As would be true for virtually any Virginia town founded in the 1700s, the historic district also contains many gracious homes — and several old tobacco warehouses!

An interesting review of the area's long and rich history is provided by the **Bedford City/County Museum**. The museum's displays include artifacts from Indian times to the present. Included are period clothing and memorabilia from both the Revolutionary and Civil Wars. The museum is also noted for its genealogy library.

Out in the county is Thomas Jefferson's summer retreat, **Poplar Forest** (begun in 1806). Designed and built by Jefferson, the creative octagonal structure remains open to the public while undergoing restoration.

The surrounding countryside offers a wealth of recreational opportunities — trout and smallmouth-bass fishing, apple picking, sunbathing on the sandy beach at **Smith Mountain Lake State Park**. Back in town, the productions of the award-winning **Little Town Players** represent community theater at its best.

SPECIAL FEATURES

• About 10 miles north of Bedford is one of the stops, named the **Peaks of Otter**, of the venerable **Blue Ridge Parkway**. The incredible beauty of the location can be enjoyed from nature trails, wildflower walks and picnic and camping sites. There is an excellent lodge with dining room, gift shop and other amenities.

• A replica of Syria, Israel, and Jordan at the time of Christ has been created on 400 acres at **Holy Land U.S.A.**, near Bedford (individual and guided tours).

> *Bedford is home to the largest yellow poplar tree in the world.*

WHERE TO STAY

Bedford House, 422 Avenel Ave., (703) 586-5050. Turn-of-century home with fine antiques, full breakfasts, "Virginia hospitality." $$

Otter's Den, Rt. 2 (Box 160 E), (703) 586-2204. Renovated 18th-century log cabin in Blue Ridge Mts., full "country" breakfasts. $$

WHERE TO EAT

Peaks of Otter Lodge, Blue Ridge Pkwy. & VA 43, (703) 586-1081. View of Peaks of Otter, American menu, Virginia specialties. $ to $$.

FURTHER INFORMATION

Bedford Area Chamber of Commerce, 305 East Main St., Bedford, VA 24523, (800) 933-9535.

DIRECTIONS

From Roanoke, US 460 east to Bedford.

CHINCOTEAGUE, VIRGINIA

Population: 3,572

Chincoteague's charm comes in part from its location on an inviting island off Virginia's **Eastern Shore Peninsula**, and in part from its long association with wildlife, especially the abundant waterfowl and the famous Chincoteague ponies.

Chincoteague shares an island 7 miles long and 1 1/2 miles wide with marshes, pastures, and other open spaces. The village's history, going as far back as the 1670s, has largely centered on gathering food from the sea — oysters, clams and fish. The village/island has developed as a resort in more recent times and offers excellent accommodations, restaurants (see below), shops and boutiques. The shops are known for their wildfowl carvings and their paintings and photographs of wildlife.

As the name suggests, the **Oyster and Maritime Museum** is designed to tell about the island's oyster and seafood industry. A diorama of the channel area, live exhibits of marine life, and implements used in oyster farming are among the items featured.

Chincoteague is also the gateway to **Chincoteague National Widlife Refuge** and the **Assateague Island National Seashore.** Located at the southern end of Assateague Island, the wildlife refuge is home to over 260 species of birds and, among other animals, the Chincoteague ponies. According to legend (reinforced by Spanish archival evidence), the ponies descend from survivors of a wrecked Spanish galleon. Larger than real ponies but smaller than most horses, the animals won fame in Marguerite Henry's book, *Misty of Chincoteague.* Although allowed to roam wild, they are provided with regular veterinary care and plenty of good food. Land and water tours of the refuge are available.

The Assateague Island National Seashore occupies the only barrier island on Virginia's Eastern Shore that is open to the public. In addition to unspoiled woodlands, marshes and sand dunes, the seashore offers more than 37 miles of beautiful, open beaches. The 145-foot tower of the **Assateague Lighthouse,** one of the few structures on the island, was built in 1857.

Along with the boating, swimming, fishing and beachcombing that might be expected around coastal islands, Chincoteague and Assateague Islands offer birdwatching, biking along wilderness trails, crabbing and shellfishing.

> *The sale of young ponies from the south (that is, Virginia) portion of the national seashore provides funds for the local firemen—and also the occasion for a carnival.*
>
> *Unlike the rest of Virginia's Eastern Shore, Chincoteaque Island maintained its association and commerce with the Union during the Civil War.*

WHERE TO STAY

The Garden and the Sea, P. O. Box 275 (New Church), (804) 824-0672. European-style country inn, antiques and Oriental rugs, private baths, afternoon teas, restaurant. $$$

The Little Traveler Inn, 4106 Main St., (804) 336-5436. 1848 home of island's first doctor, Federal-style antiques, brick courtyard with fountain. $$$

The Main Street House B&B, 4356 Main St., (804) 336-6030. Victorian home of former wildlife refuge manager, wildlife art and carvings. $$ to $$$

Miss Molly's Inn B&B, 4141 Main St., (804) 336-6686. 1886 home on bay, full breakfasts, afternoon teas, porches for enjoying the breeze. $$$

The Watson House B&B, 4240 Main St., (804) 336-1564. Restored country Victorian home, private baths, full breakfasts, afternoon teas, bicycles. $$ to $$$

WHERE TO EAT

Note: Chincoteague is understandably blessed with a good number of excellent seafood restaurants. The three below were randomly selected.

The Beachway Restaurant, Maddox Blvd., (804) 336-5590. Lobsters, soft shell crabs, raw oysters and clams, steaks, solarium garden room. $$

Bill's Seafood Restaurant, 4040 Main St., (804) 336-5831. Fresh "jumbo" flounder the specialty. $$

The Village Restaurant & Lounge, 6576 Maddox Blvd., (804) 336-5120. Overlooking Chincoteague, fresh local seafood. $$

FURTHER INFORMATION

Chincoteague Chamber of Commerce, P. O. Box 258, Chincoteague, VA 23336, (804) 336-6161.

DIRECTIONS

From Norfolk, US 13 north (via Chesakpeake Bay Bridge/Tunnel) to VA 175, VA 175 east to Chincoteague.

LEXINGTON, VIRGINIA

Population: 6,959 (including students)

Home to the hallowed halls of **Washington and Lee University** and the **Virginia Military Institute (VMI)**, Lexington is among the South's most historic towns. Nestled in the glorious **Shenandoah Valley**, and boasting a solid collection of restored 19th-century buildings, Lexington is also one of the South's most beautiful towns.

Washington and Lee and VMI are both National Historical Landmarks. Washington and Lee, founded in 1749, is a highly respected small liberal arts college and law school. The college's most famous president was Robert E. Lee, who took over as head immediately after the Civil War (1865-1870). Probably the most visited building on campus is the **Lee Chapel** (1867), which contains the office (preserved) Lee used when he was the college's president. Also in the chapel are Edward V. Valentine's statue of Lee, Lee's burial place, and Charles W. Peale's famous portrait of George Washington. The 1842 **Lee-Jackson House** was a campus residence of both Stonewall Jackson and General Lee.

Adjacent VMI was the country's first state-supported military college (1839). The college's most famous professor was Stonewall Jackson, its most famous alumnus, George C. Marshall. The **VMI Museum** recalls the history of the college by focusing on the lives of its alums and faculty. Included in the exhibits are the bullet-pierced raincoat that Stonewall Jackson wore at Chancellorsville, 19th-century firearms and daguerreotypes, and uniforms and other items that provide a glimpse of cadet life.

The **George C. Marshall Museum and Library,** also on the VMI campus, features an electric map of World War II, Marshall's Nobel Peace Prize, the Academy Award Oscar won by the movie *Patton*, and other mementos of the great general's life.

Two sites associated with Stonewall Jackson are the antebellum **Stonewall Jackson Home,** a simple brick townhouse (1801) containing many of Jackson's personal possessions (tours), and the **Stonewall Jackson Memorial Cemetery** (1797), location of Jackson's final resting place and also of Edward V. Valentine's 1891 statue honoring the general. The cemetery also contains the graves of Confederate veterans and two Virginia governors.

Lexington is known for its historic downtown and residential areas. The town is designed for relaxed touring, on foot or maybe on a narrated carriage ride. The CoC distributes a self-guided walking tour brochure that lists 42 historic sites. The many lovely old Virginia homes date from the last two decades of the 18th century and from virtually every decade of the 19th, especially the 1840s. Among important non-residential structures are a group of offices, known as **Lawyers Row,** built in the 1880s, and the 1845 Greek Revival **Lexington Presbyterian Church.**

The two theaters of the **Lenfest Center for the Performing Arts,** on the Washington and Lee campus, stage a variety of plays, musicals, concerts and recitals. In the summer, the unique outdoor **Theater at Lime Kiln** presents concerts and original stage productions.

Hikers will enjoy both the two-mile walking trail through Lexington's beautiful **Woods Creek Park** and the seven-mile **Chessie Nature Trail,** which winds from Lexington to Buena Vista alongside the **Maury River.**

SPECIAL FEATURES

• Lexington is only minutes away from the **Blue Ridge Parkway,** the **Goshen Pass** (a beautiful three-mile mountain gorge), and famous **Natural Bridge,** a spectacular 215-ft.-high limestone arch.

• Horse shows and auctions are mong the attractions of the nearby 400-acre **Virginia Horse Center.**

> *VMI's military heritage is colorfully displayed on most Fridays during the school year, when at 4:00 p.m. the cadets parade.*
>
> *Thomas Jonathan "Stonewall" Jackson taught natural philosophy (physics) and military tactics at VMI for ten years prior to the Civil War.*

WHERE TO STAY

Fassifern, Rt. 5 (Box 87), (703) 463-1013. Circa 1867 country manor home in park-like setting, private baths. $$$

Lavender Hill Farm, Rt. 1 (Box 515), (800) 446-4240. Restored circa 1790 farmhouse on working sheep farm, private baths, full breakfasts, picnics/dinners available to guests. $$

Llewellyn Lodge, 603 S. Main St., (800) 882-1145. Brick colonial home near historic district, private baths, full "gourmet" breakfasts. $$ to $$$

Historic Country Inns of Lexington, 11 N. Main St., (703) 463-2044: **Maple Hall** — restored plantation home (circa 1850) on National Register, antiques, fireplaces, private baths, pool, tennis. $$$; **Alexander-Withrow House** and **McCampbell Inn** — restored homes (circa 1789 and 1809, respectively) in historic district, antiques, private baths, TV, amenities of Maple Hall available. $$$

WHERE TO EAT

Harbs' Bistro, 19 W. Washington St., (703) 464-1900. Fresh-baked breads, "gourmet" soups, candlelight dinners, outdoor patio. $

Inn at Union Run, R.D. #3 (Box 68), (703) 463-9715. In late 19th-century manor house, American and European cuisine, seasonal specialties, reservations required. $$

Maple Hall (see above). Dining in historic country inn, reservations preferred. $$

Virginia House, 722 S. Main St., (703) 463-3643. Southern-style cooking, fried or baked country-cured ham, homemade desserts. $

The Willson-Walker House, 30 N. Main St., (703) 463-3020. In circa 1820 home, antique furnishings, creative American cuisine, outdoor dining, reservations suggested. $ to $$

FURTHER INFORMATION

Lexington Visitor Center, 102 E. Washington St., Lexington, VA 24450, (703) 463-3777.

DIRECTIONS

From Roanoke, I 81 north to exit 188, west 2 miles to Lexington.

WILLIAMSBURG, VIRGINIA

Population: 11,530

A model of restoration and reconstruction respected round the world, the capital of England's largest colony in America has been — and continues to be — retrieved from the 18th century. To understand and appreciate Williamsburg, it must be remembered that, for many people, the town was never a place of drudgery, of daily routine. Williamsburg was a place of government, of education, of intellectual discussion. It was also a place of balls, gambling and other amusements for visiting members of Virginia's landed gentry. It was a lovely and pleasurable place, just as it is now.

The main artery of **Colonial Williamsburg** is **Duke of Gloucester Street**. Anchoring the western end of the street is the **College of William and Mary**, at the eastern end is the **Capitol**, and overlooking a mall not far from the street's midpoint is the **Governor's Palace**. On and about Duke of Gloucester Street are over 500 restored or reconstructed public buildings, homes, taverns and stores. The buildings, covering 173 acres, are placed about large gardens and greens, giving the town a wonderful (and deliberate) sense of spaciousness.

Check in first at the visitors bureau for admission and other information. Additional information is available throughout the restoration from costumed colonial interpreters. Do not try to do the town and its environs (see below) in a day — allow at least three days. Carriage rides add romance and relax tired feet.

Chartered in 1693, the College of William and Mary is the second oldest college in the country. Two of the most interesting attractions are the restored **Wren Building**, the oldest college building in the country, and the **Muscarelle Museum of Art**, known for the quality and variety of its changing exhibitions.

The **Governor's Palace** (1708-1720), restored and one of the town's (and nation's) landmarks, was home to seven British governors and Virginia's first two governors. The gardens are beautiful, especially in the spring. Among the rooms of the reconstructed **Capitol** (1705), another landmark, is the **Chamber of the General Court**, one of the country's most beautiful courtrooms.

Three other well-known structures are the **Bruton Parish Church** (1715), in continuous use since its construction, the restored **Magazine** (1715), and **Raleigh Tavern**, popular in the 18th century as well as today for its billiard room. The restored town contains a number of gracious, architecturally important homes.

Although the restored area is itself a vast living museum, Colonial Williamsburg is also home to two outstanding enclosed museums. The **Abby Aldrich Rockefeller Folk Art Center** features an incomparable collection of American folk art. The **DeWitt Wallace Decorative Arts Gallery** displays English and American silver, glass, paintings, costumes, furniture, textiles, prints, ceramics, rare maps and other treasures.

Artisans and tradespeople demonstrate 18th-century silversmithing, baking, basket weaving, blacksmithing, furniture making, wig making, bookbinding, gun making and other skills. The products of their efforts are displayed and offered for sale in quaint restored shops.

The **Virginia Shakespeare Festival**, at the College of William and Mary, stages productions during the summer months. Visitors to Williamsburg may enjoy golfing, tennis, and swimming.

SPECIAL FEATURES

• The two other members of the **Historic Triangle, Jamestown** and **Yorktown**, are connected to Williamsburg by the **Colonial Parkway**. Jamestown, the site of the country's English beginnings (1607), is administered by the **Colonial National Historical Park**. Here there are a visitor center, museum, remains of a 1639 church, and several other historical attractions.

• **Jamestown Settlement** is a living history museum depicting life in Jamestown during the early settlement years. Included are the re-created palisaded fort and replicas of three ships that first brought settlers from England.

• **Yorktown**, also administered by the Colonial National Historical Park, is the site of the famous British defeat. The **Yorktown Victory Center**, a battlefield museum, features several excellent indoor exhibits and, outdoors, a re-created Continental Army encampment. Self-guided auto tours begin here.

•Along the banks of the **James River** are magnificent plantation homes, many graced by gardens and lovely antiques. Open to the public are **Berkeley, Carter's Grove, Edgewood, Evelynton, Sherwood Forest** and **Shirley plantations.**
•**Busch Gardens,** one of the country's most beautiful theme parks, boasts nine European hamlets, each with its own food, entertainment, etc., and a variety of thrilling rides.

> *The restoration and rebuilding of Williamsburg, spearheaded by Rev. W. A. R. Goodwin and John D. Rockefeller, Jr., began in the late 1920s.*
> *Visitors to the Governor's Palace are often surprised by the communal nature of the royal privy.*

WHERE TO STAY

Applewood Colonial B&B, 605 Richmond Rd., (800) 899-2753. Flemish bond brick house, colonial decor, fireplaces, private baths, afternoon tea. $$$
Colonial Capital B&B, 501 Richmond Rd., (800) 776-0570. Colonial Revival home, antiques, private baths, full breakfasts, afternoon tea/wine, patio, bikes. $$$
Newport House B&B, 710 S. Henry St., (804) 229-1775. Home designed in 1756, period furnishings, private baths, full breakfasts with historic recipes, colonial dancing in ballroom Tues. evenings. $$$
Williamsburg Manor B&B, 600 Richmond Rd., (800) 422-8011. Brick Colonial Revival home, period furnishings, private baths, "lavish" breakfasts. $$$
Williamsburg Sampler B&B, 922 Jamestown Rd., (800) 722-1169. 18th-century plantation-style colonial home, pewter and samplers, private baths, "scrumptuous" breakfasts, travel awards. $$$

WHERE TO EAT

Note: The following four restaurants are housed in restored or reconstructed buildings in the restored area. All offer colonial dishes and 18th-century furnishings. Colonial balladeers entertain diners in several. Call (800) 828-3767 for reservations (required for dinner) and information.

Chowning's Tavern, Duke of Gloucester St. $ to $$
Christiana Campbell's Tavern, Waller St. $ to $$
King's Arms Tavern, Duke of Gloucester St. $$
Shields Tavern, Duke of Gloucester St. $ to $$

The Regency Dining Room, in Williamsburg Inn, Francis St., (804) 229-1000. Elegant dining room, regional specialties, fresh seafood, award-winning. $$$
The Trellis (in Merchants Square), Duke of Gloucester St., (804) 229-8610. Fresh seafood, mesquite-grilled dishes, outdoor dining, musicians on weekends, reservations suggested. $$

FURTHER INFORMATION

The Williamsburg Area Convention and Visitors Bureau, P. O. Drawer GB, Williamsburg, VA 23187, (800) 368-6511.

DIRECTIONS

From Richmond, I 64 east to Williamsburg exits.

WASHINGTON

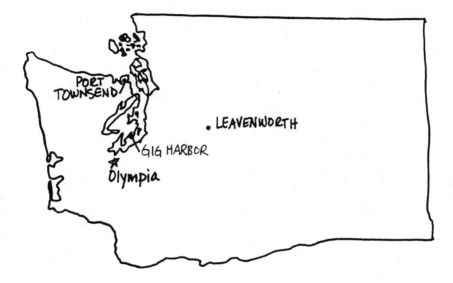

GIG HARBOR, WASHINGTON

Population: 3,236

Though only 15 minutes from Tacoma across the **Tacoma Narrows Bridge,** picturesque **Gig Harbor** is a town with genuine small-town character and friendliness. With a local theater group, music association, jazz festival, summer art festival and more, the town is artsy in the best community sense of the word.

Lining the colorful harbor is **Harbor View Avenue,** address to waterfront restaurants and an assortment of sophisticated shops and galleries. The harbor itself boasts a working fishing fleet of more than 30 boats and excellent anchorage and public moorage for pleasure craft.

The view of **Mount Rainier** from Gig Harbor is one of the most breathtaking in the country. The scene's dominant colors, made especially brilliant by the clear air, are the blues of the sky and water, the greens of the pines, and looming above and away, the whites of majestic Mount Rainier's snows. The boats in the harbor add to the whites and the blues.

With the smell of saltwater in the air, Gig Harbor has an almost literal marine flavor. The flavor doesn't stop with seafood and the usual nautical themes in artwork and decoration, however: One of the bed and breakfasts is in fact on a ship (see below), and the town is home to a very fine mariners museum:

The **Puget Sound Mariners' Museum** arranges its displays under such categories as Spanish-American War, Coast Artillery Corps (old U.S. Army), light ships and houses, tugboating, and the historic U.S. Lifesaving Service. Among the items displayed are pieces of eight off a Spanish galleon and unequalled collections of antique rope knives and boarding cutlasses.

SPECIAL FEATURES

• **Purdy Spit,** 5 miles north, is the place to go for windsurfing, beachcombing and clamming.

> *Gig Harbor has been called "the Sausalito of the North."*
> *Although evergreens predominate, the area also has maple trees and, hence,*
> *October color.*

WHERE TO STAY

The Parsonage, 4107 Burnham Dr., (206) 851-8654. Old parsonage, close to harbor and shops. $$ to $$$

The Pillars, 6606 Soundview Dr., (206) 851-6644. Old mansion, private baths, indoor pool and Jacuzzi, views of water and mountains. $$$

Tall Ship Krestine, 3311 Harborview Dr., (206) 858-9395. Cabins for 2 to 6 on board unique 1904 tall ship. $$ to $$$

WHERE TO EAT

North by Northwest, 4916 Peacock Hill Ave. NW, (206) 851-3134. Tuscan cuisine served in old mansion. $$

Tides Tavern, Harbor View Ave., (206) 858-3982. On dock with deck, fish and chips, light fare, micro-brewery beer. $

FURTHER INFORMATION

Gig Harbor/Peninsula Area Chamber of Commerce, 3125 Judson Street, Gig Harbor, WA 98335, (206) 851-6865.

DIRECTIONS

From Tacoma, WA 16 north 7 miles to Gig Harbor.

LEAVENWORTH, WASHINGTON

Population: 1,692

Lining the streets of **Leavenworth** are colorful Bavarian buildings with signs announcing "Andreas Keller," "Pension Einer," "Bosch Garten," Bergdorf Gallerie," "Die Jewellen Kiste" and dozens of other businesses. The architecture is authentic — some of it in fact was the work of a German designer. The cheerful baskets of flowers hanging from the old (and original) street lamps are distinctly Old World. The dishes in some of the restaurants are genuinely German, in taste as well as name. And although the snow-covered peaks in the background are not the Alps, they are indisputably alpine.

Leavenworth is a true American success story, albeit with a non-American flavor. With its once prosperous lumber and railroad industries gone, Leavenworth needed help. Then, in the 1960s several townspeople began to remodel their businesses using Bavarian styles, styles inspired by the lovely Cascade Mountain setting. The idea caught on — although not without controversy—and over the years the town was gradually Bavarianized and revitalized. Today even condominiums, drive-in banks and motor inns display a Bavarian motif.

Many visitors to the *Bavarian Village of Leavenworth* enjoy the outdoors during the earlier hours of the day and then browse in the shops and relax in the restaurants and pubs during the later hours. The list of outdoor activities seems endless: downhill and cross-country skiing, whitewater or scenery-watching rafting down the **Wenatchee River**, wilderness and scenic canoe trips, guided downhill bicycle trips, rock climbing, fly fishing. For those wishing more passive pursuits there are helicopter tours of the **Cascades** and dog-sled tours. Neighboring farms and ranches offer old-fashioned sleigh rides, horse-drawn hayrides, horseback rides and buggy rides.

The list of unique shops also appears endless; there are well over 70 of them. Their offerings describe every conceivable category of arts, crafts, gifts, clothing, foods and furnishings. Some of the items are American, with emphasis on the Northwest; some are European — for example, Bavarian wax art, Bavarian clothing and German steins.

SPECIAL FEATURE

• East of town, along **US 2**, are some of the world's most important pear and apple orchards. Several of the orchards maintain seasonal fruit stands.

> *The use of authentic Bavarian designs meant that city building codes governing rooflines and other features had to be changed.*

WHERE TO STAY

All Seasons River Inn, 8751 Icicle River Rd., (509) 548-1425. On the river, spacious rooms, private baths, fireplaces, "gourmet" breakfasts. $$$

Cashmere Country Inn, 5801 Pioneer, (509) 782-4212. 1907 farmhouse, pool & hot tub, private baths, "country" breakfasts. $$$

The Haus Rohrbach Pension, 12882 Ranger Rd. (509) 548-7024. European country charm, scenic views, pool & hot tub, full breakfasts. $$$

Pine River Ranch, 19668 WA 207, (509) 763-3959. Spectacular views, fireplaces, hot tubs, acres to ski or hike. $$ to $$$

Run of the River, 9308 E. Leavenworth Rd., (800) 288-6491. Quintessential NW log B&B inn, panoramic views, hand-hewn log beds and furniture, private baths, "bountiful" breakfasts. $$$

WHERE TO EAT

Edel Haus Inn, 320 9th St., (509) 548-4412. New American restaurant in classic old home, all foods prepared from scratch, outdoor seating. $

The Pewter Pot Restaurant, 124 1/2 Cottage Ave. (Cashmere), (509) 782-2036. Homemade bread/pies/desserts, soups, salads, traditional dinners. $$

Reiner's Gasthaus, 829 Front St., (509) 548-5111. Schweinesschintzel mit Kartoffelsalat, Ungarissches Gulyas mit Spatzle. $

Scandia, 217 8th St., (509) 548-5226. Fresh seafood, smorgasbord, Scandinavian chef, Sunday Champagne Brunch. $

Terrace Bistro, 200 8th St., (509) 548-4193. International cuisine, homemade pastries, balcony & patio seating. $$

FURTHER INFORMATION

Leavenworth Chamber of Commerce, P. O. Box 327, Leavenworth, WA 98826, (509) 548-5807.

DIRECTIONS

From Seattle, I 405 north to WA 522, WA 522 east to US 2, US 2 east to Leavenworth.

PORT TOWNSEND, WASHINGTON

Population: 7,001

Prosperous from its lumber trade with booming California, **Port Townsend** was just as important in the 1880s as the Port of Seattle, also on **Puget Sound**. Businesses flourished and mansions rose. But the train never came to Port Townsend, and that and several other fateful developments drove Seattle to greatness and froze Port Townsend in time. A hundred years later Port Townsend has the largest collection of Victorian buildings north of San Francisco. And it is one of only four towns in the country designated a Victorian Seaport by the National Historic Register.

Sailboats and other craft still move about the harbor of the old port town. The facades of the buildings on **Water Street**, Port Townsend's downtown, are authentically Victorian even if the specialty shops, galleries and restaurants within are not. Many of the buildings in **Uptown**, on the other side of the bluff, are also original, and here too shops, galleries and restaurants beckon. Elsewhere in the older parts of town are Victorian-era churches, cottages and mansions. The CoC's historic tour map lists 72 sites. There is much Victoriana to see, and the interested visitor is well-advised to take one of the van or historical sidewalk tours.

Of special note downtown is the 1889 **Hastings Building**, the first building in town to sport a two-story court with skylight. On the bluff behind is the restored **Old Bell Tower** (1890). The **Jefferson County Courthouse** (1892), one of the two oldest courthouses in the state, is behind the bluff. The building's clock tower is a landmark, offshore as well as in town.

Port Townsend is probably best known for its many fine restored Victorian homes. So many of these are now bed and breakfasts that the town is sometimes nicknamed the *bed and breakfast capital of Washington.* An expanded listing of bed and breakfasts that are also of architectural and/or historic interest is given under "Where to Stay" below.

There are two houses of special historic interest that are open to the public but are not bed and breakfasts. One is the 1868 **Rothschild House**, a state heritage site on the National Register of Historic Places. Most of the house's furnishings, carpets and wall papers are original. The second house is the **Commanding Officer's Quarters** at **Fort Worden State Park** (see below). This beautiful 1904 home has been carefully and authentically restored and refurnished.

SPECIAL FEATURES

• **Fort Worden State Park** adjoins the town on the north. Turn-of-the-century Fort Worden was built as part of a Puget Sound defense system. On the grounds are restored officers' houses, barracks, parade grounds and artillery bunkers.

• The fort is also home to the **Centrum Foundation**, a non-profit organization that promotes the arts. Many varieties of Washington's state flower, the rhododendron, are on display in the **Centennial Rhododendron Garden**, also on the grounds.

Uptown in Fort Townsend was established so that Victorian women could shop somewhere other than the rowdy downtown waterfront area.

The bell in St. Paul's Episcopal Church (1865) was donated by a ship's captain on condition that it be rung in foggy weather to warn vessels.

WHERE TO STAY

Ann Starrett Mansion Inn B&B, 744 Clay St., (800) 321-0644. Fine 1889 example of classic Victorian stick-style architecture, beautiful views, private baths, full breakfasts. $$$ (tours by appt.)

F. W. Hastings House/Old Consulate Inn, 313 Walker at Washington, (206) 385-6753. Fine 1889 example of Queen Anne style, private baths, 7-course breakfasts. $$$ (tours by appt.)

Heritage House B&B Inn, 305 Pierce, (206) 385-6800. Classic 1880 Italianate house, water views, breakfast "a delight." $$ to $$$ (tours by appt.)

Holly Hill House, 611 Polk St., (800) 435-1454. 1872 home in heart of historic district, private baths, full breakfasts. $$$

James House B&B, 1238 Washington St., (206) 385-1238. 1891 home with five chimneys, parquet floors, commanding view of harbor. $$ to$$$

Lincoln Inn B&B, 538 Lincoln, (800) 477-4667. Built in 1888 as showplace for the DeVoe Masonry business, antiques, full breakfasts. $$$ (tours by appt.)

Rose Cottage B&B, 1310 Clay St., (206) 386-6944. Originally an 1868 duplex, private baths, beautiful views. $$$

WHERE TO EAT

Belmont Restaurant & Saloon, 925 Water St., (800) 522-3007. Casual waterfront dining in Victorian atmosphere, fresh seafood. $$

Blackberries, Fort Worden State Park, (206) 385-9950. For example, "Halibut-salmon braid with salalberry beurre rouge." $$

Manresa Castle, 7th and Sheridan sts., (800) 732-1281. Fresh local seafood and regional cuisine served in 1892 Victorian inn. $$

Randal's Restaurant, 1004 Water St., (206) 379-9659. Northwest cuisine with a "Mediterranean Flair," homemade desserts. $$

Water Street Deli, 926 Water St., (206) 385-2422. Fresh seafood, game bird, vegetarian entrees, dinner theater. $$

FURTHER INFORMATION

Port Townsend Chamber of Commerce, 2437 E. Sims Way, Port Townsend, WA 98368, (206) 385-2722.

DIRECTIONS

From Seattle, I 5 south to Olympia, US 101 north to WA 20, WA 20 north to Port Townsend.

Note: Daily high-speed ferry service between Seattle and Port Townsend is available from late April to mid-October.

WEST VIRGINIA

BERKELEY
SPRINGS

SHEPARDSTOWN

HARPERS
FERRY

Charleston

LEWISBURG

BERKELEY SPRINGS, WEST VIRGINIA

Population: 735

Nestled in the hills of West Virginia, the village of **Berkeley Springs** has the distinction of being the country's first spa and "summer White House." George Washington and other early presidents used to come here to bathe in the warm mineral waters and to promenade and relax with friends. In fact, Washington — along with three signers of the Declaration of Independence, four signers of the Constitution, five Revolutionary generals, etc. — bought lots here when the town was platted in 1776. The place has been a resort ever since.

Today Berkeley Springs consists of two parts, tiny **Berkeley Springs State Park** and the also tiny town of **Bath**. Within the state park, springs discharge about 2,000 gallons of clear, odorless mineral water per minute at a temperature of 74.3 degrees Fahrenheit. The park's two bathhouses allow the visitor a choice among a Roman bath in an individual sunken pool, a soak in a conventional tub and, in the summer, a plunge in a swimming pool. The **Roman Bath House** has been in service as a bathhouse since its construction around 1815. A museum on the second floor provides an excellent introduction to the park and its history.

The town of Bath, historically postmarked "Berkeley Springs" to avoid confusion with another Bath (in Virginia), has a number of quaint late 19th century structures, some of them now bed and breakfasts (see below). Markers identify the village's first platted lots and their owners. The village and its setting are especially popular with artists.

SPECIAL FEATURE

• The overlook at **Prospect Peak**, five miles west of town on **WV 9**, offers one of the most spectacular views in the East.

> *The colors used throughout the state park—yellow, cream and green—are original colors of the Federal period.*
> *The large wooden hotels that visitors to the springs used to stay at have all disappeared, often through fire.*

WHERE TO STAY

Aaron's Acre, 501 Johnson Mill Rd., (304) 258-4079. Restored early 1900s home, wrap-around porch. $$$

The Country Inn, 207 S. Washington St., (800) 822-6630. Colonial-style inn adjoining park, spa, restaurant, garden. $ to $$$

Highlawn Inn, 304 Market St., (304) 258-5700. Restored Victorian home, veranda overlooking town. $$$

The Manor, 415 Fairfax St., (304) 258-1522. Exquisitely detailed 1878 manor house, full country breakfast. $$ to $$$

On the Banks Guesthouse, 304 Martinsburg Rd., (304) 258-2134. 1875 home with mountain view, library, music room. $$ to $$$

WHERE TO EAT

The Country Inn (see above). Country charm, rustic bar, live entertainment on weekends. $$

Tari's Premiere Cafe & Inn, 123 N. Washington St., (304) 258-1196. Daily specials, pasta, fresh seafood, chicken. $

FURTHER INFORMATION

Berkeley Springs-Morgan County Chamber of Commerce, 304 Fairfax Street, Berkeley Springs, WV 25411, (304) 258-3738.

DIRECTIONS

From Washington (D.C.), I 270 north to Frederick (MD), I 70 (through Hagerstown, MD) to exit 1, US 522 south to Berkeley Springs.

HARPERS FERRY, WEST VIRGINIA

Population: about 308

Harpers Ferry is a photogenic little town situated in the **Blue Ridge Mountains** at the confluence of the Potomac and Shenandoah rivers. On a visit here in 1783, Thomas Jefferson described the view from the summit of (now) Jefferson Rock "worth a voyage across the Atlantic." Today a National Historical Park, Harpers Ferry's early to mid 19th-century architecture seems to compliment the scenery. Some of the town's streets look much as they did 140 years ago.

In the 1790s George Washington selected Harpers Ferry as a site for a national armory. Later, during the 1830s, both the **Chesapeake & Ohio Canal** and **Baltimore & Ohio Railroad** came through town. By the middle of the 19th century, Harpers Ferry had become an important arms-producing and transportation center with a population several times what it is today.

Then came John Brown's famous 1859 raid followed in a few months by the Civil War. The armory was burned in 1861 to keep it from falling into Confederate hands; the rest of the town suffered, in spirit as well as structure, during the war years as control swung between the North and the South. A series of floods in the late 1800s pretty much put an end to any remaining hope that Harpers Ferry might revitalize. The little town and its buildings stood still and abandoned.

Many of the buildings have been restored by the National Park Service; others are undergoing, or will undergo, restoration. The best way to see Harpers Ferry is to park at the visitors center and take a shuttle bus to the **Lower Town.** The center offers talks by park rangers, conducted tours and information on self-guided tours.

Many of the town's (and park's) restored buildings have exhibits and media presentations. Of special interest are the Stagecoach Inn (1826-1834), which serves as the park's information center/bookstore; the **Master Armorer's House** (1858), now a gun-making museum; and the **Harper House** (1775-1782), the oldest surviving structure in the park. The **Dry Goods Store** (1812) has been restored to look like an 1850s dry goods store. Also of interest is the **Confectionery** (1844-1857), once the home of one of Harper Ferry's most respected citizens. Two of the town's restored buildings house museums that recall the lives and suffering of the townspeople during the Civil War.

On **Camp Hill** are several buildings, constructed in the 1840s and 1850s, that once served as homes for armory officials. Although damaged in the Civil War, they were rebuilt after the war and used to establish **Storer College**, a school for freed blacks. Storer College operated between 1869 and 1955.

The **John Brown Wax Museum**, housed in a historic building, traces the career of the controversial Abolitionist with figures and scenes made life-like with electronic lighting, sound and animation. Other points of interest in Harpers Ferry include the still-active **St. Peter's Catholic Church** (1830s, remodeled 1890s) and the **Appalachian Trail Conference Visitors Center**, which distributes information and items relating to the country's best-known footpath.

Harpers Ferry and its scenic surroundings support a rich variety of sports and other activities. White-water rafting, canoeing and tubing are popular on the area's rivers and streams. The restored **Chesapeake & Ohio Canal Towpath** offers great hiking and bicycling. Hikers will find a number of other mapped trails as well, including the Appalachian Trail. Rumor has it that the small-mouth bass fishing doesn't get much better. The same goes for the antique hunting.

The remnants of 19th-century factories and waterways may be explored on **Virginius Island** on the **Shenandoah River**. The National Park Service maintains (and publishes a guide to) an island trail.

SPECIAL FEATURES
  • The National Park Service's **Maryland Heights Trail** leads to Civil War batteries and fort ruins — and a series of magnificent views.
  • Five minutes to the west is historic **Charles Town**, laid out by George Washington's brother Charles. The tree-lined streets of the town are bordered by many lovely old homes, churches and other buildings. Not far from Charles Town is delightful little **Middleway**, also historic.

> *Members of the Lewis and Clark expedition carried arms made by Harper Ferry's armory.*
>
> *A popular way to see Harpers Ferry is by an evening "ghost tour." Check locally for information.*

WHERE TO STAY
  The Cottonwood Inn B&B, Rt. 2 (Box 61-S) (Charles Town), (304) 725-3371. In quiet country setting, private baths, TV, full country breakfasts, afternoon teas. $$$
  The Gilbert House B&B, P. O. Box 1104 (Charles Town), (304) 725-0637. Circa 1760 Georgian stone house on National Register, private baths, antiques, full breakfasts. $$$
  Ranson-Armory House B&B, P. O. Box 280, (304) 535-2142. 1830 home with Victorian touches, mountain views, private baths, full country breakfasts, refreshments. $$ to $$$

Hilltop House, P. O. Box 930, (800) 338-8319. Historic stone inn on mountain top, dining room. $$ to $$$

Lee-Stonewall Inn, 1141 Washington St., (304) 535-2532. Circa 1795 Georgian/Federal home on National Register, fireplaces, private baths, "hearty" country breakfasts. $$$

WHERE TO EAT

The Anvil Restaurant, 1270 Washington St., (304) 535-2582. Broiled Seafood Saffron, Shrimp and Mussels Cajun. $$

Country Cafe & General Store, 711 Washington St. (Bolivar), (304) 535-2327. Widely known for sandwiches. $

FURTHER INFORMATION

Jefferson County Visitor & Convention Bureau, P. O. Box A, Harpers Ferry, WV 25425, (800) 848-8687; (Zip for Charles Town: 25414).

DIRECTIONS

From Washington (DC), I 270 northwest to Frederick, US 340 west to Harpers Ferry.

LEWISBURG, WEST VIRGINIA

Population: 3,598

It's rare for a town steeped in history and blessed with a scenic setting to show a natural continuity with time, to be more concerned with today's soccer game than with attempts to lure visitors with the contrived. But **Lewisburg** is that kind of town, the way towns used to be, at least according to the romantic. Some say the town is more 1940s than 1990s — the *real* '40s, that is.

Chartered in 1782, the town's 236-acre historic district has no fewer than 72 sites, including 50 antebellum homes and 11 buildings erected before the War of 1812. The first stop on a town tour should be the four-story **Carnegie Hall** (1902), which houses the visitors center. Funded by Andrew Carnegie and called "the other Carnegie Hall," the hall has 22 classrooms and studios, a 500-seat auditorium and a 1904 Estey pipe organ. Two other tour musts are the **Old Stone Presbyterian Church** (1796), the oldest church west of the Alleghenies remaining in continuous use, and the Colonial 1820 **John A. North House**, now home to the museum of the **Greenbrier Historical Society**. (Schedule at least 2 1/2 hours for a full walking tour of the town.)

Lewisburg's natural endowment is as rich as its history. Located in the gorgeous **Greenbrier River Valley**, Lewisburg sits amongst mountains and forests just three miles from the beautiful 126-mile unpolluted **Greenbrier River**. Evergreens, maples, rhododendrons and other flora guarantee four seasons of color.

SPECIAL FEATURES

• Hikers and bikers will find the 76-mile-long **Greenbrier River Trail** (an old C&O Railroad bed) a custom-made paradise.

• Smallmouth-bass fishing is reputed to be better in the Greenbrier River than in any other river in the country. Canoeing is also great.

> *Names scratched by soldiers wounded in the Civil War Battle of Lewisburg can be seen in a section of old plaster in the Greenbrier County Library (1834).*

WHERE TO STAY

Hie Away, 302 S. Court St., (304) 645-7718. Common Room with grand piano, full breakfast, afternoon English tea. $

The General Lewis, 301 E. Washington St., (304) 645-2600. East wing an 1834 house, antiques, worth a visit in own right. $$ to $$$

Lynn's Inn B&B, P. O. Box 40, (304) 645-2003. Shaded front porch with big rockers, country setting. $$

Minnie Manor B&B, 403 E. Washington St., (304) 645-4096. 1830 Methodist parsonage on National Register. $$

WHERE TO EAT

The Blue Moon Cafe, 110 S. Jefferson St., (304) 645-2089. Daily blackboard specials, excellent sandwiches and salads. $ to $$

Clingman's Market, 102 E. Washington St. Lunch, country cooking, very large portions, large shared tables. $

Foods & Friends, 112 W. Washington St., (304) 645-4548. American cuisine, creative entrees, daily specials. $ to $$

Julian's, S. Lafayette St., (304) 645-4145. Classical cuisine in converted Victorian home, everything from scratch. $ to $$

FURTHER INFORMATION

Lewisburg Visitor's Center, 105 Church Street, Lewisburg, WV 24901, (800) 833-2068.

DIRECTIONS

From Charleston, I 64 south to exit 169, south to Lewisburg.

SHEPHERDSTOWN, WEST VIRGINIA

Population: 1,287

Shepherdstown is an historic little college time overlooking the **Potomac River**. West Virginia's oldest town (first settled around 1730), Shepherdstown is rich in 18th- and 19th-century commercial and residential buildings. It is also quite cosmopolitan, with sophisticated shops, restaurants and entertainments.

The town is nicely positioned for regional sightseeing — and the region offers much to see, including the **Antietam National Battlefield**, historic Harpers Ferry (see selection), and some gorgeous mountain scenery.

The **Historic Shepherdstown Museum**, housed in the **Entler Hotel** (1793/1809), displays artifacts from the town's past. On the grounds is a replica of the world's first working steamboat, built and demonstrated at Shepherdstown by James Runsey in 1787. (Elsewhere in town an impressive monument to James Rumsey, built in 1917, overlooks the Potomac). Other historic structures include the **Public Library** (1800/1845), once a farmers' market, and the **Shepherd Grist Mill** (circa 1738), which boasts the oldest and largest (40 ft in diameter) cast-iron overshot waterwheel in the world (1891).

In June and July **Shepherd College's Contemporary American Theater Festival**, a professional repertory theater, presents new plays. The festival also offers a late-night improv cabaret. On-screen entertainment is provided at the restored **Old Opera House** (1909); foreign and contemporary American films are featured.

Sherpherdtown's shops offer a variety of crafts, antiques, decorative accessories, books and gifts. One of the bakeries specializes in European breads.

The restored Chesapeake & Ohio Canal Towpath is made to order for hikers and bikers (see also Harpers Ferry). Bicycle rentals are locally available.

SPECIAL FEATURES

• **Antietam National Battlefield and Cemetery** is four or so miles northeast of Shepherdstown. On September 17, 1862, more men were killed or wounded here than on any other day of the Civil War.

> *Shepherdstown, then named Mecklenburg, was the starting point for a contingent of local volunteers who hiked with considerable speed to Boston to join George Washington's Continental Army. The march is remembered as the Bee Line March.*
>
> *It was at Shepherdstown Ford where General Lee's army recrossed the Potomac after withdrawing from Antietam.*

WHERE TO STAY

The Bavarian Inn and Lodge, Rt. 1 (Box 30), (304) 876-2551. Bavarian Alpine chalets with balconies overlooking Potomac, private baths, TV and telephones, pool, tennis court. $$$

Belle Vue B&B, Rte. 1 (Box 38), (304) 876-2887. Mid 18th-century home on National Register, sweeping lawns, antiques, private baths, private entrance, a Shepherdstown landmark. $$$

Stonebrake Cottage Guest House B&B, P. O. Box 1612, (304) 876-6607. Victorian cottage with kitchen. $$$

Thomas Shepherd Inn, P. O. Box 1162, (304) 876-3715. Restored mid 19th-century Lutheran parsonage in Federal style, private baths, "bountiful" breakfasts, afternoon tea, sherry. $$$

WHERE TO EAT

Bavarian Inn and Lodge (see above). Elegant dining rooms, variety of German and American specialties, fresh seafood, game dishes. $$

The Yellow Brick Bank Restaurant, downtown, (304) 876-2208. Northern Italian and nouvelle American dishes. $ to $$

FURTHER INFORMATION

Jefferson County Convention and Visitors Bureau, P. O. Box A, Harpers Ferry, WV 25425, (800) 848-8687.

DIRECTIONS

From Baltimore, I 70 west to exit 49 (beyond Frederick), US Alt. 40 north to Boonsboro, MD 34 west to Potomac River and Shepherdstown.

WISCONSIN

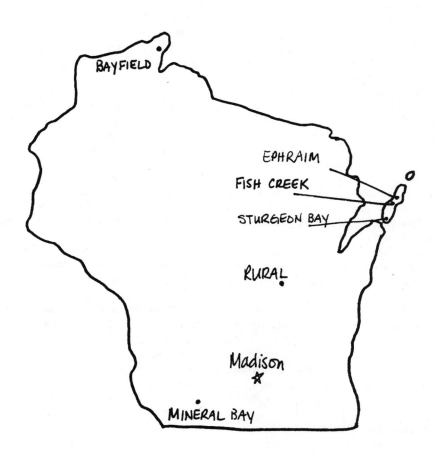

BAYFIELD

EPHRAIM

FISH CREEK

STURGEON BAY

RURAL

Madison

MINERAL BAY

BAYFIELD, WISCONSIN

Population: 686

The tiny fishing village of **Bayfield** lies on a natural harbor on the southern shore of scenic **Lake Superior**. Commercial fishing, lumbering, brownstone quarrying and tourism helped build the village, especially during the late 19th and very early 20th centuries. In the end tourism proved to be the only really reliable industry, however, and Bayfield stood still as Duluth and other cities took over. Left behind was a village containing, among other things, a delightful collection of Victorian houses.

Bayfield is today a popular summer resort for fishermen and deepwater sailors. The streets can be explored by foot or bicycle. Many of the old homes are listed on the National Register; some have been restored and opened as bed and breakfast inns (see below). One of the town's most interesting indoor stops is the **Booth Cooperage**, where visitors can watch the crafting of barrels. The cooperage is at once a factory and museum.

Offshore are the 21 pristine islands of **Apostle Islands National Lakeshore**. The islands are guarded by six picturesque lighthouses. Information on the lighthouses and other features of the lakeshore can be obtained at the **Apostle Islands National Lakeshore Headquarters**, housed in the brownstone **Old Bayfield County Courthouse** (1894).

The beauty of the Apostle Islands and the lighthouses (all built before 1874) can be experienced by private or excursion boat. A lighthouse tour is one of several excursion options; check with the CoC for schedules and other tour information.

Bayfield has a kind of "satellite" resort, because a 22nd island, **Madeline**, is big enough to support its own village (**La Pointe**) and other attractions. Access to **Madeline Island** (Population:150) is made interesting by Bayfield's northern latitude. A ferry suffices for the warmer months. During the winter, however, the thickness of the ice makes it possible to drive a car to the island. Pine trees are laid on the ice to mark the way. During months when the ice is less thick, people are carried back and forth by a wind sled driven by a large propellor.

SPECIAL FEATURE

• **Madeline Island** is home to an historical museum, a state park with nature trails and sailboat charters, and a challenging 18-hole golf course. The historical museum, comprising four historic log buildings, preserves artifacts from the island's Indian, fur-trading, missionary and later eras. Bus tours of the island are available from late June to early October.

Swimming does occur in Lake Superior, but because of the temperature most of the swimmers are children.

The first lighthouse authorized in these waters (1852) was mistakenly constructed on the wrong island.

WHERE TO STAY

Baywood Place, 20 N. Third St., (715) 779-3690. Gabled 1930s-style home, private baths, "deliciously unique" full breakfasts. $$

Cooper Hill House, P. O. Box 1288, (715) 779-5060. 1888 home, antiques and family heirlooms, private baths, quiet. $$ to $$$

First Street Inn, P. O. Box 768, (800) 245-3072. Originally a Victorian livery and boarding house, full breakfasts, restaurant. $ to $$$

Old Rittenhouse Inn, P. O. Box 584, (715) 779-5111. In three historic homes, working fireplaces, private baths, full or continental breakfasts, public dining room, one of Wisconsin's finest. $$$

WHERE TO EAT

Note: Bayfield has its own delicacies: homegrown raspberries and deep-fried whitefish livers. Depending on the age of the fish and skill of the cook, the flavor of the livers can vary from fishy and strong to delicately delicious.

Greunke's Restaurant, (see First Street Inn above). American cooking, Lake Superior whitefish and trout, low-calorie entrees. $$

Old Rittenhouse Inn, (see above). Regional specialities, one of Wisconsin's best, reservations advised. $$$

Winnie's Hungry Mariner, 117 Rittenhouse Ave., (715) 779-3958. American and Italian dishes, antique decorations. $

FURTHER INFORMATION

Bayfield Chamber of Commerce, P. O. Box 138, Bayfield, WI 54814, (715) 779-3334.

DIRECTIONS

From Duluth (MN), US 53 south to WI 13, WI 13 east to Bayfield.

EPHRAIM/FISH CREEK, WISCONSIN

Populations: 200/200

Door County and its tiny harbor villages of Ephraim and Fish Creek are Wisconsin's answer to New England. Both villages have fine old white clapboard houses and inns and attract cyclists and other tourists with their upscale shops and magnificant fall foliage. Both also look out over blue water, shelter yachts in their harbors and offer sailing cruises.

Maybe departing a little from some New England harbor towns, both back against scenic bluffs. And because they lie on the Green Bay, or west, side of the Door Peninsula, both depart dramatically from New England by enjoying sunsets over the water rather than sunrises. Indeed, some of the areas along the main road in Ephraim are kept undeveloped just to maintain the open views of the water and the spectacular sunsets.

Separated by five miles, Ephraim and Fish Creek are similar, but they're hardly twins. Ephraim is dry and Fish Creek is wet (this alone gives each a different character), Ephraim stretches along the water and Fish Creek is compact, Ephraim has more historic buildings and Fish Creek has more shops, galleries and cultural events. Both are delightfully New England (except in price).

Ephraim has several historic structures that are open to the public. The best known is the **Anderson Store**, a restored 1858 general store that displays merchandise from the early 20th century. Two other buildings are the 1869 **Pioneer School**, which has desks and other artifacts of 1920s vintage, and the **Anderson Barn Museum** (ca. 1880), which features historic exhibits and a permanent art collection.

Door County is famous for its strawberries, cherries and apples — late May is the time to see the blooms. The county is also famous for its windsurfing and other water sports. Bicycle, sailboat, canoe, sea kayak and cross-country ski rentals are available; so are sailboat and sea kayak lessons.

SPECIAL FEATURES

• **Peninsula State Park**, which lies between the two villages, offers breathtaking views of Green Bay from its limestone bluffs. The park is home to the charming **Eagle Bluff Lighthouse** (1868), also a museum; the **American Folklore Theater**, a professional theater company that does summer musicals; and the beautiful 18-hole **Peninsula Park Course**.

• The oldest professional summer stock company in the country, the **Peninsula Players**, performs in the Theater-in-a-Garden, an open-to-air theater south of Fish Creek.

> To do a "Door County Fish Boil," boil new potatoes and baby onions (optional) in a cauldron over an open fire until they're nearly done, add Lake Michigan whitefish or trout and, finally, stoke the fire with kerosene and boil unwanted "fishy" oils off the top. Serve with coleslaw and cherry pie.

WHERE TO STAY

The Ephraim Inn, 9994 Pioneer Ln., (414) 854-4515. Renovated 1908 home, harbor views, private baths, full breakfasts. $$$

French Country Inn of Ephraim, P. O. Box 129, (414) 854-4001. 1912 "summer cottage" in garden setting, French country decor. $$ to $$$

Thorp House Inn, P. O. Box 490 (Fish Creek), (414) 868-2444. Historic guest house, harbor view, antique-filled rooms, private baths. $$$

The Whistling Swan Inn, P. O. Box 193 (Fish Creek), (414) 868-3442. Historic inn, antiques, private baths, full breakfasts. $$$

The White Gull Inn, P. O. Box 160 (Fish Creek), (414) 868-3517. Turn-of-century inn, antique-decorated rooms, private baths, cottages, public dining room. $$ to $$$

WHERE TO EAT

The C&C Supper Club, Main & Spruce sts. (Fish Creek), (414) 868-3412. Steaks, seafood, house specialties, nightly specials. $ to $$

Edgewater Dining Room, 10040 WI 42 (Ephraim), (414) 854-4034. Overlooking harbor, Door County Fish Boil, reservations advised. $ to $$

Kortes' English Inn, WI 42 between villages, (414) 868-3076. Tableside flambe, Old English atmosphere, one of best in region. $$

White Gull Inn (see above). Fish boils, steaks, Beef Wellington, Shrimp and Artichoke Romano, home baking. $$

Wilson's Restaurant & Ice Cream Parlor, WI 42 (Ephraim), (414) 854-2041. Established 1906, famous ice cream, lighter fare. $

FURTHER INFORMATION

Door County Chamber of Commerce, P. O. Box 406, Surgeon Bay, WI 54235, (800) 527-3529.

DIRECTIONS

From Milwaukee, I 43 north to exit 185 (Green Bay), WI 57 north to Sturgeon Bay, WI 42 north to Fish Creek.

MINERAL POINT, WISCONSIN

Population: 2,428

People from **Mineral Point** traveling in England have been known to remark on the similarity between parts of that country and the rolling, green countryside of their Wisconsin homes. The pastoral beauty of southwestern Wisconsin does indeed recall the beauty of rural England, but there is more to the similarity than that. Families from Cornwall (England) settled in Mineral Point following the discovery of lead early in the 19th century. Bringing with them the skills of the stonemason as well as the miner, the settlers built rock houses similar to those of their native Cornwall. Many of these houses survive, and continue even today to impart a certain English character to Mineral Point.

The hilly, winding streets of Mineral Point carry the similarity to parts of England even further. And so does the state historical society's **Pendarvis Complex,** a group of six restored Cornish miners' cottages built in the 1840s.

The architectural character and variety of many of Mineral Point's others buildings are much more American. The styles range from early log through Federal to Victorian and Italian Renaissance. Of special note are the Italianate **Gundry House,** now a museum owned and operated by the local historical society, and the **Mineral Point Theatre,** a vaudeville and performing arts house with full proscenium and balcony, built in 1914. The latter's magnificent 400-seat auditorium is still used for movie presentations, performances by a local theater group, and other events. A driving-tour brochure focusing on these and other important buildings in Mineral Point is distributed by the visitors bureau.

Mineral Point has been respected as an art center since the 1940s. Over 30 artists and artesans display their work in 11 (at last count) galleries, studios and shops. The town's woodworkers enjoy an especially wide following. Many of the weavers demonstrate their craft at **The Looms,** a spinning and weaving museum. The town also boasts a large number of individual and group antique shops.

The various studios and shops are scattered about town. Some are on **High Street** (the English name for a main street). Others are in **Shake Rag Valley** (more formally, "Shake Rag Under the Hill"), a collection of restored buildings in Mineral Point's oldest trade and crafts district. The markets of **Shake Rag Alley** share their pretty valley location with nicely landscaped grounds and an historic spring.

SPECIAL FEATURES

• North of Mineral Point is the **House on the Rock,** a contemporary 14-room house built on top of a tower of rock. The house is the original structure of a 200-acre complex featuring such attractions as a gas-lit Main Street, the world's largest carousel, a collection of animated music machines, a miniature circus and a collection of 250 doll houses. Billed as Wisconsin's number-one tourist attraction, some visitors describe the exhibits as unique and fascinating, others as overwhelming, even dizzying.

• North of the House on the Rock, near **Spring Green,** is Frank Lloyd Wright's famous home, **Taliesin East** (open to the public).

> *Early miners in Mineral Point dug out burrows resembling badger holes in the hillsides for shelter. Hence the Badger State, Wisconsin's nickname.*
>
> *A Cornish pasty (PASS tee) usually consists of beef, potatoes and onions sealed in a flakey crust. The Cornish dessert, Figgy Hobbin, consists of a pastry crust with raisins, nuts and other sweets served with a caramel sauce. These and other Cornish items are available locally.*

WHERE TO STAY

The Duke House B&B, 618 Maiden St., (608) 987-2821. Restored 1870 home, fine antiques, "hospitality since 1983." $$

The Old Granary Inn, 1760 Sandy Rock Rd., (608) 967-2140. Spectacular valley setting, hiking, fireplace or porch sitting, full breakfasts. $$ to $$$

Knudson's Guest House, 415 Ridge St., (608) 987-2733. Antiques, private baths, TV, Amish quilts, full breakfasts. $$

The Wm. A. Jones House B&B, 215 Ridge St., (608) 987-2337. Elegant turn-of-century mansion, full breakfasts. $$

Wilson House Inn, 110 Dodge St., (608) 987-3600. 1853 home in historic district, antiques, full breakfasts. $$

WHERE TO EAT

Ovens of Brittany (in Chesterfield Inn), S. Commerce St., (608) 987-3682. One of Wisconsin's best, dining indoors or out. $

FURTHER INFORMATION

Mineral Point Visitors Bureau, P. O. Box 78V, Mineral Point, WI, 53565, (608) 987-3201.

DIRECTIONS

From Madison, US 151 west (via Dodgeville) to Mineral Point.

RURAL, WISCONSIN

Population: ca. 250

In tiny **Rural**, the **Crystal River** twists and turns through back yards, front yards, sometimes both yards. Whenever and wherever you step outside, you're probably going to see this beautiful little river. During the warmer months you can even sit on your porch or in your gazebo and wave at the passing skiffs and canoes. And whenever you walk down the street — and walking is what people do — you're going to cross a bridge.

This idyllic place, now a National Historic District, is the only restored intact village in Wisconsin that was settled by immigrants from the British Isles. Many of the lovely homes dates from the 1850s. Following a not uncommon scenario for charming towns, Rural was bypassed by the railroad and thereby condemned to be frozen in time.

The village measures no more than about two by four blocks. The commercial area is pretty much restricted to one genuinely old-fashioned general store and maybe one or two antique and craft shops. The rest of the village consists of homes, and all but a half dozen date from another era. The homes and intertwining river are exceptionally beautiful when the trees are in their October colors.

To the east of the village is the **Red Mill**, an old mill (1855) that today boasts the largest waterwheel in the state. Close by is a covered bridge authentically constructed in 1970 from original plans. The site also includes a gift shop and a quaint chapel popular for weddings.

Rural is just downstream from Wisconsin's renowned **Chain O'Lakes**, a chain of 22 scenic spring-fed lakes. The lakes can be toured by cruise boats or canoe — if you go very far by canoe, you'll eventually wind back through Rural.

SPECIAL FEATURES

• The **Hutchinson House** in nearby **Waupaca** is an 1854 Greek Revival mansion overlooking a lake. The grand old house, now a museum, can be visited by appointment.

• Miles of hiking and groomed ski trails can be pursued at **Hartman Creek State Park**, a few miles northwest of town. Among the park's attractions are sandy swimming beaches and facilities for winter camping.

WHERE TO STAY

Crystal River B&B, 1369 Rural Rd. (Waupaca, WI), (715) 258-5333. 1853 riverside home, fireplaces, queen-sized antique beds, gazebo. $$ to $$$

Thomas Pipe Inn, 11032 Pipe Rd. (Waupaca, WI), (715) 824-3161. Restored 1855 stagecoach inn in heart of Amish country. $$ to $$$

Whippoorwill Acres B&B, N. 1702 East Rd. (Waupaca, WI), (715) 256-0373. 80 acres of forest/rolling meadows, sundeck, full breakfasts. $$ to $$$

WHERE TO EAT

Oakwood, 1040 W. Fulton St. (Waupaca, WI), (715) 258-0181. Cajun dishes, steaks, stir-fry. $ to $$

Simpson's, 222 S. Main St. (Waupaca, WI), (715) 258-2330. Famous for seafood, home-baked breads and desserts. $ to $$

The **Wheel House Restaurant**, Chain O'Lakes area, (715) 258-8289. Sandwiches and lighter fare. **$**

FURTHER INFORMATION
   Innkeepers, Crystal River B&B, 1369 Rural Rd., Waupaca, WI 54981, (715) 258-5333.

DIRECTIONS
   From Milwaukee, US 41 north to Oshkosh, WI 110 northwest to US 10, US 10 west to Waupaca, WI 22 south to Rural.

STURGEON BAY, WISCONSIN
Population: 9,176

Marking the 250-mile shoreline of Wisconsin's scenic **Door Peninsula** are cliffs, rocky coves, harbors and little villages that are reminiscent of New England (see Ephraim and Fish Creek selection). In the peninsula's interior are some of Wisconsin's famous cherry and apple orchards. Straddling an isthmus half-way up the peninsula, 40 miles from its tip, **Sturgeon Bay** is ideally situated as a home base for touring this delightful area.

Decades of sawmills, stone quarries, an ice industry, shipbuilding and, most recently, tourism have brought prosperity to Sturgeon Bay and left a legacy of handsome buildings. There are over 100 buildings of historic or special architectural interest in the town; 42 are within two historic districts. The information center publishes an historic tour map for strollers, bikers and drivers wishing a self-guided tour. Many of the buildings were built during the last decade of the 19th and first decade of the 20th centuries. The styles range from those of the Victorian period to Craftsman and American four-square.

Sturgeon Bay has two good regional history museums. Among the displays of the **Door County Historical Museum** are a turn-of-the-century fire station with antique fire trucks, a replica of an early Door County home, and exhibits depicting the history of shipbuilding in Door County. The two-story **Maritime Museum** features boats from the early part of the 20th century as well as an actual 1907 Great Lakes pilothouse.

Helping to uphold Door County's traditional stress on the arts, the **Miller Art Center** maintains a permanent collection of 20th-century Wisconsin art and sponsors a series of changing exhibits. The center also maintains a performing arts schedule. Sturgeon Bay is home to a number of art, craft and antique shops.

Four-hour van tours of Door County depart regularly from Sturgeon Bay. Surrounded as it is by water and beautiful beaches, the Sturgeon Bay area offers a long list of water sports, including snorkeling, scuba diving and sailing. For those more interested in indoor pursuits, there are guided tours of a micro-brewery and a winery.

SPECIAL FEATURE
• A magnificent view of **Door County** and **Green Bay** may be enjoyed from the observation platform at Potawatomi State Park, just northwest of town.

> *The King of Spain and the late Shah of Iran owned yachts that were built in Sturgeon Bay.*

WHERE TO STAY
The Gray Goose B&B, 4258 Bay Shore Dr., (414) 743-9011. Civil War home in quiet wooded setting, antique-filled rooms, water/sunset view, full "gourmet" breakfasts. $$ to $$$

Inn at Cedar Crossing, 336 Louisiana St., (414) 743-4200. Antiques, whirlpools, fireplaces, private baths, refreshments, restaurant. $$$

Scofield House B&B, P. O. Box 761, (414) 743-7727. Restored 3-story Victorian home, fine antiques, private baths, full gourmet breakfasts, "treats." $$ to $$$

White Lace Inn, 16 N. 5th Ave., (414) 743-1105. Large Victorian home, down comforters, fireplaces, private baths, double whirlpools. $$ to $$$

Whitefish Bay Farm, 3831 Clark Lake Rd., (414) 743-1560. Restored 1908 American four-square farmhouse on working farm, private baths, full breakfasts. $$ to $$$

WHERE TO EAT
Dal Santo's Restaurant, 341-1/2 N. Third Ave., (414) 743-6100. In historic railroad depot, pizzas, pastas, entrees. $ to $$

Inn at Cedar Crossing (see above). Victorian-era dining rooms, creative evening menu, fresh homemade fare, scratch bakery, fine wines/libations. $$

Mill Supper Club, WI 42 & 57, (414) 743-5044. Fresh perch and whitefish, family-style chicken, fish boils, nightly specials. $

FURTHER INFORMATION
Sturgeon Bay Area Information Center, P. O. Box 212, Sturgeon Bay, WI 54235, (414) 743-4456.

DIRECTIONS
From Milwaukee, I 43 north to exit 185 (Green Bay), WI 57 north to Sturgeon Bay.

WYOMING

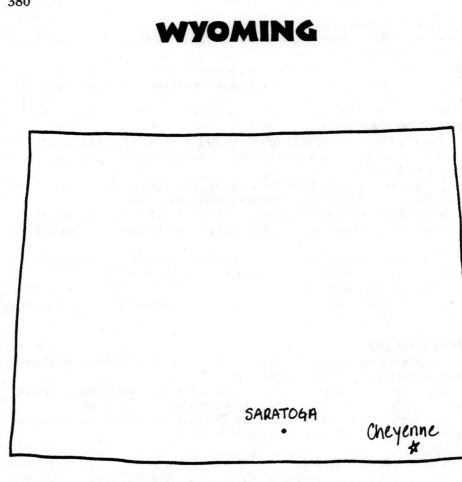

SARATOGA
•

Cheyenne
☆

SARATOGA, WYOMING

Population: 1,969

Few towns this side of the Hollywood screen can compete with **Saratoga's** *genuine* Western character and majestic Rocky Mountain setting. Away from the interstates and main tourist arteries, the town is large enough to be alive, yet small enough to be more concerned about gossip than crime. Stagecoaches used to stop in front of the old Hotel Wolf (see below). There are still people around who can tell personal stories — truthful ones — about the Old West.

Most people come here for the scenery and the outdoors, but Saratoga has sights of its own. Its natural hot springs (the town was named after its New York cousin and its springs) may be enjoyed in a year-round public pool area. There are also several good art galleries and interesting gift shops. The **Saratoga Museum**, located in the old **Union Pacific Railroad Depot** (1915), exhibits, among other things, railroad memorabilia, a country store, a pioneer home and a land office. On the museum's grounds are a caboose and restored sheep wagon.

One of the town's most popular sights is the **Saratoga National Fish Hatchery** (five miles north). Dating back to 1915, the hatchery raises several kinds of trout, including rainbow and the endangered Greenback cutthroat trout, for stocking. Trout eggs are shipped to other hatcheries. For example, millions of lake trout eggs have been shipped to Great Lakes hatcheries.

Situated on the banks of the **North Platte River**, a blue-ribbon trout fishery, the town's motto reads *Where the Trout Leap in Main Street* (and before the advent of flood control, they did). Fishing is understandably the town's most popular activity, but baited by an especially beautiful golf course (open to public), golfing isn't far behind. Whitewater boating, float trips, cross-country skiing and kayaking are also popular. The **Medicine Bow National Forest** offers a wealth of trails for hiking and backpacking.

One of the best ways to see this beautiful country is to take advantage of the knowledge and experience of an outfitter — Saratoga has many to choose from. Fishing float trips, horseback fishing trips, tours of historic mining towns, trail rides and guided snowmobile rides are just a few of the adventures that can be safely undertaken with the aid of an outfitter.

SPECIAL FEATURES

• The **Grand Encampment Museum** in **Encampment**, 20 or so miles south of Saratoga, uses authentic buildings to recreate a Western community. Included among the buildings and collections are U.S. Forest Service memorabilia, a hat shop, the Palace Bakery, the Lake Creek Stage Station and a homestead house. A two-story outhouse reminds visitors that the snows in this part of the world can drift well above ground level.

• **WY 130** between **Saratoga** and **Laramie** has been designated a **National Forest Scenic Byway** (closed winters). There are several spectacular loop tours in and around the **Medicine Bow National Forest**. Inquire locally for maps and instructions.

Hikers along major creeks in the neighboring mountains will encounter groups of old log cabins known locally as "tie hack camps." "Tie hacks" were men who produced axe-hewn railroad ties (during the period between 1868 and 1939).

Thomas Edison, a member of the Henry Draper Eclipse Expedition, got the idea for the electric light bulb in 1878 at Battle Lake (WY 70, south of Saratoga).

WHERE TO STAY

The Hood House, P. O. Box 492, (307) 326-8901. Restored 1892 Saratoga family home, fishing on owner's ranch by special arrangement. $ to $$

Hotel Wolf, P. O. Box 1298, (307) 326-5525. Restored 1893 hotel, on National Register, restaurant and lounge. $ to $$

WHERE TO EAT

Hotel Wolf (see above). Prime rib, famous Wolf Steak, chicken, seafood, homemade desserts, reservations preferred. $ to $$

FURTHER INFORMATION

Saratoga-Platte Valley Chamber of Commerce, P. O. Box 1095, Saratoga, WY 82331, (307) 326-8855.

DIRECTIONS

From Cheyenne, I 80 west (via Laramie) to exit 235, WY 130 south to Saratoga.

ALSO RECOMMENDED
Other Towns and Villages Nominated for their Charm

ALABAMA
Demopolis
Fairhope
Lownsdesboro
Marion

ALASKA
Sitka
Skagway
Talkeetna
Valdez

ARIZONA
Ajo
Carefree
Jerome
Tombstone
Wickenburg

ARKANSAS
Hardy
Mountain View
Scott
Washington

CALIFORNIA
Cambria
Quincy
San Juan Bautista
St. Helena

COLORADO
Estes Park
Georgetown
Leadville
Redstone

CONNECTICUT
Madison
Pomfret/Woodstock
Salisbury
West Cornwall

DELAWARE
Arden
Bethel

Delaware City
Lewes

FLORIDA
Cabbage Key/Useppa Island
Mt. Dora
Palm Beach
Starke

GEORGIA
Hiawasee
Newnan
Pine Mt./Warm Springs
Washington

HAWAII
Hanalei, Kauai
Kailua Kona, Hawaii
Kilauea, Kauai
Lahaina, Maui

IDAHO
Lava Hot Springs
McCall
Sandpoint

ILLINOIS
Bishop Hil
Mt. Carroll
Petersburg (New Salem)
Woodstock

INDIANA
Dana
Fountain City
Spring Mill Village

IOWA
Amana Colonies
Bellevue
Walnut
West Branch

KANSAS
Abilene
Elk Falls

Wilson
Yoder

KENTUCKY
Danville
Maysville/Washington
Olive Hill
Shelbyville

LOUISIANA
Covington
Franklin
New Roads
St. Martinville

MAINE
Bar Harbor
Castine
Northeast Harbor
Wiscasset

MARYLAND
Chestertown
New Market
Oxford
Solomons

MASSACHUSETTS
Chatham
Concord
Hyannis
Williamstown

MICHIGAN
Calumet
Petoskey
St. Clair
South Haven

MINNESOTA
Lanesboro
Mantorville
New Prague
Northfield

MISSISSIPPI
Carrollton
Corinth
French Camp
Kosciusko

MISSOURI
Bethel
Kimmswick
Steelville
Weston

MONTANA
Bigfork
Big Timber
Stevensville
Whitefish

NEBRASKA
Arthur
Gothenburg
Valentine
Wayne

NEVADA
Eureka
Lamoille
Unionvile
Virginia City

NEW HAMPSHIRE
Center Harbor
Hancock
Jackson
Jaffrey

NEW JERSEY
Batsto
Lambertville
Princeton
Salem

NEW MEXICO
The Acoma Pueblo
Cimarron
Cloudcroft
Ruidoso

NEW YORK
Annandale-on-Hudson
East Hampton
Hammondsport
Wyoming

NORTH CAROLINA
Bath

Cashiers
Dillsboro
Manteo

NORTH DAKOTA
Devils Lake
Kenmare
Walhalla

OHIO
Bath
Bellevue
Milan
Oberlin

OKLAHOMA
Elk City
Hominy
Sulphur

OREGON
Hood River
Jacksonville
Newberg
Yachats

PENNSYLVANIA
Boalsburg
Mechanicsburg
Punxsutawney
Shippensburg

RHODE ISLAND
Chepachet
Kingston Village
Little Compton
North Scituate

SOUTH CAROLINA
Cheraw
Edgefield
Georgetown
McClellanville

SOUTH DAKOTA
Hot Springs
Milbank
Pierre
Spearfish

TENNESSEE
Bell Buckle
Franklin

LaGrange
Rogersville

TEXAS
Albany
Alpine
Columbus
Ft. Stockton

UTAH
Garden City/Laketown
Midway
Springdale
Torrey

VERMONT
Grafton
Newfane
Weston
Woodstock

VIRGINIA
Middleburg
Monterey
Strasburg
Warm Springs/Hot Springs

WASHINGTON
Chelan
Ilwaco
La Conner
Winthrop

WEST VIRGINIA
Elkins
Marlinton
Martinsburg
Sistersville

WISCONSIN
Alma
Cedarburg
Hudson
Portage

WYOMING
Afton
Alpine
Cody
Meeteetse

INDEX

FROM THE AUTHOR -
WE WANT YOUR INPUT!

It's possible that things may have changed in some of the towns and villages I've selected by the time you visit. If changes have occurred, please let me know. And if you disagree with one of my recommendations, I'd like to hear that too. The address is listed below.

FROM THE PUBLISHER

Our goal is to provide you with a guide book that is second to none. As Larry reminds you above, however, things do change: phone numbers, prices, addresses, quality of food served, value, etc. Should you come across any new information, we'd appreciate hearing from you. No item is too small for us, so if you have any recommendations or suggested changes, please write us.

The address is:

Larry Brown
c/o Open Road Publishing
P.O. Box 11249
Cleveland Park Station
Washington, DC 20008

TRAVEL NOTES

TRAVEL NOTES

TRAVEL NOTES

TRAVEL NOTES

TRAVEL NOTES

TRAVEL NOTES

YOUR PASSPORT TO GREAT TRAVEL!
FROM OPEN ROAD PUBLISHING

THE CLASSIC CENTRAL AMERICA GUIDES

COSTA RICA GUIDE by Paul Glassman, 5th Ed. Glassman's classic travel guide to Costa Rica remains the standard against which all others must be judged. Discover great accommodations, reliable restaurants, pristine beaches, and incredible diving, fishing, and other water sports. Revised and updated. **$14.95**

BELIZE GUIDE by Paul Glassman, 6th Ed. This guide has quickly become the book of choice for Belize travelers. Perhaps the finest spot for Caribbean scuba diving and sport fishing, Belize's picture-perfect palm trees, Mayan ruins, tropical forests, uncrowded beaches, and fantastic water sports have made it one of the most popular Caribbean travel destinations. Revised and updated. **$13.95**

HONDURAS AND BAY ISLANDS GUIDE by J.P. Panet with Leah Hart and Paul Glassman, 2nd Ed. Open Road's superior series of Central America travel guides continues with the revised look at this beautiful land. **$13.95**

GUATEMALA GUIDE by Paul Glassman, 8th Ed. Glassman's treatment of colorful Guatemala remains the single best source in print. **$16.95**

OTHER TITLES OF INTEREST

PARIS GUIDE by Robert F. Howe and Diane Huntley. Brings you the heart of the romantic City of Light, plus new attractions, hotels, cafes, and great activities. **$13.95**

CHINA GUIDE by Ruth Lor Malloy, 8th Ed. More than 700 pages of expert travel advice, local customs, money-saving tips, great things to see and do, and hundreds of destinations in Asia's emerging giant. All new sections on Beijing, Shangahi, Xi'an, and much more! **$17.95**

SOUTHERN MEXICO AND YUCATAN GUIDE by Eric Hamovitch. Complete coverage of beautiful southern Mexico and the Yucatan peninsula. Discover terrific beaches, majestic Mayan ruins, great water sports, and the latest on hotels, restaurants, activities, nightlife, sports and more! Available Fall 1994. **$14.95**

WALT DISNEY WORLD AND ORLANDO THEME PARKS by Jay Fenster. *The* complete guide to Disney World and all of Orlando's great theme parks (including Sea World, MGM Studios, Busch Gardens, Church Street Station, Spaceport USA, and more), shows you every attraction, ride, show, shop, and nightclub they contain. Includes 64 money-savings tips for hotel, airfare, restaurant, attractions, and ride discounts. **$12.95**

LAS VEGAS GUIDE by Ed Kranmar and Avery Cardoza. Great selection of hotels, restaurants, excursions, shopping, plus more pages of gambling advice than any other Vegas guide. **$5.95**

PLEASE USE ORDER FORM ON NEXT PAGE

ORDER FORM

Name and Address: _____

_____

_____

_____ Zip Code: _____

Quantity	Title	Price

Total Before Shipping _____

Shipping/Handling _____

TOTAL _____

Please include price of book plus shipping and handling For shipping and handling, please add $3.00 for the first book, and $1.00 for each book thereafter. Ask about our discounts for special order bulk purchases.

ORDER FROM: **OPEN ROAD PUBLISHING**
P.O. Box 11249, Cleveland Park Station, Washington, D.C. 20008